Introduction to Academic and Career Opportunities in Psychology

First Edition

Edited by
Emilio Ulloa and
Kristen Cole

Bassim Hamadeh, CEO and Publisher
Christopher Foster, General Vice President
Michael Simpson, Vice President of Acquisitions
Jessica Knott, Managing Editor
Kevin Fahey, Cognella Marketing Manager
Jess Busch, Senior Graphic Designer
Seidy Cruz, Acquisitions Editor
Sarah Wheeler, Project Editor
Stephanie Sandler, Licensing Associate

First published in the United States of America in 2013 by Cognella, Inc.

Printed in the United States of America

ISBN: 978-1-62131-274-1 (pbk)/ 978-1-62131-275-8 (br)

www.cognella.com 800.200.3908

Contents

SECTION FOUR: PSYCHOLOGY-RELATED JOBS 107

Section One

Introduction to the Field of Psychology

We, the editors of this collection, firmly believe it to be the responsibility of psychology educators to prepare their students for the application of psychology in both their personal and professional lives. One way to do this is to inform them about academic and career opportunities in psychology. We believe that as psychology majors you will learn, refine, and develop the skills and aptitudes needed to be successful in your personal and professional pursuits. Pursuing a degree in psychology will reward you with expanded knowledge of human behavior, an aptitude in synthesizing and understanding data and statistics, critical thinking and interpersonal skills, and a broad awareness of ethics, all of which will leave you well positioned for the next step in life, whatever it may be. Our aim with this collection is to provide you with information to complement your education in psychology. We bring together web resources, government data, magazine and journal articles, book chapters, and reports. We also provide narratives and professional profiles to help put much of this information in the proper context. This first set of readings is the starting point, and is designed to give the psychology major a basic overview of the discipline and the occupational options available to you. It begins with overview documents from the American Psychological Association, and includes readings that address many of the "myths" that lay people entertain about our discipline. These readings also introduce you to how culture plays a role in our discipline and provide tips for success as a student of psychology.

What Psychology Is

American Psychological Association

Why people do the things they do is an age-old question. However, psychology—the science concerned with behavior, in both human and nonhuman animals—first appeared in the 1870s. Despite its youth, it is a broad discipline, essentially spanning subject matter from biology to sociology. Psychologists have doctoral degrees. They study the intersection of two critical relationships: one between brain function and behavior, and another between the environment and behavior. As scientists, psychologists follow scientific methods, using careful observation, experimentation, and analysis. But psychologists also need to be creative in the way they apply scientific findings.

Psychologists frequently are innovators, evolving new approaches from established knowledge to meet the changing needs of people, organizations, and societies. They develop theories and test them through their research. As this research yields new information, these findings become part of the body of knowledge that practitioners call on in their work with clients and patients, as well as with organizations and communities. Psychology is a tremendously varied field. Psychologists conduct both basic and applied research, serve as consultants to communities and organizations, diagnose and treat people, and teach future psychologists and those who will pursue other disciplines. They test intelligence and personality. Many psychologists work as health care providers. They assess behavioral and mental function and well-being, study how human beings relate to each other and also to machines, and work to improve these relationships. And because the United States is undergoing sizable change in its population makeup, psychologists provide important knowledge and skills to help better understand diverse cultures.

Many psychologists work independently and also team up with other professionals—for example, with other scientists, physicians, lawyers, school personnel, computer experts, engineers, policymakers, and managers—to contribute to every area of society. Thus, we find them in laboratories, hospitals, courtrooms, schools and universities, community health centers, prisons, and corporate offices.

Psychologists traditionally study both normal and abnormal functioning and treat individuals with mental and emotional problems. They also concentrate on behaviors that affect the mental and emotional health and mental functioning of healthy human beings. For example, psychologists work with patients to help them change behaviors that are having negative effects on their physical health. They work with business executives, performers, and athletes to reduce stress and improve performance.

They advise lawyers on jury selection and collaborate with educators on school reform. Immediately following a disaster, such as a plane crash or bombing, psychologists help victims and bystanders recover from the trauma, or shock, of the event. They team with law enforcement and public health officials to analyze the causes of such events and prevent their recurrence. Involved in all aspects of our fast-paced world, psychologists must keep up with what's happening all around us. When you're a psychologist, your education never ends.

As has long been true, opportunities in psychology for those with graduate degrees will be more plentiful and at a higher level than for those with undergraduate degrees. An undergraduate degree remains excellent preparation for continued graduate work in psychology or in another field, such as business, medicine, or computer science. Many employers are interested in the skills that psychology majors bring to collecting, analyzing, and interpreting data and their experience with statistics and experimental design.

Opportunities for people with advanced degrees in psychology are expanding in number as well as in scope. The move toward preventing illness rather than merely diagnosing and treating it requires people to learn how to make healthy behavior a routine part of living. Indeed, many of the problems facing society today are problems of behavior—for example, chronic health conditions or disease, drug addiction, poor personal relationships, violence at home and in the street, and the harm we do to our environment. Psychologists contribute solutions to problems through careful collection of data, analysis of data, and development of intervention strategies—in other words, by applying scientific principles, the hallmark of psychology.

In addition, an aging America is leading to more research and practice in adapting our homes and workplaces for older people. The promises of the electronic revolution demand more user-friendly technologies and training. More two-career families in the workplace spur employers to accommodate the needs of families. Psychologists are helping to make the changes that are needed. The diversity in America today calls for psychologists to develop and refine treatments and approaches to meet the unique needs of different racial and ethnic groups. Furthermore, research advances in learning and memory, and the integration of physical and mental health care, make psychology more exciting than ever.

Most psychologists say they love their work. They cite the variety of daily tasks and the flexibility of their schedules. They are thrilled by the exciting changes taking place in the field—from adapting technology to benefit humans, to working as part of primary health care teams. They are endeavoring to provide answers to research questions in such diverse areas as prevention, perception, and learning, and they are using new technology and knowledge to train the next generation. It is an exciting time to be a psychologist.

Some of the Subfields in Psychology

Psychologists specialize in a host of different areas within the field and identify themselves by many different labels. A sampling of those focal areas is presented to give you an idea of the breadth of psychology's scholarship and applications.

The field of psychology encompasses both *research,* through which we learn fundamental things about human and animal behavior, and *practice,* through which that knowledge is applied in helping to solve problems and promote healthy human development. In each of the subfields there are psychologists who work primarily as researchers, others who work primarily as practitioners, and many who do both (scientist–practitioners). Indeed, one of psychology's most unique and important characteristics is its coupling of science and practice, which stimulates continual advancement of both. Additionally, many psychologists teach psychology in academic institutions, from high schools to graduate programs in universities.

Clinical psychologists assess and treat mental, emotional, and behavioral disorders. These range from short-term crises, such as difficulties resulting from adolescent rebellion, to more severe, chronic conditions such as schizophrenia. Some clinical psychologists treat specific problems exclusively, such as phobias or clinical depression. Others focus on specific populations—for instance, youths; families or couples; ethnic minority groups; gay, lesbian, bisexual, and transgender individuals; or older people. They also consult with physicians on physical problems that have underlying psychological causes.

Cognitive and perceptual psychologists study human perception, thinking, and memory. Cognitive psychologists are interested in questions such as, how the mind represents reality, how people learn, and how people understand and produce language. Cognitive psychologists also study reasoning, judgment, and decision making. Cognitive and perceptual psychologists frequently collaborate with behavioral neuroscientists to understand the biological bases of perception or cognition or with researchers in other areas of psychology to better understand the cognitive biases in the thinking of people with depression, for example.

Community psychologists work to strengthen the abilities of communities, settings, organizations, and broader social systems to meet people's needs. They help people access resources and collaborate with others to improve their lives and communities. Instead of helping individuals cope with negative circumstances (e.g., trauma, poverty), community psychologists help empower people to change those circumstances, prevent problems, and develop stronger communities. Examples of community psychology interventions include improving support for hurricane victims, partnering with neighborhoods to prevent crime, collaborating with schools to prevent bylling, adn helping change policies to imprave health outcomes. Community psychologists blend research and practice, partnering with diverse citizens to plan and implement community changes, advance social justice, and use research to inform and evaluate this work.

Counseling psychologists help people recognize their strengths and resources to cope with everyday problems and serious adversity. They do counseling/psychotherapy, teaching, and scientific research with individuals of all ages, families, and organizations (e.g., schools, hospitals, businesses). Counseling psychologists help people understand and take action on career and work problems. They pay attention to how problems and people differ across the life span, and they have great respect for the influence of differences among people (such as race, gender, sexual orientation, religion, disability status) on psychological well-being. They believe that behavior is affected by many things, including qualities of the individual (e.g., psychological, physical, or spiritual factors) and factors in the person's environment (e.g., family, society, and cultural groups).

Developmental psychologists study the psychological development of the human being that takes place throughout life. Until recently, the primary focus was on childhood and adolescence, the most formative years. But as life expectancy in this country approaches 80 years, developmental psychologists are becoming increasingly interested in aging, especially in researching and developing ways to help older people stay as independent as possible.

Educational psychologists concentrate on how effective teaching and learning take place. They consider a variety of factors, such as human abilities, student motivation, and the effect on the classroom of the diverse races, ethnicities, and cultures that makes up America.

Engineering psychologists conduct research on how people work best with machines. For example, how can a computer be designed to prevent fatigue and eye strain? What arrangement of an assembly line makes production most efficient? What is a reasonable workload? Most engineering psychologists work in industry, but some are employed by the government, particularly the Department of Defense. They are often known as human factors specialists.

Environmental psychologists study the dynamics of person–environment interactions. They define the term *environment* very broadly, including all that is natural on the planet as well as built environments, social settings, cultural groups, and informational environments. They examine behavior evolving at various scales and from various processes (e.g., localization, globalization). They have a broad and inherently multidisciplinary focus. They recognize the need to be problem oriented, coordination as needed with researchers and practitioners in the other fields of psychology, in related disciplines (e.g., sociology, anthropology, biology, ecology), as well as in the design fields (e.g., regional, urban, and community planning; landscape architecture; architecture; and engineering).

Environmental psychologist explore such issues as common property resource management, the effect of environment stress on human effectiveness and well-being, the characteristics of restorative environments, and human information processing. They also foster conservation behavior, helping people to craft durable behavioral responses to emerging biophysical limits.

Evolutionary psychologists study how evolutionary principles such as mutation, adaptation, and selective fitness influence human thought, feeling, and behavior. Because of their focus on genetically shaped behaviors that influence an organism's chances of survival, evolutionary psychologists study mating, aggression, helping behavior, and communication. Evolutionary psychologists are particularly interested in paradoxes and problems of evolution. For example, some behaviors that were highly adaptive in our evolutionary past may no longer be adaptive in the modern world.

Experimental psychologists are interested in a wide range of psychological phenomena, including cognitive processes, comparative psychology (cross-species comparisons), and learning and conditioning. They study both human and nonhuman animals with respect to their abilities to detect what is happening in a particular environment and to acquire and maintain responses to what is happening.

Experimental psychologists work with the empirical method (collecting data) and the manipulation of variables within the laboratory as a way of understanding certain phenomena and advancing scientific knowledge. In addition to working in academic settings, experimental psychologists work in places as diverse as manufacturing settings, zoos, and engineering firms.

Forensic psychologists apply psychological principles to legal issues. Their expertise is often essential within the judicial system. They can, for example, help a judge decide which parent should have custody of a child or evaluate a defendant's mental competence to stand trial. Forensic psychologists also conduct research on jury behavior or eyewitness testimony. Some forensic psychologists are trained in both psychology and the law.

Health psychologists specialize in how biological, psychological, and social factors affect health and illness. They study how patients handle illness, why some people don't follow medical advice, and the most effective ways to control pain or to change poor health habits. They also develop health care strategies that foster emotional and physical well-being.

Health psychologists team up with other health care professionals in independent practice and in hospitals to provide patients with complete health care. They educate health care professionals about psychological problems that arise from the pain and stress of illness and about symptoms that may seem to be physical in origin but actually have psychological causes. They also investigate issues that affect a large segment of society, and develop and implement programs to deal with these problems. Examples include teenage pregnancy, substance abuse, risky sexual behaviors, smoking, lack of exercise, and poor diet.

Industrial/organizational (I/O) psychologists apply psychological principles and research methods to the work place in the interest of improving productivity, health, and the quality of work life. Many serve as human resources specialists, helping organizations with staffing, training, and employee development. They may provide employers with testing and other valid selection procedures in their hiring and promotion processes. Others work as management consultants in such areas as strategic planning, quality management, and coping with organizational change.

Neuropsychologists (and behavioral neuropsychologists) explore the relationships between brain systems and behavior. For example, behavioral neuropsychologists may study the way the brain creates and stores memories, or how various diseases and injuries of the brain affect emotion, perception, and behavior. They design tasks to study normal brain functions with imaging techniques such as positron emission tomography (PET), single photon emission computed tomography (SPECT), and functional magnetic resonance imaging (fMRI).

Clinical neuropsychologists also assess and treat people. And with the dramatic increase in the number of survivors of traumatic brain injury, neuropsychologists are working with health care teams to help brain-injured people resume productive lives.

Quantitative and measurement psychologists focus on methods and techniques for designing experiments and analyzing psychological data. Some develop new methods for performing analysis; others create research strategies to assess the effect of social and educational programs and psychological treatment. They develop and evaluate mathematical models for psychological tests. They also propose methods for evaluating the quality and fairness of the tests.

Rehabilitation psychologists work with stroke and accident victims, people with mental retardation, and those with developmental disabilities caused by such conditions as cerebral palsy, epilepsy, and autism. They help clients adapt to their situation and improve their situation and improve their lives, and they frequently work with other health care professionals. They deal with issues of personal adjustment, interpersonal relations, the work world, and pain management.

Rehabilitation psychologists are also involved in public health programs to prevent disabilities, including those caused by violence and substance abuse. And they testify in court as expert witnesses about the causes and effects of a disability and a person's rehabilitation needs.

School psychologists are engaged in the delivery of comprehensive psychological services to children, adolescents, and families in schools and other applied settings. They assess and counsel students, consult with parents and school staff, and conduct behavioral interventions when appropriate. Most school districts employ psychologists full time.

Social psychologists study how a person's mental life and behavior are shaped by interactions with other people. They are interested in all aspects of interpersonal relationships, including both individual and group influences, and seek ways to improve such interactions. For example, their research helps us understand how people form attitudes toward others, and when these are harmful—as in the case of prejudice—suggests ways to change them.

Social psychologists are found in a variety of settings, from academic institutions (where they teach and conduct research), to advertising agencies (where they study consumer attitudes and preferences), to businesses and government agencies (where they help with a variety of problems in organization and management).

Sports psychologists help athletes refine their focus on competition goals, become more motivated, and learn to deal with the anxiety and fear of failure that often accompany competition. The field is growing as sports of all kinds become more competitive and attract younger children.

American Psychological Association Divisions List

American Psychological Association

This list of 56 divisions within the American Psychological Association (APA) is a good example of the variety of topics that comprise the expansive field of psychology. Membership in a division is optional for APA members. Many of the groups offer meetings, conferences, trainings, awards, scholarships, newsletters, journals, and social gatherings. Browse through the list and notice what peaks your interest.

1 – Society for General Psychology
2 – Society for the Teaching of Psychology
3 – Experimental Psychology
5 – Evaluation, Measurement, and Statistics
6 – Behavioral Neuroscience and Comparative Psychology
7 – Developmental Psychology
8 – Society for Personality and Social Psychology
9 – Society for the Psychological Study of Social Issues
10 – Society for the Psychology of Aesthetics, Creativity and the Arts
12 – Society of Clinical Psychology
13 – Society of Consulting Psychology
14 – Society for Industrial and Organizational Psychology
15 – Educational Psychology
16 – School Psychology
17 – Society of Counseling Psychology
18 – Psychologists in Public Service
19 – Society for Military Psychology
20 – Adult Development and Aging
21 – Applied Experimental and Engineering Psychology

22 – Rehabilitation Psychology
23 – Society for Consumer Psychology
24 – Society for Theoretical and Philosophical Psychology
25 – Behavior Analysis
26 – Society for the History of Psychology
27 – Society for Community Research and Action
28 – Psychopharmacology and Substance Abuse
29 – Psychotherapy
30 – Society of Psychological Hypnosis
31 – State, Provincial, and Territorial Psychological Association Affairs
32 – Society for Humanistic Psychology
33 – Intellectual and Developmental Disabilities
34 – Society for Environmental, Population and Conservation Psychology
35 – Society for the Psychology of Women
36 – Psychology of Religion
37 – Society for Child and Family Policy and Practice
38 – Health Psychology
39 – Psychoanalysis
40 – Clinical Neuropsychology
41 – American Psychology-Law Society
42 – Psychologists in Independent Practice
43 – Society for Family Psychology
44 – Society for the Psychological Study of Lesbian, Gay, Bisexual and Transgender Issues
45 – Society for the Psychological Study of Ethnic Minority Issues
46 – Media Psychology
47 – Exercise and Sport Psychology
48 – Society for the study of Peace, Conflict, and Violence: Peace Psychology Division
49 – Society of Group Psychology and Group Psychotherapy
50 – Society of Addiction Psychology
51 – Society for the Study of Men and Masculinity
52 – International Psychology
53 – Society of Clinical Child and Adolescent Psychology
54 – Society of Pediatric Psychology
55 – American Society for the Advancement of Pharmacotherapy
56 – Trauma Psychology

Dispelling the Myths and Misconceptions About Majoring in Psychology

By Kristen Cole

Many college students have unanswered questions and significant misconceptions about majoring in psychology. This article provides some answers to those questions and clarification of some common myths regarding one of the most popular majors of undergraduate students in the United States.

1. Majoring in psychology teaches you to analyze people.

As a psychology major in an undergraduate program, you will be taught to analyze research studies and data, critically think about information presented, and remain curious about the cause and effect of many behavioral phenomena. While you will not be taught how to analyze people in depth as a clinical psychologist might, you will learn why people do some of the things they do. It's a common experience that when a psychologist is introduced to someone new in a social setting, that new person often responds by saying, "Oh, are you going to analyze me now?" If one is referring to having the skills to think critically and remain curious, the proper answer is a resounding "Yes, I am!" However, most psychologists are not busy psychoanalyzing (interpreting how current behavior is driven by past experiences and unconscious drives) everyone they meet. Rest assured there is no scientific evidence that psychologists have telepathic or mind-reading abilities.

2. You can't get a job with a bachelor's degree in psychology.

I completely disagree! It is shameful to admit that as undergraduate psychology majors in a reputable university, my classmates and I were often told by our psychology professors that we would never get a job in the field of psychology (and they even went as far as suggesting we change our major!). While it is true that a doctoral degree is required to be licensed as a clinical psychologist, it is certainly possible to work at the entry level in the field of psychology with a bachelor's degree. In fact, of those graduating, only approximately 20% of psychology majors plan to go directly to graduate school (American Psychological Association Center for Workforce Studies, 2008). Many agencies, clinics, research centers, institutions, community centers, and hospitals treating individuals with psychological distress and mental illness have positions available for those with college educations who are good communicators, empathic, ethical, responsible, and reliable. Graduating with a bachelor's degree in psychology could also lead to a variety of non-psychology–related jobs including sales, marketing, human resources, administration, management, animal training, caretaking, and teaching. As with many professions, being proficient in a second or third language significantly increases employment opportunities in the field of psychology.

3. You can't get a job in the field of psychology until you complete at least a bachelor's degree.

There are numerous jobs in the field of psychology that do not require a bachelor's degree. Certificate of Achievement programs are an excellent way to start working in the field of psychology before completing a college degree. If a person is interested in working with alcoholics and drug addicts in recovery, a certificate can be earned before even completing an associate's degree. Typically, the Certificate in Alcohol and Other Drug Studies programs require a student to complete a number of courses and supervised internships (this could vary, depending on local regulations). A state exam is then taken, and the certificate is awarded. Individuals may work in recovery settings, or even have their own private practice. An emerging area likely to offer ample job opportunities in the near future is gerontology. A person may earn a Certificate in Gerontology by completing specific courses, depending on the academic institution's requirements. Such a certificate provides a person applying for entry-level jobs working with the aging population an advantage over those applying without the certificate. Another certificate that is emerging in the field is that of a mental health worker. Completion of this type of certificate provides a foundation for working with psychologically distressed individuals and families in entry-level mental health positions. An advantage of a certificate program is that some of the courses are likely to apply to graduation requirements if a person continues on to complete an associate's or bachelor's degree. Furthermore, some certificate programs are stackable, in that course requirements overlap and apply to several certificate programs.

4. You can't earn a decent living in the field of psychology.

I suppose this is determined by how each of us defines "decent living." The field of psychology is one in which the more education (degrees and certificates) you earn, the more job opportunities you have, thus the more money you can make. Overall, it's not a career path that many millionaires travel. Yet most people in the field can comfortably support their families and lifestyles. The specific area of psychology with the highest salary earning potential is Industrial-Organizational Psychology (U.S. Bureau of Labor Statistics, 2010), which is the application of psychological principles to the business industry. For many people attracted to the field of psychology, helping others and making a difference in people's lives are truly priceless benefits of the work.

5. If you major in psychology, you will be stuck doing counseling forever.

In fact, many professional psychologists do not provide direct counseling services to individuals, and the majority of them work in businesses, governmental agencies, and colleges as researchers, instructors, and consultants (U.S. Bureau of Labor Statistics, 2010). An exciting aspect of the field of psychology is that there are so many areas to focus on and so many areas of specialty, that there is no reason to be bored throughout an entire career. The flexibility in the field of psychology allows for changing areas of focus, training, and experience. For example, a person might start working in the clinical psychology field (therapist), and then transition into the research field (researcher), then transition into the academic field (instructor), and then transition into the business field (consultant). It is a versatile and flexible career that allows a person to work in many different settings with many different populations. It also is possible to work abroad.

6. Majoring in psychology is easy; it's just common sense and not a "real" science.

Psychology is the scientific study of behavior and mental processes. Many psychology classes are quite challenging, and they are based on scientific research and findings. The discipline of psychology merges areas of research and practice. That is, the researcher shares findings with the practitioner, and the practitioner informs the researcher what is needed. Psychology majors are trained in science and theory and develop a foundation in both of these areas. Psychology majors are required to develop understanding and skills in research methods, experimental techniques and ethics, and statistical analyses, in order to fully comprehend the empirical findings in the field. Acquiring such skills is highly valued by most occupations. Although it may seem like common sense that people behave the way they do, it is scientific research conducted in the field and in laboratories that helps us separate truth from "conventional wisdom," identify and explain both "normal" and "abnormal" behavior, and confirm the most effective ways to help people and change behavior and thought patterns.

7. The terms psychotherapist, psychologist and psychiatrist are all the same.

To the contrary, there are significant differences. In most states, a psychotherapist is likely to have a master's degree in counseling or clinical psychology. A psychologist is typically required to complete a doctorate level program in psychology. A psychiatrist completes medical school, and later specializes in the field of psychology during clinical residency. Psychotherapists and clinical psychologists are extensively trained in counseling and treating psychological disorders. Clinical psychologists are further trained in assessing an individual's emotional and mental state, and may conduct formal psychological evaluations using empirically validated tests and measures. Psychiatrists are allowed to prescribe medications, while psychotherapists and psychologists in most states are not allowed to do so. Most psychiatrists focus their work on the medicine-based treatment of individuals, rather than counseling them, yet there are those who provide both counseling and medical treatment. At all levels, there are licensing agencies in each state that are designed to protect consumers by establishing a minimum level of proficiency required before working with the public. While the roles of each of these mental health practitioners differ, they often work together as a multidisciplinary team when helping clients.

8. Anyone can get admitted to graduate school in psychology.

Although only 20% of bachelor's degree psychology majors enter graduate school in psychology, it is quite competitive. It is important during your undergraduate years to have a high grade point average (minimum 3.0), experience in research, participation in academic clubs (such as Psi Beta or Psi Chi), involvement in student organizations, volunteer experience, completion of internships, attendance at conferences, and strong letters of recommendation from faculty who are familiar with your level of work and your academic and career goals. In addition, when you apply to graduate school, you are likely to be required to take the Graduate Record Exam (GRE). High scores on the GRE are valued by many graduate programs. It is important to plan ahead and acquire as many experiences as possible before applying to graduate school so that you will be a strong candidate for admission.

9. Working with mentally ill people is a dangerous job.

Unfortunately, this is a common misconception that television shows and the news media industry have conveyed to the public, and one that perpetuates the negative stigma of mental illness. Many television shows exaggerate the symptoms and violent behavior of mentally ill characters in order to make the storyline interesting and captivating. A news broadcast is more likely to highlight an act of violence by a mentally ill individual (which is not common), than to show the countless times mentally ill individuals are safe with others or how often they are victims of violence or abuse. Highly sensational behaviors attract viewers, which increases ratings and income for the television networks. Most people with severe delusions and hallucinations are so afraid of others that they are more likely to avoid people and run away than to aggressively assault them.

10. The psychology major is really for women, not for men.

While women currently represent approximately 75% of undergraduate psychology majors and more women earn doctorate degrees in psychology than men (National Science Foundation, 2008; Snyder, Dillow, and Hoffman, 2008), this has not always been the case. Historically, the field of psychology was predominantly composed of male researchers, theorists, and clinicians. As women were provided more opportunities for college-level education in the United States, there was a gradual increase in the amount of women studying, researching, and practicing psychology. It is a myth that women are "better" at psychology because they are more "intuitive." The scientific study of psychology requires advanced skills in critical thinking, analytical reasoning, intellectual curiosity, reading comprehension, professional writing, and openness to new experiences. If you posses these skills, you are likely to enjoy studying psychology regardless of your gender.

References

American Psychological Association Center for Workforce Studies. (2008). Frequently Asked Questions. Retrieved from http ://www.apa.org/workforce/about/faq.aspx#II.6

National Science Foundation. (2008). An Overview of Science, Engineering, and Health Graduates: 2006. Retrieved from http://www.nsf.gov/statistics/infbrief/nsf08304/

Snyder, T. D., Dillow, S. A., and Hoffman, C. M. (2008). Digest of Educational Statistics: 2007 (NCES 2008-022). Washington, DC: National Center for Education Statistics, Institute of Education Sciences, U.S. Department of Education. Retrieved from http://nces.ed.gov/pubsearch/pubsinfo.asp?pubid=2008022

U.S. Bureau of Labor Statistics. (2010), Occupational Outlook Handbook. Washington, DC: U.S. Government Printing Office.

How to Succeed as a Student in Psychology

By Christine T. Chambers

As Chair of the CPA Section for Students, I received many e-mails from students asking for advice about how to get into grad school, how to apply for internship, and how to find a job in psychology. While these questions came from students at all stages of their psychology careers, there was remarkable similarly in the kinds of answers and advice I was providing. As I step down as the Chair of the CPA Section for Students, I thought it would be a good time to stop and reflect on my last nine years as a psychology student and summarize some of what has worked for me (no guarantees provided!).

1. Become involved in research early on. One of the major factors that had a positive impact on my ability to succeed in graduate school was becoming actively involved in research as an undergraduate student. I was fortunate to complete my undergraduate degree in a psychology department that provided many opportunities for undergraduates to become involved in research and to work with a researcher who welcomed undergraduates into his lab. Seek out opportunities to complete research projects as an undergraduate student, either as a summer project, directed studies, or honours thesis. It was as an undergraduate student that I became "hooked" on research (prior to that, I had always wanted to be a full-time clinician). It's never too early to start.
2. Love (or at least most of the time, really like) what you do. Choose an area in psychology that you feel passionate about. It may take you a while to figure out what that area is. Read, talk to faculty, and think about what intrigued you most from your psychology courses. If you're not having fun and feeling excited by what you do (realizing that no matter what you choose, there will be ups and downs), it's going to be a long road!
3. Attend academic conferences. I attended my first psychology conference as a 3rd year undergraduate student (a CPA meeting in Charlottetown). It was a very positive and exciting experience for me. As a graduate student, I invested quite a bit of time (and money!) attending conferences. I tried to attend two meetings per year, usually a general meeting (like CPA) and then a more specific meeting directly related to my research. Conferences provide the opportunity to network, present your research, and hear what others are doing. I still leave conferences feeling excited and motivated about my work and new friends made. (But don't attend so many conferences that it interferes with #5 below!).
4. Find your family of mentors. As you progress through your psychology studies, identify

individuals who you can trust and rely on for support. Rather than replacing mentors as you move from school to school or program to program, add them to your family of mentors. I now have a trusted group of psychologists (and other professionals) who I have added to my "family" through undergrad, graduate, practicum, and internship experiences. I value the different perspectives and input that these various individuals provide.

5. Finish what you start. This is critical. Whether it is finishing some data coding, writing up your thesis, or simply returning a phone call or sending a paper to someone that you said you would. Follow through on what you say you will—if you can't, be upfront and let the person know. You may think that, if they don't mention it, they have forgotten about it—they won't! A sign of a good researcher, clinician, and teacher is someone who can finish what they start.
6. Don't let critical feedback crush you. I once received (what I perceived to be) a very critical comment from a faculty member. It came at the worst of times. ... I was physically and emotionally exhausted from 3 months of studying for my comprehensive exams, had just mailed off 13 internship applications, and was in the throes of data collection for my dissertation. For some reason, the comment really wounded me. I have heard many stories from other students describing similar experiences. I ended up taking a "break" from psychology for a few weeks to reassess whether this was the direction I wanted to take with my life. Fortunately, I decided it was. But the experience taught me to extract the constructive part out of such comments (e.g., what can I do to improve myself to prevent against such further feedback?) but then to let it go.
7. Believe in yourself. At times when you feel that no one believes in you, it's important that you do! Don't put limits on yourself. Does this sound familiar? "I think I can" "I think I can" "I think I can"...
8. Be enthusiastic. A colleague recently told me that he was so delighted by my enthusiastic reaction to an invitation to work on a project together, that he couldn't wait to ask me to do something else. Show people when you are excited—but don't fake it if you're not.
9. Apply for everything. I can't stress this enough. There are lots of student awards out there. Many students don't bother applying because they think they won't be competitive. I can tell you that I know I have won awards that I was the only applicant for! Applying takes little effort (often a CV and a letter) but the benefits can be huge. It is great practice for future grant writing and it gets your name and work out there.
10. Be involved—but know your limits. It's good to join committees, etc., but don't overburden yourself so that you can't follow through on your commitments. The CPA Section for Students offers a number of opportunities for students to become involved (e.g., as an undergraduate or graduate student rep). These can be very rewarding experiences.
11. Join associations. Student rates to join associations are reasonable and (I think) eligible as a deduction on your taxes. Association newsletters often provide very useful and helpful information for students. Be sure to join general associations (e.g., CPA, APA) as well as more focused societies.
12. Be collaborative—not competitive. Learning to work together effectively as a team is an important skill to learn. It's more fun to work together as a team.
13. Set goals for yourself. Setting goals (and more importantly) means and time lines to actually achieve these goals are very important. Review these goals with your supervisor to make sure that you are on track.
14. Take time to stop and smell the roses. Enjoy being a grad student. But also know when it is time to take a break. There is no perfect recipe for success—every person is different. Talk to other students and people you admire. Find out what has worked for them. Then put it together into something that will work for you. Good luck!

On the Growth and Continuing Importance of Cross-Cultural Psychology

By Walter J. Lonner

The concepts of culture, ethnicity, diversity, and the misused term "race" (Segall, 1999) have been part of psychology's vocabulary for many years—even going back to Wilhelm Wundt and his interest in *Volkerpsychologie* (Folk Psychology) and the 11 volumes he published under that title. But it wasn't until about the mid-1960s that a convergence of independent events and efforts led to what has been called the "modern movement" in cross-cultural psychology (see Adamopoulos and Lonner, in press). This confluence of activities and initiatives led to the creation, in 1972, of the International Association of Cross-Cultural Psychology (IACCP), an organization consisting of approximately 800 psychologists from some 70 countries. These individuals strongly identify with IACCP and its basic mission of extending psychology's horizons beyond the traditional Euro-American sphere that has dominated the discipline for many years. IACCP holds both international and regional meetings, and is central to organizational and professional matters. The 25th anniversary conference was held at Western Washington University in 1998, marking the first time that IACCP has met in the United States (Lonner, Dinnel, Forgays, and Hayes, 1999). Interested individuals are invited to learn more about these structural characteristics by visiting IACCP's website at http://www.iaccp.org. However, in this brief article I will comment primarily on problems of a conceptual and methodological nature that the introduction of culture poses. These problems are often complex, but cross-cultural psychologists excitedly rise to the challenge of solving them. My comments may also be useful to students and faculty who wish to become more actively involved in dealing with culture and ethnicity in the psychological curriculum.

Enriching Psychology's Scientific Content by Extending Its Boundaries

Most cross-cultural psychologists share the opinion that the only way psychology can reach the highest level of scientific achievement and influence, on par with sciences such as chemistry and physics, is to extend its investigations to all corners of the world. Indeed, if generalizability is a necessary ingredient of what defines a "true" science, then one may ask if psychology falls somewhat short when compared with the so-called "hard" sciences. Consider some facts. The vast majority of psychological research ever conducted has been in the Western world (primarily the United States, the U.K., Canada, and their territorial,

Walter J. Lonner, "On the Growth and Continuing Importance of Cross-Cultural Psychology," *Eye on Psi Chi*, vol. 4, no. 3, pp. 22–26.

scientific, philosophical, and linguistic extensions). And, most psychologists who have ever lived are from these same areas. This striking imbalance has created what has been called a problem of W.A.S.P. proportions—not an acronym for the familiar White Anglo-Saxon Protestant but rather for Western Academic Scientific Psychology, with its mantra of logical positivism and linear thinking and its penchant for basing a sizable percentage of its scientific foundations on participation in research by conscripted "samples of convenience" or "grab" samples known somewhat pejoratively as the American College Sophomore. Thus psychology has received accusations of being both culture-bound (largely restricted to the industrialized Western world) and culture-blind. For example, often left out of the equation in most psychological investigations are different family structures, different values placed on children, radically different views of causality, considerable variation in cognition and perception as a function of different ecologies, the effect of different languages on intricate psychological processes, and demands placed on the individual in a rapidly changing world populated by a crazy-quilt of human beings who identify with one or more of the world's approximately 4,000 psycho-linguistic groups. The list of shortcomings could go on and on. Moreover, many of these accusations and concerns can be just as valid within countries such as the United States with its many different cultural and ethnic groups. Despite the "melting pot" ideology for which the U.S. is known and its motto of "e pluribus unum" (out of many, one), this country prides itself on diversity and even makes efforts to celebrate its multicultural and multiethnic citizenry.

Lest the reader assume at this point that I am a curmudgeonly and antiestablishment psychologist with an ax to grind, that is assuredly not the case. I have been teaching psychology in a solid department at a fine little university to quite able (and overwhelmingly White and generally privileged American) students for about 32 years. I enjoy psychology and think that it's an indispensable discipline that does what it can, often creatively, to understand the human mind and to contribute to the solution of human problems. With the exception of two culture-oriented courses that I designed years ago, I have been using "mainstream" textbooks and carrying on like almost any other Anglo faculty member. Professionally, I believe that nothing is more important than providing students with a solid foundation in the entire range of topics covered in basic psychology. Like my cross-cultural brethren, however, I also believe that psychology can and must stick its neck out further to test the limits of its so-called laws and theories that are often touted as universal without first exposing them to the cauldron of other cultures, languages, and worldviews. By sticking its neck out and testing the limits of psychological theory, by subjecting an important hypothesis to people in other places, and by creatively integrating culture and all that it entails in sophisticated research, psychology will be enormously enriched. A large number of questions may be asked in the search for commonalities or universals. For example, are laws of learning, memory, perception, and other basic processes as applicable in Afghanistan, Benin, Chile, Egypt, and indeed anywhere else on the planet as they are in Anaheim, Chattanooga, or Bellingham, Washington, where I live? If not, what accounts for variations? Is conformity the same everywhere? Is depression to be understood in exactly the same way in all corners of the world? Open an introductory psychology text to four or five pages at random (perhaps excluding statistics and basic physiological processes—but don't close the book on how culture may influence those, either) and ask yourself if the topics on those pages are culturally invariant. And if you are convinced that they are, what is your evidence?

Why Many Psychologists Ignore or Resist the Challenge of Incorporating

Culture in Their Work

There are many reasons why psychologists may not want to get involved with other cultures. Formidable methodological problems (see below) may inhibit many scholars, and difficulties in acquiring adequate funding for research is another reason that may result in researchers deciding to stay home to enjoy the comfortable and familiar trappings of their own laboratories, language, customs, and values. Some researchers may decide that there's enough "on their plates" to study in their own part of the world, with many believing that behavior occurring elsewhere is insufficiently salient to their homegrown research to be of much help. Also, in some psychology departments there may be little incentive to deal with the "outer world" because such research may not conform to the kind of scientific orthodoxy that is rewarded in tenure and promotion decisions. During my career, however, this has not been an issue. I am fortunate to work in a department that has not only provided thousands of students with a solid grounding in psychology, but also strives to "walk the walk" when it comes to culture's influence on thought and behavior. More than half of the faculty in our 25-member department are associates of our Center for Cross-Cultural Research. Another inhibiting factor has been a tendency for many people to compartmentalize disciplines, which carries with it the argument that the study of culture should be left to the anthropologists and sociologists. Moreover, many instructors may shy away from cultural topics either because they don't have time in their already jam-packed syllabi or feel ill-prepared to deal with the complexities of culture. Who wants to appear ill-informed in front of admiring students?

Another factor that is particularly dampening to the growth of psychology, and which can be perniciously ethnocentric, is the absolutistic map of the world—the belief that laws of human behavior, wherever they may be established, transcend cultures. In its extreme form *absolutism* would contend that human "cultures" constitute nothing more than a thin veneer that just barely mask a broad spectrum of universal laws governing thought and behavior. The obverse of this view is the doctrine of *radical relativism*. Relativists believe that behavior and thought can only be understood in the intricate context of specific ecocultural systems. Radical relativists hold the view that everything about the human condition is based on the social constructionist argument that mind and culture make each other up, and that the pattern is never repeated. Consequently, they would argue, it is impossible to make comparisons across cultures. The view that culture and mind are co-constructed is held by a growing number of psychologists who identify with the closely related perspective known as *cultural psychology* (e.g., Cole, 1996; Miller, 1997). Not surprisingly, most cross-cultural psychologists tend to find comfort in the middle or compromise position of *universalism*—the *a priori* belief that there is considerable continuity in all human thought and behavior, and *also* the conviction that culture plays an enormously important moderating or mediating role in most domains of psychology. Indeed, it could be argued that culture is *antecedent* to all thought and behavior. Many psychologists have discussed these matters (see Lonner and Adamopoulos, 1994, and Adamopoulos and Lonner, in press, for reviews of various positions). To get a firm grasp of these arguments and perspectives one would have to consult volumes of writing and analysis that have accumulated during the past 35 years (see below).

What Do Cross-Cultural Psychologists Do, and Why?

Cross-cultural psychology, which can be described as psychology "writ large," has the same goals as mainstream psychology. Indeed, cross-cultural psychologists would hardly disagree with the definition of psychology and the listing of its goals as found, for instance, in standard introductory psychology texts (e.g., psychology is the systematic study of human thought and behavior). In a very real sense cross-cultural psychology is not a separate, fractionated "field" unto itself but a methodological approach, on par with the experimental, physiological, quantitative, and clinical approaches. The special nature of cross-cultural psychology requires, as noted earlier, that the challenges of rather trenchant methodological problems be met. For example, problems of equivalence (conceptual, linguistic, and metric) must be solved. Also, various problems associated with sampling require creative solutions. In a sophisticated research design, one must ask important questions: Which cultures are to be studied, and why? Which communities and individuals should be selected, and why? And precisely which behaviors should receive detailed attention? These are difficult matters to confront effectively and convincingly. However, there are excellent overviews of how to define and approach methodological problems (e.g., Berry et al., 1997, and van de Vijver and Leung, 1997).

The breadth of what cross-cultural psychologists study is astonishing, and it reflects the heterogeneity of mainstream psychology. Thus we see how emotions are regulated differently in various cultures, how anxiety is manifested and controlled as a function of family type, how culture shapes conceptions of the self, and whether writing Chinese characters affect performance on various Piagetian tasks. Cross-cultural psychologists study the consequences of rapid relocation, they try to determine if Gypsy children develop intellectually like other children, and they attempt to assess if and how cultural beliefs affect recovery from radical surgery. They frequently attempt to determine if human personality is structured in basically the same way everywhere, and if age-related declines in cognition are pancultural. It is clear that any psychological topic or concept can be extended to other cultures and tested to determine how safe it may be to generalize.

Resources and Perspectives Are Abundant

This brief overview has barely scratched the surface in describing historical and methodological perspectives in cross-cultural psychology. A recent article in the *American Psychologist* gives a more comprehensive account of the developments in this area (Segall, Lonner, and Berry, 1998). A wealth of information is available to those who are interested. For instance, to get a good flavor of contemporary research in this area one could peruse the bimonthly *Journal of Cross-Cultural Psychology,* which is the flagship publication. For overviews of the field and its various activities, the six-volume *Handbook of Cross-Cultural Psychology* (Triandis et al., 1980) and the three-volume second edition of the *Handbook* (Berry et al., 1997) should be consulted. A number of books, many explicitly written for undergraduates, are available. They include Brislin (2000), Lonner and Malpass (1994), Matsumoto (2000), and Segall, Dasen, Berry, and Poortinga (1999). The forthcoming single-volume *Handbook of Culture and Psychology* (Matsumoto, in press) contains numerous research perspectives. Additional commentaries on the teaching of cross-cultural psychology are given in Lonner (in press), which appears in an APA-sponsored book concerned with teaching about diversity and multicultural aspects of psychology. About 30 years ago there were very few resources and readings in this area. The current situation is remarkably different. The small explosion of scholarly activities under the aegis of cross-cultural psychology has been rather breathtaking.

We stand on the threshold of the new millennium. With it comes the exciting promise of building and maintaining a more vibrant and inclusive psychology—a psychology that consults all that is human on this shrinking big blue marble we call earth. The initiatives and perspectives provided by a growing number of psychologists with a passionate interest in expanding psychology's horizons have been explained briefly. The future of psychology is in the hands of members of Psi Chi and all the other younger psychologists throughout the world. I am optimistic about the future of psychology and am confident that cross-cultural psychology will continue to play an influential role as our important discipline continues to mature and to expand its vistas to the fullest possible extent.

References

Adamopoulos, J., and Lonner, W. J. (in press). Historical perspectives and theoretical critique of psychology and culture. In D. Matsumoto (Ed.), *Handbook of culture and psychology.* Cambridge: Oxford University Press.

Berry, J. W., Poortinga, Y. H., Pandey, J., Dasen, P. R., Saraswathi, T. S., Segall, M. H., and Kagicibasi, C. (Eds.). (1997). *Handbook of cross-cultural psychology* (2nd ed., Vols. 1-3). Needham Heights, MA: Allyn and Bacon.

Brislin, R. (2000). *Understanding culture's influence on behavior* (2nd ed.). Fort Worth, TX: Harcourt Brace.

Cole, M. (1996). *Cultural psychology: A once and future discipline.* Cambridge, MA: Belknap/Harvard.

Lonner, W. J. (in press). Teaching cross-cultural psychology. In P. Bronstein and K. Quina (Eds.), *Teaching a psychology of people: Resources for gender and multicultural awareness.* Washington, DC: American Psychological Association.

Lonner, W. J., and Adamopoulos, J. (1994). Absolutism, relativism, and universalism in the study of human behavior. In W. J. Lonner and R. S. Malpass (Eds.), *Psychology and culture* (pp. 129-134). Needham Heights, MA: Allyn and Bacon.

Lonner, W. J., Dinnel, D. L., Forgays, D. K., and Hayes, S. A. (Eds.). (1999). *Merging past, present, and future in cross-cultural psychology: Selected proceedings of the 14th International Congress of the International Association for Cross-Cultural Psychology.* Lisse, The Netherlands: Swets and Zeitlinger.

Lonner, W. J., and Malpass, R. S. (Eds.). (1994). *Psychology and culture.* Needham Heights, MA: Allyn and Bacon.

Matsumoto, D. R. (2000). Culture and psychology (2nd ed.). Pacific Grove, CA: Brooks/Cole. Matsumoto, D. R. (Ed.). (in press). *Handbook of culture and psychology.* New York: Oxford University Press.

Miller, J. G. (1997). Theoretical issues in cultural psychology. In J. W. Berry, Y. H. Poortinga, and J. Pandey (Eds.), *Handbook of cross-cultural psychology: Vol. 1. Theory and method* (2nd ed., pp. 85-128). Boston: Allyn and Bacon.

Segall, M. H. (1999). Why is there still racism if there is no such thing as "race." In W. J. Lonner, D. L. Dinnel, D. K. Forgays, and S. A. Hayes (Eds.), *Merging past, present, and future in cross-cultural psychology: Selected proceedings of the 14th International Congress of the International Association for Cross-Cultural Psychology.* Lisse, The Netherlands: Swets and Zeitlinger.

Segall, M. H., Dasen, P. R., Berry, J. W., and Poortinga, Y. H. (1999). *Human behavior in global perspective: An introduction to cross-cultural psychology* (2nd ed). Boston: Allyn and Bacon.

Segall, M. H., Lonner, W. J., and Berry, J. W. (1998). Cross-cultural psychology as a scholarly discipline: On the flowering of culture in behavioral research. *American Psychologist, 53,* 1101-1110.

Triandis, H. C., Lambert, W. W., Berry, J. W., Lonner, W. J., Heron, A., Brislin, R. W., and Draguns, J. G. (Eds.). (1980). *Handbook of cross-cultural psychology* (Vols. 1-6). Boston: Allyn and Bacon.

van de Vijver, F. J. R., and Leung, K. (1997). *Methods and data analysis for cross-cultural research.* Thousand Oaks, CA: Sage.

Section One

Personal Reflections

1. Is there a subfield of psychology that you did not know about before reading this section? Explain.
2. Before reading this section, what myths on majoring in psychology did you believe? Explain. Has your mind changed about the myths?
3. What influenced your decision to study psychology in college?
4. Is your college grade-point average an accurate reflection of your interest in psychology? Why or why not?
5. List two areas where you are academically strong and two areas where you are academically weak. What can you do to strengthen your academic weaknesses?
6. Why are you attending college? What is your goal?
7. Of the fourteen suggestions for succeeding as a psychology student in the "How to succeed as a student in psychology" article (Chambers), list two that you are already doing. Explain.
8. Of the fourteen suggestions for succeeding as a psychology student in the "How to succeed as a student in psychology" article (Chambers), list two that you need to do more often. Explain.

Section Two

The Psychology Student Experience

Whether you are at a small liberal arts college or a large state university, the psychology student experience can on occasion feel disconnected. It might seem that what you are learning in lectures isn't quite connecting, and perhaps the relevance of it all is lost. There are, however, many things you can do to avoid that feeling and make the most of your undergraduate experience. We have compiled suggestions for you from different perspectives that, taken together, will help you maximize your time as a student. Don't wait until your senior, junior, or even sophomore year to get involved with the discipline. The benefits of getting involved are explored in the section that follows. While the focus of this text is on occupational options after (and while) earning the bachelor's and advanced degrees in psychology (and in some cases, related disciplines), this next section concentrates exclusively on the undergraduate experience itself. Don't think you have the time to get involved because you have to work? How about working in the field now? Want to avoid making the undergraduate mistakes made by many others? We've got tips for you. Want to get familiar with psychology-related student organizations? We have a few to tell you about. Want to know more about what psychology has to say about culture and ethnicity? We have some helpful information.

This section is broken down into three major subsections. First, we provide information on finding psychology-related work BEFORE you earn a degree in psychology. Here you will find information about associate degrees and certificate programs that can earn you money while you work on your education. Next, we provide some guidance, do's and don'ts, and helpful tips for navigating your undergraduate experience as a psychology major. We hope the information helps you to better enjoy your educational experience, along with preparing you well for your next steps after the bachelor's degree. Lastly, we share some information from ethnic minority students on their experiences with an education in psychology, information we believe to be important for both minority and nonminority students to read.

Oh Yes, You Can!

Working in the Field of Psychology Before or While Earning a College Degree

By Kristen Cole

People often believe that in order to work in the field of psychology, one must earn a graduate level college degree. It is true that the more education and training a person attains in this field, the more available job opportunities become. However, there are many ways to be employed in the field of psychology before earning a college degree, and there are many benefits to working in the field of psychology while earning a college degree. Doing so allows a person to earn income, gain experience, clarify career goals, create a network of professional contacts in the field, and enhance qualifications for applying to colleges and graduate schools. This article describes numerous and varied types of potential employment to consider for those who want to work in an entry-level job in the field of psychology before or while earning a college degree. The areas covered include: mental health, research, business and marketing, social services, health psychology, community psychology, and other psychology-related fields. You will note that often the job duties and tasks of entry-level and paraprofessional positions overlap with those of certified and licensed professionals. In addition, a description of psychology-related Certificates of Achievement is provided, which can provide specialized training and education for those entering the psychology workforce.

Mental Health

There are many opportunities for employment in the mental health arena where one can gain experience working with clients, families, community members, and mental health professionals. The types of entry-level work in this area include conducting intake interviews, assessing behavior, keeping records, peer-counseling, crisis intervention, transportation of clients, recording attendance, participating in activities with clients, and being a liaison between a family and a client or between a family and staff. An effective way to search for such positions is to identify the mental health services agencies in your area and explore their websites for employment opportunities. Such agencies include psychiatric hospitals, crisis homes, homeless shelters, community mental health centers, group homes, vocational rehabilitation centers, and specialty treatment centers (for developmental disorders, Alzheimer's disease, eating disorders, chemical dependency, etc). The following are typical job titles of entry-level mental health positions:

Mental Health Worker
Mental Health Associate
Mental Health Assistant
Mental Health Counselor
Mental Health Technician
Behavior Health Technician
Psychiatric Technician (may be licensed in some states)
Substance Abuse Counselor Assistant
Certified Alcohol and Drug Counselor Associate
Adolescent Care Technician
Child Care Worker
Behavior Analyst
Residential Counselor
Group Home Counselor
Rehabilitation Counselor Assistant
Independent Life Skills Coach
Certified Prevention Specialist

Recommended college courses: General Psychology, Abnormal Psychology, Behavioral Psychology, Introduction to Counseling, Principles of Learning, Field Placement in Psychological Services

Research

If you live in an area with colleges and universities, you are at an advantage for gaining experience working in the research psychology field. Many psychology research scholars are thrilled to have help designing and conducting their research projects. Explore the types of research being conducted on a campus near you by searching their psychology department website. Contact the research team, and inquire if there is a paid research assistant position available. If not, offer to volunteer your time and energy in their laboratory. It is often the case that when a research team sees a volunteer who is a skilled worker and enthusiastic about the projects, they will offer a paid position as their funding permits. Other places to explore research opportunities include biotechnology companies that design medication and treatment for psychological disorders, research hospitals that conduct research in the public health arena, and government, military, and social services agencies that collect data on behavioral health issues. The following are typical job titles of entry-level psychology research positions:

Social Sciences Research Assistant
Statistical Assistant
Biostatistician
Clinical Data Assistant
Clinical Trial Assistant
Laboratory Assistant
Field Service Technician
Quality Assurance Assistant

Recommended college courses: General Psychology, Research Methods, Behavioral Science Statistics, Behavioral Psychology, Physiological Psychology

Business and Marketing

Many people who major in psychology enter careers that combine psychological principles of human behavior with business management. This is referred to as the Industrial-Organizational Psychology field. Psychology classes provide education about group dynamics, personalities, worker productivity, and the effectiveness of certain types of reinforcement. These are all essential to the business and marketing field. The following are typical job titles of entry-level industrial-organizational psychology positions:

Salesperson
Advertising Assistant
Public Relations Assistant
Hospitality Services Assistant
Customer Service Representative
Human Services Assistant
Marketing Research Assistant

Marketing Assistant
Focus Group Facilitator
Human Resources Assistant
Job Skills Developer
Occupational Health and Services Assistant
Occupational Health and Safety Specialist
Product Promoter
Real Estate Agent
Fund-Raising Coordinator

Recommended college courses: General Psychology, Introduction to Industrial-Organizational Psychology, Principles of Learning, Behavioral Psychology, Research Methods, Behavioral Science Statistics

Social Services

Most social services agencies have adopted the biopsychosocial perspective of health and healing, which recognizes that illness and wellness are multifaceted. This perspective is influenced by physiology, mental and emotional states, life experiences, and support resources. Thus, working in the social services field of psychology at the entry level can be a great opportunity to integrate various perspectives while helping people and assisting in developing programs and systems. Many counties have a health and human services agency, which is a great place to start looking for job opportunities. In addition, community organizations are often in need of empathic and motivated workers to assist licensed and certified professionals with their job tasks and responsibilities. Such organizations include social welfare agencies, correctional facilities, court-ordered programs, community programs, mental health task force programs, homeless shelters, and special needs programs. Use their websites to explore job postings. The following are typical job titles of entry-level social services positions:

Child Protection Worker Assistant
Social Services Assistant
Social Worker Assistant
Case Management Aide
Case Worker
Client Conservator
Client Advocate
Supervision of Court-ordered Child Visitations
Family Services Worker
Crisis Center Worker
Youth Worker
Child Care Worker Assistant
Teacher's Aide
Juvenile Detention Worker
Life Skills Coach

Recommended college courses: General Psychology, Principles of Learning, Behavioral Psychology, Lifespan Development, Abnormal Psychology, Introduction to Counseling, Field Placement in Psychological Services, Research Methods, Behavioral Science Statistics

Health Psychology

For people interested in the medical and psychological fields as they relate to human behavior, health psychology may be a good match. It combines physiological and psychological principles of understanding and treating many human conditions by recognizing the relationship among emotions, behavior, stress, and illness. Sites that often utilize such entry-level workers include hospitals, stress-management treatment programs, diabetes centers, pain management clinics, elder care facilities, college peer-education programs, infectious disease clinics, smoking cessation programs, and oncology treatment centers. The following are typical job titles of entry-level health psychology positions:

Behavioral Health Educator
Health Care Technician

Patient Care Specialist
Gerontology Aide
Hospital Patient Services Representative
Public Health Worker
Public Health Educator
Home Health Aide
Nutrition Worker
Group Exercise Aide
Physical Therapy Aide

Recommended college courses: General Psychology, Principles of Learning, Behavioral Psychology, Lifespan Development, Abnormal Psychology, Physiological Psychology, Human Sexual Behavior, Introduction to Counseling, Introduction to Health and Lifestyle

Community Psychology

A holistic view of human behavior includes recognizing the impact that environment and community have upon people. Community psychology recognizes this interaction and seeks to improve the quality of life for people and the entire community. This involves assessing community needs, developing community prevention and intervention programs, providing open access to community resources, and active participation by community members in establishing guidelines, policies, interventions, and resources. By fostering a sense of community among its residents, social action takes place to enhance the quality of life and social justice for all. Entry-level community psychology jobs are likely to be found by searching local neighborhood watch programs, violence prevention programs, youth delinquency prevention and intervention programs, community research programs, promotion of wellness centers, suicide prevention centers, school-based bullying prevention programs, social change organizations, community clubhouses, and programs promoting sobriety and civil behavior on college campuses. The following are typical job titles of entry-level community psychology positions:

Community Outreach Specialist
Community Services Manager
Community Health Worker
Community Support Worker
Recreational Counselor Assistant
Camp Counselor
Community Distribution Assistant

Recommended college courses: General Psychology, Principles of Learning, Behavioral Psychology, Lifespan Development, Abnormal Psychology, Introduction to Counseling, Introduction to Community Psychology, Introduction to Health and Lifestyle, Research Methods

Other Related Areas

The principles learned in psychology classes can be applied to areas of work that do not seem directly associated with the scientific study of behavior. Assisting children and adults with educational, occupational, and interpersonal development is likely to draw upon such a knowledge based. Caring for and training animals also requires a basic understanding of learning and behavior. The following are typical job titles of other types of entry-level positions that relate to the field of psychology:

Animal Trainer Assistant
Veterinary Assistant
Teacher Aide/Assistant
Academic Tutor

Recommended college courses: General Psychology, Principles of Learning, Behavioral Psychology, Lifespan Development

Certificates of Achievement

Certificates of Achievement are vocational technical training programs that provide specific education and training in a field with the goal of promoting employment at the entry level. They are usually offered at community colleges, do not require general education completion, and can be earned before completing a college degree. They are often stackable, in that a specific course may be applied to more than one certificate. Having a Certificate of Achievement makes a person more competitive in the workforce when applying for entry-level jobs. They are an effective way to take a step forward on your psychology career path early in your journey. The following are titles of Certificates of Achievement relating to the field of psychology; most require completing between 10–30 semester units. For more information about Certificates of Achievement, consult your local community college catalog.

Mental Health Worker
Child Development Worker
Youth Development Worker
Community Health Worker
Gerontology Worker
Human Services Worker
Alcohol and Other Drug Studies Counselor

In summary, there are many entry-level jobs in the field of psychology, but it takes initiative and exploration to find them. Do not be discouraged by so-called experts in the field who warn that you must earn a doctoral degree to work in this field. It is simply not true. As you embark upon your vocational journey through the fascinating work world of psychology, be aware of what is desired by those in hiring positions. When researching what employers expect from psychology graduates, Landrum and Harrold (2003) found that employers value the following abilities and skills in their employees: "listening skills, desire and ability to learn, willingness to learn new and important skills, getting along with others, and ability to work with others as part of a work team." Keep these skills in mind when starting your paraprofessional career in the field of psychology. Be sure to maintain a strong work ethic, effective communication skills, and a positive attitude. Establishing collegial relationships and networking in this field is one of the most productive ways to advance into positions and responsibilities you would like to obtain. See the opportunities and seize them. There are many options for working in the field of psychology before or while earning a college degree if you put effort into finding them. Job satisfaction is often high when we do what we love and love what we do. Go for it!

Reference

Landrum, R., and Harrold, R. (2003). What Employers Want from Psychology Graduates. Teaching of Psychology, vol. 30, no. 2, 131–53 .

Psychology Major! What Are You Going to Do With That? Strategies for Maximizing Your Degree

By Derek E. Zeigler and Lindsay M. Orchowski

In any economic climate, it is important that individuals pursuing a career in psychology understand how to maximize their major, explore potential career paths, and market their skills. However, undergraduates majoring in psychology are often posed the question, "Psychology major! What are you going to do with that?" The general public, as well as current majors, are often unaware of potential career paths for individuals with an undergraduate psychology degree. Another common misperception is that psychology majors have a narrow and limited array of career options. For example, people frequently assume that psychology majors must pursue graduate training to use their degree. These misunderstandings limit students' ability to strategically tailor their major to match their personal interests and advance their career aspirations. The purpose of this paper is to debunk myths surrounding career paths in psychology and provide practical suggestions for maximizing an undergraduate psychology degree and marketing the degree to potential employers.

Skills Acquired by Psychology Majors

Similar to other individuals with liberal arts degrees, psychology majors are well trained in problem-solving, research skills, contextual awareness, and critical evaluation. Psychology majors are especially well suited for employment in fields that emphasize (a) communication skills, (b) analytical skills, (c) problem-solving skills, (d) teamwork, (e) flexibility, and (f) compassion. It is important that psychology majors are aware that their training is well-suited to a number of careers, and that they market themselves accordingly. Lloyd (1997) identified eight essential skills that employers seek when considering an individual for a job; these include (a) having a sense of curiosity and working well with others (i.e., adaptability); (b) quickly extracting important information from readings and data (i.e., analysis skills); (c) concisely conveying ideas in writing and when speaking; (d) database management skills; (e) ability to judge appropriate behavior (i.e., group interaction skills); (f) ability to achieve personal goals within an organizational structure; (g) ability to absorb new information; and (h) taking responsibility for achieving goals (i.e., self-management). Many of these skills are already integrated into the curriculum of a psychology major.

Regardless of the specialization pursued, psychology majors generally know how to ask good questions, develop ways to test hypotheses, and analyze data in light of coexisting cultural and societal paradigms.

The training in the scientific method, statistics, and hypothesis testing that forms the foundation of psychological science is highly valuable to employers. Majors are also well trained in recognizing the importance of human diversity and multiculturalism. Psychology majors are often well-skilled in "perspective taking" and tend to keep in mind how human behavior is constructed by multiple, complex, interacting, and intersecting influences. Psychology majors also obtain their degree within a larger liberal arts curriculum. The breadth of courses required by liberal arts majors offers students extensive experiences to gain skills in comparative analysis, conducting research, and creating persuasive and well-developed arguments. Furthermore, as a component of a liberal arts degree, undergraduates are often required to take classes within the Modern Language Department. Multilingual employees are increasingly in demand. Studying a language abroad can also provide students with a unique immersion experience into a culture different from their own. It can be helpful to keep these experiences and skills in mind when drafting cover letters to potential employers.

Common Career Paths in Psychology and Related Fields

Most individuals who complete a psychology degree do not seek careers in professional practice or pursue advanced training (O'Hara, 2005). Among those individuals who do pursue graduate study in psychology, however, only 50% obtain an advanced degree in clinical or counseling psychology (O'Hara, 2005). Many students are not aware that it is not necessary to obtain a Doctor of Philosophy (PhD) degree in clinical or counseling psychology to practice as a mental health care provider. Completing the Masters of Education (MEd) or Doctor of Psychology (PsyD) degree can also enable an individual to become licensed to practice as a mental health care provider. Other options for career paths in mental health care provision include completing advanced training in marriage and family therapy, social work, or school psychology. It is also important to note that just as many individuals seek advanced degrees in other areas of psychology as seek degrees in clinical and counseling psychology (O'Hara, 2005). These advanced degrees include, but are not limited to, the areas of developmental, experimental, social, industrial/organizational, and cognitive psychology.

There is also a range of potential careers well-suited to psychology majors that do not require advanced training. Because of the breadth of training within the degree, psychology majors seek employment in a wide variety of fields. Ample work is available for individuals with a BA or BS in psychology in the areas of residential care, social and human services, human resource management, or teaching (DeGalan and Lambert, 2006). Psychology majors often seek employment in the following areas: (a) state and national human services agencies, (b) shelters, (c) nursing homes, (d) correctional facilities, (e) juvenile detention centers, (f) group homes, (g) human resources, (h) advertising, (i) business, (j) public relations, (k) student affairs (e.g. admissions, residential life, student activities), (l) education (e.g., child care worker, teacher's aide), (m) scientific research (e.g., market research, opinion surveys), and (n) academic research and teaching (DeGalan and Lambert, 2006). According to Campbell (2008), most organizations today feel they need employees with a variety of educational backgrounds. Psychology majors' understanding of human behavior—coupled with their generally strong scientific and liberal arts educational foundation—makes them a particularly desirable new hire (Campbell, 2008).

To work towards employment in the business field, psychology majors may want to explore a few business classes as well as coursework in industrial/organizational psychology. Some majors may consider pursuing a business minor in order to demonstrate to future employers their specific knowledge and training in the business field, as well as their commitment to a career in business.

Exploring Your Interests

Lloyd (1997) suggests that students are often confused and unfocused about their career and academic goals for two reasons: (a) they don't have much information about the variety of career/academic options available or what these may require, and (b) they don't know themselves very well, at least with respect to how personal qualities may be related to career options. Therefore, knowing yourself, your interests, and your goals should be the psyche behind the psych major. The wide range of opportunities offered to a psychology undergraduate through a liberal arts degree allows students to explore their interests while building a strong foundation that future employers will find desirable.

Strategy #1: Narrow your interests and develop a tailored degree. As an undergraduate, learning what you don't like to do is just as important as learning what you do like to do. Psychology majors have significant freedom to explore classes in many different departments. Opportunities to choose courses from other departments (e.g., cross-listed courses) aren't to be thought of as a lack of scope in the degree, but rather an opportunity to discover multidisciplinary interests. The field of psychology has considerable overlap with several other disciplines, especially sociology, criminal justice, women's studies, and mathematics. Enrolling in cross-listed courses may help students discover ways to tailor and personalize their major. For example, math and computer science courses may have useful overlap for students interested in cognitive psychology. Social work classes may be especially intriguing to students interested in clinical and social psychology. Pursuing a minor in a related field can also assist majors in tailoring their degree. Some majors may learn early on that they are interested in child and adolescent development, behavior, and psychopathology, and can build on this knowledge by pursuing volunteer, research, and employment opportunities that allow them to gain advanced training.

Strategy #2: Develop mentoring relationships. College campuses offer a seemingly endless array of individuals with diverse and extensive expertise. Connections with mentors can be very valuable for career development. Beyond simply fulfilling requirements for graduation, a mentoring relationship can help to ensure that you are making the most of your degree. Thus, it can be helpful to develop one with an advisor or another relevant professional early on in the undergraduate degree process. Even if your advisors are not a match for your career interests, they can help to connect you with other professionals who have similar interests to your own. Additionally, it has been our experience that graduate students, although very busy, can also be particularly helpful when it comes to providing feedback on navigating the graduate school application process, helping students to realize various career paths in psychology, and providing an insider's view on what graduate training is like. Aside from helping you to explore and narrow your career interests, mentors can also serve as references for future employers or write letters of recommendation. The quality of a recommendation or reference reflects how well your mentor knows you, as well as the quality of your work and demonstrated desire and motivation for future employment.

Strategy #3: Pursue additional research, volunteer, and leadership opportunities. In addition to helping you test drive a career, an internship gives you relevant job experience to include on your resume. You not only learn more about the particular field, but you also gain a job reference (O'Hara, 2005). Participating in such a position will help you determine if your specific interest is a reasonable choice. For example, some may find counseling very interesting, but later learn that they have difficulty being patient with individuals. It is helpful to understand what the practical components of a career choice will be like before applying for your first position or committing to graduate study!

Working in a research laboratory is an excellent way to discover likes and dislikes in the field of psychology. And notably, faculty and graduate students are often searching for help from undergraduates to assist with data processing, data entry, or participant recruitment for experiments. A simple expression of interest via email to a faculty member or graduate student will likely initiate this process. The primary objective of laboratory research is to see a behind-the-scenes view of how psychological research is conducted. Students will also realize whether the research is of interest to them. Dealing and caring for collected data is also an essential learning experience in a laboratory, and requires patience, persistence, and a careful work ethic.

Being proactive in the laboratory can provide you with not only the nuts and bolts of psychological science, but also exposure to how a psychological research program functions and evolves over time. We encourage undergraduates who volunteer in the laboratory to (a) stick with it to learn the basic skills of laboratory work; and then (b) be proactive about pursuing additional responsibilities, developing their own research projects with advisors and graduate student mentors, and gathering an array of laboratory experiences beyond working on one project. After establishing yourself as a reliable contributor to the research laboratory, larger opportunities to work more collaboratively with faculty or graduate students will often present themselves. These opportunities may come in the form of facilitating a peer-based intervention, assisting on a poster or paper presentation, or collaborating with a professor or peer on an article for publication. All of these opportunities, although time-consuming, can expand your repertoire of skills and help you hone in on your career interest.

Joining an organization such as Psi Chi, the International Honor Society in Psychology, or becoming a student member of a national, regional, or specialized psychological organization, not only demonstrates your commitment to the field of psychology, but also provides a range of helpful career-relevant resources. Participation in group activities around campus can also help to develop your people skills. Even if these groups or activities are not psychology-related, they still reflect a willingness to be involved with group tasks. If you are an events planner or hold a position within a campus organization (i.e., treasurer, activities chair), for example, you may also show how these skills are a good match for the requirements of a desired position (O'Hara, 2005).

Strategy #4: Be strategic. Employers tend to believe that your past academic and professional behavior can predict your behavior in the work setting. Because there are so many opportunities for undergraduates, it is important to pick the ones that are the best fit for you—and not just the most convenient! Therefore, be strategic in locating opportunities that are a good match for further developing your interests. Successful applicants—for a job or graduate school—should be able to communicate in their application why they are driven to the position, what training experiences and classes have taught them about being a good fit for the particular specialization, and also in what area of psychology they would like to develop an expertise through the position.

Conclusion

There is no one way to pursue a psychology major! The strong science background of a psychology major prepares students to pursue a range of careers, and the flexibility of the degree enables students to tailor their degree to reflect their specialized career interests. Nonetheless, students can maximize their psychology major by knowing the strengths of the major, taking advantage of diverse, cross-disciplinary course offerings, partaking in training experiences, networking among faculty, volunteering in laboratory research or clinical activities, and joining peer organizations. By being strategic about the courses that you take, the types of activities you engage in throughout your college experience, and persistent in exploring new interests and expanding existing passions, you can maximize your psychology degree to make yourself a competitive candidate for the career path of your choice.

What Is Psi Beta?

By Jerry Rudmann

Psi Beta® is the national honor society in psychology for community and junior colleges. It is the first two-year college honor society approved for membership in the Association of College Honor Societies, which regulates membership requirements. The mission of Psi Beta is professional development of psychology students through promotion and recognition of excellence in scholarship, leadership, research, and community service. The society functions as a federation of chapters located at accredited two-year colleges. Psychology students become members through chapters at their colleges. The chapters are operated by the Psi Beta student members and faculty advisors. A National Council composed of Psi Beta advisors guides the affairs of the organization and determines policy. The national office in California coordinates and records activities and maintains membership files. Psi Beta participates with other organizations at American Psychological Association (APA), Association for Psychological Science (APS), and regional conventions. The mission of Psi Beta Honor Society is to promote professional development of psychology students in two-year colleges through promotion and recognition of excellence in scholarship, leadership, research, and community service.

Psi Beta provides a means of national recognition by providing

- awareness of the honor by Psi Chi, the APA, APS, and psychology departments at colleges and universities
- verification of membership for references throughout member's lifetime
- eligibility for national research awards (Pearson / Psi Beta research paper awards are $500, $300, and $200)
- eligibility for national community service, chapter, college life project, or faculty advisor awards
- publication of membership and activities in the nationally distributed *Psi Beta Newsletter,* which is preserved in the National Archives of Psychology
- opportunities for ethnic minority students to participate in mentoring leadership programs

Psi Beta offers the experience of operating a chapter and provides opportunities to acquire leadership skills, interact with faculty outside the classroom, learn more about the professional and educational choices available, meet outstanding professionals in psychology, participate in community service, meet peers with similar interests, and communicate with other Psi Beta members online on the national Psi Beta member Web site. Psi Beta membership contributes to the member's confidence and feeling of self-worth. Psi Beta offers the opportunity to participate in national, regional, and local psychological association programs, including paper and poster presentations. Psi Beta student members are eligible for student affiliate membership in APA and APS. Psi Beta membership meets one of the requirements for entrance at the GS-7 level (2 levels higher) in numerous occupations in the Federal service.

Membership is obtained through a local Psi Beta chapter and is open to faculty members of the department(s) sponsoring the chapter and to students who

1. are enrolled at an accredited two-year college with a Psi Beta chapter
2. rank in the top 35% or have an overall GPA of 3.0 (in a 4.0 system), whichever is higher, and have at least a "B" average in psychology (your chapter may set higher standards)
3. have completed at least two quarters or one semester of a psychology or psychology-based course and 12 semester hours or the equivalent quarter hours total college credit
4. have demonstrated a genuine interest in psychology and high standards of personal behavior and integrity
5. have been approved by the chapter and received a written invitation to membership
6. have signed a completed membership registration card accepting Psi Beta's bylaws and policies
7. have paid the once-in-a-lifetime national registration fee of $50

Further information is available at http://psibeta.org

Welcome to Psi Chi

Psi Chi

Psi Chi is the International Honor Society in Psychology, founded in 1929 for the purposes of encouraging, stimulating, and maintaining excellence in scholarship, and advancing the science of psychology. Membership is open to graduate and undergraduate men and women who are making the study of psychology one of their major interests, and who meet the minimum qualifications. Psi Chi is a member of the Association of College Honor Societies and is an affiliate of the American Psychological Association (APA) and the Association for Psychological Science (APS). Psi Chi's sister honor society is Psi Beta, the national honor society in psychology for community and junior colleges.

Psi Chi functions as a federation of chapters located at over 1,090 senior colleges and universities in the USA, Canada and Ireland. The Central Office is located in Chattanooga, Tennessee. A Board of Directors, composed of psychologists who are Psi Chi members and are elected by the chapters, guides the affairs of the organization and sets policy with the approval of the chapters.

Psi Chi serves two major goals—one immediate and visibly rewarding to the individual member, the other slower and more difficult to accomplish, but offering greater rewards in the long run. The first of these is the Society's obligation to provide **academic recognition** to its inductees by the mere fact of membership. The second goal is the obligation of each of the Society's local chapters to nurture the spark of that accomplishment by offering a climate congenial to members' **creative development.** For example, the chapters make active attempts to nourish and stimulate professional growth through programs designed to augment and enhance the regular curriculum and to provide practical experience and fellowship through affiliation with the chapter. In addition, the international organization provides programs to help achieve these goals, including Society and regional conventions held annually in conjunction with the psychological associations, research award competitions, and certificate recognition programs.

The Society publishes a quarterly magazine, *Eye on Psi Chi*, which helps to unite the members, inform them, and recognize their contributions and accomplishments. The quarterly *Psi Chi Journal of Undergraduate Research* fosters and rewards the scholarly efforts of undergraduate psychology students and provides a valuable learning experience by introducing them to the publishing and review process.

Students become members by joining the chapter at the school where they are enrolled. Psi Chi chapters are operated by student officers and faculty advisors. Together they select and induct the members and carry out the goals of the Society. All chapters register their inductees at the Central Office, where membership records are preserved for reference purposes. The total number of memberships registered at the Central Office is now over 500,000 lifetime members. Many of these members have gone on to distinguished careers in psychology.

Psychology Education and Training from Culture-Specific and Multiracial Perspectives

People of African Descent

By Faye Belgrave

Historical Perspectives

Consistent with Sankofa—"in order to move forward one must look back"—an appreciation of the history of Blacks in psychology can help us to understand the contemporary psychological experiences of Blacks in the United States. Robert Guthrie's (1976/1998) book, *Even the Rat Was White*, provides an excellent description of how Blacks have been treated within the discipline of psychology. The book includes a historical account of how Blacks have been studied over the previous 2 centuries. Guthrie discussed the role of European researchers in perpetrating theories of racial inferiority and cites studies from physical anthropology and Galton's eugenics on the inheritability of intelligence. Guthrie also provided a thorough discussion of American scientists' contributions to scientific racism by reviewing work by Jensen and more recent work by Herrnstein and Murray (i.e., The Bell Curve, 1994) implying an intellectual inferiority of Blacks.

According to Guthrie (1976/1998), during the first half of the 20th century, most of the research on Blacks by American psychologists compared Blacks with Whites on physical, cognitive, emotional, and behavioral attributes. The general conclusions of these studies were that Blacks were intellectually inferior to Whites, more psychologically dysfunctional, and had more social and behavioral problems. This negative comparative paradigm in research continues today.

During the last half of the 20th century, more Blacks were trained as psychologists, and thus there have been some notable shifts in the study of Black psychology. In 1968, the Association of Black Psychologists (ABPsi) was formed. One goal then that continues today is to disseminate accurate information on the psychology of people of African descent. To this end, ABPsi has also recently initiated an International Congress on Licensure, Certification, and Proficiency in Black Psychology to certify professionals in Black psychology (for further information, please see www.abpsi.org).

During the emergent period of Black psychology, studies were conducted on how a history of racism and oppression in this country shaped who Blacks are today and how Blacks are portrayed. Akbar (2004) noted that this type of study was reactionary and did not acknowledge the contribution of African culture. More recent studies address topics such as resiliency and protective cultural attributes to elucidate how Blacks have survived and thrived under less than optimal conditions. Many of these studies have been published in the *Journal of Black Psychology.*

Cultural Values and Worldviews

Also critical to an understanding of the psychology of Blacks is an understanding of the Africentric worldview. Africentric psychology considers that people of African descent share a common culture consisting of values, beliefs, and ways of behaving, some of which can be summarized by the following:

- ***Spirituality*** is the most fundamental dimension of the Africentric worldview. It is a belief in a being or force greater than self. Among many people of African descent, spirituality is woven into all aspects of one's life.
- ***Collectivism*** values interdependence and cooperation. A person is motivated to work for the well-being of the group rather than for him- or herself. Persons who are collectivistic in orientation will consider the impact of their decisions on significant others prior to acting.
- ***Time orientation*** within African culture considers the past and present to be as important as the future. Time is not seen as a concrete commodity defined by a clock; rather, time is flexible and experienced subjectively. There is less need to impose one's own time on others.
- ***Sensitivity to affect and emotional cues*** acknowledges the emotional and affective states of self and others. The emotional needs of others are linked to one's own emotional well-being. This value is reflected in the saying, "I am well if you are well."
- ***Balance and harmony*** with nature assumes that one lives in harmony with nature and does not control or conquer nature. These beliefs reinforce the importance of respecting all creatures and creations.

Some of these dimensions of the Africentric worldview are shared with other ethnic minority groups in this country (Zea, Quezada, & Belgrave, 1996). For example, worldview beliefs regarding collectivism, spirituality, and harmony with nature are also found among people of Asian, Latino/a, and Native American descent. (For further information about the Africentric worldview, see the books cited in the Culture-Specific Teaching Tools and Recommendations section.)

Barriers to Culture-Specific Education

There are several barriers to the training and education of Blacks. One barrier that remains is the relatively low number of Black psychologists in doctoral training programs. In 2005, racial/ethnic minority faculty represented approximately 12.4% of full-time psychology faculty. Because all ethnic minority faculty are included in this figure, the number of African American faculty is much lower (APA, 2007). In a 2000 survey of first-year graduate students, 7.2% were African American (Pate, 2001). Clearly, Blacks are underrepresented in the academy. The limited number of African American faculty in psychology departments, especially graduate departments, may be one reason why the pipeline for graduate training in psychology is limited. African American faculty may encourage research on topics of concern to African Americans, assist in recruitment and retention of African American students, and teach classes and integrate material on African Americans in the curricula of courses taught.

In the academy, related problems are the extra demands and responsibilities that Blacks and other ethnic minority faculty often have because of their small numbers within academic psychology and training departments. In addition to regular classroom teaching, African American faculty often chair and serve as members of thesis and dissertation committees, are responsible for diversity training within their departments, and disproportionately serve on departmental and other committees within the university as ethnic minority representatives. Tokenism is often the culprit. Further, because many African American psychologists conduct applied and community-based work, they are also involved in community programming and services to African Americans.

In summary, a major barrier to the training and education of Blacks is the relatively low number of African American psychologists in doctoral training programs and their overinvolvement with institutional responsibilities. They are caught between a "rock and a hard place"—trying to advance their professional careers, engage with local community groups, and meet institutional expectations.

Future Directions

While some progress has been made in psychology regarding teaching about persons of African descent, much more needs to be done. Unfortunately, many psychologists complete their training with little or no knowledge of how to work effectively with Black people and institutions in Black communities and little or no appreciation for those who do. Universal and culturally inappropriate models are being used to train and educate those who will, in turn, provide training, supervision, and clinical services to Blacks.

One suggestion is for universities and departments to offer a core education and training program (courses, curriculum integration, seminars, etc.) on the psychology of Blacks and other ethnic minorities. Allocation of departmental and university resources to support such a program would be needed. Rewards and incentives could be provided for faculty and other staff who implement these programs.

African American and other ethnic/racial minority faculty should not be solely responsible for educating and training on ethnic minority issues. All faculty need to be trained in order to train others competently. Unfortunately, at most universities only lip service has been paid to this matter, and very few resources are spent on training everyone to be culturally competent.

Students should be required to show proficiency.

Preliminary and comprehensive exams should examine the extent to which the student is prepared to work with Blacks and other ethnic minorities. Of course, one cannot expect students to be proficient if they have not had training in this area. Dissertations and theses involving Black participants should be examined for cultural competence. This can be done by making sure that an individual trained in multicultural issues is a member of the committee or by having an outside reviewer.

It is noteworthy that ABPsi has initiated a program where certification in proficiency on Blacks may be obtained. Many of the classes are offered during the annual conference of the ABPsi. (For further information on this certification program, see www.abpsi.org.)

References

Akbar, N. (2004). The evolution of human psychology for African Americans. In R. Jones (Ed.), *Black psychology* pp. 17-40). Hampton, VA: Cobb & Henry.

American Psychological Association, Office of Ethnic Minority Affairs. (2007). *Communique*. Retrieved from http://www.apa. rg/pi/oema/

Azibo, D. A. (1997). *African psychology in historical perspective and related commentary.* Trenton, NJ: African World Press.

Belgrave, F. Z., & Allison, K. W. (2006). *African American psychology: From Africa to America.* Thousand Oaks: Sage.

Bronstein, P., & Quina, K. (Eds.). (2003). *Teaching gender and multicultural awareness: Resources for the psychology classroom.* Washington, DC: American Psychological Association.

Fairchild, H., Whiten, L., & Richards, H. (2003). Teaching African American psychology. In P. Bronstein & K. Quina (Eds.), *Teaching gender and multicultural awareness: Resources for the psychology classroom* (pp. 195-206). Washington, DC: American Psychological Association.

Grieco, E. M., & Cassidy, R. C. (2001). Overview of race and Hispanic origin. *Census 2000 Brief.* Retrieved June 13, 2009, from www.census.gov/prod/2001pubs/c2kbr01-1.pdf

Grills, C. (2004). African psychology. In R. L. Jones (Ed.), *Black psychology* (4th ed., pp. 93-115). Hampton, VA: Cobb & Henry.

Guthrie, R.V. (1998). Even the rat was white: A *historical view of psychology* (2nd ed.). Needham Heights, MA: Allyn & Bacon. (Original work published 1976)

Herrnstein, R. J., & Murray, C. (1994). *The bell curve: Intelligence and class structure in American life.* New York: Free Press. Jones, R. (Ed.). (1991). *Black psychology* (3rd ed.). Berkeley, CA: Cobb & Henry.

Kambon, K. (1998). *African/Black psychology in the American context: An African-entered approach.* Tallahassee, FL: Nubian Nation.

Nobles, W. (1991). African philosophy: Foundations for *Black psychology*. In R. Jones (Ed.), Black psychology (pp. 47-57). Berkeley, CA: Cobb & Henry.

Pate, W. E. (2001). Analyses of data from *Graduate Study in Psychology*: 1999-2000 Washington, DC: American Psychological Association, Research Office. Retrieved June 12, 2009, from http://research.apa.org/grad00contents. html#demstudfrom

U.S. Census Bureau. (2001, August 13). Majority of African Americans live in 10 states. U.S. *Census Bureau* News. Retrieved June 13, 2009, from www.census.gov/Press-Release/ www/releases/archives/population/000437.html

U.S. Census Bureau. (2008, December 2). Facts for features: Black (African American) History Month, February 2009. *U.S. Census Bureau News*. Retrieved June 13, 2009, from www. census.gov/Press-Release/www/releases/archives/cb09ff-01.pdf

Wilson, M. N., Greene-Bates, C., McKim, L., Simmons, F., Askew, T., Curry-El, J., et al. (1995). African American family life: The dynamics of interactions, relationships, and roles. In. M. Wilson (Ed.), *African American family life: Its structural and ecological aspects* (pp. 5-21). San Francisco: Jossey-Bass.

Zea, M. C., Quezada, T., & Belgrave, F. Z. (1996). Limitations of an acultural health psychology: Reconstructing the African influence on Latino culture and health-related behaviors. In J. Garcia & M.C. Zea (Eds.), *Psychological interventions and research with Latino populations* (pp. 255-266). Boston: Allyn & Bacon.

American Indian, Alaska Native, and Native Hawaiian People

By Beth Boyd

Historical Perspectives

When teaching about the indigenous people of the United States, one must understand the history and impact of U.S. government policies. Although every tribal nation has its own unique sociopolitical history and experiences with the mainstream culture, all Native people and communities have been affected in devastating ways. A few historical events and their consequences are discussed in the following sections.

Policies of Genocide

It is estimated that prior to contact with Europeans, Native people numbered approximately 15 million in North America. Between 1500 and 1900, federal policies of extermination, removal, relocation, and assimilation led to the death of roughly 95% of the population. Many Native people died because they had no immunity to diseases that unintentionally came from Europe, but there are also numerous reports of deliberate introduction of smallpox-infected blankets in Native communities as a form of biological warfare (Stiffarm & Lane, 1992). As American settlers moved westward, tribes were forced to move further west. In 1830, the U.S. Congress passed the Indian Removal Act, which allowed for the relocation of tens of thousands of Native people west of the Mississippi River. These forced relocations resulted in the deaths of thousands of Native people. The Trail of Tears relocation of five tribes from the southeast to "Indian Territory" (what would later become Oklahoma) resulted in the deaths of approximately 8,000 Cherokee, 6,000 Choctaw, and 50% of the Creek, Seminole, and Chickasaw nations. On the Great Plains, when nomadic tribes resisted confinement to reservations, President Jackson issued an order to kill as many buffalo as possible to cut off the tribes' main source of food and force them onto reservations. Thousands died from hunger, disease, and encounters with military forces.

In the late 19th century, federal policy focused on "civilization" and assimilation of Native people. During this time, it was thought that the "Indian problem" could be solved by assimilating Native people into the mainstream American culture. Thousands of Native children were sent to boarding schools run by the U.S. Bureau of Indian Affairs (BIA) or Christian missions in an attempt to eradicate their Native cultures and languages through what might be called Western sociocultural and educational "reprogramming."

Threats of incarceration and restriction of food and supplies were often used to force families to send their children to boarding schools far from their homes. Children were given English names, punished for speaking their languages or practicing their cultures, and many experienced severe physical, sexual, and emotional abuse. Children often did not see their families for years, and when they returned to their communities, they had no experience of living in families and were ill prepared to live within their culture and community with a positive sense of themselves as Native people. Children, parents, and their home communities experienced a devastating sense of estrangement.

Millions of acres of communally held tribal lands were opened up for White settlement when Congress passed the Dawes Act of 1887, which allotted 160 acres of land to individual Native families who agreed to register and Anglicize their names. The Urban Indian Relocation Program, begun in 1952 by the BIA, promised to relocate Native families to large urban areas and provide vocational training. Many of these programs did not materialize, and although many relocated families eventually returned to their reservations, approximately 64% of Native people still live in urban areas.

In Alaska, Native villages came into contact with Russian fur traders in the late 1700s. They experienced devastating disease epidemics and losses of land, resources, and subsistence lifestyle. The Alaska territory was purchased by the United States in 1867, and an influx of whalers, fur traders, gold miners, settlers, and missionaries ensued. The BIA began removing Alaska Native children from their villages to boarding schools in the 1940s, creating the same trauma experienced by American Indian people. Alaska became a state in 1958, but Native Alaskans continue to lose access to their traditional ways of life.

The Native Hawaiian experience has been similar to that of Native Americans and Alaska Natives. Prior to the arrival of Captain Cook in the Hawaiian islands in 1778, the Native Hawaiian population is estimated to have been 800,000 to 1 million (Akau, 1998). By 1893, when the last reigning sovereign, Queen Liliuokalani, was illegally overthrown, the population had declined to approximately 40,000 because of the introduction of previously unknown diseases such as gonorrhea, syphilis, and leprosy. The arrival of Protestant missionaries beginning in 1820 led to devastating losses of land, culture, and language. Today, tremendous disparities in health, mental health, education, and income for Native Hawaiians and their descendents mirror those of Native Americans and Alaska Natives.

Loss of Cultural and Spiritual Ways

The traumatic losses that generations of Native people have experienced have been described as the American Indian "holocaust" (Brave Heart & DeBruyn, 1998) and meet the United Nations definition of genocide. The devastation of loss was compounded because traditional spiritual and ceremonial ways of healing were outlawed by U.S. policy until 1978, leaving Native people with no mechanism for healing from these historical traumas. The resulting "historical trauma response" includes high levels of substance abuse, suicide, depression, anxiety, low self-esteem, anger, difficulty recognizing and expressing emotions, and unresolved historical grief.

Today, Native people have the highest poverty rate of any ethnic group in the United States and experience serious health disparities compared with other Americans, including infant mortality (2.3 times higher), diabetes (2.6 times higher), liver disease (3 times higher), sexually transmitted diseases (6 times higher), unintentional injuries (2 times higher), and youth suicide (3 times higher). The Indian Health Service, charged with providing health and mental health services for members of federally recognized tribes, estimates that federal appropriations provide only 55% of what is needed for adequate services (Indian Health Service, 2007). However, to truly understand this picture, one must remember the historical context in which these conditions developed and recognize the tremendous resiliency of Native people. It is the specific tribal cultures, values, and worldviews of American Indian and Alaska Native people that provide the most important source of this resiliency.

Cultural Values and Worldviews

There are a number of key cultural values that should be understood when teaching about the Native people of the United States. Although each tribal group has its own specific culture and value system, there are some values that are common across tribes and interconnected. Some of these include connection, family, respect, spirituality, harmony and balance, community well-being, and generativity.

Connection

Native people value their connection and relationship to all of life. This includes all forms of life: animal, human, and "inanimate." Although each nation has a name in its own language for a supreme spiritual being and its own creation stories, there is a common belief that all living things share the essence of the Creator, making all living things related to one another. Strong cultural identity and emphasis on intergenerational relationships and community well-being have contributed to Native peoples' resiliency for generations. Connection transcends death, as Native people view the relatives who have gone before them as part of their lives and relationships with ancestors as helping to guide present-day actions.

Family

Family is very important and often means a large, extended, multigenerational family. Understanding where one comes from and the role one plays as a relative is very important. In many Native kinship systems, closer relationship roles are assigned to what would be considered extended family in mainstream American culture. For example, a woman's sisters and a man's brothers are all considered "mother" and "father" to their children. Parents' siblings are all considered grandparents. Thus, family relationships among "extended family" are considered much closer and more defined than in non-Native cultures.

Respect

Respect is highly valued for life, for the natural world, for one's place in the natural world, and for each other. Elders are held with great respect because of their wealth of experience and knowledge. Their wisdom is sought out and highly respected. Children are considered sacred and respected as the future of the tribe.

Spirituality

Spirituality is seen as something much more than what one believes; rather, it is a way of living. Each tribe has its own cosmologies, practices, and ceremonies, and spirituality is integrated into every aspect of social and cultural life. There is no word in most Native languages for religion because spirituality is not understood to be separate from the rest of life. Native peoples' strong sense of spirituality has promoted resilience by giving meaning to difficult times and reaffirming connectedness. However, it should be noted that individuals may still ascribe to a designated faith-based group.

Balance and Harmony

Native people value balance within the self and harmony and interdependence with the environment. Wellness is understood as a delicate balance between the equally important physical, mental, emotional, and spiritual parts of the whole person. Illness, adversity, and difficult times are understood as a lack of balance, and healing involves reestablishing the balance and creating harmony within the self, with others, and with the environment. This emphasis on balance is important in understanding Native peoples' view of the planet as well. The relationship between humans and all of the natural world is considered sacred and must always reflect balance and harmony.

Community Well-Being

Tribes are collectivistic societies, and this presents difficulties when trying to survive within the larger U.S. culture, which strongly values individualism. Decisions in Native communities are often made by consensus and for the overall good of the group. As all things are related, there is an understanding that one's actions have an impact on others. What happens to one individual, happens to the whole community. Self-governance within tribes is also in place to act on behalf of the tribal community.

Generativity

Native people recognize a responsibility to promote the next generation's well-being. Native elders teach that each decision of the present must be considered in terms of the impact it will have on the next seven generations. This value of generativity protects and ensures the healthy continuation of the community and the tribe. For example, Native people recognize the responsibility of those who live in the present to preserve the physical environment for the generations yet to come.

Barriers to Culture-Specific Education

American Indians, Alaska Natives, and Native Hawaiians have largely been invisible in American education and within the field of psychology. As with other ethnic minority groups in the United States, the most important reason for this is the lack of full and accurate information within educational curricula about Native people, both historically and in a contemporary context. Native people may be discussed in history textbooks but only as required to tell the White story. Portrayals of Native Americans, Alaska Natives, and Native Hawaiians are often stereotypical, inaccurate, or outdated. Despite ample evidence of the historical inaccuracy of well-known American myths (e.g., the Thanksgiving story), these stories continue to be taught as they have for generations. In addition, information is not presented from a Native perspective. For example, history textbooks have finally replaced the term *manifest destiny* with terms such as *westward movement*. However, if the story were to be told from the perspective of Northern Cheyenne people, the terminology might be *invasion from the east*. Contemporary Native thought, social, political, or economic issues, literature, art, language, cosmology, or culture are rarely mentioned outside of specific "ethnic studies" courses. These inaccuracies and stereotypes continue to have an impact on psychology, as it is impossible to understand people's behavior and mental well-being without understanding their sociopolitical history and realities.

Native American psychologists are more likely to integrate Native issues into the psychology curriculum and training experiences. However, Native Americans account for less than 1% of all psychologists. There are fewer than 200 Native psychologists in the United States, and only about 14 new degrees are granted each year to Native American psychologists. In 2003/2004, 596 Native Americans received bachelor's degrees in psychology (<1% of total degrees awarded) (National Science Foundation, 2007).

Native Americans and Alaska Natives are under-represented in the psychological research literature, and much of the existing research focuses on differences between Native people and White people. For many years, research was conceptualized, implemented, interpreted, and disseminated without any input from the community or consideration of cultural issues. Many studies pathologized Native people and had a damaging effect on Native communities. As a result, many tribes have closed their communities to outside researchers. Research can be valuable to communities but it must be done from the communities' perspective with regard to topic, methods, and dissemination.

In recent years, tribes have begun to establish tribal review boards, contract with researchers to conduct research of value to the community, and retain control of how that information is disseminated. The tribal participatory research model (Fisher & Ball, 2002) is one example of research that is conducted entirely in concert with the tribe, with community input in every aspect of the process. Some tribes may require researchers to complete cultural responsiveness training specific to that tribe before doing any work in the community. The studies that result from this type of collaboration will do much to bring American Indian and Alaska Native issues into the psychological literature and result in better education concerning Native Americans.

Future Directions

Students and educators must examine their knowledge of and assumptions about Native Americans, Alaska Natives, and Native Hawaiians. We must be cognizant of the fact that much of what we "know" about Native people and their culture, history, and experience is what we have learned in standard textbooks, educational curricula, and published research. These texts, courses, and studies have typically "glossed" over differences between nations and even perpetuated inaccuracies and stereotypes. They have not presented Native American, Alaska Native, and Native Hawaiian issues from the perspectives of Native people themselves.

Future training and education concerning Native American, Alaska Native, and Native Hawaiian people and communities must be culture specific. As educators, we must recognize and acknowledge the mistakes of the past and commit to making psychology education about real people, with real lives, living in real cultures. To do this, we must become knowledgeable about the specific groups we are addressing. We need to develop relationships with people from within the culture who can guide and advise us in teach in this material. Finally, we need to make sure that the Native voice comes through in our education and training about Native people. In these ways, we can help psychology become a field that is truly culturally responsive to American Indian, Alaska Native, and Native Hawaiian people.

References

Akau, M. (1998). Ke Ala Ola Pono: The Native Hawaiian community's effort to heal itself. *Pacific Health Dialog,* 5, 232-238.

Brave Heart, M. Y. H., & DeBruyn, L. M. (1998). The American Indian holocaust: Healing historical unresolved grief. *American Indian & Alaska Native Mental Health Research,* 8, 56-78.

Fisher, P., & Ball, T. (2002). The Indian Family Wellness Project: An application of the tribal participatory research model. *Prevention Science,* 3, 235-240.

Indian Health Service. (2007). *Facts on Indian health disparities.* Rockville, MD: Indian Health Service, Office of the Director. Retrieved from http://info.ihs.gov/Files/DispritiesFacts- Jan2006.pdf

National Science Foundation. (2007, January). *Science and engineering degrees, by race/ethnicity of recipients:* 1995-2004 (NSF 07-308). Arlington, Va: Author.

Stiffarm, L. A., & Lane, P., Jr. (1992). The demography of native North America: A question of American Indian survival. In M. A. Jaimes (Ed.), *The state of Native America: Genocide, colonization, and resistance* (pp. 23-53). Boston: South End Press.

Trimble, J. E., & Dickson, R. (2005). Ethnic gloss. In C. B. Fisher & R. M. Lerner (Eds.), *Encyclopedia of applied developmental science* (Vol. 1, pp. 412-415). Thousand Oaks, CA: Sage.

U.S. Census Bureau. (2002). *The American Indian and Alaska Native population*: 2000. Retrieved June 3, 2007, from www. census.gov/prod/2002pubs/c2kbr01 15.pdf

U.S. Department of the Interior. (2002, July 12). Indian entities recognized and eligible to receive services from the United States Bureau of Indian affairs [Notice]. *Federal Register,* 67(134).

American Indians and Alaska Natives in Psychology

By Damian A. McShane

The Need for American Indian Psychologists

Although many young American Indians may come into contact with American Indian teachers, nurses, social workers, or lawyers, few know American Indian psychologists. However. job opportunities on reservations and in urban areas are increasingly available to qualified American Indian applicants trained in psychology. Counselors in alcohol-related programs, diagnosticians in school systems, and therapists for mental health programs are in demand by the Indian Health Service, the Bureau of Indian Affairs, tribal organizations. and public institutions serving American Indian populations. There is a great need for adequately trained administrators for these psychologically oriented programs. The scarcity of American Indian psychologists exists partly because of special difficulties faced by American Indian students. The purpose of this chapter is to identify common obstacles and to suggest ways of overcoming them.

Common Obstacles Faced by American Indian Students

American Indian students face difficulties in college as a result of cultural differences. Values, identity, aspirations and motivations, ability to cope with change, academic preparation, and interpersonal relationships are often cited as areas in which American Indian students differ from other students.

Values. Many American Indian students have difficulty in coping with the challenges of college because they come from cultures that hold educational values different from those of the dominant culture. For example, some American Indian students may learn to view excelling in school as standing above peers and thus undesirable. Yet, achievement may be viewed as a means of becoming competent enough to do something useful for the world, community, family, or self. Often young American Indians are confused by conflicting values and arrive at school without a clear. unified sense of their own values. Furthermore. American Indians lack experience with realistic role models, have little personal contact with adults who can help them make career decisions, or have had little experience fulfilling responsible roles. Not having a consistent value system already worked out often means that the student must spend significant emotional energy to develop one, thus distracting him or her from what personal resources should be applied toward school achievement. The ability to organize and direct your energies, which arises from knowledge of your own values, is essential to success in college.

Identity. American Indian students may often wonder whether friends and family like them or whether the skills they have or are acquiring are important to parents and peers. They may end up doubting their self-worth. Such students may not have a detailed knowledge of their community history and culture or a clear geographical center, such as a place to call home. These uncertainties typically are only symptoms of low self-esteem, which can undermine the confidence and energy the student needs to succeed in college.

Aspirations and motivations. American Indian students may lack professional role models who are psychological service providers in their community whom the students can emulate. Alcoholism, developmental disabilities, divorce, and foster placement of children within the reservation or urban neighborhood are a few of the problems common in American Indian communities. Currently there are few American Indians who are trained as psychological service providers to resolve these problems; therefore, American Indian students have little opportunity to observe what psychologists do and thus have no impetus to aspire to psychology.

Coping with change. Coping with change is critical to the success or failure of American Indian students. Enmeshed in relationships between two disparate cultures, American Indian students are pressured to relinquish their cultural identity; struggle to maintain their cultural integrity while becoming part of the dominant culture; reject the dominant culture by withdrawing or resisting actively or passively; or experience the dominant culture only marginally. These forces can significantly hinder the relationships between personal aspirations and effective use of the educational system. For example. many American Indian students return home to participate in traditional activities or ceremonies during times that are also critical to their studies. Other students become embroiled in political issues to such a degree that their academic performance suffers.

Academic preparation. Many American Indian students simply may not have adequate academic preparation to enable them to succeed in college. Appropriate writing, language, and mathematical skills are particularly important for training in psychology. This lack of preparation may be the case especially for those students who are bilingual.

Interpersonal relationships. American Indian students often come to universities from communal settings with prominent ideological. rather than technical goals. Although the importance of family and tribal relations on the reservation cannot be overemphasized, the interpersonal aspects of college life often take a back seat to the need to learn technical skills of acquiring facts and information, thinking abstractly outside the context of social life, and communicating with individuals who are not only strangers but whose status and interpersonal relationships with students are undefined. This sort of isolation from interwoven familial and group life can create a sense of alienation.

Overcoming Obstacles to Success in Psychology

Tribal cultural norms differ from those of the larger American society; the success of American Indian students often depends on their ability to reconcile cultural differences. Therefore, as a American Indian student, you must develop a clear value framework. Although there are many points of conflict between tribal cultural norms and the expectations of the larger society, there are also points of harmony between the two. These points need to be emphasized. You need to come to grips with issues of competition versus cooperation, public performance and public discussion of making mistakes, time deadlines, direct and indirect handling of differences of opinion, reacting to constructive criticism, and so on. You should prepare yourself to cope with different kinds of behavior or performance that may be expected of you in college. Your study of psychology may help you see your way through this.

It has been shown that American Indian students who have high self-esteem and a strong sense of identity are more likely to succeed in college. A clear sense of identity often results from an understanding of community history and culture, a sense of home, and a perception of the current and future needs and directions important to the tribal community and to the student's potential place in that future.

A perception of community needs can provide American Indian students with the aspiration to become psychologists. This aspiration can be strengthened by finding and spending time with individuals who are doing what you would like to be trained in to do in psychology. You might help a school psychologist who works with children who have disabilities, a counselor who runs an after-care resource program for alcohol abusers, or a mental health counselor who facilitates a support group. Observing, examining, and discussing specific role and skill requirements (as well as what it takes to acquire the necessary knowledge and skills) with an experienced professional will help you refine your career and schooling expectations.

Once at the university you should secure a mentor relationship with an advanced student or teacher in your area of study. This mentor not only can become the model who can guide you but also the ally upon whom you can rely on to prevent and resolve crises. Often, advisers are assigned randomly to incoming students. However, as you get to know a variety of teachers and university staff, you will find an individual with whom you are most comfortable or who would be good role model. Whether the adviser and mentor are the same person, it is very important for you to secure this relationship and to cultivate it.

As early as possible, join university groups that will provide you with interpersonal and professional relationships. The psychology club, student associations (American Indian and others), sports teams, and social groups are all possibilities. Schedule periodic visits home so that they do not interfere with school but still meet your personal needs to restore family and tribal group relationships. Talk and write to family and friends to help them understand what you are doing and to maintain the interpersonal ties that you have with your community. Volunteer for work in areas related to psychology in your tribal community during school breaks to keep in touch as well as to expand your academic development.

Succeeding as an American Indian Psychologist

American Indian students who have been successful in college have been able to adapt to a variety of situations or circumstances into which they are thrust. Whether situational distractions are long-distance travel, ending a friendship, death or illness in the family, or financial hardship, American Indian students who succeed are those who have the strongest commitment to a specific goal that is important to them. They are able to clarify potentially conflicting values, such as learning the old ways versus moving up the ladder of success, maintaining anonymity versus individual visibility in excellence, harmony versus mastery. Some American Indian students have initiated cooperative study groups, which have challenged the belief that being ruggedly and individually competitive is necessary for academic success. Other students have learned to be selective about particular political issues and action before they take priority over academic preparation. It is, as always, important for you to maintain a balance.

There is a great need for trained American Indian psychologists. Many job openings in all parts of the country have gone unfilled because of the lack of qualified American Indian applicants. Your eventual success as a American Indian psychologist begins with your being able to adjust and cope with the demands and forces of the academic life. Once you have succeeded there, the world is wide open for your talents as a psychologist.

Psychology Education and Training From Culture-Specific and Multiracial Perspectives

Latinos

Latinas/os and Their Communities

By Alberta M. Gloria and Jeanett Castellanos

Historical Perspectives

The saying or dicho *el pasado deja huellas* (the past leaves impression) underscores the importance of knowing a community's history in order to accurately understand its current experiences. Identifying key events contextualizes Latina/o realties and provides insight into their reactions and responses to current conditions and policies (e.g., immigration, education)—for example, knowing the impact of broken treaties (e.g., Treaty of Guadalupe Hildago, 1846) and of laws that have benefited the United States at the expense of Latinas/os (e.g., Foraker Act, 1900; Operation Wetback, 1954) and have been central to current conditions and barriers to upward mobility in many Latina/o communities. These laws have perpetuated marginalization and a sense of disconnection for many Latina/o groups, often contributing to a dynamic sense of distrust toward the government and reinforcing a hostlike exchange between the United States and Latinas/os, which affect their daily encounters (e.g., racial profiling). In addition, some groups have been negatively targeted (e.g., Mexicans), whereas others (e.g., Cubans) have received transition services given their refugee status. However, these efforts have been selective and differential among Latina/o refugee groups (e.g., Guatemalan). Finally, it is important to recognize that although laws may be ethnic-specific for Latinas/os, previous and current laws adversely affect the entire group.

Cultural Values and Worldviews

The multicultural counseling competencies model posits three domains for professional effectiveness:

(a) self-awareness of values, biases, and assumptions;

(b) knowledge of the worldview of the "others"; and

(c) synergistic articulation of strategies and interventions (Arredondo et al., 1996; Sue, Arredondo, & McDavis, 1992).

A significant consideration for educators, researchers, and practitioners when working with any cultural/ethnic group is to understand their worldviews—that is, their beliefs, values, traditions, and so forth. Although not all Latinas/os similarly adhere to or place importance on the following cultural values, these are often considered to be core values for Latinas/os (Santiago Rivera, Arredondo, & Gallardo Cooper, 2002):

- *Familia*, or family, is a primary aspect of Latinas/os' lives and values *(familismo).* Familismo involves loyalty, solidarity, cooperation, and reciprocity among family members and is physically manifested through extended kinship systems that include nuclear, extended, and nonrelated family members. For many, familia is the primary natural support system that provides physical, emotional, and social support. In addition, families generally have the flexibility to incorporate new members (e.g., children, elders, and visitors from the homeland) and withstand change. Because interdependence is a critical aspect of family, group needs will often supersede individual needs.
- Closely related to familismo is the approach of caring for and having responsibility to *comunidad* (community). Such responsibility is manifested through *compadrazgo*, or coparentage, of children within families and communities as *padrinos* (godfathers) or madrinas (godmothers). *Comadres* and *comprades* define the individuals in these special relationships. Within these interpersonal connections, family is responsible for providing direction and care (e.g., spiritual, financial) for one another. The process of compadrazgo manifests at special events (e.g., baptisms) and constitutes life-long relationships that tie together and expand the family. In good times and bad, comadres and compadres are sources of comfort and support.
- Central to these interactions are core values in which *personalismo* emphasizes the importance of personal connections and *simpatia* directs these interactions toward the harmonious and pleasing. Personalismo is an orientation in which people are more primary and tasks or events are secondary. Such interactions emphasize dignity and respect for self and others despite personal or social status. As such, personal warmth and genuineness characterize interactions. Similarly, simpatia engenders respectful and harmonious interactions and interpersonal behaviors. The development of trust, intimacy, loyalty, and familiarity within a relationship is the development of *confianza* (trustworthiness).
- The personal comfort in relationships ultimately allows for the expression of friendship based on mutual understanding and appreciation and *respeto* (respect). It is within relationships characterized by *son de confianza* (can be trusted) that individuals freely express *carino* (affection and care) via verbal and nonverbal (e.g., hug, touch of the arm) endearments. Respect within relationships acknowledges the personal power one has, regardless of the degree of power held. It is important that an individual be *una persona bien educada*, or a person who was taught by his or her parents the importance of respect and of being well mannered within personal and public relationships.
- Many Latinas/os hold the worldview that individuals are open systems in which all persons and things are interrelated, as reflected in community and family. Such an approach centralizes group identity and responsibility, which is described in the cultural literature as *allocentrism.* In particular, strong identity with family heritage is stressed, as the group helps to maintain balance between the individual and the larger world or the supernatural. Within this system, the presence of *espiritualidad* (spiritualism) and mind/ body interconnections are emphasized. Similarly, the belief in a higher power connecting and providing meaning to daily life is fundamental to many Latinas/ os (Ramirez, 1998). In many respects, this world-

view perspective emanates from the indigenous, tribal roots of Latinas/os.

Barriers to Culture-Specific Education and Counseling

Provision of effective and culturally competent counseling services for Latina/o clients and communities may be hindered by elements that range from the structural (e.g., societal stereotypes and institutional barriers) to the individual. That is, mental health practitioners' and administrators' lack of understanding of cultural values and worldviews and an unwillingness to exercise cultural flexibility and new learning become gatekeeping forces. Identification of these barriers is a starting point to making changes that engage Latinas/os in counseling.

Institutional Barriers to Counseling

- Counselors-in-training are not provided opportunities to conduct services and/or receive supervision of counseling in Spanish.
- Counseling services focus solely on individuals rather than on key systems such as family, social support (e.g., neighbors, comadres, church and/or priests and ministers), and other indigenous beliefs (e.g., spiritism).
- The role of the counselor is perceived unidimensionally rather than as a continuum of roles (e.g., community advocate, consultant).

Educational Barriers to Counseling

- Instructors teach about culture rather than teach from a cultural approach when instructing about Latinas/os and other racial and ethnic minority communities.
- Specific introductory or advanced courses on Latina/o psychology are rarely provided.
- Community research on and for Latinas/os is perceived as social service and not "real research" and is often overlooked and undervalued at training sites.

Interpersonal Barriers to Counseling

- Clinicians' interactions are steeped in stereotypes and misperceptions of Latina/o values, beliefs, and practices. A lack of cultural empathy will likely lead to relational inequities. Interaction styles (e.g., greeting with hug or kiss) are often misperceived as unethical.
- Clinicians often react/respond inappropriately regarding Latina/o clients' gifts (e.g., *pan dulces*, bag of oranges) or invitations to attend family events (e.g., *Quinceanera*).
- Latina/o clients may feel judged based on their appearance, language proficiency, or knowledge of the counseling process.
- A strong sense of *confianza* is not established to allow the client or clinician to engage fully in the therapeutic relationship (e.g., overfocus on paperwork rather than relationship building). *La pladtica* (small talk) is a culture-specific method that can be used with many first-time participants in mental health counseling.

Future Directions

Implications for Continuing and Graduate Education

With the increasing need for competent and effective services, future considerations for graduate training, continuing education experiences, and workplace issues warrant exploration. It is through the systemic integration and collaboration of different levels of training and education that effective services result. Broad implications for the field as well as specific implications for each service entity and/or provider are suggested.

Implications for Training Programs/Departments

- Hire and maintain culturally proficient faculty who understand racial and ethnic minority experiences, particularly Latinas/os. Have multiple faculty who can teach culture-specific classes and infuse diversity and multicultural perspectives into all courses (e.g., research methods, assessment, theory, supervision).
- Require a general multicultural counseling course as well as an ethnic-specific course (e.g., Latina/o psychology).
- Bridge multicultural learning worldwide. Make use of technology (e.g., video streaming) for national and international scholars to "enter the classroom."
- Create partnerships between the program/department and Latina/o communities to establish training opportunities (e.g., practica) for students and resources for the needs and concerns of Latina/o individuals and families.

Continuing Education Experience and Implications for the Field

- Expand the continuing education credits to equally address awareness, knowledge, and skills about Latina/o individuals and their communities.
- Create continuing education credits regarding the provision of supervision to clinicians who are providing services for Latina/o clients.
- Attend Spanish language training programs to enhance counseling competence for the provision of mental health services with Latinas/os.
- Attend conferences and organizational meetings that specifically focus on Latinas/os (e.g., National Latina/o Psychological Association, American Association of Hispanics in Higher Education).
- Refer to Latina/o journals such as the *Journal of Hispanics in Higher Education and the Hispanic Journal of Behavioral Sciences. The Journal of Multicultural Counseling and Development and Cultural Diversity and Ethnic Minority Psychology* are also relevant sources.

Workplace Considerations and Implications for the Field

- Collaborate with nonprofit and local Latina/o community centers to provide workshops and lectures about Latina/o communities, needs, and availability of resources.
- Provide services outside of the agency at satellite centers that are centrally located within Latina/o communities (e.g., churches, community center).

Implications for Agency Directors

- Incorporate a biannual or annual review of staff members to ensure minimum cultural competence to work with Latinas/os and other members of diverse communities.
- Hold case conferences that include multidisciplinary teams (e.g., psychiatry, social work) to share perspectives that address Latina/o clients and considerations.
- As agency director, establish your own community-based advisory council.
- Establish a community liaison committee where agency staff meet with Latina/o community members to plan a strategic response for community needs.

Learning is a lifelong process that extends beyond the classroom and incorporates multiple roles and functions as educator, practitioner, and learner. Requiring personal commitment and investment, the call for cultural competence must occur at all levels of education and training, including both prevention and intervention efforts. The issues and needs of Latina/o individuals and their communities can be approached by collectively addressing organizational infrastructures, integrating Latina/o-specific pedagogy, attending to specific interpersonal interactions, and reflecting on personal experiences.

References

Arredondo, P., Toporek, R., Brown, S. P., Jones, J., Locke, D. C., Sanchez, J., & Stadler,H. (1996). Operationalization of the multicultural counseling competencies. *Journal of Multicultural Counseling and Development*, 24, 42-78.

Ramirez, M. (1998). *Multicultural/multiracial psychology: Mestizo perspectives in personality and mental health.* Northvale, NJ: Jason Aronson.

Santiago Rivera, A. L., Arredondo, P., & Gallardo Cooper, M. (2002). *Counseling Latinos and la familia: A practical guide*. Thousand Oaks, CA: Sage.

Sue, D. W., Arredondo, P., & McDavis, R. (1992). Multicultural competencies and standards: A call to the profession. *Journal of Counseling & Development,* 70, 477-486.

U.S. Census Bureau. (2007, July 16). *Facts for features* (CB07 FF.14). Retrieved from http://www.census.gov/Press-Release/www/2007/cb07ff-14.pdf

Recommended Readings

Atkinson, D. R., Thompson, C. E., & Grant, S. K. (1993). A three-dimensional model for counseling racial/ethnic minorities. *The Counseling Psychologist,* 21, 257-277.

Casas, J. M., & Pytluk, S. D. (1995). Hispanic identity development: Implications for research and practice. In J. G., Ponterotto, J. M. Casas, L. A. Suzuki, & C. M. Alexander (Eds.), *Handbook of multicultural counseling* (pp. 155-180). Thousand Oaks, CA: Sage.

Espin, O. M. (1997). *Latina realities: Essays on healing, migration, and sexuality.* Boulder, CO: Westview Press.

Falicov, C. J. (1998). Latino families in therapy: *A guide to multicultural practice.* New York: Guildford Press.

Gonzalez, J. (2000). Harvest of empire: *A history of Latina/os in America.* New York: Viking Penguin.

Velasquez, R. J., Arellano, L. M., & McNeill, B. W. (2004). (Eds.). *The handbook of Chicana/o psychology and mental health.* Mahwah, NJ: Erlbaum.

Asian Americans in Psychology

By Richard M. Suinn

Obstacles Facing Asian Americans Considering Psychology

As an Asian American student majoring in psychology. you will need to deal with a variety of issues. Assuming that your family retains an Asian cultural orientation, you may be faced with a feeling that they think you are majoring in a marginal field. In some Asian languages, there is no exact word for psychology. Psychology in many Asian countries today is still struggling for recognition. You may need to be prepared to share your knowledge with your parents, grandparents, and aunts and uncles in terms they can understand. In some instances, the scholarliness of the field can convey that it is intellectually appropriate. In others, the various graduate specialties highlight job opportunities. In other instances, the growing body of knowledge directly relevant to psychology and topics concerning ethnic minorities can provide a contact point. In some cases, the presence of a faculty member who is Asian American conveys a certain reassurance that the field is a valid one. However, if your family expresses concern, you will need to be prepared to express you own reasons for selecting psychology. If you have chosen psychology for the right reasons, prepare yourself to be patient and understanding of your family's concerns. Their interest is stirred by their desire for you to have the best life possible with your talents.

Keep open the possibility; however, that you may really have not selected psychology appropriately. … [T]here are a variety of fields and professions that assist people. Social workers, attorneys, nurses, day-care personnel, teachers, and ministers are all in the business of helping people. You should use all your personal and local resources to help you decide about your major and what career direction you wish to take. … It might be helpful to look at the educational history of a distinguished Asian American psychologist in order to see what directions he took to arrive at choosing psychology as his major and career.

Profile of an Asian American Psychologist

After a successful academic high school education, he enrolled in a local university. However, beyond knowing that he was a natural for more academic studies, he really did not have any strong sense for a major and had not received any vocational counseling. Being bright and competent, he soon learned, did not guarantee making a sophisticated vocational choice. The world of science became his immediate, though not well-considered, choice. He declared a medical technology major on the admission application, changed to physics on the day of freshman orientation, then to chemistry by the start of classes. One semester of chemistry was enough for him to realize that he had best look elsewhere.

What was going on? First, his selection of science, including the early medical science choice, reflected family standards. There was no explicit pressure on him to become a doctor, but he knew that by choosing a medical science degree, his folks would be pleased. Additionally, there was a sense that majoring in another field would mean wasting intelligence on unchallenging ventures. The standard was to achieve the highest levels; society and family defined sCience as representing such levels.

Selecting psychology as his major, then, came about because he realized that intellectual curiosity can be channeled into curiosity about the human being. The interest in orderliness that was the attraction to the formulas of chemistry fit some of the course content of psychology as well, such as the paradigms of Hullian learning and the psychometric methods and concepts underlying psychological test construction. A major event was discovering that he did not need to choose a field that was worthwhile or valuable or respectable as defined by society's stereotypes. He realized that psychology is indeed a science and has specialties ranging from the applied science to theory construction to mathematical and statistical developments. The topic of psychology is always the human being; the laws that are developed inevitably are relevant to people. At the same time, there is an important role for the student who is less interested in relating to people and more interested in the laboratory or even in computer simulations.

To consider psychology as a major, as this psychologist did, may be difficult for the majority of Asian American students. The bunching up of Asian American students in the engineering and science majors today is due to a number of factors. Many of these students are following their aptitudes for mathematics, or physics, or engineering. A number have been encouraged by earlier successes in science fairs and have therefore given less attention to their equal competencies in less-reinforced skills. Some are responding to the stereotype that Asian American students are truly scholarly and are less outgoing. Possibly there is still the desire to succeed and to accept the current societal definitions of what fields are considered valuable and worthwhile. Parents who have themselves been in business or nonscientific occupations tend to hope that their children will carry the family name to further levels of achievement.

On Being an Asian American Student

Studies of ethnic minorities have recognized the importance of identity. Because you look different from the majority culture, you have to confront this difference for yourself. If your family retains traditional values, you may already be evaluating where your identity falls. Some Asian Americans elect to have an Asian background and value system as their primary identity. For others, a purely Western orientation has been chosen. In some cases, biculturalism is more descriptive. Such Asian Americans may feel more kinship with other Asians and Asian values but also accept certain Western standards and aspirations. None of these approaches to identity are without gratifications and conflict. You may be faced with making decisions in college in terms of your identity.

As more and more universities accept that ethnic minorities contribute important diversity to their campuses and view such diversity as a positive part of the educational experience for all students, your minority status can become a source of visibility.

Although you may not feel Asian or different, or may wish to go unnoticed, you may occasionally find your ethnicity identified, such as in a sociology course on culture. Interested faculty may assume that you are an expert in not only Asian values, but also Asian philosophy and Asian history. If you have become personally comfortable with your ethnicity, then such interest would be relatively easy to handle. If you are knowledgeable about Asian affairs, then you can share your knowledge; if you are not, you can discuss the stereotype that assumed that you are an expert and how you feel about being viewed in this manner. If you have not resolved your identity, then the experience might become a valuable stimulus for you to introspect more on the matter.

Asian American students tend to shy away from viewing themselves as minorities. The term may connote negative perceptions that Asian Americans wish to avoid, such as being poor, underprivileged, militant, or foreign. Asian Americans are physically different in appearance; others do react to these differences; there are stereotypes, some of which are intentionally derogatory; there has been evidence of overt prejudice. But being labeled as an ethnic minority does not simply suggest negative association. Asians do have a separate cultural history with special values. that can be identified within the United States. Thus Asian Americans do fit the two definitions of an ethnic minority: a group with physically distinctive features that are different from those of the dominant culture that has maintained certain unique cultural mores or traditions; and a subgroup that has experienced discrimination (for instance, Asian Americans receive less income even though their educational levels are higher).

The Obligations and Privileges of Being Asian

You will be involved in certain situations by being Asian, even if you dress, eat, talk, and behave as a Westerner. If another dormitory resident is experiencing personal difficulties in adjusting and is an Asian American, you might be asked to offer support. You will need to wrestle with your feelings about this. Spend time clarifying your own feelings, then decide how to respond. Ultimately, your major contribution might be in just offering to be a friend. As an example, an Asian American intern was rushed into the psychiatric ward by a frantic psychiatrist, on the premise that the intern could communicate in Chinese to a newly admitted Asian patient. Although the intern was Asian American, he was not bilingual. So the request was as inappropriate as asking a person from Washington State advice on predicting volcanic eruptions, just because Mount Saint Helens once erupted in Washington. For the patient's sake, the intern did locate a friend who could converse in the right dialect. Later the intern did concede that he regained some respect for the psychiatrist for at least being sensitive enough to try to do something rather than ignoring the patient entirely.

You may inherit the positive stereotype associated with Asians, which includes being hardworking, responsible, quietly efficient, well mannered, and studious. If this stereotype fits you, it will help you go far in clubs, committees, and organizations. If not, and the circumstances warrant, you may need to enable others to recognize you for what you are as an individual. Your major effort may be solely to achieve being understood as a unique person, irrespective of how this relates to general minority issues.

In some settings, including graduate admissions or applications for scholarships, your special status as an ethnic minority may be important. How do you deal with this? What you are facing may be the mixed issue of personal identity, personal values and commitments, or personal philosophy. If you are bicultural or Asian in identity, you would permit yourself to be recognized in this way. If you feel you are primarily Western but believe that you can serve as a model to others by doing well with scholarship or succeeding in training, you may feel comfortable in the circumstance. On the other hand, if your personal philosophy is to refuse any special treatment, or you believe that your personal characteristics should not influence decisions, you might not have any interest in such opportunities. The limited resources such as scholarships or specialized training programs such as those in cross-cultural psychology should require the student applicant to prove his or her unique ethnic identity via activities. Yet, in many settings, Asian Americans do not receive their rightful share of services, financial support, or training simply because of a failure to apply or a distorted sense of pride at not being needy or a minority.

Ethnicity in Psychology

Until recently. the study of ethnicity did not receive the acceptance it rightfully deserved. However, several events have occurred. First, professional journals and conferences have now accepted research, symposia, and workshops on ethnicity as a variable influencing human performance and achievement. Second, volumes are now appearing on cross-cultural or culturally sensitive counseling and psychotherapy. Third, courses devoted to minority content and research are now offered in many universities, treating the subject as legitimate scientific findings rather then as a social advocacy issue. Fourth, the American Psychological Association (APA) membership formally recognized the importance of ethnicity by forming the Board of Ethnic Minority Affairs, which takes leadership in matters such as identifying ethnic minority resources, devdoping ideas for education and training, initiating further scientific research endeavors, and promoting culturally sensitive delivery systems. The membership has elected two minority persons to be presidents of APA. Fifth, in addition to participating in the efforts of APA, Asian American psychologists have also organized their own professional association, the Asian American Psychological Association. And finally, the National Institute of Mental Health sponsored the National Asian American Psychology Training Conference, in recognition of the importance and needs of Asian American psychologists.

Studying Ethnicity Within Psychology

In the event that you wish to become involved in ethnicity studies, there are many avenues for you to pursue regardless of what specialty you elect within tbe field of psychology. For example, if you eventually specialize in the branch of experimental psychology dealing with cognitions or information processing, you might eventually study the influence of bilingualism on concept formation or decision making among Asian Americans. If you select work in developmental psychology, you might examine the role of family approaches to discipline as they relate to performance of Asian American children. If you become interested in clinical psychology, you could devote attention to the ways in which different cultures provide coping resources or the effects of folk treatment approaches for abnormal behaviors.

How can you best prepare for your future studies in etbnic psychology? As a start, discover your roots. Find out how your parents' generation perceives and thinks about life, what values are involved in their decisions, and how their decisions are made. Engage in those aspects of tradition that offer you more perspective, such as an Asian church. Observe your familial environment with fresh eyes: Are there activities that represent culture and meanings you had overlooked? Seek out and compare reactions of Asian Americans and non-Asians to the same events, to learn about similarities and differences. Furtber, be alert for those who can provide oral histories, an intriguing source of information that may not be found in books.

On campus, take advantage of Asian American student services or Asian American student organizations. Remember that the student services are not only for students in academic or financial trouble, but can be a locus for people sharing similar ethnic characteristics. It can also be a resource for achieving more information, such as arranging for visits from Asian touring performance groups, or for special speakers, or for involvement with research projects. Do not overlook the non-Asian faculty and students who are doing things that may stimulate your own growth and identity. The professor who teaches Asian literature, philosophy, or geology may provide insights, even though he or she might not be Asian. People of other ethnic backgrounds might engage you in discussions about their own thoughts or beliefs that can raise topics equally important to you.

Find out who has written on subjects of interest to you by talking to faculty. Start to identify common tbemes, conflicts, or issues that psychologists are studying related to Asian Americans. See if you can identify recurring names of experts, especially those who are themselves Asian Americans. Engage in projects that lead you to become involved. Help plan activities or locate resources for an Asian Awareness Week, including defining the goals you think should be met by this endeavor. Select a term paper topic associated with ethnicity for your courses in and outside of psychology. Volunteer to do special studies research projects with a faculty member who is sympathetic and interested in ethnicity. Enroll in courses that offer a scientific foundation from different viewpoints, such as sociology, anthropology, literature, philosophy, and political science. If you are not bilingual, you may consider some exposure to conversational language classes.

If you live in a community with a large Asian population, do volunteer work in nursing homes, crisis centers, or Asian American counseling centers. Attend case conferences, training presentations, or public speeches in Asian psychology sponsored by the community agency. Befriend an Asian American graduate student. Find out about his or her plans and interests in psychology. Seek advice about undergraduate experiences and what opportunities to take advantage of before graduation. Establish links with major organizations. Ask to be on the mailing list of groups, such as APA's Board of Ethnic Minority Affairs. Become a student member of the Asian American Psychological Association and attend meetings. And finally, by all means retain a balance. Ethnic psychology does not exist in a vacuum. Learn all you can about the basic foundation material of psychology, then expand your horizons to include material on ethnicity and continue to let your horizons expand!

Psychology Education and Training from Culture-Specific and Multiracial Perspectives

Asian Americans

Asian American People and Their Communities

By Karen L. Suyemoto and Alvin N. Alvarez

Historical Perspectives

The history of Asian Americans is characterized by exclusion and racialization, both legally and socially. Waves of Asians from various Asian home countries (China, Japan, Korea, Philippines, etc.) were encouraged to come to the United States as temporary workers to address labor needs (e.g., sugar plantations, railroads, mining), but a variety of laws aimed to prevent them from becoming citizens or from accessing economic and social resources (e.g., the Foreign Miners Tax of 1852, the Chinese Exclusion Act of 1892, the Gentlemen's Agreement of 1907, the Alien Land Act of 1913, the Asiatic Barred Zone Act of 1917, the Cable Act of 1922, etc.).

Social and economic organizations and movements also aimed to exclude or oppress Asian immigrants and Asian Americans (e.g., the "Chinese must go" movement in California in the late 1800s; the Asiatic Exclusion League in the early 1900s; segregated schools in the 1800s and 1900s; the burning of boats by the KKK of Texas to symbolize their opposition to Vietnamese refugee resettlement programs in the early 1980s; the anti-Japanese sentiment in the automobile industry, culminating in the murder of Vincent Chin in 1982; the "Dotbusters" in New Jersey and New York in the late 1980s). In addition to legal and social exclusions aimed specifically at Asian immigrants and Asian Americans, people of Asian heritage like Black and Native Americans (whether citizen or not) were seen as inferior and were subject to similar oppressive practices such as not being able to testify against White Americans in court or not being able to intermarry with White Americans.

The history and current experiences of Asian Americans are also strongly affected by the United States' involvement in war and its interactions with and foreign policy regarding Asian nations. Some of the most oppressive practices against Asian Americans were related to war, such as the concentration camps[1] for the Japanese Americans. In contrast, the same war also shaped the creation of more positive views of Chinese immigrants and Chinese Americans and contributed to changes in exclusion laws. In addition, the composition of Asian Americans has been strongly shaped by war (e.g., North vs. South Korean immigrants to the United States, Asian "warbrides," Vietnamese and Cambodian refugees, Amerasians from Vietnam, etc.). The attitudes of many Asian Americans toward the United States and toward other Asian ethnic groups have also been affected by war. And the image that the current average American has of "Asian American" has also likely been shaped by war.

[1] The use of "concentration camp" is controversial because of the links to the Nazi death camps—clearly the U.S. concentration camps were not death camps. The Encyclopaedia Britannica states that concentration camps are "for political prisoners and members of national or minority groups who are confined for reasons of state security, exploitation, or punishment, usually by executive decree or military order. Persons are placed in such camps often on the basis of identification with a particular ethnic or political group rather than as individuals and without benefit either of indictment or fair trial" (http://search.eb.com/eb/article-9025072). To not use the actual term maintains the mythology that the U.S. has never had these types of camps. In addition, as the web page of the Japanese American National Museum notes, the term concentration camp is the one that was used by U.S. officials, including President Franklin D. Roosevelt, at the time; the government quickly changed its public language to make the camps more acceptable (see http://www.janm.org/nrc/accfact.php): "Even Supreme Court Justice Owen J. Roberts declared on December 18, 1944, so-called 'relocation centers,' [were] a euphemism for concentration camps.' The detention orders were called 'civilian exclusion orders,' and American citizens were referred to as 'non-aliens.' This extensive and persistent use of euphemisms not only worked to sidetrack legal and constitutional challenges but, more insidiously, functioned to gain the cooperation of its victims as well as deceive the American and worldwide public."

Overall, the history of Asian Americans in the United States is generally a history of immigrants and refugees rather than of colonization or slavery. However, any statement about Asian Americans as a whole frequently emphasizes the diversity of the group and the difficulty with aggregation: The history of Filipino Americans, for example, is that of colonization rather than of immigration. Myths and misperceptions about Asian Americans are frequently related to overaggregation, as described more fully below.

Cultural Values and Worldviews

As implied by the previous discussion of heterogeneity and diversity, there is considerable discussion among social scientists about whether there is a pan-Asian ethnicity—that is, cultural variables common to most or all Asian ethnic groups. Given that there is very limited (although growing) research on specific ethnic groups (e.g., ethnic groups within Southeast Asians, South Asians, Filipinos), we are not yet able to know whether values from different Asian ethnicities are more similar to each other than to ethnicities from other racial groups. Furthermore, it is frequently difficult to determine whether comparative value differences between racial groups (e.g., Asian Americans compared with European Americans) are due to ethnic heritage or racial experiences in the United States.

With these limitations in mind, the research to date suggests that Asian Americans (particularly those from cultural heritages associated with East Asian countries) are more likely than European Americans to have a collectivistic orientation in which group interests, achievements, and relational harmony are valued more than individual interests, achievement, or needs and desires. This collectivistic orientation is frequently associated with the following values and experiences:

- Emphasis on maintaining harmonious relationships, which may be reflected in higher abasement and affiliation, avoidance of conflict, less assertiveness and autonomy, strong family cohesion, more conformity, and external locus of control.
- Reciprocal obligations through hierarchical relationships, which may be reflected in respect of authority, emphasis on obligation, less expressiveness, more formality, high control from authority while simultaneously fostering internal conscience and control in the service of the group.
- High context communication, which tends to be indirect, sensitive to social cues, and characterized by less verbalized expression, less assertiveness, less extroversion, and possibly related to increased social anxiety when in low-context communication environments. High-context communication relies on shared understandings of history, culture, and social expectations, so that meanings are conveyed indirectly through these understandings rather than directly in the words or content of the communication.

Nevertheless, Asian Americans may vary considerably in how much they endorse or exhibit these characteristics due to acculturation and personal variability. Asian Americans also vary considerably in the extent to which they identify as "Asian American." Racialization and U.S. racial categorizations may or may not be familiar to Asian immigrants or U.S.-born Asian Americans. Indeed, given their relatively recent immigration, many Asian Americans identify primarily or solely with their specific ethnicity. Others may recognize a different racial and/or political identity as Asian American in addition to a specific ethnic identity. Still others may endorse a pan-Asian American ethnic identity with or without an associated Asian American racial identity.

In contrast to the tendency to treat race and ethnicity as interchangeable, it is important to recognize that race (i.e., Asian American) and ethnicity (e.g., Chinese, Filipino, etc.) are differentiated although related identities and reference groups. Examples of this differentiation include a Korean transracial adoptee who has a strong racial identity as Asian American but whose ethnic identity may be Italian American, similar to that of her adoptive parents, or a Chinese American immigrant with a strong ethnic identity as Chinese but minimal racial identity as an Asian American.

Consequently, educators and students are encouraged to (a) explore in significantly more depth the range of values and worldviews of diverse Asian American ethnicities and their impacts on psychological processes; (b) use caution in applying cultural generalities to "Asian Americans" and consider interacting variables such as specific ethnicity, acculturation, ethnic identity, racial identity, and gender; (c) understand issues related to research methodologies, including the comparative nature of psychological research; (d) consider whether ethnic cultural heritage, racialized experience in the United States, or both might be contributing to differences between groups in values and worldviews; and (e) recognize that an individual's identification with race and ethnicity is critical to understanding within-group differences in Asian Americans.

Barriers to Culture-Specific Education

Education within the United States, and within psychology specifically, has traditionally been Eurocentric in both content and pedagogy. Thus, the largest historical barrier to racial and cultural-specific education about Asian Americans has been a basic lack of attention to the impacts of racial and cultural differences.

Minimal Research

Asian American psychology is a relatively new area within psychology and within education, reflecting educational reforms and changes in social attitudes since the civil rights movement. In general, psychologists continue to focus on European American samples and/or fail to significantly incorporate explorations of the impacts of race and culture. While the research in Asian American psychology has increased substantially in recent years, there is still a dearth of information. Moreover, when research does include Asian Americans, researchers often fail to address within-group variability.

Dissemination of Research

Even when research is available, textbooks and other educational resources frequently fail to include such research or place information about racial and ethnic minorities only in a separate chapter. Although information related to the specific psychological impacts of race and culture for Asian Americans may be appropriately placed in a separate chapter, information about racial and cultural diversity also needs to be integrated into all basic content areas.

Educators' Awareness

Despite a desire to be more racially and culturally sensitive, educators who have been educated within a Eurocentric system often lack an understanding of race and culture in general and of Asian Americans in particular. Educators may know how to evaluate a textbook on the basis of inclusion of basic psychological concepts that are "canon" yet have little experience or consciousness of the need to evaluate a textbook or a curriculum in regard to its inclusion of information about Asian Americans. Furthermore, when issues of race and culture are framed as "add-ons," educators may perceive them as "competing" with other content rather than as integral to the exploration of this content and as contributing important depth and generalizability.

Limited Numbers of Psychologists of Color

Until recently, Asian Americans have been underrepresented in the field of psychology. The National Center for Education Statistics (NCES; U.S. Department of Education, 2005) indicated that 5.2% of the doctoral degrees in psychology conferred in 2000-2001 were to Asian Americans. In contrast, only 3.3% of the doctoral degrees in psychology conferred in 1990-1991 were to Asian Americans. The NCES notes that even this seeming increase might be misleading, as many Asians converted from temporary visas to permanent visas in the mid-1990s, perhaps accounting for the increase. Because there has been a historical underrepresentation of Asian Americans in the field, the ability to critique the existing literature and to give voice to the experiences of Asian Americans from within the community, as both scholars and educators, has been inhibited.

Racial Paradigm

The absence of Asian Americans from the curriculum also reflects the manner in which Asian Americans are regarded and situated within this country's racial discourse. In effect, Asian Americans are rendered racially invisible insofar as race is narrowly constructed within a Black-White paradigm, and Asian Americans are perceived as being shielded from issues of race and racism due to their presumed educational and economic "success," as reflected in the model minority myth.

Future Directions

The effective integration of the psychological experiences of Asian Americans into the curriculum cannot be reduced to an understanding of research findings and facts and their insertion in a single lesson. It is equally important, if not more so, that educators and students develop insights into their own assumptions and knowledge of these communities and be equipped with the ability to critically analyze the complexity and limitations of the information to which they are exposed. In effect, the resources and information provided in this chapter should be regarded as the initial catalyst for a more in-depth and ongoing exploration about the Asian American community.

References And Recommended Readings

Alvarez, A. N., & Chen, G. A. (in press). Organizational applications of racial identity theory: An Asian American perspective. In C. Thompson & R. Carter (Eds.), *Racial identity theory: Applications to individual, group, and organizational intervention* (2nd ed.). New York: Wiley.

Fong, T. P. (2001). *The contemporary Asian American experience: Beyond the model minority myth* (2nd ed.). Upper Saddle River, NJ: Prentice Hall.

Lai, E., & Arguelles, D. (Eds.). (2003). *The new face of Asian Pacific America: Numbers, diversity, and change in the 21st century.* San Francisco: Asian Week.

Lee, E. (1997). *Working with Asian Americans: A guide for clinicians.* New York: Guilford Press.

Leong, F. T. L., Inman, A. G., Ebreo, A., Yang, L. H., Kinoshita, L. M., & Fu, M. (2006). *Handbook of Asian American psychology* (2nd ed.). Thousand Oaks, CA: Sage.

Lorenzo, M. K., Frost, A. K., & Reinherz, H. Z. (2000). Social and emotional functioning of older Asian American adolescents. *Child & Adolescent Social Work Journal*, 17, 289-304.

Matusmoto, D. (2000). People: *Psychology from a cultural perspective.* Long Grove, IL: Waveland Press.

Suyemoto, K. L. (2002). Redefining "Asian American" identity: Reflections on differentiating ethnic and racial identities for Asian American individuals and communities. In L. Zhan (Ed.), *Asian Americans: Vulnerable populations, model interventions, and clarifying agendas* (pp. 195-231). Boston: Jones and Bartlett.

Suyemoto, K. L., Tawa, J., Kim, G. S., Day, S. C., Lambe, S. A., Nguyen, P. T. & AhnAllen, J. M. (2009). Integrating disciplines for transformative education in health services: Strategies and effects. In L. Zhan (Ed), *Asian American voices: Engaging, empowering, and enabling* (pp. 209-228). New York: NLN Press.

Tewari, N., & Alvarez, A. N. (2008). *Asian American psychology: Current perspectives.* Mahwah, NJ: Erlbaum.

Tuan, M. (1998). *Forever foreigners or honorary Whites.* New Brunswick, NJ: Rutgers University Press.

Uba, L. (1994). Asian Americans: *Personality patterns, identity, and mental health.* New York: Guilford Press.

U.S. Department of Education. (2005). *Statistical profile of persons receiving doctor's degrees in the social sciences: Selected years, 1979-80 through 2002-03.* Retrieved November 27, 2006, from http://nces.ed.gov/programs/digest/d05/tables/dt05_301.asp

Wu, J. Y., & Song, M. (2000). *Asian American studies: A reader.* New Brunswick, NJ: Rutgers University Press.

Section Two

Personal Reflections

1. Before reading this section, what was your opinion on being able to work in the psychology field without a graduate degree? Has your opinion changed? Explain.
2. Which strategy in the "Psychology Major! What are you going to do with that?" article (Zeigler and Orchowski) do you plan to use during your time in college? Explain.
3. Does your campus have a career and/or transfer center that you can visit? If so, where is it located and what is the procedure for having an appointment with a career/transfer counselor?
4. Does your college have a Psi Beta or a Psi Chi club? Do you qualify to join?
5. Go to the website **www.apa.org.** Click on "Psychology Topics" and then click an area that interests you. What did you discover? Further explore the website and describe one aspect of it that may be helpful to you during your college career.
6. Go to the website **www.psychologicalscience.org.** Explore the website and describe two aspects of it that may be helpful to you during your college career.
7. Go to the website **www.allconferences.com/Science/Psychology/**. Identify two future or past conferences cited that interest you.
8. Based on the readings in this section, what are some of the common obstacles facing people of color studying in the field of psychology? Explain.

Section Three

Gaining Experience in the Field of Psychology

Students (and their parents) often ask why is it that many people believe you can't do anything with a bachelor's degree in psychology (this is a myth; see Section One for a discussion of common myths and misperceptions of psychology). We believe this might be true for only a subset of psychology majors—those who don't acquire relevant experience while in school. Relevant experience is important, not only to prepare for a career in psychology but, perhaps more important, to help you make an informed decision on what career in psychology you are best suited to pursue. Many of the guest speaker professionals visiting our classes have described the experience of believing strongly about the type of career they would pursue or the population they knew they wanted to work with (e.g., young children)—that is, until they actually tried it. Gaining experience as a student may help you learn more about what you like and don't like before you invest too much in a particular career path. As a student it can be easy to fall into the trap of focusing all your energy on going to class and earning good grades, while completely ignoring the opportunities available to you for relevant, career-related experience. In fact, many professors encourage students to gain experience as early as possible and they underscore how critical such experience is to complementing the undergraduate experience. Want to know more? Want tips on how to clinch that job or internship? This section of the collection will help you in exploring various types of opportunities such as working as a teaching assistant or a research assistant, moves that can bolster both your resume and graduate school applications.

Maximizing Undergraduate Opportunities

The Value of Research and Other Experiences

By R. Eric Landrum

These extracurricular activities give you an opportunity to increase your skills in applying the psychological principles you are learning in the classroom. Also, reading about research results and being involved in collecting data and actually doing research are different. By being involved, you give your psychology faculty more opportunities to get to know you and become familiar with your professional abilities and potential, perhaps leading to strong letters of recommendation. Whether you're looking for a job with your bachelor's degree or looking for admission into graduate school, you need to be competitive. If you can take advantage of some of the opportunities presented in this article, you'll be well on your way to achieving a competitive edge. Remember, each year over 70,000 students in the United States receive their bachelor's degree in psychology—what will you do to stand out from the crowd and gain the competitive edge?

Perhaps the best source for opportunities in your department is to consult with the faculty and fellow students in your department. Since your department is going to be the source of most of the opportunities, start there. Some students in psychology are shy or reluctant to approach faculty about the opportunities available; while you may be uncomfortable in approaching faculty members, the reality is that you must conquer this fear in order to reap the benefits of your undergraduate education. Course work is important, and good grades are very important, but you'll need to be more than a good "book student" in order to be successful in psychology. I would strongly suggest that you consider serving as a research assistant for at least one member of your psychology department.

Research Assistantships

What is a research assistantship? It is an opportunity for undergraduate students to assist a faculty member (or members) in a program of research. When you serve as a research assistant (RA), you'll actually be involved in *doing* research rather than reading about it in a textbook or journal article. Typically you receive academic credit for serving as a research assistant; in limited cases, faculty may be able to offer you wages for serving as an RA. There are a number of advantages to serving as a research assistant:

- Acquisition of skills and knowledge not easily gained in the classroom

- Opportunity to work one-on-one with a faculty member
- Opportunity to contribute to the advancements of the science of psychology
- Exposure to general research techniques helpful for pursuing later graduate work
- Opportunity to practice written and oral communication skills by preparing for and attending professional conferences and preparing and submitting manuscripts for publication
- Cultivation of a mentoring relationship with a faculty member that will be helpful for acquiring letters of recommendation

What does a research assistant do? This is best answered by asking the faculty member directly. Although the answers will vary, the following list describes some of the general tasks and duties that you may be asked to perform:

- Administer study sessions with research participants (this procedure is called data collection, or "running subjects").
- Score and/or code the collected data, and enter them into a spreadsheet (e.g., Excel) or statistical analysis program (e.g., SPSS).
- Conduct literature searches using resources like *PsycINFO* and Social Sciences Citation Index; search your local library database for books and periodicals; make copies of articles available; order unavailable resources through interlibrary loan.
- Work with the faculty member to develop new research ideas. Often these ideas are developed from research just completed, the need that arises from a particular situation, or reviews of the existing literature.
- Attend lab meetings with other undergraduate research assistants, discuss research ideas, collaborate on projects.
- Use word processing, spreadsheet, scheduling, and statistical analysis programs to perform research-related tasks.
- Work on project outcomes so they can be submitted for presentations at local or regional conferences, prepare abstracts. If accepted, work on poster or oral presentations of the research materials for presentation at professional conferences.
- Collaborate with faculty members to submit work to an appropriate journal to share the results with the scientific community.

Your commitment to serve as a research assistant is substantial—you will be given some responsibility to see that the research gets done. It is a serious commitment that should not be taken lightly. By watching you complete tasks and by observing you take on more and more responsibility, your faculty mentor will have plenty of good things to write about in those letters of recommendation. If you don't take the commitment seriously, if you make repeated mistakes on important tasks, then the recommendations the faculty member can make will be weakened. (*Important tip:* You know how students talk about the faculty, right? Well, faculty talk about students. You may sour the pool of faculty from which to draw if you do an incredibly poor job for one faculty member—we talk too!)

So I've convinced you that becoming a research assistant is a good idea. How do you get involved as a research assistant? Here are some suggestions:

- Look at the listing of departmental faculty and explore their research interests. If you *really* want to impress a faculty member, do a *PsycINFO* search on them (i.e., an author search), find out what they have published, and read one or two of those articles. Then mention that you've done this while meeting with the faculty member. They will be impressed—trust me.
- Then, make appointments with faculty members, preferably during their posted office hours, to discuss research possibilities. (*Another important tip:* Faculty are quirky. They may want you to e-mail them first, they may want a separate

appointment to talk about research, or they may only want to talk about research during their office hours. Try to figure out the quirks ahead of time by talking to other students.)
- When you meet with the faculty members, be yourself. Let them know that you are willing to work hard on their program of research. Ask them about the specific requirements that they expect from their research assistants. You'll want to know about the duration of the project, what your responsibilities will be, grading practices, weekly time commitment, etc. Also, what length of commitment is the faculty member looking for? Some may want RA help only for a semester, some will ask for a one-year commitment, and some may want longer. Some may want you to have completed certain courses, such as Statistical Methods, Research Methods, or Experimental Design. You might need to think and plan ahead in order to work with particular faculty members.
- Remember, you are making a commitment to the faculty member, and the faculty member is making a commitment to you. Do not take this commitment lightly.

If you have the opportunity, try to get involved as a research assistant. If you do not have the opportunity, try to create it. When you work with a faculty member on a research project, it is a mutually beneficial relationship. What does the faculty member get out of this relationship? He or she gets a hard-working, eager student to do some of the labor-intensive portions of any research project. Many faculty, especially those at institutions that do not have a graduate program in psychology, depend on undergraduate students to help further their own research agenda. If this research culture does not exist at your school, try to develop it. Find that student-friendly faculty member who realizes how important the research opportunity is to you, and chances are you'll find a way to collaborate on some sort of research project. What do faculty think students get from the research assistant experience? Former undergraduate student Lisa Nelsen and I surveyed faculty members in undergraduate psychology programs and asked faculty to rate the importance of 40 potential outcomes from serving as an RA (Landrum and Nelsen, in press). The top 10 most important outcomes faculty believe students reap from serving as an RA are (1) an opportunity to enhance critical thinking skills, (2) preparation for graduate school, (3) gaining an enthusiasm for the research process, (4) participation in the data collection process, (5) improving writing ability, (6) the ability to conduct literature searches, (7) developing a one-to-one relationship with a professor, (8) influencing decisions about attending graduate school or not, (9) having the ability to ask effective research questions, and (10) seeing the research process from beginning to end. Faculty value working with students in this capacity.

Teaching Assistantships

It is important to realize that there are other opportunities that may be available to you as an undergraduate that will help you maximize your skills and abilities and help you achieve that competitive edge. What about being a teaching assistant? Serving as a teaching assistant is typically much less involved and time-consuming than being a research assistant. Usually, a teaching assistant helps a faculty member for one semester (or term) in the administration of a specific course, such as Introduction to Psychology or Statistical Methods. You might have a number of different responsibilities as a teaching assistant, depending on the instructor, the course, the history of the institution in utilizing teaching assistants, etc. Below is a list of some of the tasks you might be asked to do:

- Attend class and take notes so that students have a resource available to get notes when they miss class.

- Hold office hours during which you may conduct tutoring sessions, review notes with students, review class assignments before they are due, and answer class-related questions.
- Help to proctor exams, help to grade exams and/or term papers, and help to enter these scores in the instructor's grade book.
- Hold general review sessions prior to tests where groups of students can receive supplemental instruction regarding course-related topics.
- Help the instructor in the general administration and completion of the course to provide the best experience possible for enrolled students.

The teaching assistantship is an excellent way to build a mentoring relationship with a faculty member. Almost certainly during the course of the semester, a situation will occur where you can step in and provide some real assistance to a faculty member teaching a course. These are the types of events that faculty members will be thankful for and may write about in a letter of recommendation. Also, many of our students tell us that sitting in on the general psychology course is a great study strategy when they prepare for the GRE Advanced Test in Psychology. There are significant benefits for those who serve as a teaching assistant. If you are faced with a choice of serving as a research assistant or as a teaching assistant, try to do both. You'll be busy, but you'll gain valuable skills, abilities, and knowledge for your future.

Field Experiences and Internships

Field experiences and internships are opportunities to learn about and apply psychological principles outside the classroom and in the field. These placements are in agencies that relate to some aspect of human behavior—hence, you can imagine that many places are possible internship sites. They also differ from teaching and research assistantships in that a nonfaculty member at the placement site typically supervises field experiences. A faculty member usually serves as the campus coordinator of the field experience or internship program. In some instances, if an internship opportunity is not available to meet your needs, you may be able to arrange your own specialized internship.

What are the benefits of participating in an internship? The following list was compiled from Jessen (1988), Mount Saint Vincent University (1998), and the University of Michigan at Dearborn (1998):

- Practical, on-the-job experience
- Development of professional and personal confidence, responsibility, and maturity
- Understanding of the realities of the work world
- Acquisition of human relations skills
- Opportunity to examine a career choice closely and make professional contacts
- Opportunity to test the ideas learned in the classroom out in the field
- Opportunity to make contacts with potential employers
- Enhancement of classroom experiences
- Learning what careers not to pursue
- Development of skills that are difficult to learn and practice in the classroom
- College credit
- Possible earnings to help offset college expenses

How do you find out about field experiences and internships? There is probably a key faculty member in your department who makes sure that internship sites are suitable, establishes the policies and procedures for working with agencies, ensures that grades are submitted on time, handles inquiries from internship supervisors, etc. Find that person. Most departments have some well-established connections with agencies in and around your community; if you want to do something where the relationship is not established, you may have to do more of the groundwork yourself. This latter approach gives you the chance to show some initiative and really demonstrate to your internship site your willingness to work hard and persevere at the task.

What will you do as an intern? Ideally, you'll get a realistic glimpse of the types of tasks necessary for success in a particular office or agency. Where appropriate, you will have the opportunity to acquire new skills and hone those that you already have. Internships are not designed to provide agencies with extra office staff or gophers, although you may occasionally be asked to help pitch in when agencies are under time and budget constraints. Although you might not be running a group therapy session, you might sit in on such a session and help facilitate that session under the supervision of appropriately trained and licensed personnel. In addition to these tasks, there may be group supervisory sessions if your site has multiple interns, and your on-campus faculty internship coordinator may ask that you keep a weekly journal of your intern experiences (Jessen, 1988).

Although most students have an invigorating internship experience, we have known some students who come back from an internship with the conclusion "I definitely do not want to do that for my entire career." This decision is a very valuable outcome of the internship process. Although it is unfortunate that the student didn't enjoy the internship process, it is better to have an unsatisfying 16-week internship experience than to go to a graduate program to get a degree to enter a job that leads to misery.

Organizational Involvement

The opportunities discussed in this chapter (research assistant, teaching assistant, field experience, and internship) all focus on skill and ability development. Organizational involvement also provides the chance to enhance knowledge about the discipline and to find opportunities to network within it. On a regional or national level you can become involved in organizations designed for students, and/or join organizations (as a student affiliate) designed for psychology professionals.

The best-known organization explicitly designed for psychology students is Psi Chi, the National Honor Society in Psychology (www.psichi.org). Psi Chi has grown into an impressive organization benefiting students on many levels. Involvement in your local chapter can lead to opportunities to develop leadership skills, and Psi Chi members are often the most involved and well-connected psychology students around. On the regional and national levels, Psi Chi has various offerings. At major regional and national conferences held each year, Psi Chi has an important presence in promoting the scholarly achievements of undergraduate psychology students. Psi Chi has a long tradition of providing student-friendly programming at these conferences. Yes, this author was a Psi Chi member as an undergraduate and also chapter president (sounds like the Hair Club for Men!). There may also be a psychology club on campus. Usually, these clubs are open to anyone with an interest in psychology, and members do not have to be psychology majors. Often, students who are unable to join Psi Chi can be active and involved as members of the local psychology club. On campuses where both groups exist, they often coordinate activities and opportunities for the benefit of all students interested in psychology.

One last recommendation is that you get involved in activities in your own department! Often during the academic year your department may sponsor guest speakers, or faculty members may participate in some sort of colloquium series. As a student, you want your faculty to be supportive of your efforts; you also need to be supportive of the faculty. Attending such presentations also gives you a chance to hear about faculty research, which might interest you and lead to an opportunity to serve as a research assistant. Perhaps hearing about research being conducted at a local homeless shelter might inspire you to think about an internship opportunity. Attending these departmental events shows your commitment to psychology and your general interest in the happenings of the department. Taking advantage of the opportunities highlighted in this article should lead to a more well-rounded education and give you the skills, abilities, and knowledge to make you more marketable with your bachelor's degree and better qualified as a candidate for graduate school. It's up to you to seize the opportunity—now go make it happen!

References

Jessen, B. C. (1988). Field experience for undergraduate psychology students. In P. J. Wood (Ed.), *Is psychology for them? A guide to undergraduate advising* (pp. 79-84). Washington, DC: American Psychological Association.

Landrum, R. E., and Nelsen, L. R. (in press). *The undergraduate research assistantship: An analysis of the benefits.* Teaching of Psychology. Mount Saint Vincent University. (1998). Benefits to the co-op student. [Online]. Retrieved on December 1, 1998, at http://serf.msvu.ca/coop/st_ben.htm

University of Michigan at Dearborn. (1998). *Benefits to the student.* [Online]. Retrieved December 1, 1998, at http://www-personal.umd.umich.edu/~pdjones/benef_s.html [now available: http://casl.umd.umich.edu/casl_stubenefits.html]

Undergraduate Research

Getting Involved and Getting into Graduate School (A Student's Perspective)

By Scott F. Grover

Undergraduate research can make the difference between admission or rejection to graduate school. In fact, many graduate schools are starting to require research experience. Recent research on admissions to APA accredited doctoral programs has shown that research experience and commitment to research were the most important factors in the admissions decision (Munoz-Dunbar and Stanton, 1999). Also, nearly 75% of PhD programs in psychology require experimental methods and research design courses (Mayne, Norcross, and Sayette, 1994). Nearly all of the programs require conceptual statistical knowledge and expect students to know how to be able to apply such knowledge. So where can one gain such experience and technical knowledge?

Research provides a good opportunity to gain experience and develop important skills. Research regarding admissions to PhD programs in experimental, clinical, counseling, and school psychology found that field placements and internship experiences are not as important as GPA, GRE scores, letters of recommendation, and research experience (Landrum, Jeglum, and Cashin, 1994; Purdy, Reinehr, and Swartz, 1989). The message is clear that a scholarly research project can set apart a serious candidate for graduate school. Research experience can give an applicant an advantage and the skills needed to not only get into graduate school but to succeed in graduate school. Graduate schools are starting to make it clear that it is not enough to have textbook knowledge of research methods and design; they require hands-on practical research experience. In fact, when applying to several graduate schools I found that some of them actually require applicants to have had some form of research experience for their application to be considered.

I was motivated to do research primarily because I was told it looked good to graduate schools. I was surprised to find that I not only enjoyed the work but was also reaping the rewards of my hard work for months to come. My involvement in research began by becoming educated on the research being conducted by one of my professors and simply expressing interest to that professor. Psychology professors often need bright motivated students to help conduct research projects. Ask around to find out if a professor is looking for a research assistant; you can usually receive academic credit for assisting with research. Research projects are an opportunity to learn valuable statistical skills that are highly desirable in the workplace. Many organizations in the community often will hire students to conduct research or statistical analyses.

Gain Experience in the Field

It is important for students to know what they intend to study when applying for graduate school. Graduate schools will ask applicants to explain in their statement of purpose what kind of work they are interested in. Some students find they enjoy designing and conducting a research project, while others prefer working with people in a clinical capacity. Research experience can be helpful in determining whether to pursue research or clinical work in graduate school. This can be very important because most graduate schools tend to be oriented towards either research or clinical work. Research provides a good opportunity to figure out what research interests one has and in what field. Also, most applications ask which professors you might want to work with; knowing your own research interests is crucial to matching yourself to a faculty member.

Student research has several advantages that are worth mentioning. Student research is more accessible and typically consists of smaller, quicker projects. These projects can help build a strong vita with numerous conference presentations and publications. However, student research has several shortcomings which include a general lack of funding and lack of technical experience on the researcher's part such as research design or statistical errors.

Get a Mentor

Faculty-led research may make up for many of the shortcomings of student research. There is a marked difference in the quality of research when the research is done collaboratively with a professor that has experience, funding, and contacts. A research project's scope will generally increase in terms of resources, length, and overall quality when undertaken with a professor in a student's department. For example, the research that I was involved in was financed by a grant from the Council for Christian Colleges and Universities (CCCU).

Recent research has shown the merits of getting involved in a professor's research project. A study done looking at the student/professor mentor relationship (Koch, 2002) reported, "students who were mentored were subsequently more productive in terms of scholarly output (e.g. conference presentations, publications). Those who were mentored also felt better prepared for either their current work position or graduate school" (p. 36).

Present or Publish Research

Research gives the student an opportunity to show graduate schools a student's specific research interests and scholarly potential through presentations and publications. Research with a professor often can lead to a conference presentation or a journal publication. A very good way to increase one's chances of admission to graduate school is publishing an article or empirical paper. There are many undergraduate journals that will publish student research, are relatively easy to find, and are worth pursuing. It may be too ambitious as an undergraduate to try to publish in an APA journal. It does take time to prepare a manuscript for publication, but it would be great practice for eventually writing a dissertation or other scholarly work. Graduate schools look highly upon research experience and publication/conference presentations because they are believed to be reliable predictors of future success in graduate school. Graduate schools look for these things: a student who has a high level of motivation, interest in the field, and scholarly potential. Research experience and publication or conference presentations are used often as subjective measures of choosing a candidate for graduate school and are given a good deal of weight along with objective measures such as GPA and GRE scores. A published study asked graduate institutions about their procedures for selecting applicants and they responded by placing heavy emphases on research experience (Landrum et. al., 2004).

Be Proactive

Research is an opportunity to be visible in a student's department. Being active in their department is one thing that students can easily do to increase their chances of graduate school admission. Research experience and being active in the department can have financial advantages as well. As a result of my research experience and activity in the psychology department at Point Loma Nazarene University, I received a large scholarship from the psychology department. Graduate schools also look for students at the top of the department as evidenced by departmental scholarships and conference presentations (Keith-Spiegel and Wiederman, 2000).

An often overlooked advantage of research is getting the opportunity to know a professor on a personal level outside of the classroom. As a result, the professor is often more willing to write a favorable letter of recommendation. Letters of recommendation are given a lot of weight in most graduate school admission processes. Strong letters of recommendation can often make up for other areas of weakness (Keith-Spiegel, 1991).

Network, Network, Network

Collaborative research can allow a student to attend a conference and meet and network with professionals in the field of psychology. Many colleges and universities will have a budget for students to attend conferences and present their research. As a student, take advantage of this opportunity to present research.

Research can facilitate networking and meeting researchers and professors from graduate schools you might be interested in. Conferences can provide an opportunity to link up with graduate school professors that have the same and similar interests as you.

For example, the research that I was involved in allowed me to meet and work with a professor from a graduate institution that I was interested in attending. I made a connection with a professor who shared research interests with me, and he offered to make a favorable comment to the admissions committee on my behalf.

Research experience and networking can prove to be a valuable asset when it comes time to apply for graduate school. The opportunity to talk with professors at conferences and see what their research interests are can be advantageous for determining not only a career path but also to determine the right graduate school program for you. For example, you may meet an expert neurocognitive scientist who is doing brain research with a functional MRI machine at Arizona State University. This would be important to know when choosing where to apply if you're interested in neurobiological research. Another example is when a research project allowed me to meet with professors and researchers from various universities around the country. Through this experience I got an idea of what their graduate programs emphasized and learned of their projects and interests. This information was very helpful when choosing which schools to apply to and was helpful with the application process itself. These conversations can also be helpful when writing your personal statement and mentioning the professors' names and their ongoing research projects. These kinds of details make a difference and show admissions committees that you are serious about graduate study.

These interactions can also be helpful in getting information about the topics of research, which professors are involved in research, who is competing for grants, who has received grants, and who would have money to hire you as a research assistant. Networking can payoff and if I am hired, I would receive a research assistantship and half tuition scholarship. Knowing professors' projects and funding for projects are important things to consider when choosing a graduate school. For example, I have been networking with a professor through my research who is in the process of receiving a million dollar grant and is interested in hiring me as a research assistant; if it works out, I would receive a large stipend. Research experience can equip a student with the technical skills and the experience to not only get into a quality graduate program but to succeed in it. Research experience often can provide many ways for students to distinguish themselves and increase their chances of admission to graduate school.

Research can also broaden students' perspectives and open the door for various professional opportunities. Research experience is by far one of the most worthwhile ventures that undergraduates can undertake to further their professional and personal goals of continuing graduate education.

Four things to do to increase one's chances of graduate school admission:

- Get involved in research
- Network with professionals in the field
- Attend conferences
- Present a poster or paper at a conference

References

Keith-Spiegel, P. (1991). *The complete guide to graduate school admission: Psychology and related fields.* Hillsdale, NJ: Erlbaum.

Keith-Spiegel, P., and Wiederman, M. W. (2000). *The complete guide to graduate school admission: Psychology, counseling, and related professions* (2nd. ed.). Mahwah, NJ: Erlbaum.

Koch, C. (2002, Spring). Getting involved by getting a mentor. *Eye on Psi Chi, 6*(3), 28, 36.

Landrum, E. R., Jeglum, E. B., and Cashin, J. R. (2004). The decision-making processes of graduate admissions committees in psychology. *Journal of Social Behavior and Personality, 9,* 239-248.

Mayne, T. J., Norcross, J. C., and Sayette, M. A. (1994). Admission requirements, acceptance rates, and financial assistance in clinical psychology programs: Diversity across the practice research continuum. *American Psychologist, 49,* 806-811.

Munoz-Dunbar, R., and Stanton, A. L. (1999). Ethnic diversity in clinical psychology: Recruitment and admission practices among doctoral programs. *Teaching of Psychology, 26,* 259-263

Purdy, J. E., Reinehr, R. C., and Swartz, J. D. (1989). Graduate admissions criteria of leading psychology departments. *American Psychologist, 44,* 960-961.

Getting "Real-World" Psychology-Related Experience

By Amira Rezec Wegenek and William Buskist

As you continue to take courses in psychology and perhaps start to read more about the different psychology career paths that you may wish to consider, it may not he immediately clear to you how the knowledge that you have gained in the classroom relates to potential work settings. In fact, the majority of psychology courses emphasize the teaching of psychological theory and practice rather than emphasizing the connection between psychological theories and their real-world applications outside of academia. The connections are there, of course, but are not always made explicit, which is why being proactive and seeking out opportunities to apply your knowledge and talents in extracurricular activities is so important. You can make connections between classroom material and the real world through firsthand experience as a volunteer or intern in a psychology-related position. In addition, internship, volunteer, and practicum experience can be helpful in making you a desirable candidate for admissions to graduate programs. Many of the skills that you can attain through these sorts of positions may help prepare you for graduate study. In fact, it is highly advised that students applying to clinical psychology or doctor of psychology (PsyD) graduate school programs seek internship, volunteer, and practicum experience in clinical settings before applying.

These experiences will also allow you to try out different job settings and work environments, which is a wonderful way to find out whether a potential line of work, or even working with a particular population, might suit you. As a volunteer or intern, you will also gain valuable skills that can add to your personal and professional development. The many communication, writing, computer, and other skills that you can hone in these positions will undoubtedly be great additions to include on your résumé and graduate school admission applications.

Which Volunteer Positions Suit Psychology Majors Well?

Volunteer positions related to psychology can be found in a wide range of settings. If you are interested in clinical psychology, you may be more interested in a volunteer position related to counseling or psychological health. A volunteer position within a company's human resources department might better suit you if you are considering a career path in industrial-organizational psychology. Volunteering to work with children might be best for psychology majors who want a career in child development. Exhibit 6.1

presents a partial list of settings in which psychology students commonly volunteer.

Most of the types of work settings and organizations listed in Exhibit 6.1 can be found in your local phone book. It takes only a few minutes to place a call and inquire about volunteer possibilities. Because many counties offer such community services, you may also contact your county governance offices to find out whether they have a volunteer placement and referral service, although some colleges even provide this service at their career services center. (Actually your school's career services center may be the best place to start your search for a volunteer position.) Alternatively, you may want to look into using an Internet-based volunteer service to help match you with a site that is seeking volunteers. The following is a partial list of web sites that match volunteer interests with appropriate corresponding organizations:

- *Cool Works Volunteerism* (http://www.coolworks.com/volunteer/). This site lists resources that can help you to find a volunteer position and is organized regionally.
- *Global Volunteers* (http://www.globalvolunteers.org). This site offers an international volunteer matching service.
- *Smart Volunteer* (http://www.smartvolunteer.org). This company offers a national volunteer matching service.
- *U.S. Government National Volunteer* (http://www.volunteer.gov/gov/). This site lets you choose your state and find volunteer opportunities in your own area that are sponsored by different government agencies.
- *Volunteer Match* (http://www.volunteermatch.org). This site offers a national volunteer matching service.

In addition, you may wish to consult Silvia, Delaney, and Marcovitch's (2009) book to learn more about the kinds of activities you may wish to participate in as an undergraduate psychology major.

EXHIBIT 6.1

Common Volunteer Settings for Psychology Majors:

- Hospitals
- Day treatment centers for eating disorders
- Day treatment centers for substance abuse
- Substance abuse treatment centers
- Residential facilities for the elderly
- Senior centers
- Residential facilities for youth
- Teen and youth centers
- Teen and youth hotlines
- Tutoring centers for children
- Summer enrichment programs for children
- Psychologist-psychiatrist offices
- Nonprofit agencies serving the mentally ill and their families (e.g., National Alliance on Mental
- Illness)
- Halfway houses
- Shelters for women or children in distress
- Support group organizations (e.g., support groups for grieving families)
- County social services agencies (e.g., child and family services, helping a case manager)
- Private social services agencies (e.g., helping adults or children with disabilities)
- Rehabilitation centers for those who have suffered stroke or other brain injury
- Research laboratories within colleges (see Chapter 5) or companies
- District attorney's offices
- HIV prevention programs
- Alcohol abuse prevention programs on college campuses
- Student health advocacy groups on college campuses
- Domestic abuse prevention programs

Is a Volunteer Position Right for You?

There are some important things to keep in mind before taking on the responsibility and commitment involved with volunteer positions. First, most volunteer positions are not paid and are not meant to lead to paying positions. If you need to spend your time outside of school earning money, take this point into account and consider finding a part-time job or paid internship related to psychology instead

Second, before you agree to take on a position, be sure to ask questions about the time commitment involved. Does the organization require a certain minimum number of hours per week from its volunteers? How much of a long-term commitment would you be making by taking on this position? Time commitments can vary widely from one position to another. For example, volunteer positions such as assisting with a field research project or an ongoing support group require a lengthier time commitment than perhaps assisting with a summer camp program. They both require lengthy training and repeated meetings over a longer period of time. Assess your existing time commitments and ask yourself how much time you have available each week and whether you can stick with a volunteer position over the long term.

Third, you should also ask for a description of the expected duties required in the volunteer position. It is important to make sure that at least some of the required duties will allow for you to gain the type of experience that you seek to achieve as a volunteer. For example, if you hope to learn more about behavior analysis by working closely with animals and trainers as a volunteer at a zoo, you will want to be sure that at least some of your volunteer duties involve this kind of experience. What a shame it would be to find out that your duties were far from working with the actual animals or observing trainers but included instead only cleaning up after animals or interacting with zoo patrons. Being clear about what you are signing on for before you start will help ensure that you enjoy your volunteer position and get the type of experience that

EXHIBIT 6.2

One Student's Perspective:

Annie H., BS, doctoral candidate in clinical psychology, University of California, San Diego, "Why I Am Glad I Volunteered in a Clinical Psychology Setting"

As an undergraduate psychology major, I wanted to be a clinical psychologist but I was not sure what area of clinical psychology to select as my specialty. I decided to serve as a volunteer in the Family Mental Health Program at the local Veteran's Affairs hospital. My duties did not involve counseling people, of course, but I was in an environment that allowed me to learn much about what life as a clinical psychologist might be like.

I am glad I volunteered because it helped to solidify my decision to pursue a graduate degree in clinical psychology and to choose my specialty research and clinical area of couple therapy. As a volunteer, I got the opportunity to work with couple therapists with different types of training, including doctoral-level psychologists, psychology interns, marital and family therapists, and marriage and family therapist trainees. I got to see what they did firsthand by participating in clinical roundtable meetings and viewing videotapes of therapy sessions in which I could watch couple therapists in action. Volunteering at this site allowed me to learn about different models and frameworks of couple therapy, network with clinical psychologists and other professionals, assist in conducting couple relationship research, and show graduate school admissions committees that I was serious about becoming a psychologist.

you want. Read more about one student's experience volunteering in a clinical setting in Exhibit 6.2.

What Is the Difference Between a Volunteer Position and an Internship?

A volunteer position is more loosely defined than an internship position and does not involve any sort of compensation or educational component. Internships are usually work or service opportunities with an educational component and typically involve clearly defined projects and goals, a set time frame, and possible pay. Student interns gain professional experience related to their major or career goal in an occupational area they are considering. An internship usually involves working in a professional setting under the guidance and supervision of practicing professionals. For this reason, working as an intern is a great way to "test drive" possible careers and pick up directly marketable skills. An internship usually requires a level of responsibility that allows a student to develop new skills.

Internships can be paid (via salary or stipend) or unpaid and can sometimes be incorporated into the college curriculum for course credit. Although some students might be less than thrilled to work for no pay, some employers use internships as a way to test out potential employees. Whether this is company policy or not, your experience within an organization can give you an edge over other applicants when you later apply for positions within the organization.

An internship provides students with the opportunity to gain skills that will make them more marketable in the workforce and may lead to valuable professional contacts. Internships also are a useful way for recent graduates to bridge the gap between school and the professional world. Internships provide students with a sense of how the work world differs from the academic world. Interns learn about the inner workings of an organization and about the work schedules, duties, and, roles of professionals within it, which is valuable knowledge for students who may not have had much work experience within an organization or company. Internships can also benefit students who are already in the workforce but are considering changing careers and are not ready to make a permanent commitment. Internship listings can usually be found posted in all of the same places that similar employment opportunities are posted. You may wish to check whether your college career services center has separate listings of internships or even an internship placement program. Popular job search sites also list internship opportunities. For example, check out the following web sites:

http://www.monster.com
http://www.careerbuilder.com
http://www.jobsearchusa.org
http://www.jobs.com
http://www.indeed.com

A few other popular online sites that provide a multitude of internship listings in different fields are as follows:

http://www.internjobs.com
http://www.internshipprograms.com
http://www.job-hunt.org/interns.shtml
http://www.wetfeet.com

To read about how an internship helped shape one professional's career and how a volunteer position helped form the basis of one student's career decisions, read Exhibits 6.3 and 6.4.

How Can You Make the Most of Your Volunteer Position or Internship on Paper?

Serving as a volunteer or an intern for an organization speaks to what kind of person you are to employers and graduate schools considering your application.

EXHIBIT 6.3

One Professional's Perspective

Michelle Donovan, Ph.D., People Analytics Team Member at Google, Inc., "A Fulfilling Career in Industrial-Organizational Psychology"

During my doctoral program, I was selected for an internship at a company called Personnel Decisions Research Institutes in Washington, DC, that consisted of two major projects. The first was to help design a survey to measure adaptability and administer it at several Army bases. The data that we collected resulted in an award-winning paper presented at the annual meeting of the Society of Industrial/Organizational Psychology (SIOP; http://www.siop.org). It was really gratifying to be recognized in front of the more than 3,000 attendees. Our second project was conducting a job analysis at a government agency in which we conducted interviews, studied people's jobs, and trained them on computer software, which helped them describe their jobs. It was during this internship that I fell in love with the idea of working as an industrial-organizational (I/O) psychologist in an applied setting. When I returned to Illinois to finish my doctorate, there was no turning back. I wanted to finish my dissertation, get my doctorate, and start working in this field.

My first job after my doctorate was at a small consulting firm in the San Francisco Bay area called Terranova Consulting Group. At Terranova, I worked on a wide variety of projects—a training needs analysis survey for a biotech company; human resource audits for startups in the Silicon Valley; and job analysis projects for various companies to help them understand what their people did and how to select, train, develop, and manage them in those jobs. I found the projects that I enjoyed most were organizational surveys. The idealist in me loved the idea that I could capture "the voice of the people," apply some unique skills (analyzing the data and creating a presentation to tell the story), and then convince leaders to take action to improve the work environment based on the data. So when I saw an opening at Intel Corporation called "survey researcher," which involved managing surveys full time, I decided to have an informational interview with them to learn more. That informational interview turned into a job offer, and I spent the next several years at Intel working on surveys, focus groups, and other projects related to human resource data and metrics to help inform important decisions and strategies (e.g., How do we retain people? What should our company look like in the future?).

After 6 years at Intel, I moved on and found my next job at Google through a person I met networking. I have been with Google for 2 years now, where I am part of a team called People Analytics. Although Google's mission is to organize the world's information and make it universally accessible and useful, the mission of People Analytics is to organize information on Google users and make it accessible and useful to our leaders, managers, and in some cases to Googlers themselves (as Google employees are called). Our goal is to ensure that all people-related decisions are based on data—not an easy task because we make hundreds of people-related decisions a day.

My specific role is to manage our survey program, which includes our annual survey sent worldwide to over 20,000 Googlers. I also manage a small team that helps collect and analyze data, such as surveys and focus groups (we call them "roundtables" at Google so they do not sound scary and people actually show up). Our group is responsible for not merely gathering the data, but also for making sure that data influences

EXHIBIT 6.3 (cont'd)

change—real and meaningful change. After just 3 months at Google, I made recommendations based on some data I analyzed, and when I presented to two directors, they said, "Yes, do it!" In moments like that, I feel a part of something very special—helping to make Google a better place to work. Granted, some of the changes our data has led to are small (e.g., new fitness courses based on a fitness survey), but some are bigger and more far reaching (a much greater emphasis on career development for Googlers and fundamental changes in the compensation and benefits we offer).

Over the years and ever since that first internship, I have had the privilege of studying many different kinds of jobs, including assembly line workers, salespeople, soldiers, security guards, ordnance officers, analysts, managers, software and hardware engineers, chefs, and chief executive officers. What I know for sure is that although every job is unique and fulfilling in its own way, the job of an I/O psychologist is still the best fit for me.

It suggests that you are a person who takes initiative, seeks to learn, and desires to serve others. It also implies that you have gained skills that are relevant to the professional world. In fact, experience as a volunteer or intern can serve as a foot in the door to achieving your first paid position in the workforce if you are someone who otherwise lacks past work experience. After you have served as a volunteer or intern within an organization for some period of time, it is both appropriate and beneficial for you to include a description of this experience on your résumé and/or graduate school application. You can describe volunteer work on your résumé by listing the organization's name and location, your functional title, the dates of your work, your supervisor's name and contact information, and a description of your duties. Of course, be sure to indicate that you served as a volunteer if that is not clearly indicated by the functional title you provide.

Merely including the dates and title of your position is not enough to ensure that employers and graduate schools get an adequate picture of you and the talents that you may have developed or demonstrated as a volunteer or intern. You should take the time to craft your résumé and applications so that the specific skills that you acquired or practiced in your position are highlighted. You need to present your volunteer or internship experience in a way that will have the most impact on your résumé or graduate school applications.

When writing a résumé or describing your experience in a graduate school application, it is best to use action verbs that accurately reflect the skills and duties involved in your volunteer or intern position. Action verbs are great to use in résumés and applications because they capture interest, have a stronger impact on the reader than passive wording, and more accurately reflect your experience. For example, if you were to list on your résumé that you were a "teen hotline volunteer," you may simply write, "Responsibilities included: answering phone calls and increasing teen hotline calls." However, this description is not specific enough to show that you gained experience in counseling, making decisions independently, and leading others to a successful outcome. It would be more powerful and better reflect these skills if you described your duties as follows:

> Responsibilities included: answered hotline calls, counseled teens in noncrisis situations, screened calls for crisis situations and determined whether callers should be referred for professional help, and planned and led a campaign to increase hotline awareness that resulted in a 20% call increase.

EXHIBIT 6.4

One Student's Perspective

Tannia Henetz, BA, doctoral student, Stanford University, "How Volunteering as an Undergraduate Teaching Assistant Helped Me"

During my years as an undergraduate psychology student, I tried to take advantage of all the opportunities my major had to offer: courses and seminars, research positions, and organizations such as Psi Chi. However, of all my adventures in psychology, I look back with special fondness on the time I spent volunteering as an undergraduate teaching assistant (TA). I loved being a TA, and after my first time doing it, I found myself assisting with multiple courses in some capacity or another from spring of my sophomore year to graduation. The courses were all quite different from one another, and the experience never became tiresome. Each new subject or group of students brought new challenges and perspectives. Teaching—yes, good moments and bad, stresses and rewards—added a dimension to my studies that both enhanced and complemented my other adventures in psychology, and I wholeheartedly recommend that you consider trying it yourself. One unexpected benefit of being a TA was interpersonal in nature. It offered the opportunity and great satisfaction of spending time with people who shared my interests and goals. I will always be grateful to have found, in those opportunities, a group of truly exceptional instructors and graduate student TAs who served as an inspiration and eventually became my mentors, colleagues, and good friends. The dedication to teaching that I witnessed during those sessions was simply infectious.

When you are a TA, you learn a lot! First, you are exposed to the ins and outs of teaching a course. You might prepare materials, class web sites, and readings; collaborate to write and grade tests; and hold office hours, section, and/or review sessions. You also form a deeper understanding of the material you are presenting in class. If you get to give a lecture—fear of suffering humiliation while in the front of a lecture hall full of people is not the only motivator for increased understanding, but it helps—your insights will expand beyond the limits of your own introspection as you respond to the collective curiosity of all your students.

Serving as a TA was also an excellent way for me to explore, and ultimately prepare for, potential career paths after graduation. I was considering graduate school with an eye toward a future in academia. However, how could I be sure my chosen path would actually suit my talents and interests? I needed experience. I set out to try as many of the activities I expected to encounter in my graduate career as I could, particularly research and teaching. As an undergraduate TA, I got a glimpse of my potential future in graduate school and felt more informed when the time came to make my decision about life after college. There is no denying that teaching is a welcome addition to a résumé or curriculum vita, regardless of what you plan to do with your psychology degree. Teaching experience demonstrates responsibility, a collaborative ethic, and the ability to communicate ideas successfully to a wide audience—all pluses for a future employer or adviser.

Table 6.1 Desirable Qualities in Job Applicants and Related Action Verbs

Desirable quality	Related action verbs
Public speaking	Briefed, communicated, informed, lectured, persuaded, presented, proposed, showed
Communication—Interpersonal and written	Advised, assembled, briefed, clarified, communicated, composed, condensed, constructed, counseled, demonstrated, directed, documented, drafted, edited, facilitated, illustrated, informed, interpreted, negotiated, persuaded, presented, proposed, prepared, qualified, reviewed, revised, resolved, simplified
Writing (reports and proposals)	Briefed, clarified, compiled, defined, generated, informed, interpreted, maintained, modified, summarized, submitted, synthesized, translated, verified, wrote
Statistics, Mathematical reasoning, and computer skills	Analyzed, balanced, budgeted, calculated, classified, compared, computed, estimated, evaluated, examined, formulated, financed, gathered, integrated, interpreted, measured, mapped, observed, obtained, predicted, processed, projected, quantified, questioned, recorded, reinforced, researched, studied, summarized, tabulated, tested
Teamwork skills	Assisted, collaborated, counseled, empowered, encouraged, enforced, facilitated, guided, helped, instructed, motivated, participated, oversaw, represented, resolved, reinforced, served, supported
Motivation	Achieved, acted, administered, applied, assembled, attained, built, completed, conducted, constructed, coordinated, created, demonstrated, earned, improved, introduced, invented, met, realized, received, repaired, solved, undertook, spearheaded, utilized
Flexibility	Adapted, improvised, learned, introduced, invented, modified, took over, undertook
Ability to think independently and make decisions	Administered, allocated, assessed, averted, classified, conceptualized, consolidated, controlled, decided, defined, determined, developed, devised, diagnosed, eliminated, identified, implemented, initiated, innovated, installed, realized, performed, proposed, questioned, produced, repaired, verified
Organizational skills	Arranged, collected, coordinated, identified, improved, maintained, organized, planned, streamlined, synthesized, systematized, simplified
Leadership skills	Empowered, encouraged, advised, coached, conducted, counseled, controlled, coordinated, directed, guided, handled, headed, instituted, led, managed, motivated, monitored, oversaw, planned, realized, showed, supervised, taught, trained, undertook, served, staffed, supported

Note. Data from Edwards and Smith (1988), Appleby (1997), DeGalan and Lambert (1995), Lock (1988), and Kuther (2003).

You can see that the use of more descriptive action verbs, the past tense, and specifics (e.g., the percentage increase in calls) in the revised description of duties gets across much more information about what you actually did and achieved in your volunteer role than the original version.

[...] there are specific characteristics and qualities that graduate schools generally seek in applicants. The same is true of employers: Some of the qualities that employers value are those skills that graduate programs value as well (e.g., oral and written communication skills, motivation, organizational skills [...]). In preparing to write your own résumé and application materials, you should identify not only the skills related to the specific job or graduate program to which you are applying, but also the general positive qualities you possess as an individual. Table 6.1 presents the general qualities that many employers who hire psychology graduates find appealing in an applicant. In the right-hand column, you will find action verbs related to each of the general desirable qualities presented on the left. The goal is to choose the words that best describe how you demonstrated the desirable qualities in the left column as a volunteer, intern, or employee in your résumé, graduate school application, or job application.

The Undergraduate Psychology Internship

Benefits, Selection, and Making the Most of Your Experience

By Todd J. Walter

The number of baccalaureate graduates in psychology has substantially increased over the last 20 years and so too has the competition for admission into psychology-related graduate programs (Landrum and Clark, 2005). Aside from traditional course requirements and electives in the undergraduate psychology curriculum, fieldwork such as undergraduate internships have been highly regarded by psychology graduates and can significantly impact graduates' vocational or graduate school placements (Grocer and Kohout, 1997; Prerost, 1981). Accordingly, whether internships are required, an elective, or can be developed (e.g., independent study) as part of one's undergraduate study, it is worth considering how an internship can enhance your undergraduate study and preparations for postbaccalaureate placement.

You may perceive participating in an internship with anticipation, ambivalence, or even trepidation. Regarding the latter, uncertainty about what to expect, how the internship will affect you, and whether you are prepared for such paraprofessional opportunities is understandably daunting. In an effort to allay some of these concerns and make your internship an optimal experience, I identify the following benefits and recommendations for obtaining and making the most out of your internship experience.

Personal and Professional Benefits

- **Internships can help you clarify your interests and goals.** Given the competitiveness of graduate admissions and the job market, not to mention the considerable investment in time and energy required to apply for these endeavors, an internship can provide you with an experiential opportunity to evaluate and clarify your career interests and goals before embarking on your postbaccalaureate endeavors.
- **Internships can promote skill development.** Internships can offer you the opportunity to develop skills that may enhance your professional development including your candidacy to acquire postbaccalaureate job placement at that internship or related settings.
- **Internships can enable you to network.** Internships can afford you the opportunity to network with professionals and agency personnel that may be of value in subsequent vocational placement.

- **Internships can enhance the quality of your graduate school candidacy.** Landrum and Clark (2005) reported that graduate admissions committees give the highest importance to letters of recommendation and statements of goals and objectives, while some place the highest importance on clinically-related service. The internship can provide you an additional resource for letters of recommendation via your supervisor, can enhance your statement of goals and objectives by relating how your internship experiences may have shaped or clarified your goals, and may provide you a competitive advantage for some graduate programs.
- **Internships can enable you to apply what you have learned.** Internships may afford you an opportunity to enrich your classroom learning through real-world application of the information that you have acquired.
- **Internships can enhance your awareness of your attributes.** The challenges and responsibilities associated with internship may enhance your awareness of and enable you to better evaluate your personal and professional strengths and weaknesses in need of further development.

Strategies for Obtaining Internship Placements

While your undergraduate psychology program may have a list of prospective internship placements, you should play an active role in identifying and securing placements. Many students underestimate this responsibility, yet given the benefits of internship, it is vital that students be selective of placements that are in keeping with their interests and goals.

- **Begin your internship search at least 2-3 months in advance.** Many students underestimate how time consuming obtaining an internship can be. Faculty may need to contact prospective internship sites to confirm availability for placement, you may need to apply for placement and be required to interview and submit letters of recommendation, and contractual agreements between your institution and the internship placement may need to be processed.
- **Consult with faculty about your goals and interests.** Faculty may be able to help you clarify your interests, they may be aware of appropriate agencies from previous internship placements, and they may be able to make recommendations per your abilities, interests, and goals.
- **Consult with your institution's Career Services and/or Alumni Relations office.** The Career Services office may keep a record of not only potential employers, but also potential fieldwork and volunteer opportunities. The Alumni Relations office may have contact information for alumni in your field of interest who may be helpful in facilitating internship placements in the settings in which they work or with which they are familiar.
- **Consult former interns.** Previous interns at your institution can offer information about what to expect, what internships to avoid if there have been problems, and advice for making the most out of the internship.
- **Investigate settings in which you may want to work or study.** Consider internships in agencies that may offer you subsequent employment, or opportunities that may be available at graduate schools that you are considering. The latter may offer internships with professionals of interest to you in clinics or on projects related to your goals in graduate study.
- **Search the Internet.** Numerous websites (see Additional Resources for Identifying Internships) provide resources and links to undergraduate internship opportunities in psychology and related fields, both domestic and abroad.

- **Investigate "nontraditional" internship placements.** Mental health, medical/hospital, and human/social service agencies are traditionally common internship placements for psychology undergraduates (VandeCreek and Fleischer, 1984). However, internship placements in forensic (e.g., correctional settings, judicial settings), business, advertising and marketing, public relations, education, human resources, and administrative settings may be available to you and in keeping with your goals and interests.
- **Be assertive in pursuing internships.** Exhibiting initiative in contacting prospective internship placements can make a favorable impression on your faculty as well as the prospective internship personnel/supervisor.
- **Anticipate meeting with the prospective internship's staff.** Internships may require you to meet with them in advance (e.g., an interview). This meeting can be vital in your securing placement at that site and you should dress in a professionally appropriate manner. You should also be prepared to answer questions about your education and goals, comment on how you may be able to assist that particular internship placement, and ask questions about the internship including its functions and the role that you may play.
- **Discern your need for appropriate insurance coverage before starting internship.** Illness or injury sustained on internship may not qualify for coverage via workman's compensation or via your educational institution. If not already required of you, obtain your own health insurance coverage to provide you peace of mind and security in the unlikely event that you should need it. Likewise, because malpractice claims may not be covered under the umbrella of standard university insurance coverage, you should consult with your internship supervisor or faculty coordinator/sponsor regarding the need for and availability of liability insurance coverage through your institution. Individual student liability coverage is available for APA student-affiliates at www.apait.org for a nominal fee.

Tips for Making the Most of the Internship

The following recommendations may enable you to maximize the benefits and minimize problems associated with your internship.

- **Complete as many hours as possible.** Participating for a minimum amount of time on internship can compromise the breadth of educational and networking opportunities that could be of benefit to you. Greater participation can enable you to acquire a better understanding for how the internship placement operates, the roles of its staff, the training and attributes that are necessary for such roles, and the staff's familiarity with you.
- **Participate in multiple internships.** Participating in different internships across semesters/quarters, as opposed to completing just one, can afford you greater opportunities to test your personal hypotheses of careers that are in keeping with your interests and abilities.
- **Get actively involved.** As an undergraduate student there may be limits to what activities you can participate in during internship. Nevertheless, the internship represents a shift from being a consumer of education in the classroom to active learning via providing service to others. You should avoid being relegated to mere observation and discuss with your supervisor the most meaningful ways you can participate in the internship.
- **Identify your goals, expectations, and responsibilities at the start.** Mutually agreed upon

written expectations, goals, and responsibilities with your supervisor can minimize misunderstandings and dissatisfaction, can provide a focus and a reminder throughout the internship of your goals to be accomplished, and can be a basis for your supervisor to evaluate you upon its completion (Wrobel and Ogilvy, 2003).

- **Establish the parameters of supervision.** Your supervisor may have little formal training or experience in supervision (especially to undergraduate interns). At the onset of your internship, you should meet with your supervisor to clarify your expectations for supervision including where, when, and how it will be conducted. Formally structured and ongoing supervision has been associated with more positive student outcomes (Kantrowitz, Mitchell, and Davidson, 1982; Morris and Haas, 1984).
- **Utilize supervision effectively.** Supervision is your opportunity to ask questions not only about the functions of the internship and its staff, but also about your progress. Assertively seeking constructive feedback is often regarded as a sign of maturity and can be instrumental in your personal and professional development.
- **Avoid being "sidelined" and consult with your faculty sponsor/coordinator as necessary.** Your supervisor may have work-related priorities that overshadow your educational needs and limit his or her availability to you. While often inevitable, you should discuss your concerns with your supervisor as well as the possibility of identifying "alternate supervisors" (e.g., other staff) that you can go to for supervision, and/or consult with faculty for assistance if your supervisor's lack of availability persists (Murray, 2003).
- **Plan in advance to terminate your internship.** Because most internship placements do not operate on semester or quarterly periods, supervisors may lose track of when your internship will end. Discussing the imminent completion of your internship with your supervisor, preferably a few weeks in advance, can serve as a reminder to review what internship goals you have and have not accomplished and what you can meaningfully accomplish in the remaining time, help your supervisor and internship placement prepare for the transition of your absence, allow you timely guidance on how to terminate with your clients appropriately (if applicable), prompt you to request letters of recommendation from them (if applicable), and provide you with a more satisfactory and professionally appropriate termination with your supervisor and other personnel.

Regardless of whether the undergraduate internship is a requirement or an elective of your program's curriculum, participating in such experiences can be especially valuable to you. If your program does not offer fieldwork opportunities, strongly consider volunteering at a setting that is of interest to you and consider the preceding recommendations when establishing and making the most out of your volunteer opportunity.

Additional Resources for Identifying Internships

American Psychological Association. (n.d.). *Undergraduate research opportunities and internships.* Retrieved November 1, 2006, from http://www.apa.org/science/undergradopps.html

North Carolina A and T State University. (n.d.). *Directory of international internships.* Retrieved November 2, 2006, from the Office of International Programs Website: http://www.ncat.edu/~oip/directory_internships.htm

Pennsylvania State College. (n.d.). *Locating an internship—print resources.* Retrieved November 5, 2006, from the College of Liberal Arts Website:

http://www.la.psu.edu/CLA-Internships/print_resources.shtml

References

Grocer, S., and Kohout, J. (1997). *The 1995 APA survey of 1992 baccalaureate recipients.* Washington, DC: American Psychological Association.

Kantrowitz, R., Mitchell, C., and Davidson, W.S., II. (1982). Varying formats of teaching undergraduate field courses: An experimental examination. *Teaching of Psychology, 9,* 186188.

Landrum, R. E., and Clark, J. (2005). Graduate admissions criteria in psychology: An update. *Psychological Reports, 97,* 481-484.

Morris, S. B., and Haas, L. J. (1984). Evaluating undergraduate field placements: An empirical approach. *Teaching of Psychology, 11,* 166-168.

Murray, B. (2003). Making supervision work for you. *gradPSYCH, 1,* 24-25.

Prerost, F. J. (1981). Post-graduation educational and occupational choices of psychology undergraduate internship participants: Issues for the psychology profession. *Teaching of Psychology, 8,* 221-223.

VandeCreek, L., and Fleischer, M. (1984). The role of internship in the undergraduate *Teaching of Psychology, 11,*

Wrobel, T. A., and Ogilvy, J. P. (2003, August). *Undergraduate internship contracts: Issues to consider.* Poster session presented at the annual meeting of the American Psychological Association, Toronto, Canada.

Section Three

Personal Reflections

1. Does your college offer research assistant opportunities?
2. Does your college offer teaching assistant opportunities?
3. Does your college offer field placement or internship opportunities?
4. List five volunteer settings of interest from Exhibit 6.1 in the "Getting Real World Psychology-Related Experience" article (Wegenek and Buskist).
5. Go to the website **www.volunteermatch.org**.
    - In the middle of the page, click on ADVANCED.
    - Enter your zip code in the LOCATION box.
    - Click on all the CAUSE AREAS that you are interested in exploring.
    - Click on SEARCH.

    Find two volunteer positions of interest and describe each.
6. If you were to take on a volunteer position, how much time per month would you realistically have to devote to it? What days and times in the week would you be available?
7. Using Table 6.1 in the "Getting Real World Psychology-Related Experience" article (Wegenek and Buskist), list two desirable qualities in job applicants that you possess. Explain.
8. Using Table 6.1 in the "Getting Real World Psychology-Related Experience" article (Wegenek and Buskist), list one desirable quality in job applicants that you do not yet possess and would like to improve. Explain.

Section Four

Psychology-Related Jobs

When the authors meet psychology students or prospective psychology students for the first time, we have a set of questions we will inevitably ask them. We start by asking if they have heard that you can't do anything with an undergraduate degree in psychology. There is almost always a unified "yes" from everyone asked. It has the potential to be a very sobering conversation. Some students will share that their friends and family aren't sure what jobs a psychology major is qualified to do—they've heard that you will have a hard time being employed with a degree so broad that employers don't think you have any specialized skills. We then usually ask them why they chose the psychology major anyway? That's when we hear the excitement in their voice, the passion in their words, and the intellectual curiosity that fueled their commitment. The truth is that the rumor is simply not true. Yes, completing an undergraduate degree in psychology doesn't train you to be a psychologist. But it does teach you about human behavior, through lectures and coursework, and it sharpens your critical thinking, deductive reasoning, and quantitative analysis skills through research methods, research experience, and statistical training. It gives you the opportunity to practice your communication skills, both orally and in writing. It hones what, for many of you, is an innate desire to help others, or a deep intellectual curiosity about how humans think and behave with and toward each other. These are not only skills and qualities that employers value in their employees; they are also the foundations for professional careers in the helping profession and in psychological science. We complement the previous sections that focused on education with a large group of readings that investigate careers in psychology. Included are resources for understanding the many types of jobs available at different levels of education in the discipline (bachelor's, master's, and doctorate), and for understanding how these positions are compensated. There are articles to help explain academic and nonacademic jobs in psychology, as well as both traditional and nontraditional jobs in psychology. We highlight some examples of psychologists doing very interesting things with their education. These profiles are good examples of the creative ways in which an education in psychology can be applied. We believe it is important for future professionals in psychology to hear about the professional experiences of people from ethnic minority backgrounds. As such, we bring you some thoughts about the profession of psychology from a different cultural perspective. Lastly, we believe it is important for psychologists of all ethnic and cultural backgrounds to recognize and understand how issues of culture and ethnicity play out in the practice of psychology. The section ends with sources that bring into perspective some of the common ethnic and cultural issues that psychologists frequently confront.

Popular Jobs for Psychology Majors

PayScale.com

If you major in psychology, you're likely to work directly with people. From mental health counseling to human resource work, your understanding of human behavior will help you excel in the most demanding settings. To see your job options, check out PayScale's list of the most popular jobs for psychology majors.

Methodology

Jobs ranked by popularity among graduates. Annual pay for Bachelors graduates without higher degrees from all colleges. See full methodology for more.

All data is limited to those with a Bachelor's degree and no higher degrees who work full-time in the United States. Jobs are listed in order of relative

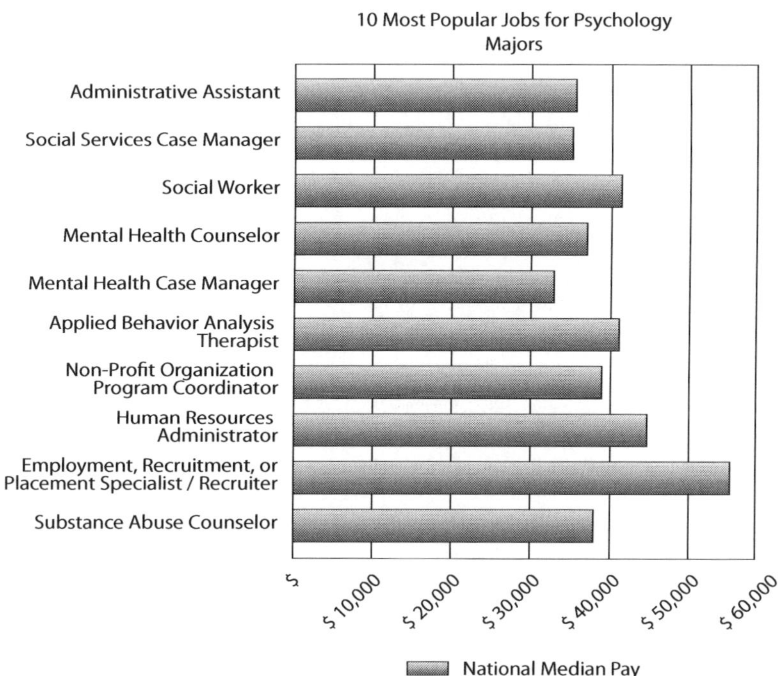

popularity amongst graduates with a Bachelor's degree in the given major from any college. Median salary for each job title is for individuals with any major who have a typical amount of experience at that job. Salary is the sum of compensation from base salary, bonuses, profit sharing, commissions, and overtime, if applicable. Salary does not include equity (stock) compensation. This chart is based upon PayScale Salary Survey data, and may not represent all individuals in these categories.

Popular Jobs for Psychology Majors	**National Median Pay**
Social Services Case Manager	$34,900
Social Worker	$41,000
Mental Health Counselor	$36,500
Mental Health Case Manager	$32,800
Applied Behavior Analysis Therapist	$40,700
Non-Profit Organization Program Coordinator	$38,600
Human Resources Administrator	$44,500
Employment, Recruitment, or Placement Specialist/Recruiter	$54,800
Substance Abuse Counselor	$37,500
Non-Profit Organization Program Manager	$49,200
Medical Research Assistant	$34,000
Mental Health Technician	$31,300
Medical Case Manager	$57,800
Clinical Research Coordinator	$60,700
Qualified Mental Retardation Professional	$34,200
Daycare Teacher	$23,400
Child, Family, or School Social Worker	$39,000
College/University Academic Advisor	$37,200
Supportive Residential Counselor	$28,600
Psychiatric Technician	$34,000
Family Service Worker	$35,200
Social Services Director	$43,200
Home Health Aide	$22,300
Crisis Counselor	$35,400

Psychology

Scientific Problem Solvers

American Psychological Association

The Job Outlook

Psychology graduates generally report being pleased that what they studied in school has helped prepare them for both life and work. As a woman who opened her own business shortly after earning a baccalaureate in psychology stated, "After all, psychology is the business of life." Although the majority of those with bachelor's degrees in psychology work in areas other than psychology, they continue to be excited by the changes taking place in the field that relate to what they are now doing.

The U.S. Bureau of Labor Statistics (BLS, 2011) expects that opportunities in psychology will continue to grow over the next decade. "Job prospects should be the best for people who have a doctoral degree from a leading university in … [a] field such as clinical, counseling, or health, and those with a specialist or doctoral degree in school psychology. … Employment will grow because of increased demand for psychological services in schools, hospitals, social service agencies, mental health centers, substance abuse treatment clinics, consulting firms, and private companies." The push to place health service provider psychologists in community health clinics and as core participants in health care practices will provide opportunities. Psychologists are also needed to work with an aging population and one that is diversifying rapidly.

According to the BLS (2011), "the demand for school psychologists will be driven by a growing awareness of how students' mental health and behavioral problems, such as bullying, affect learning. School psychologists will be needed for general student counseling on a variety of other issues, including working with students with disabilities or with special needs, tackling drug abuse, and consulting and managing personal crisis."

Although psychologists may compete with providers from other disciplines such as psychiatry, clinical nursing, social work, and counseling, "clinical psychologists will continue to be needed to help with the rising health care costs associated with unhealthy lifestyles, such as smoking, alcoholism, and obesity, which have made prevention and treatment more critical. There also will be increased need for psychologists to work with returning veterans" (BLS, 2011).

The BLS also states that "industrial-organizational psychologists can help employers understand their organizations better and sort out restructuring so as to help boost worker productivity and retention rates in a wide range of businesses. Industrial-organizational psychologists will help companies deal with issues such as workplace diversity and antidiscrimination policies.

Companies also will use psychologists' expertise in survey design, analysis, and research to develop tools for marketing evaluation and statistical analysis." The need for psychologists' abilities in applied research settings and activities such as survey and market research will be particularly acute in the next decade.

Widespread retirement of government employees at both the state and federal levels will provide openings over the next decade across the board for psychologists, particularly in research, administration, and management roles. Opportunities will be available at all degree levels but particularly at the doctoral level.

U.S. Department of Labor, Bureau of Labor Statistics. (2011). *Occupational outlook handbook* (2010–2011 ed.). Retrieved from http://wMv.bls.gov/oco/ocoso56.htm

Doctoral Graduates

Analyses of 2000 Doctorate Employment Survey data from the American Psychological Association's (APA) Center for Workforce Studies (Michalski, Kohout, Wicherski, & Hart, 2011) found that 72% of responding psychologists who earned their doctorates in 2008–2009 secured their first choice when looking for a job. In addition, at least 73% of the respondents were employed within 3 months of receiving the doctorate. Nearly 40% rated the job market as "good" or as "excellent" and 35% as "fair." Just over three fourths of respondents to the 2009 online survey (the most recent study available) said that they were not underemployed. As might be expected, the highest paid and greatest range of jobs in psychology are available to those with doctorates in psychology. Unemployment and underemployment levels remain below those noted for other scientists and engineers. Few drop out of the field.

In general, career opportunities and employment settings have not varied greatly from those of the previous decade, although the prototype solo clinical practice is less common today than it was a decade or more ago. According to data from the Doctorate Employment Survey (see Table 3 in Michalski et al., 2011), the leading full-time employment settings for those with new doctorates in psychology in 2009 were universities/4-year colleges (25.9%) and hospitals/ other human services (25%). Other human service settings included university/college counseling centers, outpatient clinics, and primary care offices or community health centers. About 16% of new doctorates worked in government/VA medical center settings, 10% in business/nonprofit settings, 8% in schools/other educational settings, 6% in medical schools/other academic settings, and slightly less than 6% in independent practice (see chart on p. 14).

Master's Graduates

While the doctoral degree is the standard for independent research or practice in psychology, the number of psychology students who pursue a terminal master's degree has increased sixfold since 1960; master's degrees totaled at least 21,400 in 2008 (National Center for Health Statistics [NCES], 2009). Just under one fifth of master's graduates were full-time students in 2000, and 56% were employed outside psychology (National Science Foundation, 2000).

Graduates with a master's degree in psychology may qualify for positions in school and I/O psychology, although in most states they will be prohibited from using "psychologist" as their job or professional title. By APA policy and licensing laws, the term psychologist is reserved for individuals with doctoral education and training. Master's degree holders with several years of experience in business and industry can obtain jobs in consulting and marketing research, while other master's degree holders may find jobs in government, universities, or the private sector as counselors, researchers, data collectors, and analysts. Today, most master's degrees in psychology are awarded in clinical, counseling, and I/O psychology. Two of these three fields—counseling and I/O psychology—enjoy established occupational niches.

Persons with master's degrees often work under the direction of a doctoral psychologist, especially in clinical, counseling, school, and testing and measurement psychology.

Some jobs in industry—for example, in organizational development and survey research—are held by both doctoral- and master's-level graduates. But industry and government jobs that focus on compensation, training, data analysis, and general personnel issues are often filled by those with master's degrees in psychology.

Bachelor's Graduates

According to the CIRP [Cooperative Institutional Research Program] Freshman Survey (Higher Education Research Institute, 2008), psychology was the second most popular undergraduate field in 2008, chosen by 5.1% of incoming freshmen. Only general biology was more popular (chosen by 5.2% of incoming freshmen). When regarded as a single field and not as a constellation of fields (as are business, biology, or education), psychology outdrew all other fields. In 2008, 92,587 students graduated with a bachelor's degree in psychology—although many had no plans to pursue a career as a psychologist (NCES, 2009). Some students stop with a bachelor's degree in psychology and find work related to their college major (e.g., they may be assistants in rehabilitation centers). If they meet state certification requirements, they may be able to teach psychology in high schools.

The study of psychology at the bachelor's degree level is also good preparation for many other professions. In 2008, 5% of recipients of bachelor's degrees in psychology were working in psychology or in an occupation related to psychology. Of the small proportion working in psychology, over 80% were in educational settings, broadly defined.

People with bachelor's degrees in psychology often possess good research and writing skills, are good problem solvers, and have well-developed, higher level thinking abilities when it comes to analyzing, synthesizing, and evaluating information. Many find jobs in administrative support, public affairs, education, business, sales, service industries, health, the biological sciences, and computer programming. They may also work as employment counselors, correction counselor trainees, interviewers, personnel analysts, probation officers, and writers.

Sources

Higher Education Research Institute. (2008). *2008 CIRP Freshman Survey*. (Available from http: //www.heri.ucla.edu)

Michalski, D., Kohout, J., Wicherski, M., & Hart. B. (2011). *2009 Doctorate Employment Survey*. Retrieved from the APA website: http://www.apa.org/workforce/publications/09-doc-empl/index.aspx

National Science Foundation, Division of Science Resource Statistics. (2006). *National Survey of Recent College Graduates, 2006* (Table 2). Retrieved from http://www.nsf.gov/statistics/nsf10318/pdf/tabo2.pdf

U. S. Department of Education, National Center for Education Statistics. (2009). *Digest of education statistics* (Table 315). Retrieved from http://nces.ed.gov/programs/digest/do9/tables/dto9_315.asp

What Psychologists Do And Where They Do It

Psychology is an extraordinarily diverse field with hundreds of career paths. Some specialties, like caring for people with mental and emotional disorders, are familiar to most of us. Others, like helping with the design of advanced computer systems or studying how we remember things, are less well known.

What all psychologists have in common is a shared interest in the minds and behaviors of both human and nonhuman animals. In their work, psychologists draw on an ever-expanding body of scientific knowledge about how we think, act, and feel, and they apply the information to their areas of expertise.

Many psychologists work in more than one setting. For instance, college professors often consult for industry or see clients on a part-time basis. Although it is possible to identify a host of different work settings, for the purpose of this booklet, we'll consider some of the most prominent examples.

Where Psychologists Work

Work Setting	Percentage of Doctorate-Holding Psychologists Working Within Industry
University/4-year college	25.9%
Medical school/other academic	6.3%
Schools/other educational	8.1%
Independent practice	5.7%
Hospital/other health service	25%
Government/VA medical center	16.3%
Business/nonprofit	10.4%

Note. The chart represents employment settings for those with recent doctorates in psychology. Totals amount to 97% due to rounding and exclusion of 17 "not specified" responses. Adapted from D. Michalski, J. Kohout, M. Wicherski, & B. Hart (2011), *2009 Doctorate Employment Survey* (Table 3). Retrieved from the APA website: http://www.apa.org/workforce/publications/09-doc-empl/table-3.pdf

PSYCHOLOGISTS CONDUCT RESEARCH

Many psychologists conduct research that runs the gamut from studies of basic brain functions to individual behavior to the behavior of complex social organizations. Subjects of such scientific study include nonhuman animals, human infants, both well-functioning and emotionally disturbed people, older persons, students, workers, and just about every other population one can imagine. Some research takes place in laboratories where the study conditions can be carefully controlled; some is carried out in the field, such as the workplace, the highway, schools, and hospitals, where behavior is studied as it occurs naturally.

Much of the laboratory research is conducted in universities, government agencies (such as the National Institutes of Health and the armed services), and private research organizations. Whereas most psychological scientists are engaged in the actual planning and conduct of research, some are employed in management or administration—usually after having served as active researchers.

DR. LINDA M. BARTOSHUK

Psychophysics psychologist, researcher, and university professor

I am a psychologist and Bushnell Professor at the University of Florida (UF). I direct human research in the UF Center for Smell and Taste and collaborate with food scientists and plant geneticists working to make fruits and vegetables more palatable. I study taste and the genetic and pathological conditions that affect taste and thus alter a variety of behaviors (dietary choice, smoking, drinking) affecting health.

I earned my BA at Carleton College. Although I began my college career as an astronomy major, my courses in astronomy got me interested in people's abilities to compare the brightness of stars, and that led to my interest in the senses. I switched my major to psychology. After receiving my PhD from Brown University, I worked at the Natick Army Research labs (where research related to food for military personnel is conducted), then went to the Pierce Foundation and Yale University in New Haven, CT, and am now at the University of Florida in Gainesville.

Psychology contributes to health in significant ways. As an academic working in the health professions, I have collaborated with dentists and physicians in using psychophysics to quantify symptoms, thereby advancing the understanding of disorders in my field (taste/oral pain) and promoting patient well-being. Psychology and the science supporting it have never been more relevant to the world around us.

I spend a typical workday at my computer and with patients. My students and I design experiments to study the sense of taste, run the experiments, and then analyze the data. Sometimes I serve as a subject in experiments, because I never do an experiment on another person that has not been done on me first.

I believe that to be a psychologist, a good background in mathematics and science is useful, and you need to observe the world around you and yourself. Behavior is fascinating. Psychology includes many subspecialties. The more you learn about them, the easier it will be to pick an area that will use your skills and give you great satisfaction.

I love being a psychologist. We study the behavior we see, but we know how to look beneath the surface to explore mechanisms. We are sophisticated and tolerant thinkers, yet we recognize nonsense. We have an impact on the lives of real people, and we care about them. To me, there is no better way to spend one's life. ... I feel very lucky to be able to do the work that I love. The best advice that I ever gave myself was to go with my heart!

Adapted from "Cool Careers in Science: Meet Linda Bartoshuk." *Scientific American Frontiers Archives: Fall 1990 to Spring 2000.* Retrieved from http://www.pbs.org/safarchive/5_cool/53c_bartoshuklitml

Dr. Robert Rescorla

University professor and research psychologist who studies how we learn

Dr. Robert Rescorla became a psychologist because he likes puzzles. "You see a phenomenon and try to understand it," he says. "I like the logic of designing an experiment, developing a hypothesis, and testing your ideas." Dr. Rescorla studies his favorite phenomenon, learning, at the University of Pennsylvania, where he directs undergraduate studies in psychology and is Christopher H. Browne Distinguished Professor in Psychology. Throughout his career, he has discovered and defined the ways that animals (including humans) learn, especially by the power of association.

His love of research was sparked at Swarthmore College, where one professor encouraged students to conduct their own experiments in visual perception. Recalls Dr. Rescorla, "It was exciting to be the first person in the world to know the answer to something."

After graduating in 1902, he earned a PhD in psychology in 1900 at the University of Pennsylvania. Inspired by a book by one of the field's early researchers, Dr. Rescorla and Dr. Richard Solomon embarked on a classic series of experiments on the mechanisms of learned fear. Their findings have helped to shape effective therapies for treating phobia and other anxiety disorders.

Dr. Rescorla began his teaching career at Yale University. In 1981, he returned to the University of Pennsylvania, where in 1980 he was appointed the James M. Skinner Professor of Science. He studies not only how animals and humans learn that one stimulus signals another, but also how they learn that this relationship no longer holds. Dr. Rescorla also figured out how to measure the strength of learning, the key to documenting his observations.

This lifelong researcher has seen his work help to relieve human suffering. Armed with insights into associative learning, clinical psychologists have developed ways to "extinguish" the phobias that develop when people learn to fear a stimulus because it signals a painful experience.

Dr. Rescorla encourages more undergraduate research because, as he learned. "Once you do it, you're hooked." At Penn, he has chaired the psychology department and been dean of the College of Arts and Sciences. He was elected to the Society- of Experimental Psychologists in 1975 and to the National Academy of Sciences in 1985.

For students considering psychology, he recommends a broad liberal arts education and adds, "Take the psychology intro course, and then sample broadly around it so you can find out what psychology is, whether it's right for you, and what particular topic within it grabs you."

Dr. Rescorla also urges students to study more biology and math. "Psychology increasingly has a biological component—not just in the laboratory but in the applied world, for various therapies. Plus, you will need more of a quantitative background."

Dr. Stanley Sue

Clinical psychologist, researcher, and university professor

I am a professor of psychology and the director of the Center for Excellence in Diversity at Palo Alto University. Unlike psychologists who specialize in a technique or a theory, I specialize in a population. Much of my work focuses on Asian American and ethnic minority clients, who often have special needs, especially if they immigrated to the United States.

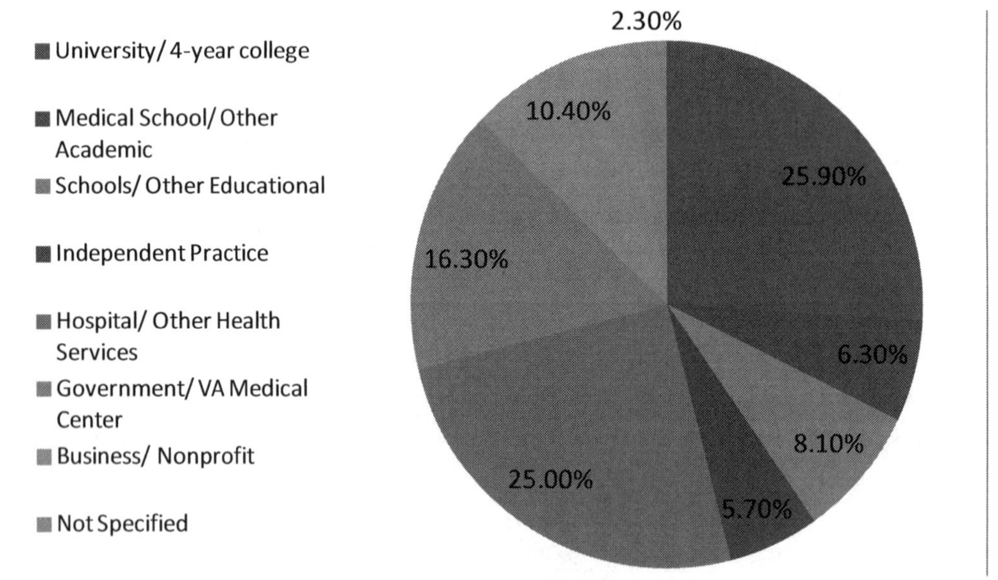

Where Psychologists Work

Source: Data for psychologists working full time adapted from the National Science Foundation *Note. The chart represents employment settings for those with recent doctorates in psychology. Adapted from 1). Michalski, J. Kohout, M. Wlcherski, & B. Hart (2011), 2009 Doctorate Employment Survey (Table 3). Retrieved from the APA website: http://www. apa.org/workf0rce/publicati0ns/o9-doc-empl/table-3.pdf.*

I went to an all-boys technical high school and wanted to be a television repairman. Within a year, I became disinterested in electronics and woodworking, so I switched schools and tried to prepare myself for college. Along the way, I decided I wanted to become a clinical psychologist even though I was quite naive and didn't know what a clinical psychologist actually did. But I remember always watching a television program called *The Eleventh Hour* that featured both a psychiatrist and a psychologist and thinking that this is what I wanted to do.

I told my father that I was interested in psychology, particularly clinical psychology. He's Chinese from the old country and couldn't understand what a psychologist does and how one could make a living at it. But I persisted and went to the University of Oregon to major in psychology and then to the University of California, Los Angeles for graduate work. Since then, my three brothers have gone into psychology. The oldest brother even married a psychologist!

At the Palo Alto University center, we focus on cultural and group issues involving diversity dimensions such as ethnicity; race; lesbian, gay, bisexual, and transgender issues; gender; and social class. We conduct research, develop programs to promote diversity, integrate such issues into our courses, and recruit and train students to work effectively with diverse groups.

My particular area of interest is to study rates of mental disorders among Chinese people in the United States. Little is known about Asian Americans in this regard. Many people have said that Chinese and other Asian Americans don't have many mental health problems. But we know that they have problems just like any other group of people, although there are some differences in the distribution of disorders.

What we have found generally, however, is that Asian Americans tend to underutilize mental health services and that those who do use the services tend to be very disturbed. This means that Asian American people with mild disturbances tend not to come in until their problems are serious.

We're also trying to determine the factors related to mental disturbances among some Chinese people in this country and the factors that seem to insulate others in this population from mental problems. Several researchers at the center are also studying parent-child conflicts in Asian American families to see if the conflicts are different from those affecting other ethnic families and to identify ways to resolve the conflicts. Other investigators are looking at husband- wife problems to ascertain if they're unique because of cultural differences. One researcher has developed a scale that measures "loss of face," which is a particularly important concept for people of Asian descent; fear of losing face affects how they behave. We are also going to look at how to improve the delivery of effective mental health services to Asian Americans.

Psychologists Study Social Development

Developmental psychologists study the many behavioral and psychological changes that occur throughout the life span.

Dr. Pamela Trotman Reid

Developmental psychologist, researcher, and university professor

Developmental psychologists look at the changes that occur across an entire lifetime. It is a fantastic area because you can do so many different things. You can focus on language development, for example, and study why children's speech may not reflect their thinking. You can look at adolescents and the problems they have in establishing identity. Or you can examine families, from how they use discipline to how they develop attitudes.

There is also a growing interest in adult development and aging, partly because of the graying of

America and partly because we are beginning to realize that we don't stop growing when we reach puberty. Instead, we continue to change and develop in many areas all our lives. Developmental psychologists can investigate adult learning issues at the workplace or the effects of aging on cognition.

I was always interested in science; even as a child I had played with chemistry sets. At Howard University' in Washington, DC, I majored in chemistry and thought about becoming a medical doctor. But because so many of my friends were taking psychology as an elective, I did, too. Psychology, I learned, is about both science and the application of science to people. I fell in love with the subject, switched my major to psychology, and then went to graduate school and earned my doctorate in educational psychology.

As a researcher and professor in psychology for many years, I specialized in social development; the effects of gender and culture were my primary interest. Today, as the president of Saint Joseph College in Connecticut, I still get a great deal of pleasure from teaching and research. I enjoy helping my students prepare for leadership roles by studying how leaders develop and what factors influence their leadership styles from childhood through adulthood.

In some of my past studies, I investigated why girls act in certain ways and why boys behave in different ways. One small body of research had suggested that women and girls are typically more interested in babies than men and boys are. But all this research had been conducted on White children and adults.

So I looked at both Black and White children and found no difference between African American boys and girls! In 8- to 10-year-old middle-class children, the White girls liked the babies (they looked at them, touched them, and smiled at them), the African American girls liked the babies, and even the African American boys liked the babies. Only the White boys appeared uninterested. As often happens, the research led to more questions. Now, instead of asking why girls are more interested than boys in babies, the question became are we socializing White boys so that they don't like babies?

I also conducted research with children who lived in shelters because their families were homeless. I learned about the stresses they undergo so that we can understand how some children cope and others do not. For me, the important thing is that in psychology, you can research the questions that you are interested in, not only those that someone else has posed.

Dr. Miguel Ybarra

Counseling psychologist and director of a VA substance abuse treatment program

There are many different ways to come into the field of psychology, but the best way is to understand your strengths and what it is you want to accomplish. I started my academic career as a music major. One of my professors helped me see that my strengths, however, were in another area. I decided that there had to be a better fit for me in a different career. One day, it occurred to me that most of my friends and family would seek me out to talk about things going on in their lives. I felt I had a natural ability to help people see the options that were before them. It was at that moment that I decided to explore what I could get out of (and offer) the field of psychology.

Having to master statistics and research methodology was an intimidating prospect. In fact, the very idea of having to learn this material was so worrisome that I almost decided not to apply to graduate school at all! But once I started learning the material and applied these skills to real-life situations, it made sense and became enjoyable. Statistics became a tool I would use to actually provide the clinical services for which I was in training. This was the best part of my academic experience because the very thing that almost kept me out of a graduate program became the means to achieving my goals.

During my course work in counseling psychology at the University of Wisconsin—Madison, I was fortunate enough to have worked with one of my professors and participate in a study he was directing. The design of this project was to learn about the use of various coping strategies by middle-school students living and interacting in a multicultural setting. This experience became even more important to me when I realized that we were also searching for ways to get our findings back to the community that had agreed to participate in the study. With great enthusiasm, we presented our findings to the parents and teachers of those students at an open meeting.

Through all of this, I learned that the need for psychologists to bring cross-cultural considerations and multicultural competency to their work is increasing daily because of the changing cultural and ethnic composition of our country. As members of the larger and increasingly diverse society, we need to meet the needs of people from different backgrounds and communities, thus allowing them to build on their strengths. Also, let us not forget the role of language. We must understand the context from which language (and behavior) emanates in order to be successful psychologists, whether we are conducting research, teaching, or providing therapy.

Since completing my doctoral degree, I have worked as a full-time and part-time faculty member and have taught in undergraduate, master's, and doctoral programs and in college counseling centers. I have also been involved with the Veterans Affairs initiative to integrate mental health with primary health care; worked as a consultant for businesses and academic programs; and conducted research. Currently, I am the program director of a VA substance abuse treatment program. Each professional experience has helped to shape my own journey and has added to my satisfaction and success within the field of psychology. My best advice is to seek out diverse experiences that match your interests, be ready to transform a "not-so-great" job description into a great work experience, and never take yourself out of the running to achieve a goal you want to attain.

Psychologists Teach and Provide Services to Students

Psychologists provide a number of services—both direct and indirect—to children, youth, and families in schools at all levels, from early childhood education settings through college. Some focus on improving student learning and behavior through research on topics such as motivation and cognitive processes, while others provide psychological services within educational settings. Psychologists work within specialty areas of learning, too, such as the arts and sports.

School psychologists help students with learning or behavior problems in the classroom and serve as members of the interdisciplinary teams that develop individual educational plans for students with learning disabilities, social and emotional issues, or other special needs. They work with students and staff members on schoolwide issues such as bullying prevention, and they consult with teachers on problems in the classroom.

Dr. Sylvia Rosenfield

School psychologist, university professor, and consultant

Schools are essential to our democratic society. I find them fascinating as organizations and recognize how important they are to children's learning and mental health. I enjoy solving problems in schools and am never bored.

As an undergraduate at Cornell. I took Urie Bronfenbrenner's child development course and became aware of how much settings contribute to behavior. Years later, after obtaining my degree from the University of Wisconsin in educational psychology, with a major in school psychology, I maintained my focus on settings and learning environments. Over the course of my career, I have worked as a school psychologist in the Madison (Wisconsin) public schools and as a school psychology faculty member at Fordham University in New York City, Temple University in Philadelphia, and the University of Maryland. I have been engaged in teaching, research, and consultation with state education departments and with school systems around the country. My work has consistently been about enhancing learning environments for staff and students.

Schools today are diverse institutions, reflecting the multicultural nature of our society. There is consensus that schools have a mission to educate all students, including those of color, those with mental health and learning issues, and those whose impoverished backgrounds have limited their learning opportunities. School psychologists play a key role in this essential work. As a faculty member in Fordham University's urban school psychology program, I initiated a bilingual school psychology specialty to reflect our urban mission. We recruited and funded bilingual students and also provided all the school psychology students in the program with a better understanding of how culture and language affect teacher perceptions of students and student outcomes.

School psychologists engage in direct interaction and service to students, as well as focus on prevention (such as bullying prevention) and intervention through consulting with school staff about student concerns. My focus has been on using consultation skills to support school staff in promoting positive student outcomes, particularly for students at risk of developing more severe academic and behavior problems.

Through my work on consultation, I recognized the importance of helping schools develop structures so that staff can support their students' development more effectively and efficiently. My colleagues and I created Instructional Consultation Teams (IC Teams), which we developed at the Lab for IC Teams at the University of Maryland. We embedded evidence-based process skills and content into a team structure and figured out how to help schools implement and sustain IC Teams, which are now conducted in multiple states and school districts.

People spend a large part of their lives in school. When you return as a school psychologist, you see the schools in a new way. Helping to create healthy environments in which children and youth can flourish is a rewarding life's work.

Psychologists Promote Physical And Mental Health

Psychologists as health providers span a large and diverse spectrum of subfields. Some psychologists work alone, with patients and clients coming to the psychologist's office. Others are involved in health care teams and typically work in hospitals, medical schools, outpatient clinics, nursing homes, pain clinics, rehabilitation facilities, and community health and mental health centers.

Increasingly, psychologists in independent practice are contracting on either a part-time or a full-time basis with organizations to provide a wide range of services. For example, a psychologist can join a health practice and work with a team of other health care providers, such as physicians, nutritionists, physiotherapists, and social workers, to prevent or treat illness. This team approach, which is likely to become more common in the future, frequently includes efforts to change unhealthy behaviors and ensure that patients follow the recommended treatment. The team also helps patients cope with stress.

Psychologists also instruct students who are training to become health care professionals, such as physicians and nurses, about the psychological factors involved in illness. And they advise health care providers already in practice so that illnesses with symptoms that have a psychological component can be better diagnosed and treated.

Dr. Daniel Abrahamson

Clinical psychologist, administrator, and advocate

It's important to pick a career that suits your temperament and your likes and dislikes. I grew up in a family that values helping people who are less fortunate and less able to take care of themselves. So psychology was a natural choice for me. I studied clinical psychology in graduate school.

I also went into psychology because I thought it would provide me with more variety than any other field. I have been a practicing psychologist, an administrator, a consultant, and a researcher. I now work for the American Psychological Association (APA) as assistant executive director for state advocacy.

Before coming to APA, I was a clinical psychologist and the administrative director of a large group practice—The Traumatic Stress Institute (TSI)—in Connecticut. At TSI, my colleagues and I dealt with trauma—everything from natural disasters and industrial accidents to physical and sexual abuse. The institute is a model for independent practice because we did more than sit in an office for 50 minutes of psychotherapy with a patient—although we did that, too. But we also did research, training, and community education to help traumatized individuals get their lives back on track as quickly as possible.

At TSI, my colleagues and I valued professional involvement and advocated for public policy that provides services and secures the rights for those who have experienced traumatic events. Over time, I became more invoked in advocacy efforts on a number of fronts, primarily through my various roles in the state psychological association and also at APA.

Ultimately, I changed careers and began working full time at APA on a broad range of issues affecting the professional practice of psychology at the state and national levels. For the past several years I've worked on health care reform, changes in health finance and reimbursement as they affect psychological and mental health services, and parity in mental health insurance coverage.

All of these opportunities to advance the practice of psychology stemmed from my earlier role as a practitioner interested in contributing to the field through state advocacy efforts. It is essential more than ever that psychologists think both locally—regarding their individual practices—and globally—concerning how they can contribute to the larger world. Through involvement in a broad range of institutions (e.g., educational, health care, business/corporate, correctional, environmental systems), psychologists can have a significant impact on the psychological well-being of others.

I can't think of a single part of our culture, a single part of the world that we live in, where psychology doesn't have something to contribute. I get excited when I think that I can make a difference in somebody's life. I love the field.

Dr. Dorothy W. Cantor

Clinical psychologist in independent practice

I like to help people solve their problems. My work as a clinical psychologist with an independent practice in New Jersey allows me plenty of opportunity to do so. I help individuals from teenagers to octogenarians, and some couples, who have varied psychological or relationship concerns.

I earned my PsyD, a professional psychology doctorate, in 1970, was licensed in 1978, and since then have practiced psychodynamic therapy, which assumes that a person's early years are a critical part of his or her current problem and explores them in the context of the patient–therapist relationship.

I listen with the ear of someone who is trained to understand the dynamics of what the person is saying. If medication is indicated for the patient, I coordinate the treatment with a local psychiatrist.

Psychology wasn't my first career. I was originally trained to teach because that's what most women who went to college in the 1950s did. Beginning when my children were in preschool, I earned two master's degrees (in reading education and school psychology) at New Jersey's Kean College. I went on to earn the newly offered PsyD, a doctoral degree designed for people who want to practice psychology, at Rutgers University's Graduate School of Applied and Professional Psychology. It was important that the schools I attended be close to home so that I could combine my education with being a mom—and Rutgers is 35 minutes from home!

I earned my doctorate so that I could be licensed to have a clinical private practice. As a school psychologist, I did a lot of the assessing of problems but never got to help alleviate them.

To be a good psychologist, you should be a good listener, nonjudgmental, smart, and flexible in order to apply scientific theory to people in a nonformulaic way, which takes a certain creativity. I advise students entering the field to prepare for many years of education, all the way to the doctorate. The rewards are just so great. It's so gratifying to be helpful to people on an ongoing basis.

I am past president of the American Psychological Association and current president of the American Psychological Foundation. I've written many articles and several books, including *Women in Power* (with Dr. Toni Bernay), *What Do You Want to Do When You Grow Up?* and *Finding Your Voice*. And I've appeared as an expert on many television shows, including *Good Morning America*, *Prime Time Live*, and the *Today* show.

What lies ahead? I expect psychology to become more of a part of the bigger health care system, as people come to understand how mind and body interact. I hope that people will go for mental health checkups the way they go for physical health checkups.

As for my career, my role model was a 90-year-old psychologist who worked until her death. I plan to write a few more books. And then, as always, I'll see what opportunities present themselves. There are just so many opportunities for psychologists.

Dr. Rodney Hammond

Health psychologist and CDC violence-prevention program administrator

My passionate interest in helping people live their lives to their fullest potential is what attracted me to psychology. My early training and experiences prepared me for career opportunities that I could scarcely have imagined as an undergraduate in college. Ultimately, I identified as a health psychologist because it is a field that goes beyond traditional mental health and addresses broader health concerns.

When I started as an undergraduate at the University of Illinois at Urbana-Champaign, I hadn't decided on my major. To help finance my education, I took a part-time job in a child development research program sponsored by the psychology department. There, I observed inner-city children in settings designed to enhance their learning. I saw firsthand the contributions psychology can make, and I knew I wanted to be a psychologist.

After completing undergraduate work in psychology, I went on to earn my doctorate, focusing on children, both in school and in the community. When I graduated, there was no such thing as a health psychologist. I started as an assistant professor in a doctoral program in school psychology at the University of Tennessee. But soon I went on to direct a children's program at Meharry Medical College in Nashville. As a psychologist in a medical setting, I could help children with health problems as well as their families and physicians.

At Meharry, I was in charge of an extensive and innovative program with an interdisciplinary staff. We worked with children who had developmental disabilities, dealt with child abuse and neglect, developed partial hospitalization for children with emotional problems, and created prevention programs for youths at risk I then became assistant dean at the Wright State University School of Professional Psychology in Ohio, where I trained clinical psychologists and directed a program to prevent homicide and violence among minority youths.

Most of my career was spent at the Centers for Disease Control and Prevention (CDC), where for 15 years I served as the director of the Division of Violence Prevention at the National Center for Injury Prevention and Control (I retired in 2011). The division, with its budget of more than $100 million, manages research, surveillance, and programs in intentional injury; homicide, suicide, and youth, family, and intimate partner violence prevention; and rape and sexual assault prevention.

As director of this CDC division, I oversaw the world's largest concentration of public health experts working on violence issues and prevention. These experts come from a variety of fields, including psychology, medicine, sociology, economics, and epidemiology. I was also involved in global efforts to prevent violence through the World Health Organization and Pan American Health Organization.

Through my work, I was able to achieve a career level unprecedented by a psychologist—I was the first psychologist to serve as the director of a division of the CDC. As you can see from my experience and background, my early work as a health psychologist was the basis for—but just the beginning of—this adventure. Psychology is much more than the traditional roles you may be aware of. When you think of a career in psychology, think beyond those limited roles!

Dr. Prenda Khatri

Clinical psychologist and community health organization director

I was always interested in human behavior; it seemed to be a key component to so many aspects and issues in life. I was also strongly influenced by my father, who was both a sociologist and psychologist. When I was a child, he would talk to me about the work of Freud and B. F. Skinner. I knew words like classical conditioning and super ego before I reached the 9th grade! I wanted to contribute to society and engage in a variety of activities such as teaching, clinical practice, and research. Psychology offered the opportunity to fulfill these goals in a meaningful way.

After majoring in psychology at the University of Alabama at Birmingham, I graduated with a PhD in clinical psychology from the University of North Carolina at Chapel Hill. I completed a postdoctoral fellowship at Duke University Medical Center, which was an amazing experience. On my first day I joined the cardiac rehab team and talked to patients about health behavior change while walking on a track with them. What a shift from the traditional 50-minute therapy session! From then on I realized that the knowledge and skill base in psychology could be adapted to fit almost any setting and, moreover, could have a significant impact on a person's quality of life, health status, and overall functioning.

Today I am director of integrated care at Cherokee Health Systems (CHS), which is a comprehensive community health organization that provides integrated primary care and behavioral health services in east Tennessee. CHS is both a federally qualified health center and a community mental health center, with a mission of improving the physical and mental health of everyone in our community. As a community health organization, we see everyone in our communities regardless of their ability to pay. Therefore, we are able to bring progressive, evidenced-based health care to everyone, including people who are uninsured. Working in community health means I can fulfill my personal and professional mission to work with the underserved in our communities.

As director, I am responsible for implementing the clinical model of integrating behavioral health and primary care to optimize functioning and quality of life for our patients. I am also involved in teaching and consulting with other organizations as part of CHS's training and outreach initiatives on integrated care. I serve on teams that provide oversight and guidance regarding clinical activities and procedures within the organization. In my leadership role, I am responsible for many of CHS's wellness, chronic care, and research initiatives. As training director of CHS's APA-accredited internship program, I am closely involved with teaching, clinical supervision, and program administration.

On any given day, I may see patients, work on a grant, develop a training schedule, address operational and clinical issues that arise at any of our clinics, provide clinical supervision (i.e., supervise the work of other providers), and participate in a management meeting. I love the variety and stimulation in my work. I get to work with bright, mission-oriented individuals with a range of expertise in different fields, including medicine, behavioral health, and business management.

Working in a community health setting with a mission to the underserved provides tremendous professional and personal satisfaction. Primary care psychology offers exciting opportunities for psychologists to practice in a unique and rewarding setting. It is a significant growth area in the field. My advice to new psychologists: Work hard, be guided by a sense of mission and purpose, think outside of the box, and be open to new possibilities. You will be amazed by the opportunities that will come your way.

Dr. Carol Manning

Neuropsychologist and university professor

My doctoral degree was in clinical psychology. I do clinical work, research, and teaching at the University of Virginia. All three aspects of my career are very important to me.

For example, I work in a memory disorders clinic as part of a team of neurologists, nurses, and medical technicians. I oversee patient treatment apart from medication. What I learn in my research, I use in my clinical practice. And in my clinical practice, I learn the important questions to ask in my research.

One of my patients who has Alzheimer's disease is in a clinical drug trial involving an experimental medication. No one knows if he is receiving medication or a placebo, which is something that looks like the medication but is actually inert (i.e., an inactive substance or preparation). I assess this person periodically and also talk with his wife occasionally to determine whether his condition has changed. I test his ability to remember things, and I look to see if the kinds of judgments he makes are the same kinds of judgments you or I would make. I test his ability to know the time, date, and place—to see if he knows generally where he is. I look at his ability to copy drawings and also to remember those drawings. I also check his attention span.

I use computers to run experiments. This morning, I tested a patient's spatial memory: He had to remember where words were placed on the screen. I also use computers for statistics—to analyze what my data mean.

I teach in the Department of Neurology, and some of my work involves supervising graduate students. It's important that my students are truly interested in psychology and in the projects they're working on. They need to think creatively, be determined, and work thoroughly and carefully.

I'm helping one graduate student learn to do therapy and to assess patients. Another graduate student works with me on research studies. She helps me guide people through the research program on the computer. She analyzes data, and she's learned to do statistics and how to design studies. We write papers together for publication.

If you're interested in psychology, I'd advise you to take psychology courses as an undergraduate. And try to work in a research laboratory so that you can get some insight into what the field is really like.

Many of today's students are encouraged to take time off between undergraduate and graduate school because it's a long haul and it takes a lot of determination. Sometimes I think it's nice for people to have a break in there. It takes persistence to earn a doctorate in psychology, along with a great interest in psychological research, science, and people. It takes a long time—but I think it's well worth it!

Dr. Susan McDaniel

Clinical psychologist, family health psychologist and administrator

I was raised in the South during desegregation and have always been interested in the underlying values and behaviors that can bring different individuals, groups, or cultures together. This process is a common thread in my professional life, whether working to strengthen couples and families or in primary care teams with physicians, psychologists, and other clinicians.

My father was an obstetrician/gynecologist who loved being a physician. It was clear to me that I wanted to do meaningful, rewarding work, too. My interest in science came from him. My emotional intelligence came from my mother. Put those with the irrational events of the time I grew up in, and you have the makings of a budding psychologist.

When I went to college in the early 70s, I wanted to study stereotyping and why people generalize across groups. This led to a double major in cultural anthropology and psychology at Duke. I loved studying the effect of culture on behavior and language but thought psychology might be a more practical choice for graduate school. I was fortunate to attend the University of North Carolina at Chapel Hill in clinical psychology, working with many talented clinical and research professors, including William Stiles, with whom I did my dissertation on language (verbal response modes) in psychotherapy. Probably because of my strong southern family, I went to the University of Texas Medical Branch in Galveston for internship and worked with pioneering family psychologists Harry Goolishian and Harlene Anderson. Family therapy made immediate sense to me. It is applied anthropology—understanding individual behavior in the context of the group.

A fascination with mind-body interaction led me to accept a part-time job as a faculty member in the Department of Family Medicine at the University of Rochester (the first woman and first PhD on the faculty) in 1981. These bright, dedicated residents wanted a more organized behavioral science curriculum that would prepare them for the huge proportion of primary care practice that is psychological in nature. They were also interested in what family therapy had to offer family medicine.

Collaborating closely with family physician Thomas Campbell, we developed a practical curriculum that taught family medicine residents to evaluate the mental, behavioral, and interpersonal difficulties of their patients along with their biomedical problems. We combined the biopsychosocial approach with a family systems approach that is particularly well suited to primary care. The problems people bring to their primary care doctor aren't always physical and are often difficult to evaluate. Having systems skills to understand the individual, family, and community components is extremely helpful for assessment and successful treatment planning. It is also useful in enlisting family input and support and in promoting team functioning among the disciplines that make up the primary care team.

The Family Medicine Department has been a wonderful home. I see my own patients in the primary care setting (and see many patients who will not enter the traditional mental health system). My systemic/family skills are now put to use in promoting healthy faculty functioning, leadership coaching, and helping to transform primary care practice into patient-centered medical homes that are psychologically healthy.

The year after I joined the family medicine faculty (1982), I joined the psychiatry faculty when a family therapy training program began there. I eventually took over as division chief and developed the Institute for the Family, which has clinical, training, and research functions. We train family medicine, psychiatry, pediatric, and internal medicine residents. By design, faculty members work both in the Institute and in another clinical department (i.e., ob/gyn, pediatrics, the epilepsy center, internal medicine, family medicine) to provide behavioral health at the point of service as part of a heath care team.

Health care—patients, families, and other health professionals—needs psychologists. There is enormous opportunity for psychologists with clinical, systems, health, and research training. Some opportunities are defined and posted, others (like the coaching program) are innovative and an obvious fit with our skill set. Like my father, I have meaningful and rewarding work that I love. You can, too.

Psychologists Study the Work Environment and Performance Issues

Anywhere people work, and anything they do while at work, is of interest to psychologists. Psychologists study what makes people effective, satisfied, and motivated in their jobs; what distinguishes good workers or managers from poor ones; and what conditions of work promote high or low productivity, morale, and safety.

Some psychologists design programs for recruiting, selecting, placing, and training employees. They evaluate, monitor, and improve performance. They help make changes in the way the organization is set up. Others help design the actual tasks, tools, and environments people must deal with when doing their jobs. These specialists can also help design the products that organizations create and conduct research related to product design. For example, they play a big role in making computer hardware and software more user friendly.

Psychologists with training in mental health and health care also deal with the health and adjustment of individuals in the work setting. They work with employee assistance plans that provide help with drug or alcohol addiction problems, depression, and other disorders; they also foster healthy behavior. Others work on performance issues in areas such as sport psychology, where they may provide athletes with counseling, work with them to improve motivation and performance, explore psychological considerations in sports injuries and rehabilitation, and perform a range of tasks related to sports performance and education.

Dr. Elizabeth Kolmstetter

Industrial/organizational psychologist, researcher, and senior executive

If we're going to keep up with the "bad guys," we need to keep our workforce skills, knowledge, and competencies continuously developing. As an industrial/organizational (I/O) psychologist, I helped lead the drive to heighten airport security after September 11, 2001. This involved the largest civilian mobilization effort in the United States—to hire more than 50,000 airport screeners for the government in less than a year. The undertaking, called for in the Aviation and Transportation Security Act that President Bush signed into law soon after the attacks, sought to strengthen airport security screening by federalizing it and enhancing the workforce skill standards.

At that time, I was the director of Standards, Testing, Evaluation, and Policy for the newly formed Transportation Security Administration (TSA). I created a team of I/O psychologists, HR professionals, medical experts, and trainers to develop higher standards and the accompanying tests for screeners' cognitive, customer service, X-ray detection, and physical abilities. Using future-oriented job analyses, the team validated new post-9/11 skill standards for every aspect of the new screener rotational job design and then designed an assessment process, including automated application screening, computer-based tests, and in-person structured interviews and medical evaluations, that could process masses of applicants efficiently. Applying the newly established standards, the TSA processed more than 1.8 million applications and hired and trained about 50,000 screeners by the congressionally mandated one-year deadline. Throughout the process, the team faced many obstacles, but we did get it done—we raised the standards for the workforce and national security, and we did it against unbelievable odds.

During my nearly 6 years with the TSA, I developed numerous testing and assessment programs for screeners, law enforcement officers, and armed pilots; implemented enhanced training, including the automated Learning Management System; implemented a mandatory, annual certification program for all screeners; instituted a pay-for-performance program; and designed and implemented a career progression program for the screeners.

In 2007, I became the deputy associate director of National Intelligence for Human Capital at the Office of the Director of National Intelligence (established in 2005). I help to drive the collaboration and integration of the 17 agencies that make up the Intelligence Community (IC). My work includes setting common competency directories for the occupations of the IC, supporting culture change through common performance standards and appraisal processes, developing common leadership programs and succession management processes, establishing a consistent workforce planning template and annual process, and designing a common professional development framework and associated metrics.

It is very rewarding to know that the programs I build as an I/O psychologist touch every employee and greatly improve the workplace. I continuously see how our work directly improves the nation's ability to enhance and ensure national security during this most challenging time in our history. A lot of it has to be done with creativity and innovation.

Dr. David Sirota

Industrial/organizational psychologist and consultant

When I began my career as an industrial/organizational psychologist there was an emphasis on testing—ability testing, personality testing, and so on—in an effort to put the right person in the right job. Today, the emphasis is turning to establishing the atmosphere most conducive to productivity and quality work.

The field has become extremely influential—starting in the late 1970s—in part because of the overwhelming competition from Japan and the success of their products. Studies indicated that Japanese companies tended to manage the way I/O psychologists say people should be managed.

Most I/O psychologists maintain that people go to work wanting to do good work. Nevertheless, when we look at a company that has a problem—let's say, a drop in customers or a large turnover in labor—we see large percentages of people not working very hard. When we analyze what causes people to lose their motivation, the answer usually has to do with how they're being managed. For example, if management treats employees like children or criminals, the employees are likely to become demoralized.

I had wanted to be a psychologist since I was a psychology major at the City College of New York (I originally thought I would go into engineering). One great influence on me was my father. He was a strong union man. From him I learned that workers' opinions are very important to a company's overall well-being. While earning my doctorate in social psychology at the University of Michigan, I also became enamored of survey work at the university's Institute for Social Research.

I was an I/O psychologist for IBM for 13 years and then set up my own consulting firm, Sirota and Associates, in New York City. (I sold the firm a few years ago.) It is now called Sirota Survey Intelligence and does work for companies, government agencies, and nonprofits all over the world. Earlier in my career, I also taught at a number of universities, such as MIT and the Wharton School.

My particular branch of the field focuses on data collection. We diagnose an organization's problems by surveying people in the organization through questionnaires, informal interviews, focus groups, or a combination of all three methods. Why do employees stay with the company? What helps them produce quality' products or quality service? Do they have the right training, the right equipment, the right management, the right whatever? Does the way management treats employees cause them to feel good or bad about the company's customers? Often we interview the customers, too. All these variables constitute the heart of what we do.

We come back to management with our analysis. We try to be candid, but not abrasive, pointing out what's being done well and the opportunities for improvement. We then try to get the managers involved in coming to their own solutions.

Unlike a doctor who finds out what's wrong with you and then writes a prescription, most I/O psychologists want people to become their own doctors. We're not necessarily interested in people liking each other or becoming "nice guys," per se. Of course, it's good if they do, but what we want is for them to deal with what has to be done in terms of business objectives.

Dr. Adam Shunk

Neuropsychologist and sport psychologist

There are many different paths that may lead to a career in psychology, and many opportunities that present themselves along the way. In my case, my passion to work as a psychologist in athletics guided my journey to create my dream job.

I always knew as a child that I loved sports and wanted my career to involve athletics. I was a dedicated high school athlete who was fortunate enough to earn an athletic scholarship to the University of North Carolina. After college, I followed my passion for sports to become a professional track-and-field athlete who competed on the international circuit for 4 years. My involvement in sports and my experience as a coach helped me understand the sports culture.

Early in my academic training, I realized that I wanted to focus on positive psychology and help individuals in their pursuit of excellence. In my studies, I was drawn to biology and the relationship between brain and behavior. Although I was primarily trained as a neuropsychologist through my formal education, I emphasized and integrated sport psychology course work into my curriculum at both the undergraduate and graduate levels, and focused rotations were part of my internship and postdoctoral training. I had to be innovative in creating a training program that met formal guidelines in neuropsychology and also provided appropriate training in sport psychology. It worked out beautifully for me, as I found a career that allowed me to pursue my passion for sports and neuropsychology with a population focused on athletic achievement.

My schedule differs on a daily basis, and flexibility is an essential part of my job. For example, 2 days a week I work in an athletics setting at Purdue University, where my time is spent providing counseling and assessment services in the athletic department. As a sport psychologist, I have been trained in the applied practice of sport and performance psychology, and I work with "elite" performance issues and positive psychology applications. Another focus of sport psychology is to provide individual counseling for mental health issues and consultation services for coaches, teams, and administrators.

My job often involves travel, and I frequently work with clients on weekends and in the evenings to accommodate their busy schedules. The focus of sport psychology is to use psychological interventions to enhance athletic and overall performance. The nature of athletics creates some specialized needs for athletes, who must manage and deal with rigorous practice, workout schedules, extensive travel, injuries, fatigue, high expectations, and media exposure, in addition to normal stressors.

If you are interested in becoming a sport psychologist, you'll need to establish proficiency within the field. APA's Division 47 (Exercise and Sport Psychology) provides appropriate guidelines for establishing competency as a sport psychologist.

Pursuing my interests in neuropsychology and sport psychology has certainly been challenging, but it has taught me that if you know what you want to do, there is always a way to make it happen.

Stats on the Education and Training Measurements for Psychologists

Emilio Ulloa, ed.

Table 1. Bureau of Labor Statistics (BLS) Education and training measurements for workers by occupation

Occupation title	Most significant source of education or training	Educational attainment						
		% who have Less than high school diploma	% who have High school diploma or equivalent	% with Some college, no degree	% with Associate's degree	% with Bachelor's degree	% with Master's degree	% with Doctoral or professional degree
Sales managers	Bachelor's or higher degree, plus work experience	1.0	9.1	17.6	6.7	47.7	16.6	1.4
Medical and health services managers	Bachelor's or higher degree, plus work experience	1.3	9.0	16.1	12.8	31.1	22.5	7.1
Social and community service managers	Bachelor's degree	1.7	9.4	15.3	6.3	37.7	24.7	4.9
Employment, recruitment, and placement specialists	Bachelor's degree	1.6	13.7	22.9	9.2	37.7	13.2	1.8
Statisticians	Master's degree	0.4	1.4	4.9	3.2	28.1	38.5	23.6
Clinical, counseling, and school psychologists	Doctoral degree	0.2	0.2	0.4	0.3	4.2	43.2	51.5
Industrial-organizational psychologists	Master's degree	0.2	0.2	0.4	0.3	4.2	43.2	51.5
Social science research assistants	Associate degree	2.6	17.5	23.9	12.6	29.7	9.4	4.2
Educational, vocational, and school counselors	Master's degree	1.3	7.3	10.5	5.6	25.0	45.9	4.4
Marriage and family therapists	Master's degree	1.3	7.3	10.5	5.6	25.0	45.9	4.4
Mental health counselors	Master's degree	1.3	7.3	10.5	5.6	25.0	45.9	4.4
Rehabilitation counselors	Master's degree	1.3	7.3	10.5	5.6	25.0	45.9	4.4
Child, family, and school social workers	Bachelor's degree	1.2	6.2	10.4	6.0	42.3	32.2	1.6
Medical and public health social workers	Bachelor's degree	1.2	6.2	10.4	6.0	42.3	32.2	1.6
Mental health and substance abuse social workers	Master's degree	1.2	6.2	10.4	6.0	42.3	32.2	1.6
Probation officers and correctional treatment specialists	Bachelor's degree	2.4	15.3	20.9	9.6	37.1	13.4	1.3
Social and human service assistants	Moderate-term on-the-job training	2.4	15.3	20.9	9.6	37.1	13.4	1.3
Special education teachers, preschool, kindergarten, and elementary school	Bachelor's degree	0.4	4.6	5.9	3.8	38.3	44.9	2.1
Physicians and surgeons	First professional degree	0.2	0.3	0.4	0.4	1.0	2.3	95.3
Physician assistants	Master's degree	1.0	6.7	9.0	14.2	30.6	26.6	12.0
Occupational therapists	Master's degree	0.2	0.5	0.9	8.6	55.5	31.1	3.2
Psychiatric technicians	Postsecondary vocational award	2.5	27.8	34.1	19.0	14.1	1.4	1.1
Psychiatric aides	Short-term on-the-job training	16.0	40.6	28.3	7.2	5.8	1.3	0.9
Real estate brokers	Work experience in a related occupation	1.5	15.4	28.4	9.6	34.6	8.5	2.0
Real estate sales agents	Postsecondary vocational award	1.5	15.4	28.4	9.6	34.6	8.5	2.0
Secretaries, except legal, medical, and executive	Moderate-term on-the-job training	2.6	33.0	34.6	13.1	14.1	2.1	0.4
Airline pilots, copilots, and flight engineers	Bachelor's degree	0.6	6.3	12.9	8.3	59.2	11.1	1.6

Emilio Ulloa, ed., "Condensed Version of Table 1.11 Education and Training Measurements for Workers 25 Years and Older by Detailed Occupation, 2008," bls.gov.

Doctorate Employment Survey for Psychologists

By Marlene Wicherski, Daniel Michalski, and Jessica Kohout

Table 1: Demographic Characteristics of 2009 Doctorate Recipients in Psychology by Employment Status

	Employment Status										Total
	Employed Full Time		Employed Part Time		Postdoctoral Fellow		Unemployed, Seeking Employment		Unemployed, Not Seeking		N (100%)
	N	%	N	%	N	%	N	%	N	%	
N=	785	63.0	64	7.5	297	23.8	48	3.9	22	1.8	1246
Gender											
Men	196	67.4	15	5.2	69	23.7	9	3.1	2	0.7	291
Women	574	61.6	73	7.8	227	24.4	39	4.2	19	2.0	932
Not Specified	15	65.2	6	26.1	1	4.3	0	0.0	1	4.3	23
Race/Ethnicity											
White	578	62.3	72	7.8	225	24.2	33	3.6	20	2.2	928
Black	44	65.7	2	3.0	15	22.4	6	9.0	0	0.0	67
Hispanic	39	59.1	5	7.6	21	31.8	1	1.5	0	0.0	66
Asian	61	70.1	5	5.7	13	18.4	4	4.6	1	1.1	87
American Indian	1	50.0	0	0.0	1	50.0	0	0.0	0	0.0	2
Pacific Islander	1	100	0	0.0	0	0.0	0	0.0	0	0.0	1
Other	9	50.0	3	16.7	5	27.8	1	5.6	0	0.0	18
Multiracial/ multiethnic	34	68.0	2	4.0	11	22.0	3	6.0	0	0.0	50
Not Specified	18	66.7	5	18.5	3	11.1	0	0.0	1	3.7	27
Age											
Under 30	202	64.1	18	5.7	82	26.0	10	3.2	3	1.0	315
30-34	352	61.6	32	5.6	154	27.0	27	4.7	6	1.1	571
35-39	99	60.0	19	11.5	37	22.4	4	2.4	6	3.6	165
40-44	44	66.7	4	6.1	14	21.2	2	3.0	2	3.0	66
45-49	27	77.7	2	5.7	6	17.1	0	0.0	0	0.0	35
50-54	25	73.5	4	11.8	1	2.9	3	8.8	1	2.9	34
55-59	15	65.2	5	21.7	2	8.7	1	4.3	0	0.0	23
60 or Older	6	50.0	3	25.0	0	0.0	0	0.0	3	25.0	12

	Employment Status										Total
	Employed Full Time		Employed Part Time		Postdoctoral Fellow		Unemployed, Seeking Employment		Unemployed, Not Seeking		N (100%)
	N	%	N	%	N	%	N	%	N	%	
Age (cont.)											
Not Specified	15	60.0	7	28.0	1	4.0	1	4.0	1	4.0	25
Mean	37		37		32		34		40		34
Standard Deviation	7		10		5		7		12		7
Sexual Orientation											
Heterosexual	670	62.9	81	7.6	261	24.5	36	3.4	18	1.7	1066
Gay	34	73.9	2	4.3	5	10.9	5	10.9	0	0.0	46
Lesbian	20	64.5	0	0.0	10	32.3	1	3.2	0	0.0	31
Bisexual	16	69.6	1	4.3	5	21.7	0	0.0	1	4.3	23
Prefer not to answer	25	58.1	4	9.3	9	20.9	3	7.0	2	4.7	43
Other	3	42.9	0	0.0	4	57.1	0	0.0	0	0.0	7
Not Specified	17	56.7	6	20.0	3	10.0	3	10.0	1	3.3	30
Perception of the Job Market											
Bleak	21	35.0	7	11.7	15	25.0	16	26.7	1	1.7	60
Poor	147	55.1	27	10.1	70	26.2	17	6.4	6	2.2	267
Fair	276	63.3	31	7.1	108	24.8	12	2.8	9	2.1	436
Good	255	70.4	23	6.4	78	21.5	2	0.6	4	1.1	362
Excellent	64	80.0	2	2.5	13	16.3	1	1.3	0	0.0	80
Not Sure	22	55.0	4	10.0	12	30.0	0	0.0	2	5.0	40
Not Specified	0	0.0	0	0.0	1	100.0	0	0.0	0	0.0	1
Sourced: 2009 Doctorate Employment Survey, APA Center for Workforce Studies. March 2011.											

Table 2: Educational Characteristics of 2009 Doctorate Receipients in Psychology by Employment Status

	Employment Status										Total
	Employed Full Time		Employed Part Time		Postdoctoral Fellow		Unemployed, Seeking Employment		Unemployed, Not Seeking		N (100%)
	N	%	N	%	N	%	N	%	N	%	
N=	785	63.0	64	7.5	297	23.8	48	3.9	22	1.8	1246
Degree(s) Earned											
PhD	594	63.4	64	6.8	229	24.4	31	3.3	19	2.0	9337
PsyD	187	62.3	30	10.0	64	21.3	16	5.3	3	1.0	300
EdD	1	33.3	0	0.0	1	33.3	1	33.3	0	0.0	3
PhD/JD	2	66.7	0	0.0	1	33.3	0	0.0	0	0.0	3
PsyD/JD	1	100.0	0	0.0	0	0.0	0	0.0	0	0.0	1
PhD/MD	0	0.0	0	0.0	1	100.0	0	0.0	0	0.0	1
PhD/RhD	0	0.0	0	0.0	1	100.0	0	0.0	0	0.0	1

	Employment Status										Total
	Employed Full Time		Employed Part Time		Postdoctoral Fellow		Unemployed, Seeking Employment		Unemployed, Not Seeking		N (100%)
	N	%	N	%	N	%	N	%	N	%	
Subfield											
Biological	4	50.0	1	12.5	2	25.0	1	12.5	0	0.0	8
Clinical	312	61.5	46	9.1	123	24.3	21	4.1	5	1.0	507
Clinical Child	34	57.6	4	6.8	18	30.5	1	1.7	2	3.4	59
Clinical Neuropsychology	9	25.0	0	0.0	24	66.7	1	2.8	2	5.6	36
Cognitive	25	61.0	2	4.9	13	31.7	1	2.4	0	0.0	41
Community	9	69.2	2	15.4	1	7.7	1	7.7	0	0.0	13
Comparative	0	0.0	0	0.0	1	100.0	0	0.0	0	0.0	1
Counseling	70	68.0	12	11.7	15	14.6	3	2.9	3	2.9	103
Developmental	36	64.3	3	5.4	12	21.4	3	5.4	2	3.6	56
Educational	36	78.3	5	10.9	3	6.5	2	4.3	0	0.0	46
Engineering	0	0.0	0	0.0	1	100.0	0	0.0	0	0.0	1
Environmental	2	100.0	0	0.0	0	0.0	0	0.0	0	0.0	2
Evolutionary	3	100.0	0	0.0	0	0.0	0	0.0	0	0.0	3
Experimental	8	36.4	0	0.0	12	54.5	1	4.5	1	4.5	22
Family	3	75.0	0	0.0	0	0.0	1	25.0	0	0.0	4
Forensic	8	66.7	1	8.3	2	16.7	1	8.3	0	0.0	12
General	7	87.5	0	0.0	0	0.0	1	12.5	0	0.0	8
Geropsychology	0	0.0	0	0.0	0	0.0	0	0.0	0	0.0	0
Health	6	33.3	2	11.1	9	0.5	0	0.0	1	5.6	18
I/O	45	80.4	2	3.6	4	7.1	5	8.9	0	0.0	56
Neurosciences	17	31.5	2	3.7	31	57.4	3	5.6	1	1.9	54
Personality	2	50.0	0	0.0	2	50.0	0	0.0	0	0.0	4
Physiological	1	100.0	0	0.0	0	0.0	0	0.0	0	0.0	1
Psycholinguistics	1	100.0	0	0.0	0	0.0	0	0.0	0	0.0	1
Psychometrics	7	100.0	0	0.0	0	0.0	0	0	0	0.0	7
Psychopharmacology	0	0.0	0	0.0	1	100.0	0	0.0	0	0.0	1
Quantitative	5	100.0	0	0.0	0	0.0	0	0.0	0	0.0	5
Rehabilitation	0	0.0	0	0.0	0	0.0	0	0.0	0	0.0	0
School	58	82.9	3	4.3	7	10.0	0	0.0	2	2.9	70
Social	53	74.6	4	5.6	10	14.1	2	2.8	2	2.8	71
Sports	1	100.0	0	0.0	0	0.0	0	0.0	0	0.0	1
Systems/ History/ Methods	0	0.0	0	0.0	0	0.0	0	0.0	0	0.0	0
Other in Psychology	10	55.6	4	22.2	3	16.7	0	0.0	1	5.6	18
Not in Psychology	1	100.0	0	0.0	0	0.0	0	0.0	0	0.0	0

	Employment Status										Total
	Employed Full Time		Employed Part Time		Postdoctoral Fellow		Unemployed, Seeking Employment		Unemployed, Not Seeking		N (100%)
	N	%	N	%	N	%	N	%	N	%	
Health Service Provider Subfields	510	62.0	70	8.5	199	24.2	29	3.5	15	1.8	823
Research and Other Fields	263	64.6	23	5.7	95	23.3	19	4.7	7	1.7	407
Not Specified	12	75.0	1	6.3	3	18.8	0	0.0	0	0.0	16
Source 2009 Doctorate Employment Survey, APA Center for Workforce Studies. March 2011.											

Table 11: Starting Salaries for Full-Time Employment Positinos: 2009 Doctorate Recipients in Psychology

Position	Employment Setting	Median	Mean	SD	N
Assistant Professor*	All Settings	56,727	59,155	14,762	130
	University Psychology Department	58,000	58,797	10,665	54
	University Education Department	57,000	58,330	8,693	19
	Other University Academic Department	60,000	59,447	10,268	12
	4-year College Psychology Department	52,000	51,103	8,286	20
Lecturer/ Instructor*	All Settings	40,909	42,212	7,768	13
Educational Administration	All Settings	71,000	72,767	20,759	13
Research	All Settings	60,000	60,767	17,535	62
	University Research Center or Institute	63,000	67,364	17,716	11
	Medical School, Psychiatry Department	45,000	50,275	12,407	12
Direct Human Services: Clinical Psychology	All Settings	61,000	60,046	15,629	175
	University Counseling Center*	60,000	56,430	8,052	14
	City/ County/ State Psychiatric Hospital	68,000	66,500	14,819	17
	VA Medical Center	71,000	70,542	7,216	28
	Group Psychological Practice	55,000	50,667	15,199	13
	Community Mental health Center or Clinic (CMHC)	49,000	48,846	10,656	28
	Criminal Justice System	80,500	73,563	14,810	16
Direct Human Services: Clinical Child Psychology	All Settings	58,500	56,643	11,036	14
Direct Human Services: Counseling Psychology	All Settings	54,200	56,533	14,945	32
Direct Human Services: School Psychology	All Settings	58,000	63,391	14,863	29
Administration of Human Services	All Settings	62,000	67,804	22,341	21
Applied Psychology	All Settings	73,332	75,304	19,038	59
	Consulting Firm	75,000	78,727	9,350	11
Other Positions	All Settings	67,000	79,191	54,085	53

Source: 2009 Doctorate Employment Survey, APA Center for Workforce Studies. March 2011.
Note. Salaries are those at the time of survey (Spring, 2010) and are represented for only those settings reported by 10 or more individuals. Figures for "All Settings" include settings reported by fewer than 10.
* Salaries in these setting are typically paid on a 9-10 month (academic year) basis. The statistics given here can be converted to their 11-12-month (calendar year) equivalents by multiplying by 11/9.

What Is Forensic Psychology? It's Not Silence of the Lambs!

By Matthew T. Huss

Forensic psychology is one of the fastest growing areas of psychology as suggested both by an increase in the practice of clinical psychology within our legal system and the increasing interest expressed by undergraduate and graduate students. However, students often become interested in the field because of sensationalistic media portrayals that may not be accurate nor offer realistic employment opportunities. Students may become disheartened to learn that certain media depictions are less than realistic but should be excited to learn about the real possibilities forensic psychology has to offer. This article will attempt to describe the field of forensic psychology, identify possible careers, and suggest relevant training opportunities.

It's difficult to turn on a television, go to the movies, or walk through a bookstore without running across a fictional portrayal of a crazed but brilliant serial or mass murderer being tracked by a psychologically sophisticated and deductively sound hero. Popular movies such as *Silence of the Lambs* and *Hannibal* and television shows like *Profiler* often depict the intersection of law enforcement and psychology in sensationalistic and dramatic fashion. If you watch the news or read a newspaper you can hear about the psychological "sketch" offered by a forensic psychologist in the latest Jeffrey Dahmer, Ted Kaczynski, or Michael McDermott trial. Our society has become increasingly fascinated with individuals who seemingly are able to perpetrate the most heinous crimes imaginable. Now is this stuff interesting?

Sure it is! Similar things got me interested in forensic psychology! We are horrified but drawn to these scenes much like we are drawn to the aftermath of a car accident. Are these depictions accurate? Probably not. Are they accurate depictions of forensic psychology? Almost never. Forensic psychologists are not able to become psychically linked with a particular killer and visualize their next move as the heroes in the movies or on television seem to do. Forensic psychology is a discipline based on the scientific practice of psychology. So, while forensic psychologists get the cool jobs, they are far from the situations often portrayed.

So What Is Forensic Psychology?

If someone told you he or she was a forensic psychologist, what would you think they do? Do they have something to do with the high school speech and debate team? Do they perform autopsies on homicide

Matthew T. Huss, "What is Forensic Psychology? It's Not Silence of the Lambs!," *Eye on Psi Chi*, vol. 5, no. 3, pp. 25–27.

victims? If you are like most people, these thoughts probably immediately came to mind. However, the origin of the word *forensic* comes from the Latin word *forum.* Forums were the public gathering places in the Roman city-states where much of the judicial process took place in the form of debates. As a result, forensic psychology deals with the intersection of psychology and the legal process.

There continues to be debate in the field about the definition and breadth of the term *forensic psychology.* Some professionals apply the term broadly to describe any intersection of the legal system and psychology (Wrightsman, 2001). However, others use the term to specifically describe the clinical practice of psychology in legal contexts (e.g., Melton, Huss, and Tomkins, 1999). For example, the American Board of Forensic Psychology and the American Psychology-Law Society (1995) define forensic psychology as:

> the professional practice by psychologists within the areas of clinical psychology, counseling psychology, neuropsychology, and school psychology, when they are engaged regularly as experts and represent themselves as such, in an activity primarily intended to provide professional psychological expertise to the judicial system. (p. 6)

Such a definition focuses the field on the mental health aspects of psychology and the law and away from the more experimental areas of jury selection and eyewitness identification. When I speak of forensic psychology, I will be focusing on the intersection of mental health, or the clinical practice of psychology, and the law. Moreover, when I speak of the law, I do not simply mean law enforcement but the legal process itself. Working with law enforcement is just one activity a forensic psychologist may undertake in a routine day.

Clinical psychologists are broadly concerned with the assessment and treatment of persons with mental disorders. They interact with people suffering from a variety of mental health problems ranging from the less severe (marital difficulties and adjustment problems) to the more severe (e.g., schizophrenia, posttraumatic stress disorder, major depression, or bipolar disorder). Clinical psychologists specializing in forensic psychology work with individuals who may present with a variety of mental illnesses and mental health issues within the context of the criminal or civil arenas of the law. Civil matters usually involve civil litigation in which a plaintiff usually brings forward a suit because they believe someone else has physically or emotionally injured them. Examples may include personal injury suits, civil commitment proceedings, child custody disputes, or workers' compensation cases. Criminal areas of forensic psychology include those situations in which an individual has committed a crime against society. Examples that necessitate the involvement of a forensic psychologist may include pleading insanity, raising issues of competency to stand trial, assessment of future violence potential during sentencing, or treatment of sex offenders.

Careers in Forensic Psychology

So what can a forensic psychologist do besides track down the bad guys and hang out with "crazy" people who eat their relatives? Forensic psychologists can be employed in a variety of settings including jails, prisons, state hospitals, federal and local law enforcement agencies, community mental health centers, juvenile detention facilities, private practice, or colleges and universities. Forensic psychologists are likely to perform a myriad of roles in these settings that are only limited by time and imagination.

For example, let's take a brief snapshot of the possible tasks a forensic psychologist may perform. Let's say a man—we'll call him Charlie—is accused of brutally murdering a family while they slept. Before he enters a plea, the court may be interested in whether Charlie possesses sufficient intellectual ability (i.e., is competent) to enter a plea (e.g., guilty or not guilty) at his initial arraignment. A forensic psychologist may be called to ascertain whether Charlie has sufficient cognitive ability to understand the nature of the charges against him and can assist in his defense. So, let's assume the court finds Charlie competent to enter a plea and stand trial for the crime. Charlie may suffer from paranoid schizophrenia, and his defense attorney may be interested in using an insanity defense. Again, you might be asked to assess whether at the time of the crime Charlie was suffering from a mental illness that made it impossible for him to understand the quality of his actions or the difference between right and wrong. Assume the outcome did not go well for Charlie and he was convicted of the murders. Before the court decides whether to sentence him to a particular period of time behind bars, you might once again be asked to evaluate him regarding his potential for future violence. The court, in deciding his ultimate sentence, may take into consideration whether it is probable and under what conditions Charlie is likely to commit future violence. Finally, it appears that Charlie has been sentenced to serve his time in the same institution where you work. It is now your job to design and implement a treatment program for Charlie in order to stabilize him while he is incarcerated and improve his chances if he is ever released. It is not likely that a forensic psychologist would be involved in every aspect of this example case, but it does give you some idea of the possibilities.

It's clear that with Charlie, forensic psychologists are asked to really get inside the mind of someone. You may have to assess an individual's current cognitive and mental abilities. You may have to play detective and attempt to assess their mental status at some point in the past. You may even be asked to predict someone's future behavior. How good of a job does your local meteorologist do at predicting whether it will rain tomorrow or not? Can you imagine how difficult it is to predict the behavior of a human being over the next 20 years of that individual's life? However, it's these challenges that offer the most excitement for students entering the field of forensic psychology.

One of the biggest enticements for students to become interested in forensic psychology is their interest in "criminal profiling." The reality is that most law enforcement agencies do not use criminal profiling procedures, and those agencies that do use similar procedures are more likely to employ law enforcement personnel than they are to employ a forensic psychologist. Criminal profiling is much more of a law enforcement technique and art form than it is a scientific process (Wrightman, 2001). Students interested in these types of careers should have a broad interest in law enforcement and not simply intend to work as a profiler, because these employment opportunities are extremely rare. Again, the sensationalistic portrayals fall a little short of the reality. Criminal profiling was conceived out of years of law enforcement experience with serial offenders and is not rooted in psychological principles. Thus, most people who conduct "profiling" are law enforcement personnel who may or may not have formal training in the behavioral sciences. More importantly, many graduate programs in forensic psychology do not favorably evaluate applications from students whose sole interest is in criminal profiling.

Training in Forensic Psychology

There are almost as many ways to be trained in forensic psychology as there are possible tasks for forensic psychologists to perform. However, the first thing that should be noted is that in order to be a forensic psychologist you have to be a good *clinical psychologist.* Also, by saying clinical psychologist I mean someone who practices psychology in some sort of mental health setting, not simply someone who has received a graduate degree in clinical psychology (see Norcross, 2000, for the distinction between clinical and counseling psychology). What I mean is that in order to become a good clinical or practicing psychologist you need a basic understanding of psychopathology, clinical assessment, and psychotherapy. You need to be able to tell the difference between a criminal and a noncriminal. The best training programs allow you to gain experience with both. Students who are only interested in learning about forensic clients and are not interested in more traditional clinical psychology areas could have some difficulty succeeding in quality clinical or counseling psychology programs. However, there are certainly programs available that will allow you to focus on forensic populations while limiting your experience with nonforensic clients.

You may have already guessed that in order to obtain a career in forensic psychology you will probably need a graduate degree, either a master's or a doctorate. You certainly might be able gain employment in an entry-level position at a forensic hospital or prison (e.g., psychological technician), but you will be very limited by your lack of education. As a result, a number of graduate programs are increasing their offering of forensic course work and practica (Bersoff et al., 1997). The number of programs specific to forensic psychology are also increasing at both the master's and doctoral levels (Melton et al., 1999).

There are several master's programs in forensic psychology at institutions such as Castleton State College, the University of Denver, John Jay College, Marymount University, and the Sage Colleges. Of course, these programs are likely to vary in quality and focus of their training. For example, some of these programs identify themselves as "forensic" psychology programs, but their focus is on the broader psycholegal field and not on the clinical practice of psychology. Students interested in forensic psychology should do a thorough job of investigating a program and asking difficult questions. How long does it take students to graduate from the program? Do graduates of the program obtain the types of jobs in which I am interested? What types of job placements or clinical practicum experiences are available? If you eventually want to obtain a PhD, is the program successful at placing students in quality PhD programs?

There also are a number of doctoral training programs at schools such as the University of Alabama, the University of Arizona, the University of Nebraska, Sam Houston State University, and Simon Fraser University, to name a few. A more comprehensive list of graduate programs in forensic psychology can be obtained by checking the American Psychology-Law Society website at *www.unl.edu/ap-ls/gradp.htm* and *www.unl.edu/ap-ls/CAREERS.htm* [WEBMASTER NOTE: This material can now be accessed at www.ap-ls.org/students/graduateIndex.html]. At the doctoral level, forensic programs can be very diverse. Programs may offer joint degrees in both clinical psychology (PhD or MA) and the law (JD or c) or simply offer specialized course work and clinical experience on the way to a PhD. It is certainly not necessary to receive a law degree in order to be a forensic psychologist. However, joint degree programs may offer some advantages to particular students. Melton et al. (1999) offer a more comprehensive discussion of the advantages and disadvantages of the different types of doctorate programs in forensic psychology.

Remember that in order to be a good forensic psychologist, you must first be a good clinical psychologist. In order to become a competent and successful forensic psychologist, you do not have to enter a forensic psychology program, though it is preferred. In fact, most forensic psychologists have not received their education in one of the select few forensic psychology programs. Obtaining admission to any APA-approved clinical or counseling doctoral program is an achievement! If you decide to pursue your training in a program that does not have a specific focus in forensics, you can obtain predoctoral training in forensically focused clinical placements. You can seek forensic training at forensic predoctoral internships such as with the Federal Bureau of Prisons or a number of mental hospitals around the country. There also are a number of postdoctoral fellowships that can be obtained after you have completed your PhD (see Bersoff et al., 1997, for a comprehensive list).

Conclusion

Simply put, forensic psychology is an awesome field! While you are probably not going to become like Special Agent Clarice Starling in *Silence of the Lambs,* there are a number of opportunities available for forensic psychologists. It's hard for me to believe that my original interest has ultimately paid off, and I get to continually learn and teach about the things that I find so interesting and challenging. Furthermore, forensic psychology has not even approached its potential. The next generation of students has a very bright future ahead of them.

References

American Board of Forensic Psychology, and American Psychology-Law Society. (1995). *Petition for the recognition of a specialty in professional psychology* [Online]. Available: http://www.unl.edu/ap-ls/petition.PDF [Webmaster's Note: Link no longer works]

Bersoff, D. N., Goodman-Delahunty, J., Grisso, J. T., Hans, V. P., Poythress, N. G., Jr., and Roesch, R. G. (1997). Training in law and psychology: Models from the Villanova Conference. *American Psychologist, 52,* 1301-1310.

Melton, G. B., Huss, M. T., and Tomkins, A. J. (1999). Training in forensic psychology and the law. In A. K. Hess and I. B. Weiner (Eds.), *Handbook of forensic psychology* (2nd ed., pp. 700-720). New York: Wiley.

Norcross, J. C. (2000, Fall). Clinical versus counseling psychology: What's the diff? *Eye on Psi Chi, 5,* 20-22.

Wrightsman, L. S. (2001). *Forensic psychology.* Belmont, CA: Wadsworth.

Industrial/Organizational Psychology as a Career

Improving Workforce Performance and Retention

By John J. Pass

So, you are thinking about pursing a career in the field of industrial/organizational (I/O) psychology. The following are two examples of what you might end up doing as an I/O psychologist:

1. A large company is experiencing high turnover in its sales department and needs to stop losing its top salespeople. The company decides to hire the consulting company that you work for as an I/O psychologist to determine the reasons for the turnover and make recommendations for improvements. You are asked to be a part of a consulting team with other members who specialize in information technology, finance, and business strategy to help solve this company's problem.
2. You work for a large company as an I/O psychologist, and the company needs to design a hiring and selection procedure for a new call center that is being opened in 6 months. The center will need to have 450 call takers hired before the opening. You are asked to join a team to help design a Web-based system that uses the best selection tools, such as cognitive-ability tests, personality inventories, and interviews, to select the most qualified people for the call taker jobs. And one other item: The call center is in India.

Sound interesting? If so, I/O psychology may be for you. If you have an orientation to business and a drive to implement programs that affect organizations and large groups of people, then industrial/ organizational psychology will be a rewarding professional area for you to pursue.

Industrial/Organizational Psychology: What Is It, Anyway?

I/O psychology is the application of psychological concepts and research findings to the workplace to improve workforce performance and retention. I/O psychology is an applied field of psychology, yet it is still based on the scientist-practitioner model; I/O psychology depends on sound research and theoretical frameworks to form the basis for the design of programs and systems that enable organizational improvements. An I/O psychologist can be either more of a practitioner, applying research findings to solve organizational problems, or more of a scientist or researcher. I/O psychologists who hold faculty positions are typically more focused on research, but the boundary between the roles is often blurred, so that I/O psychologists often pursue both.

In the research area of I/O, you might focus on developing and validating new assessment tools or evaluating the effectiveness of different types of leadership development programs. If you lean toward the practitioner side, you might work as an internal consultant, designing and developing programs while working as an employee of an organization, or you might be an external consultant, working for a consulting firm and designing and developing programs for other companies. External consultants can also be faculty members, or they can work solely for a consulting firm.

The primary objective of both the internal and external I/O consultant is to design programs that improve workforce performance and retention. The programs that I/O psychologists analyze, design, or improve are typically human resource programs and include hiring and selection, training and development, performance appraisal, and employee satisfaction and retention programs. You may be involved in executive coaching or even in market research, determining what parts of the market may offer opportunities for your company.

I/O psychologists frequently work as part of a team. Sometimes the team is rather static, as in a company department, or the team may be temporary, convened to solve some acute problem. Typically, the team analyzes a problem that needs to be worked on, makes recommendations to management, implements the recommendations, and follows up on the implementation. One of the last team problems that I worked on at IBM was to develop an online workforce skills inventory system that would identify the current skills of hundreds of thousands of employees. This type of system is used for several purposes, including enabling employees to move to jobs that are in high demand as reflected by the market or by organizational strategy changes.

Because most of the programs or systems that I/O psychologists design and implement affect employees' careers, legal and fairness issues are usually a major concern. As an I/O psychologist, you must pay attention to these concerns to avoid possible lawsuits. And while you do this type of work, your performance will be evaluated in terms of the value your implemented recommendations add to the company in saving money, producing revenue, or improving performance or productivity. You will likely have an opportunity to work on a global team. Many companies are multinational and so, more and more, the work that I/O psychologists do involves working with associates in other countries.

Preparation for the Career

You need a graduate degree to be successful in I/O psychology. A PhD will definitely lead to more opportunities and better compensation (see the Financial Compensation section later in this chap.). And if you want to be an I/O faculty member, you definitely will need a PhD. But this does not mean that if you have an MA degree in I/O psychology, you will not be able to find good I/O or human resources jobs. With a PhD, you will be more likely to conduct research and/or to design programs and improvements in large organizations, but many organizations, such as local government agencies, require only an MA degree for their I/O work. Although some states require I/O psychologists to be licensed, a license is typically required only if you are working in your own business and offering your individual services as an I/O psychologist. Nonetheless, it is a good idea to investigate any license requirements in the state in which you wish to work.

A few other points about your graduate education: Pirst, be sure to develop some level of expertise in the basic areas of I/O (selection, training and development, performance evaluation, compensation administration, consulting skills, and statistics). Second, be sure to gain some knowledge about global issues and applications, as this area is taking on greater and greater importance. Finally, a relevant internship will definitely improve your competitiveness in the job market; employers look for an internship that has provided you with actual work experience in a relevant I/O area.

Potential Work Opportunities

What does the future hold for I/O psychology in regard to opportunities for employment? Because most I/O jobs are focused on improving, in one way or another, human-re source-related functions such as selection or hiring, training and development, or workforce satisfaction and performance, these functions will obviously continue to be needed as long as there are organizations of people. But the number and types of opportunities depend on many factors such as the overall economy and the economic health of different sectors in the economy such as secondary education, the government, and the private sector.

The Bureau of Labor Statistics (see, http://www.bls.gov) estimates opportunity growth for all occupations in their Occupational Outlook Handbook. According to the Handbook, the growth of employment opportunities for psychologist positions, including I/O psychologists, will be faster than the average rate of growth when compared to all other occupations. The Bureau of Labor Statistics predicted average growth through 2012:

Industrial/organizational psychologists will be in demand to help to boost worker productivity and retention rates in a wide range of businesses. Industrial/organizational psychologists will help companies deal with issues such as workplace diversity and antidiscrimination policies. Companies also will use psychologists' expertise in survey design, analysis, and research to develop tools for marketing evaluation and statistical analysis. . . . Psychologists with extensive training in quantitative research methods and computer science may have a competitive edge over applicants without this background. {U.S. Department of Labor, 2006)

Financial Compensation

The Web site of the Society for Industrial and Organizational Psychology {SIOP; http://www.siop.org) shows the results of a salary survey of SIOP members that was conducted in 2003 (Medsker, Katkowski, and Purr, 2005). I/O psychologists with a doctorate make substantially more over the course of their careers than those with only a master's degree. Recent PhD graduates earn a median income of about $65,000, with a range of about $70,000 to about $140,000, and private sector jobs pay substantially more than university or public sector jobs. Master's degree graduates earn about one third less, on average, than their PhD counterparts. (See American Psychological Association [20051 for salary data as well as data on new doctorates from the Doctorate Employment Survey.)

My Career

My own career in I/O psychology reflects the opportunities and types of jobs that I/O psychologists have. I highlight some important tips that helped me and could well improve your opportunities and chances of success in the I/O field.

My career as an I/O psychologist has spanned some 30 years. I have worked in many different organizations, from a small consulting firm to some of the largest public and private organizations in the world. So how did I get started? First of all, after obtaining a BA in psychology, I went on to graduate school in I/O psychology for my PhD, and I was fortunate to have an excellent North Carolina State graduate advisor who had obtained a grant that provided me with invaluable experience in the area of job analysis. Job analysis refers to the systematic analysis of jobs and their constituent knowledge, skills, and abilities. The results of such analysis inform all the major human resources programs of organizations, namely hiring and selection, training and development, performance evaluation, and compensation administration. For example, if you need to hire software engineers, you need to know what types of skills and abilities the applicants for the job need and how to assess those skills and abilities.

The experience I had in graduate school and the area I specialized in led to my first job as an I/O psychologist working for the U.S. Navy Personnel Research and Development Center in San Diego. In this first job, I helped evaluate the effectiveness of the Navy's job analysis procedures that determined the responsibilities and requirements for more than 100 enlisted military jobs, from clerk to jet engine mechanic. I heard about this position because of the contacts of my graduate advisor, Bill Cunningham, an expert in the area of occupational analysis, whose own graduate advisor was Ernest McCormick, known as the father of job analysis. The Navy contacted McCormick, who contacted Cunningham, who recommended me. *Tip 1*: As with many careers, the key to success is to develop a specialty area and to have associations with key people in your field.

After about 6 years at the Navy Personnel Research and Development Center and having worked with several different Navy organizations in job analysis, an opportunity opened up for me to be the technical director of the Navy Occupational Development and Analysis Center. It was a lucky break for me because it was a terrific job in which I had a primary role in the technical and personnel leadership of an organization of 80 people that conducted job analyses for all the jobs in the Navy. This job analysis information was used to develop promotional exams and to identify required training for different Navy jobs. To get this job, I had to relocate across country and leave San Diego for Washington, DC. Although I did relocate to Washington, I kept a house in San Diego because I hoped to be able to move back there one day. *Tip 2*: Being willing to relocate will greatly improve your career opportunities.

During my 3 years as technical director in Washington, I honed my leadership and organizational skills and this experience proved to be critical for my future career. In this position, I was responsible for motivating and promoting some individuals as well as for demoting others—the tough side of a leadership position. I also had a multimillion-dollar budget to oversee and had to make sure that the money we spent to improve our procedures added significant value to the Navy. I often had to present our proposed recommendations for improvements to the management level above and convince them that our improvements would yield substantial benefits and that the job analysis information we collected would be very useful for developing promotional exams and training programs.

I was able to make many improvements for the Navy's job analysis procedures because I knew something about statistics. I was able to analyze and evaluate different procedures and make improvements that led to more effective and less expensive ways to do the organization's work. For example, we analyzed the statistical reliability (or consistency) of job analysis data collected using our survey procedures and as a result developed better survey methods that improved reliability. *Tip 3*: A sound knowledge of statistics is a relatively rare commodity in many organizations. It will enhance your ability to succeed and will always be a good selling point for opportunities that you might want to pursue,

Because I was interested in going back to San Diego, I contacted my associates back at the Navy Personnel Research and Development Center in San Diego. Again, through contacts and luck, I found myself the director of personnel systems at that organization. Through this job, I was introduced to the realm of government contractors and many well-known I/O psychologists who worked for the government in different capacities. While in this position, I started to focus more on procedures for hiring or selecting people into the Navy; this focus on selection was to become my new specialty area over the course of my remaining career.

After working for quite a few years with the Navy, which is, of course, a public sector organization, I wanted to try the private or corporate side of life as an I/O psychologist. I thought it would be more exciting and perhaps more profitable for me as well. I got my chance when, through a friend, I learned of an opportunity that led to an offer to work as an I/O psychologist in the area of selection for one of the major telephone companies in Denver, Colorado. This job provided me with the corporate experience I was looking for, and it led to one of the best jobs a corporate I/O psychologist could have: working as the head of a global selection team for IBM, one of the largest companies in the world. This was a very exciting job, and our team instituted global interviewing procedures, global on-line testing for analytical skills, and on-line assessment of personality attributes such as customer orientation skills. Our team's programs affected thousands of applicants who were hired by IBM. *Tip 4*: Getting the job you want is based on relevant experience, your reputation, your resume, and how well you interview. Work on improving these for increased success,

As my career demonstrates, there are many different and varied opportunities for I/O psychologists. Perhaps one or several of these appeal to you.

Resources

One of the best sources for additional information on the field of I/O psychology is the Society for Industrial and Organizational Psychology. The SIOP Web site (http://www.siop.org) and the Web site of American Psychological Association Division 14 (http://www.apa.org) provide information on graduate schools, license requirements, salary information for master's and PhD graduates, and job opportunities. The SIOP annual conference includes a job placement center where SIOP members can interview with many employers. If you want to pursue a career in I/O psychology, you should become a member of SIOP. According to the SIOP Web site, as of 2002, the society's membership totaled 6,117.

Let me make one other point about opportunity: As indicated, I/O psychology is closely aligned with human resource functions. As such, it provides those who go into this field with knowledge of the functions that all managers need to know. This knowledge also makes I/O psychologists competitive for general management positions, either inside or outside of the field.

Conclusion

I hope that you now have a better idea of what you might be able to do as an I/O psychologist. You can work in many types of organizations, including private, public, and global organizations, and the activities that you can choose to engage in are indeed varied and potentially rich in satisfaction.

References

American Psychological Association. (2005, May). *Salaries in psychology 2003*. Retrieved July 6, 2006, from http://research.apa.org/

Medsker, G. J., Katkowski, D. A., and Purr, D. (2005). *2003 income and employment survey results for the Society for Industrial and Organizational Psychology* (Unpublished report). Alexandria, VA: Human Resources Research Organization.

U.S. Department of Labor, Bureau of Statistics. (2006). Psychologists. Retrieved August 3, 2006, from http://www.bls.gov/oco/ocos056.htm#outlook

Sport Psychology

History, Professional Organizations, and Professional Preparation

By Karen M. Appleby

A sprinter crouches and senses the familiar feelings of butterflies in her stomach. She closes her eyes, takes a long, deep breath, and repeats to herself the words "fast, strong, smooth." She looks up, hears the gun, and BLASTS out of the blocks.

A high school cross country coach is conducting a preseason team meeting. At this meeting, he encourages each runner to think about what he wants to accomplish both during practice and during competition this season. His athletes leave the meeting with a feeling of purpose and excitement about working toward and accomplishing their goals.

A college soccer team is having a difficult season. The team has lost its last three games, and team members feel as if their conference championship title may be at risk. The athletes feel they are not communicating well on the field and lack motivation during practice. A sport psychology consultant intervenes to assess and create ways to enhance their communication skills and feelings of motivation.

All of these scenarios are examples of issues that athletes, coaches, and teams face. Stress and arousal, goal setting, and group cohesion are just a few of the topics the field of sport psychology has been designed to address. Sport psychology focuses on the psychological and emotional processes athletes and exercisers experience while pursuing both competitive sport and lifetime fitness activities. This article will introduce you to the field of sport psychology by focusing on the history of sport psychology in North America, professional organizations in the field of sport psychology, professional preparation opportunities for sport psychology professionals, and ways to learn more about sport psychology.

The History of Sport Psychology in North America

It is essential to know the historical background of an academic discipline in order to understand its current goals, purposes, and endeavors. Sport psychology in North America has a rich history that was born in the late 19th century. This section will introduce you to some of the pioneering educators and practitioners in the early days of sport psychology.

Pioneers in the field of sport psychology. The first documented pioneer in the field of sport psychology investigated the effect of social facilitation on athletes. Dr. Norman Triplett, a psychology professor at Indiana University in the late 1800s, conducted research on how the presence of others impacted the performance of cyclists. Triplett's study supported his hypothesis that cyclists often performed better when riding in pairs or groups than when riding alone

(Anshel, 2003; Weinberg and Gould, 2003). Triplett's research titled "Dynamogenic Factors in Pacemaking and Competition" was published in 1898 in the American Journal of Psychology and provided the field with the first documented research discussing how and why group dynamics impact athletic performance (for a more detailed account of Dr. Triplett's work, see Davis, Huss, and Becker, 1995).

While Triplett's work provided a foundation for sport psychology research, much of his work was conducted in the laboratory with no emphasis on the real-life application of his findings. In the 1920s, another burgeoning sport psychologist from the University of Illinois, Coleman Griffith, began developing the first sport psychology laboratory where the findings of research conducted in laboratory settings could be applied to the real-life performance of athletes (Weinberg and Gould, 2003). Griffith worked directly with both the Chicago Cubs and with Knute Rockne and the University of Notre Dame (IN) football team to enhance the performance of athletes who played on these teams (for a more detailed account of Dr. Griffith's work, see Gould and Pick, 1995).

The life work and research of other sport and psychology professionals led to the further advancement of sport psychology as an academic discipline in the mid 1960s. Professionals such as Franklin Henry (University of California, Berkley) set the stage for sport psychology to be taught and researched in academic settings (Weinberg and Gould, 2003). As sport psychology began to advance as an academic discipline, the applied aspects of sport psychology began to take root as well. Academicians such as Bruce Ogilvie (San Jose State University, CA) and Dorothy Harris (Pennsylvania State University) helped advance the praxis-oriented discipline that sport psychology is today.

Professional Organizations in Sport Psychology

The increase in the academic pursuits of sport psychology researchers and practitioners led to the need for professional organizations to support continuing education in this discipline. Currently, the following three major professional organizations help promote and advance knowledge in the field of sport psychology: (a) the Association of Applied Sport Psychology (AASP), (b) the North American Society for Psychology of Sport and Physical Activity (NASPSPA), and (c) Division 47—Exercise and Sport Psychology—of the American Psychological Association (APA).

AASP. AASP, formerly known as the Association for the Advancement of Applied Sport Psychology (AAASP), was started in 1986. AASP focuses on providing theoretical and applied information to sport psychologists, coaches, athletes, and students to increase athletic performance. AASP concentrates on three specific areas related to this goal: (a) health psychology, (b) performance enhancement/intervention, and (c) social psychology. Every year, AASP hosts a national conference that spotlights the major research that has been conducted that year and provides continuing education opportunities for academics, scientists, and students in the field. AASP also publishes a scholarly journal in the field of sport psychology: The Journal of Applied Sport Psychology. To find out more information about AASP visit www.aaasponline.org

NASPSPA. The purpose of NASPSPA is to help promote and improve the quality of both teaching and research in the field of sport psychology. NASPSPA is specifically devoted to the disciplines of sport psychology, motor behavior and development, and motor learning and control. NASPSPA hosts a national conference every year and also publishes two scholarly journals in the field of sport psychology: The Journal of Sport and Exercise Psychology and Motor Control. To find out more information about NASPSPA visit www.naspspa.org

APA Division 47. In 1987, the APA developed Division 47 which is devoted specifically to the study of exercise and sport psychology. The mission of Division 47 is to advance knowledge and disseminate information related to teaching, research, and service opportunities to students and professionals in the field of sport and exercise psychology. Furthermore, Division 47 publishes a triyearly newsletter devoted to the field of exercise and sport psychology. To find out more information about APA's Division 47 visit www.apa.org

Professional Preparation in the Field of Sport Psychology

Sport psychologists engage in many activities including, but not limited to, teaching students about the theoretical orientations and applied aspects of sport psychology, conducting research that examines the psychological parameters of participation in sport and exercise, and working directly with athletes to improve their athletic performance or enjoyment in sport (Weinberg and Gould, 2003). Professional preparation at the undergraduate and graduate level is a necessary prerequisite for any of these activities.

Undergraduate preparation. As an undergraduate student, a background in psychology or physical education is preferable. At this point in your academic career, it would be beneficial to study topics such as personality, social psychology, psychology of learning, and other core psychological subjects. If you choose to enter the field of physical education, classes such as motor development, psychological aspects of sport and exercise, adapted physical education, kinesiology, and biomechanics will introduce you to various curricular components of sport psychology. It would also be very valuable for you to engage in collaborative research with a faculty member during your undergraduate tenure. Helping with various aspects of a research project will facilitate your understanding of the research process and make you a strong candidate for graduate work.

Master's-level graduate preparation. The next step in becoming a sport psychologist is to investigate master's programs in the field of sport psychology. At the master's level, you will take courses in the psychology, sociology, and philosophy of sport that will strengthen your understanding of the various factors that impact the performance of athletes. AASP offers provisional certification for professionals at the master's level that will enable you to coach or work with athletes on performance enhancement at a basic level. Certification at this level requires 300 hours of supervised work with athletes or teams as well as educational preparation in various areas related to sport and exercise psychology. For more information on this certification process visit www.aaasponline.org

Doctoral-level graduate preparation. The final step in becoming a sport psychologist is to receive an advanced degree (PhD or EdD) in sport psychology or counseling. There are a number of educational institutions which provide a degree specifically in sport psychology. At the doctoral level, you will take courses and engage in research activities that will prepare you to develop an even stronger grasp of the complex environment of sport and exercise settings. You may also have the opportunity to work directly with athletes under the supervision of an academic mentor or advisor. At the completion of your doctoral work, you may be eligible to become an AASP Certified Consultant. This certification would allow you to work with athletes at a number of different performance levels. Certification at this level requires 400 hours of consulting work as well as educational preparation in various areas related to sport and exercise psychology. For more information on this certification process visit www.aaapsonline.org

Learning More About Sport Psychology

Today, the field of sport psychology has developed into a discipline that investigates numerous psychological aspects that impact sport and exercise participation. These aspects include, but are not limited to, confidence, body image, gender issues, anxiety and stress, goal setting, social facilitation, the impact of youth sport, the psychology of injury, burnout, and addictive behaviors in sport and exercise settings. An excellent way to find out more about the field of sport psychology is to take an introductory course in sport and exercise psychology at your college or university. This class will likely introduce you to the major areas of research and applied topics in the field and will also give you a better understanding of the techniques that sport psychologists may use with athletes.

Another excellent resource to read if you are interested in the practical application of sport psychology is Dr. Brent Rushall's article in Eye on Psi Chi titled "Some Psychological Factors for Promoting Exceptional Athletic Performance" (2000). In this article, Dr. Rushall described the complex setting of competitive sports and explains the performance enhancing power of strategies such as performance segmenting, concentration, and positive self-talk.

Sport psychology is an exciting field for anyone interested in the mental aspects of sport. Being a sport psychology professional allows you to teach, research, and apply the psychological concepts you may be learning right now to the complex and exhilarating field of sport. If you would like to help athletes sharpen their mental game, teach students how to apply psychological concepts in their coaching, or research aspects of performance enhancement, I highly recommend that you investigate the field of sport psychology.

References

Anshel, M. H. (2003). *Sport psychology: From theory to practice* (4th ed.). San Francisco, CA: Benjamin Cummings.

Davis, S. F., Huss, M. T., and Becker, A. H. (1995). Norman Triplett and the dawning of sport psychology. *The Sport Psychologist,* 9, 366–375.

Gould, D., and Pick, S. (1995). Sport psychology: The Griffith era, 1920–1940. *The Sport Psychologist,* 9, 391-405.

Rushall, B. S., (2000, Winter). Some psychological factors for promoting exceptional athletic performance. *Eye on Psi Chi,* 4 (2), 14–18, 55.

Weinberg, R. S., and Gould, D. (2003). *Foundations of sport and exercise psychology* (3rd ed.). Champaign, IL: Human Kinetics.

What Is a School Psychologist?

National Association of School Psychologists

School psychologists help children and youth succeed academically, socially, behaviorally, and emotionally. They collaborate with educators, parents, and other professionals to create safe, healthy, and supportive learning environments that strengthen connections between home, school, and the community for all students.

School psychologists are highly trained in both psychology and education, completing a minimum of a specialist-level degree program (at least 60 graduate semester hours) that includes a year-long supervised internship. This training emphasizes preparation in mental health and educational interventions, child development, learning, behavior, motivation, curriculum and instruction, assessment, consultation, collaboration, school law, and systems. School psychologists must be certified and/or licensed by the state in which they work. They also may be nationally certified by the National School Psychology Certification Board (NSPCB). The National Association of School Psychologists sets ethical and training standards for practice and service delivery.

What Do School Psychologists Do?

School Psychologists Work with Students to:

- Provide counseling, instruction, and mentoring for those struggling with social, emotional, and behavioral problems
- Increase achievement by assessing barriers to learning and determining the best instructional strategies to improve learning
- Promote wellness and resilience by reinforcing communication and social skills, problem solving, anger management, self-regulation, self-determination, and optimism
- Enhance understanding and acceptance of diverse cultures and backgrounds

School Psychologists Work with Students and Their Families to:

- Identify and address learning and behavior problems that interfere with school success
- Evaluate eligibility for special education services (within a multidisciplinary team)
- Support students' social, emotional, and behavioral health

- Teach parenting skills and enhance home–school collaboration
- Make referrals and help coordinate community support services

School Psychologists Work with Teachers to:

- Identify and resolve academic barriers to learning
- Design and implement student progress monitoring systems
- Design and implement academic and behavioral interventions
- Support effective individualized instruction
- Create positive classroom environments
- Motivate all students to engage in learning

School Psychologists Work with Administrators to:

- Collect and analyze data related to school improvement, student outcomes, and accountability requirements
- Implement school-wide prevention programs that help maintain positive school climates conducive to learning
- Promote school policies and practices that ensure the safety of all students by reducing school violence, bullying, and harassment
- Respond to crises by providing leadership, direct services, and coordination with needed community services
- Design, implement, and garner support for comprehensive school mental health programming

School Psychologists Work with Community Providers to:

- Coordinate the delivery of services to students and their families in and outside of school
- Help students transition to and from school and community learning environments, such as residential treatment or juvenile justice programs

Where School Psychologists Work

The majority of school psychologists work in schools. However, they can practice in a variety of settings including:

- Public and private schools
- Universities
- School-based health and mental health centers
- Community-based day-treatment or residential clinics and hospitals
- Juvenile justice centers
- Private practice

How Do School Psychologists Make a Difference In Schools?

All children and adolescents face problems from time to time. They may:

- Feel afraid to go to school
- Have difficulty organizing their time efficiently
- Lack effective study skills
- Fall behind in their school work
- Lack self-discipline
- Worry about family matters such as divorce and death
- Feel depressed or anxious
- Experiment with drugs and alcohol
- Think about suicide
- Worry about their sexuality
- Face difficult situations, such as applying to college, getting a job, or quitting school
- Question their aptitudes and abilities

School psychologists help children, parents, teachers, and members of the community understand and resolve these concerns. Following are examples of how school psychologists make a difference.

Helping Students with Learning Problems

Tommy's parents were concerned about his difficulty reading and writing. They feared that he would fall behind and lose confidence in himself. In school the teacher noticed that Tommy often struggled to understand what he was reading and often needed the help of his classmates to do related written work. After observing Tommy, consulting with his teacher, and gathering specific information about his skills, the school psychologist collaborated with his parents and teachers to develop a plan to improve his reading and writing. The plan worked, and Tommy's reading, writing, and confidence as a learner improved.

Helping Students Cope with Family and Life Stressors

The teacher noticed that Carla, an able student, had stopped participating in class discussions and had difficulty paying attention. The school psychologist was asked to explore why Carla's behavior had changed so much. After discovering that Carla's parents were divorcing, the school psychologist provided counseling for Carla and gave her parents suggestions for this difficult time. Carla's behavior and emotional wellbeing improved, and she felt more secure about her relationship with her parents.

Helping Students with Behavior Problems Learn New Ways to Respond

David was a high school student who often skipped class and got into fights with others. He acted out in class and had been suspended from school on various occasions. After establishing a relationship with David, the school psychologist taught him simple techniques to relax, recognize his needs, and to control his aggressive behavior. David's mother and his teacher worked together on a plan designed by the school psychologist to establish limits, recognize David's escalating tension, and improve communication. David's relationships with peers and adults improved and he began to make steady progress towards graduation.

Non-Academic Careers

American Psychological Association

A faculty position at a college or university is not the only career option for psychologists.

In response to the concerns of many psychology graduate students about the lack information on careers outside of the university setting, we began inviting psychologists with traditional training to tell us about their work in some relatively non-traditional places. The list below represents a relatively small sampling of an infinite number of careers that are possible—those who have "taken a different path" relate their own experiences of how they got to where they are now and the valuable lessons they learned along the way to employment "beyond the lab."

The following *Interesting Careers in Psychology* articles illustrate the various skill-sets and expertise that psychologists possess which are also highly valued by employers outside of academe. The non-traditional career paths represented by these personal success stories illustrate the different types of unique contributions made by psychologists in many different employment settings.

Animal Protection

- *Psychology in Animal Programs:* http://www.apa.org/careers/resources/profiles/ogden.aspx
- Jacqueline Ogden, PhD, is responsible for animal care, veterinary care, and education and science programs at Walt Disney World, and uses her academic training in human and non-human behavior constantly in meetings, conservation-related projects, and more.

Criminal Justice/Law Enforcement

- *Forensic Psychologist:* http://www.apa.org/careers/resources/profiles/pinizzotto.aspx
- As the senior scientist and forensic psychologist in the FBI's Behavioral Science Unit, Anthony J. Pinizzotto, PhD, is a liaison among academic, professional, and criminal justice agencies, participates in the scientific exploration and investigation within the FBI's Training Division, and more.

- *Police Psychology in the Federal Government*: http://www.apa.org/careers/resources/profiles/hibler.aspx
- Psychologists like Neil S. Hibler, FAClinP, make important contributions to the government in the areas of counterespionage, pre-employment selection screening, fitness for duty evaluations, crisis intervention, direct investigative/operational support, team building, training and other services.

- *Trial Consultant*: http://www.apa.org/careers/resources/profiles/stapp.aspx
- Joy Stapp, PhD, develops effective trial strategies based on empirical research for clients in many types of litigation, including antitrust, contracts, discrimination, employment, environmental, insurance, intellectual property, lender, premises and product liability, oil and gas, personal injury, securities, toxic tort, and medical, legal and professional malpractice.

Health Care

- *Clinical Neuropsychopharmacologist*: http://www.apa.org/careers/resources/profiles/katz.aspx
- Psychologist-monitors like Richard J. Katz, PhD, have been instrumental in establishing the safety and efficacy of many drugs for Alzheimer's disease, depression, anxiety, PTSD and more.

Human Resources

- *Expert Witness in Employment Discrimination Cases*: http://www.apa.org/careers/resources/profiles/weiner.aspx
- As an expert witness with the EEOC, Hilary R. Weiner, PhD, uses research to help investigators and attorneys determine whether or not employment discrimination has taken place.

Interior Design

- *Design Psychologist*: http://www.apa.org/careers/resources/profiles/painter.aspx
- Knowledge of psychology and human behavior gave Susan Lee Painter, PhD, a new way to create spaces for people by focusing on fulfilling the psychological needs of clients and users of space, rather than simply using aesthetic factors to serve as the basis for design.

Organizational Development

- *Organizational Development Consultant*: http://www.apa.org/careers/resources/profiles/smith.aspx
- As director of a consultancy firm, Philip M. Smith, PhD, oversees recruitment, assessment, management development, survey research, career counseling, and organizational change with household brand name clients on three continents.

Research

- *Experimental Psychologist in a Behavioral Science Research Firm*: http://www.apa.org/careers/resources/profiles/becker.aspx
- Organization, critical thinking, statistical analysis, good research design, and technical writing are all skills that Sunny Becker, PhD, honed in graduate school, and were the very ones she needed to succeed as a military and educational researcher.

Writing

- *Science Writer*: http://www.apa.org/careers/resources/profiles/carpenter.aspx
- Science writer Siri Carpenter's work is intellectually stimulating but broad in scope, concerns science, but not just one area of science, and allows her to do research and write, but not always about the same subject.

What Is Art Therapy?

American Art Therapy Association

Art therapy is a mental health profession that uses the creative process of art making to improve and enhance physical, mental and emotional well-being. The creative process involved in artistic self-expression helps people resolve conflicts and problems, develop interpersonal skills, reduce stress, and increase self-esteem and self-awareness. Art therapists are master's-level professionals who hold degrees in art therapy and/or a related field. The educational requirements art therapists must fulfill include coursework in theories of art therapy, counseling, and psychotherapy; individual, group, and family therapy; human and creative development; assessment and evaluation; multicultural issues; research methods; ethics and standards of practice; and practicum experience in clinical and community settings. Art therapists are also trained in applying a variety of art modalities as part of assessment and treatment, including drawing, painting, sculpture, and other visual media.

Who Can Be Helped by Art Therapy?

Art therapists work with people of all ages in many different environments to address challenging mental, physical, and social issues. They are trained to work as private practitioners and as part of treatment teams in psychiatric outpatient and inpatient programs, hospitals and community health centers, veterans' health facilities, rehabilitation programs, schools, hospices, and many other settings. Art therapy is used to treat a wide range of issues and conditions, including family and relationship issues, depression and other mental health conditions, substance abuse and addiction, abuse and domestic violence, social and emotional issues related to disability or cognitive loss, trauma, and psychosocial difficulties related to medical illnesses.

Credentialing and Licensure of Art Therapists

Art therapists who meet rigorous education and experience requirements are credentialed by the Art Therapy Credentials Board. The "Art Therapy Registration" credential (ATR) is granted to art therapists who have completed graduate education and post-graduate supervised experience requirements and the "Board Certification" credential (ATR-BC) is granted to Registered Art Therapists who pass a written examination. Credentialed art therapists are entitled to use the professional designation of ATR or ATR-BC after their name. The credentials are recognized by all states and D.C. and are maintained by meeting stringent continuing education requirements.

Five states currently license professional art therapists or creative arts therapists: Kentucky, Mississippi, New Mexico, Wisconsin, and New York. In addition, many art therapists are licensed in related mental health fields that have education and training requirements paralleling those of art therapy, such as counseling or marriage and family therapy. All states currently license professional counselors and in Pennsylvania, Massachusetts, and Texas, art therapists are specifically included in the counselor licensure laws.

What Is Sex Therapy?

American Board of Sexology

Sex Therapy is the application of professional and ethical skills to deal with the problems of sexual function of people. It assumes recognition of the concept that sexuality is of legitimate concern to professionals and that it is the right of individuals to expect expert knowledge when seeking remedies with sexual concerns. Sex Therapists and Clinical Sexologists focus their specialized skills to help individuals and/or couples to deal with their sexual concerns.

Why Is Sex Therapy Necessary?

Sex therapy is the result of relatively recent scientific attention to human sexual function and dysfunction. Out of the increased knowledge of the physiology and psychology of human sexual behavior has come a new professional appreciation for human sexual response. At a time in our society when sexuality is being more openly discussed, we are beginning to realize how uninformed many people really are about this important personal topic.

The importance of sexual function for individuals varies, of course, but for many it is closely tied in with their total concept of self identity. For these, problems in sexual function may lead to devaluation of self - "When I cannot feel good about my sexuality, how can I feel good about myself?" We are also in a time when marital and family units seem to be quite vulnerable. Concepts of these traditional relationships are being reevaluated, challenged and restructured. Alternatives to marriage are now being more openly tried and are becoming more widely accepted than at any other time in our history. Regardless of the structure of the intimate relationship shared, sexuality serves a valuable function for most couples. It becomes an expression of caring, not only for the partner, but for oneself. It can become a powerful bonding element in a relationship, which, in today's society, must withstand considerable demands on time, energy and commitment. Dissatisfaction with the sexual relationship and the loss of that shared intimacy, in many instances, may lead to negative feelings and attitudes which are destructive to the relationship. Many marriages end therefore, because of unresolved sexual differences and difficulties.

Who Goes for Sex Therapy?

The sex therapist works with a wide variety of problems related to sexuality. People seek help with such problems with arousal (impotence and frigidity), as well as problems with orgasm (either inability to climax or the inability to control ejaculation). In addition to seeking medical evaluation and treatment, many people who experience painful intercourse also seek the assistance of a sex therapist. Couples often seek help when it becomes apparent that differences exist in their sexual desires or when they sense that their sexual relationship is not growing as they would wish. The need for additional information, more effective verbal/physical communication, and for sexual enrichment lead many couples to the sex therapist's office in their quest to enhance their intimate relationship.

The qualified sex therapist is also available to those wishing to resolve troublesome sexual inhibitions or change undesirable sexual habits. People with questions about their sexual identity or sexual preferences seek out the trained sex therapist for consultation. Parents consult the therapist about the sexual curiosity and experimentation of their children and seek insight into ways to foster the healthy development of their youngsters through effective sexual education in the home. Sex therapists also assist those experiencing sexual difficulties as a result of physical disabilities or as the consequence of illness, surgery, aging or alcohol abuse.

How Does Sex Therapy Differ from Other Therapies?

Sex therapy employs many of the same basic principles as the other therapeutic modalities, but is unique in that it is an approach developed specifically for the treatment of sexual problems. That is, sex therapy is a specialized form of treatment used with one aspect of the wide range of human problems. Herein lies its value and also its limitation! Sex therapy techniques, when applied by an unskilled counselor or therapist, might focus too readily on mechanical sexual behavior, to the exclusion of the total individual and the total relationship.

Are There Limitations?

As with any therapy for personal or behavioral difficulties, sex therapy has its limitations. Although usually brief and effective with most sexual concerns, sex therapy does not offer a miracle cure for all interpersonal problems.

Success of treatment depends upon many factors, not the least of which are the nature of the problem, the motivation of the patient, the therapeutic goals and the therapist's skills. The motivated prospective patient and/or couple should choose a therapist carefully and establish realistic goals early in the counseling.

If you are not comfortable with your therapist or feel that the therapist has set unrealistic performance goals for you, discuss these concerns with him/her. All therapy depends upon trust and mutual respect, but this is particularly true when working with intimate issues of sexuality.

How Does One Know if a Sex Therapist Is Qualified?

One must realize that with any new field, a variety of definitions and expectations will exist for a time, and that a wide variety of people will claim expertise in accordance with their own definition of the field. The expectations presented here might be criticized by some as too rigid, but it is purposefully intended to present a fairly strict set of guidelines for selecting a sex therapist. Very few states license sex therapists, so the client must exercise caution and must choose wisely!

Five criteria need to be met in choosing a sex therapist. First of all, the therapist must have a sound knowledge of the anatomical and physiological bases of the sexual response. The sex therapist may, therefore, have a basic medical background or may come out of another non-medical profession but with post-graduate education in the biological aspects of human sexuality. A qualified non-medical sex therapist will usually work closely with physicians or may function as a non-physician in a medical clinic or university school of medicine.

Secondly, the qualified sex therapist must be skilled in providing counseling and psychotherapy, and most sex therapists will be found to have a sound background in psychology, psychiatry, psychiatric social work or psychiatric nursing. This background in the behavior sciences is essential to the understanding of the total individual and to the planning of an individualized treatment program. There are, however, some notable exceptions to the rule that sex therapist should have a traditional mental health training background, in that there are also highly respected and well trained sex therapists who began as clergy. These clergy, however, need to demonstrate specific post-graduate training in pastoral counseling or in equivalent psychiatric mental health areas.

The third criterion is that the sex therapist, having both biological and psychological sophistication, must be able to demonstrate extensive post-graduate training specifically within the areas of sexual function and dysfunction, sex counseling, and sex therapy. A weekend workshop or possession of a few sex therapy films does not meet this criterion, and the prospective client should feel free to ask for a list of specific training experiences in these specialized areas.

The fourth requirement to be met is that of having expertise in relationship counseling. That is, the sex therapist should also be a skilled marital, family and/or group therapist. In order to work effectively with sexual problems, the sex therapist must be able to work effectively with non-sexual relationships as well. Sexual behavior does not occur in a vacuum - it occurs within a relationship! The total relationship must, therefore, be accurately evaluated and treated.

The fifth requirement is the therapist's adherence to a strict code of ethics! Prospective clients have the right to request a copy of the therapist's ethical code before agreeing to any treatment.

How Does One Find a Qualified Sex Therapist?

Most qualified sex therapists do not depend on ads in the newspaper, as most professionals have made themselves and their credentials known to other professionals in the community. If you need a sex therapist, you might begin by consulting your family physician, gynecologist or urologist. Ask for a referral to someone your doctor has used confidently in the past. In addition to this, you might be inclined to ask a trusted clergyman for a referral. As you begin to collect information about available resources, you might then wish to turn to the telephone directory Yellow Pages, looking under such headings as "Psychologist," "Social Workers," "Marriage and Family Counselors," and elsewhere. Remember, there is probably no legislative control of the title "Sex Therapist" in your state, so simply finding the title in the phone book does not document that individual's clinical skills! In all states, however, licensing laws control who can list as a "Psychologist" or as a "Physician." A small number of states now also restrict the listings of "Social Workers" and/or "Marriage Counselors."

When calling a professional, be sure to ask questions about qualifications, experience and fees! It is recommended that you call and ask, "Do you have a specialty?" rather than stating, "I have a sex problem—can you help?"

Perhaps the most useful referrals will come from other knowledgeable professionals within your community. However, it is also helpful to be able to discover which therapists belong to recognized national professional associations having high membership requirements and enforcing rigid codes of ethics.

What Can I Expect in Sex Therapy?

Even qualified sex therapists may differ widely in their basic approaches to the treatment of sexual problems, but some generalizations can be made.

First of all, you can expect to be talking explicitly and in detail about sex. One cannot solve sexual problems by talking around them! Neither can one gain new sexual information unless clear, direct instruction is given!

Second, you might expect to be offered the opportunity to add to your knowledge by reading selected books and/or viewing clinical films designed specifically for use in sex therapy. You should not, however, do anything which you do not understand, and you must reserve for yourself the right to question the purpose of an assignment. It is your right to decline or postpone acting on the suggestions of your therapist, rather than allowing yourself to be pushed into behavior which might actually increase your discomfort. Every assignment, task, or experience presented by the therapist should fit into an understandable and acceptable treatment plan - and you have the right to question the procedures.

Third, you should expect sex therapists to be non-judgmental and to portray their own comfort in giving and receiving sexual information. While you might expect to be challenged and confronted on important issues, you should also expect to experience a respectful attitude toward those values which you do not which to change.

Fourth, unless your therapist is a licensed physician wishing to conduct a physical examination, you should not expect to be asked to disrobe in the presence of your therapist. Sexual contact between client and therapist is considered unethical and is destructive to the therapeutic relationship. Neither should you expect to be required to perform sexually with your partner in the presence of your therapist. Overt sexual activities just should not occur in your therapist's presence, even though the talk, material and the assignments must, by the nature of the problem, be specifically sexual and at times bluntly explicit.

Finally, you should feel that you are heard and adequately represented in your sexual therapy. That is, you should that you have been stereotyped as "female," as "gay," as "too old," or in any other way that interferes with your sense of unique identity within the therapeutic setting. You should feel that you are being treated as an individual, not as a category!

Sex therapy is a new, dynamic approach to very real human problems. It is based on the assumptions that sex is good, that relationships should be meaningful, and that interpersonal intimacy is a desirable goal. Sex therapy is by its nature a very sensitive treatment modality and by necessity must include respect for the client's values. It must be nonjudgmental and nonsexist, with recognition of the equal rights of man and woman to full expression and enjoyment of healthy sexual relationships.

Non-Traditional Psychology Career Profiles

By M. Dittmann

Matt Bellace, PhD

Comedian/Motivational Speaker

Bellace has mixed comedy and psychology as a motivational speaker and stand-up comedian. He has created a profitable career off his "How to get high naturally" program, which aims to empower high school and college students to choose drug- and alcohol-free lifestyles.

Career path: In June, Bellace earned his doctoral degree in clinical neuropsychology from Drexel University in Philadelphia. But he started landing gigs for motivational speaking 10 years ago and has been spreading his drug- and alcohol-free message across the country ever since.

As an undergraduate biology and psychology major at Bucknell University, Bellace began a drug and alcohol prevention college group called C.A.L.V.I.N and H.O.B.B.E.S (Creating A Lively Valuable Ingenious New Habit Of Being at Bucknell and Enjoying Sobriety), which provides college students with social and educational activities that promote fun without drugs or alcohol. Local colleges and high schools took notice of the program and asked Bellace to speak to their students. The group will celebrate its 13-year anniversary in October.

Bellace also does stand-up at comedy clubs—humor that he also ties in to his motivational speaking. For example, Bellace likes to begin his talks by cracking jokes about his life as a non-drinker in high school and college.

Work schedule: Bellace does 60 to 75 speeches and workshops a year at high schools and colleges throughout the country, sometimes squeezing in three a day. He incorporates psychology into his motivational speeches, such as by drawing from social psychology to explain how to buck peer pressure, and he uses neuropsychology to describe the effects of alcohol and drugs on brain functioning and decision-making.

Best part of his job: Bellace enjoys interacting with the students, who often share their stories of peer pressure and struggles with drugs and alcohol. "Some students don't feel connected to others or feel like they are outsiders" if they don't take drugs or drink alcohol, Bellace explains. "This [program] gives them a chance to be heard and shows them they are not alone."

Salary: National-level motivational speakers average $1,500 per lecture and big-name lecturers can pull in $3,500 to $4,000 per lecture, according to Bellace. Stand-up comedians' salaries depend on experience, he says. For example, beginners often perform for free or make about $50 per show, whereas headliners can make about $1,500 for an entire weekend of shows. Feature acts—like Bellace—bring in about $100 a show.

How you can get his job: The best way to break in to motivational speaking, Bellace says, is to have expertise in a specific area and passion about it.

"Be willing to talk about it for free because in the beginning you probably will have to," Bellace says. He also recommends joining the National Speakers Association or attending its conference or meetings (www.nsaspeaker.org).

"The skills we learn in psychology can be applied to a lot of different areas," Bellace says. "Don't be afraid to branch out. ... It can really be empowering to take something uniquely inside of you and develop it outside of psychology."

Bellace's Web site is at www.mattbellace.com.

Patricia Cowings, PhD

NASA Psychophysiologist

Cowings was the first American woman to be trained as a scientist astronaut. She was an alternate in 1979. Although she never made it to space, she has spent her 34-year career at NASA making it better for those who do. Cowings helps astronauts better adapt to space by studying the effects of gravity on human physiology and performance.

Career path: Cowings earned her psychology doctorate from the University of California, Davis, in 1973. She has worked at NASA since 1971 when she was a graduate student and received a fellowship in NASA's Graduate Research Science Program. She has served as principal investigator for a number of studies, mostly involving the autogenic-feedback training exercise (AFTE), a treatment for space motion sickness she developed and patented. AFTE teaches people to control up to 20 physiological responses—such as heart rate, skin conductance, muscle reactivity and blood pressure—to overcome motion sickness and improve performance during high-stress tasks.

Work schedule: Cowings and her team prepare astronauts to handle the physiological impact of space by teaching them AFTE. In downtimes, they run a remote training software program via the Internet to help civilian hospital patients with various conditions, such as gastrointestinal disorders. Currently, they are using AFTE at the Morehouse University School of Medicine in Atlanta, where doctors are using it to control patients' blood pressure. Research has shown that AFTE also helps with nausea and hypertension.

When Cowings teaches AFTE to astronauts, the training includes 12 sessions—each 30 minutes—to help them learn to control physiological responses. At first, they receive feedback, and then gradually they learn to control the responses on their own. For example, training might include self-suggestions to increase warmth in their hands.

Best part of her job: "Touching astronauts," she says—but not in the way it sounds. The astronauts make great test subjects "since on any metric measure of human performance, they tend to be a couple of standard deviations above the mean," she says. Astronauts are intelligent, usually holding multiple advanced degrees, and they are physically fit. "I get to see what they are like and help them" better adapt to space, she adds.

Salary: NASA scientists at her level can make around $125,000 a year. Graduate students working full time at NASA generally make $1,950 a month, and undergraduates earn $1,650 per month.

How you can get her job: "If you want to work in this area—ask," Cowings says. "You'd be surprised." For example, when she was in graduate school, she wrote a letter to psychologist Neal Miller—a pioneer of biofeedback research who discovered that people could be trained to alter bodily processes—and explained to him that he was her hero and she would love to work for him, even for free. She worked with him for one year on his biofeedback research, and they eventually worked together as co-investigators on AFTE research.

"If you're financially able, work for free to get yourself in the door," she says. Many students volunteer at NASA to gain the experience, not to mention a good letter of recommendation, she says.

Nadine O'Reilly

Special Education Coordinator

At the Paterson Charter School for Science and Technology, O'Reilly develops innovative student-oriented programs and has the chance to work with children and the community more often than the typical school psychologist. Charter schools are publicly funded schools that are generally controlled in-house by the school and not by a local school district—operating more like a private school than a traditional public school.

Career path: Last year, O'Reilly began her role as a special education coordinator at Paterson Charter School for Science and Technology, a charter middle school for low-income and urban students in Paterson, N.J. O'Reilly has a master's in educational psychology and her certification in school psychology from Montclair State University in Montclair, NJ. She is a third-year school psychology doctoral student at the Graduate School of Applied and Professional Psychology at Rutgers University.

O'Reilly also drew from her school psychology training to write "Peter Can't Eat Peanuts," a self-published children's book due out this fall about the dangers of food allergies. She wrote it in response to her own son's peanut allergies.

Work schedule: O'Reilly conducts psychological evaluations, counsels students, develops programs to meet the needs of general education and special education students, consults regularly with teachers, designs pre-referral interventions and talks with parents about how to advocate for special services for their child. O'Reilly also conducts in-service training for teachers by translating psychological research into lay terms, such as explaining research on inclusion models and attention-deficit hyperactivity disorder. As a coordinator, O'Reilly also interacts with students and administrators at the state level, which is not typical of the traditional school psychologist's position.

Best part of her job: "Ninety percent of my time is spent getting to know the students," O'Reilly says. She found that in more traditional school psychology jobs she spent more time on paperwork than with students.

Also, she enjoys being able to develop innovative programs for students. For example, she used her original dissertation idea as a pilot program on vocabulary acquisition. In the program, students learn a new word each week, apply it to a sentence and make up a rap song with that sentence. By the end of the year, they turn the words they've learned into a complete rap song and compete against other classes.

Salary: $53,000 for working four days a week during the school year. Charter schools operate on their own pay scales, independent of the larger school districts, so pay can range according to the discretion of the school.

How you can get her job: O'Reilly strongly recommends jobs in charter schools because the environments are smaller and, therefore, "there is less red tape to work through. At these start-up schools, teachers often are more amenable to working with psychologists," O'Reilly says. "You have a place to really showcase your knowledge."

To find a charter school, she recommends visiting your state's Department of Education Web site for your local charter school database as well as the National Charter School Clearinghouse Web site at www.nationalcharterschoolclearinghouse.net. She also recommends taking an education law course in graduate school because in charter schools, your responsibility as a psychologist will likely be broader than the traditional consult, test, place and counsel model.

Anthony J. Pinizzotto, PhD

Catholic Priest and Forensic Psychologist

During the day, Anthony Pinizzotto, PhD, is a forensic psychologist in the FBI's Behavioral Science Unit. In the evening, he returns to a Catholic parish and his duties as a Roman Catholic priest.

Career path: Pinizzotto became a priest in 1978 and currently serves at St. William of York Catholic Church in Stafford, Va. Before becoming a priest, he aspired to become a counselor or chaplain in a prison. To that end, he worked as an intern counselor and investigator in the correctional system in Pennsylvania. While pursuing a master's degree in the administration of justice, he joined the Metropolitan Police Department in Washington, D.C., as a uniformed reserve.

"From that point on, I realized just how interesting and exciting a career in law enforcement could be," Pinizzotto says. "I never lost my interest in counseling, and I thought I would bring together psychology and law." He holds a master's degree in forensic psychology from the John Jay College of Criminal Justice in New York City and a PhD in forensic psychology from Georgetown University. In 1988, he began working at the FBI while continuing to serve as a priest.

Work schedule: Pinizzotto carries on limited ministerial duties at the parish during the week and works full time as a senior scientist and clinical forensic psychologist at the FBI. He teaches a class in behavioral sciences at the FBI's Training Academy in Quantico, Va.

He also conducts research, such as investigating why people kill and assault police officers. In the FBI study, "Killed in the Line of Duty," he and a team of researchers interviewed 50 people who had killed law enforcement officers, investigated physical evidence from crime scenes and spoke to investigators involved to determine if certain officers were more at risk than others of being killed on duty. In particular, police officers most at risk for being killed in the line of duty were those who tended to help others, be hardworking and respected by officers and the community, Pinizzotto notes. He says these officers may be more likely to let down their guard when arresting individuals or when stopping vehicles.

Best part of his job: Pinizzotto says it's being able to integrate being a priest with his forensic psychology career. "I'm looking at the human person from various perspectives—the psychological, emotional, environmental and spiritual—in an attempt to understand why we do the things that we do," he says.

Pinizzotto says understanding the biological components of behavior is key to his jobs. Many of the FBI cases he works on involve individuals abusing alcohol or drugs. "It's better if we understand the biological components of behavior and assist law enforcement by explaining why [criminals] act the way they do," Pinizzotto says.

The same goes for his job as a community priest. His psychology background allows him to better understand the choices people make in life, he says; it also provides a spiritual outlet to cope with the effects of evil he sees in his day job.

Salary range: \$57,000 to \$85,000 for psychologists in the FBI; \$85,000 to \$125,000 for chief scientists.

How you can get his jobs: Pinizzotto encourages students to gain a variety of experiences working with supervisors of differing theoretical orientations to learn how to view problems in various ways. By gaining multiple perspectives, he says, students then can view problems more objectively—free of biases from just one orientation—when coming up with solutions. Also, he encourages students to gain exposure to law enforcement—such as by working part-time as a law enforcement officer—to be able to better relate to law enforcement officers' experiences.

"Forensic psychology gives me the opportunity to look at issues clinically as well as experimentally in order to test the hypotheses that psychologists have developed over the years," Pinizzotto says. "I see psychology as a helping profession, which is consistent with the ministry. Plus, I always liked the mystery story."

Jacqueline Ogden, PhD

Director of Animal Programs at Walt Disney World Resort

At Walt Disney World in Orlando, Fla., Ogden combines a background in animal behavior and industrial and organizational psychology to oversee the resort's animal health and welfare, visitor education and science and conservation programs. She manages teams that work with animals at Disney's Animal Kingdom, Disney's Animal Kingdom Lodge, Epcot's The Living Seas, the Tri-Circle D Ranch at Fort Wilderness and Typhoon Lagoon.

Career path: Ogden studied industrial and organizational psychology as an undergraduate, which led to a career as an office manager for four years at a sports promotion firm and then a market research firm. But she also had a passion for conservation and animals.

"Part of the reason I went to graduate school is that I wanted to combine my interests of working with people as well as doing something to support animals and conservation," she says. In 1992, she received a doctorate in general and experimental psychology from the Georgia Institute of Technology with a specialization in animal behavior and a minor in management. As a research associate with Terry Maple, PhD, a psychology professor at Georgia Tech and then-director of Zoo Atlanta, she helped design research projects, prepare grant applications and conduct data collections and analyses.

Before coming to Disney in 1997, Ogden worked as the children's zoo curator at the San Diego Zoo, where she supervised employees and designed new exhibits and interpretive materials.

Work schedule: Ogden mostly serves in administrative roles by overseeing the staff of Walt Disney animal-related programs. Her typical day includes budget analysis and other administrative tasks as well as working on initiatives to further Disney's conservation efforts. For example, she oversees programs to get Disney staff excited about animals and the environment, such as by holding an awards event each year to honor staff members who've taken a role in conservation efforts, like starting a recycling program. She aims to help individuals and the organization become more friendly to the environment.

Her team also works with the state of Florida and the U.S. Fish and Wildlife Service on such programs as turtle rehabilitation to release turtles that had been injured in the wild back into the environment following treatment. Likewise, she works with the American Zoo and Aquarium Association on such projects as "The Multi-Institutional Research Project"—which aims to assess the overall impact of zoos and aquariums on visitors' conservation-related knowledge, attitudes and behavior.

Best part of her job: "Probably the best part of my job is helping my team to do their job so we can accomplish the mission," Ogden says. "Our mission is to help inspire all of our guests to care more about wildlife."

Salary: Experts say new PhDs at zoos and aquariums earn about the same as their early-career peers in academe. According to the U.S. Bureau of Labor Statistics, wildlife biologists and zoologists working in scientific research and development services make, on average, $54,520 per year.

How you can get her job: Psychologists can become involved in a wide variety of animal and conservation-related careers at zoos and aquariums, such as animal-keeping, veterinary medicine, animal behavior research, visitor research, conservation biology and working as an educator. Ogden suggests students make contacts with professionals in the fields of conservation and zoology by joining professional organizations, such as APA, the American Zoo and Aquarium Association, the American Society of Primatologists or the Animal Behavior Society. Students might also opt to volunteer at a zoo or aquarium. "This is a great way to get your foot in the door and also to assess whether this is really a career you are interested in," Ogden says.

Victor Balaban, PhD

Epidemic Intelligence Service Officer

Epidemic Intelligence Service (EIS) officers—unofficially dubbed the "disease detectives" or the James Bonds of the medical profession—scour the country looking for clues on epidemics that could harm the nation's health or safety. In a two-year EIS postdoctoral fellowship with the Centers for Disease Control and Prevention (CDC) Division of Violence Prevention, Balaban analyzed data related to youth violence, suicide, child maltreatment, sexual violence and intimate partner violence.

Career path: After graduating with a psychology doctoral degree from Emory University, Balaban wanted to make a transition from clinical psychology to public health. He started by working with the CDC on a contract basis for about 18 months on refugee health issues with the International Emergency and Refugee Health Branch. He was at that branch during the 9/11 terrorist attacks and became involved with a mental health assessment of 8,000 public school children in New York City. After that experience, he gained epidemiology training with EIS. While his two-year fellowship with EIS ended in June, he plans to continue in public health with the CDC.

Work schedule: Balaban spent most of his time as an EIS officer conducting investigations, attending meetings, analyzing data and writing papers on such topics as elevated suicide rates in certain regions of the country.

For example, in an on-site investigation, he combined quantitative and qualitative research methods to evaluate elevated rates of youth suicide in Maine, comparing them with national suicide rates. He and his team also held focus groups with community members to gather information on the public's perceptions of the elevated suicide rates.

Balaban also investigated injuries caused from annual celebratory gunfire in Puerto Rico, in which 19 people were accidentally injured and one died when residents fired their guns in the air during 2004-2005 New Year celebrations. By analyzing law enforcement and hospital records on firearm injuries, he found a problem did exist and that, in particular, women, children and elderly people were at risk. The team provided education and prevention materials and plans to conduct further investigations on celebratory firearm injuries in the United States and other countries to identify the extent of the problem.

Best part of his job: Balaban enjoys the EIS investigations because of their real-world applications. "The work we're doing really can have an impact and help people," Balaban says. Plus, he enjoys working with disciplines outside of psychology, such as teaming with anthropologists, sociologists and physicians.

Salary: EIS salaries range from $27,000 to $58,000, depending upon qualifications and experience.

How you can get his job: "Take the initiative and show interest," Balaban says. E-mail or call public health professionals to ask how they landed their jobs and what opportunities—such as internships or research projects— are available, he advises.

He also encourages students to pursue an internship or part-time work on a public health-related project, such as through their state or county health department. For more on EIS, visit www.cdc.gov/eis.

Natalie Hamrick, PhD

Psychologist, Indiana University Department of Anesthesia

In her role as coordinator of the clinical research program, Hamrick uses her psychology background to help physicians in Indiana University's Department of

Anesthesia craft anesthesia research projects and, ultimately, get them published in peer-reviewed journals.

Career path: She graduated in 2003 with her doctoral degree in health psychology from Carnegie Mellon University. After a postdoc in behavioral oncology at the Fox Chase Cancer Center in Philadelphia, Hamrick sent her curriculum vitae to Indiana University's School of Nursing hoping to land a job in cancer research there. But instead, the anesthesia department called to ask her to head up a clinical research program.

Work schedule: Hamrick mentors the department's faculty and residents, who often have no formal training in research, to create sound studies. For example, she works with them on writing grants and developing study designs. She also offers her statistical expertise to help them analyze research data.

Besides that role, as an assistant professor she teaches an Introduction to Clinical Medicine class to first-year medical students on how to work with patients of various ages, religious beliefs and races, have good bedside manners and listen to patients' concerns.

Best part of her job: Hamrick enjoys helping physicians design medical studies— especially since, she says, they often have great ideas for research topics but just don't know how to go about studying them.

Many of these studies relate to psychology too. For example, one study she recently worked on looks at parental attachment and the advantages and disadvantages of having parents in a child's room before the patient is given anesthetic for surgery.

Furthermore, the job allows Hamrick to devote time to her own research on stress's effects on physical health—an area of study that first drew her to study psychology. For example, she is studying the effectiveness of faith-based stress management interventions for women with metastatic ovarian cancer and the validity of a quality-of-life scale for women with cancer. Hamrick's research centers on the social, behavioral and physiological factors that lead to increases in psychological stress and decreases in physical health.

Salary: $65,000

How you can get her job: Have a strong research background and get your curriculum vitae out to many places, such as university departments outside of psychology, which may lead to jobs that you didn't even consider before.

"Don't think it always has to be a tenure-track psychology position," Hamrick adds. "You can still find success and happiness in other places."

A Job List of One's Own

Creating Customized Career Information for Psychology Majors

By D.W. Rajecki

Introduction

Surveys indicate that a large number of psychology majors plan to attend graduate school (Gallucci, 1997; Rajecki, Appleby, Williams, Johnson, and Jeschke, 2005). However, other research shows that most psychology alumni enter the general job market with a BA or BS soon after graduation (Borden and Rajecki, 2000). Accordingly, whatever the future brings, undergraduates and their advisors should have access to quality information about a wide range of occupations. Of course, a good many career self-help articles, books, and Web sites already exist. Several offerings in this vein concentrate on features of relatively high-level occupations, such as university professor or practicing clinician, held by individuals with advanced degrees. But I am also attentive to various authors' statements regarding entry-level jobs said to be "of interest" to the baccalaureate holder. Regrettably, the quality of advice in this latter domain is not uniformly high, with some traditional sources simply providing long lists of job titles presumably appropriate for psychology BA/BS alumni (Rajecki, 2007). For example, plausible-sounding entries in such lists might include "child care worker," "computer operator," "psychiatric aide," "statistical assistant," and "teacher assistant." That is, these titles sound as if they could demand the skills and knowledge gained through the formal study of psychology.

Plausibility notwithstanding, for a pop quiz, how many of the five jobs in the just-mentioned list actually require anything more than on-the-job training? To phrase this question another way, how many of the five require a bachelor's degree? The answer to both questions is "None of the above." Occupations in this little collection are quite open to people with a high school education. To be sure, some university graduates hold such jobs, but clear majorities of their coworkers never attended college or did not complete a bachelor's degree (Rajecki, 2007). In short, psychology baccalaureates are technically overqualified for work in the five jobs considered in this section.

A Public Source of Job Information: O*NET

A job list would gain in information value if students and advisors had a reliable way to check on real-world employment characteristics. The good news is that anyone can quickly become a successful job sleuth by taking advantage of free services via the Internet. For instance, my claims in connection with the five

D. W. Rajecki, "A Job List of One's Own: Creating Customized Career Information for Psychology Majors," *Office of Teaching Resources in Psychology* (OTRP) online, pp. 1–7.

jobs just mentioned are based on public sources of information made available by the U.S. Department of Labor (DOL). A wonderful collection of useful data can be obtained from an online DOL service called the "Occupational Information Network," or O*NET for short. Indeed, DOL writers declare that the O*NET package is America's primary source of occupational information.

Getting the Information You Want

By any standard, O*NET is a huge program, designed to serve the needs of many types of readers including job seekers and employment professionals. This is not the place to discuss every complex facet of O*NET. For the present purpose it is sufficient to say that with just a little effort users can begin to reap bountiful harvests of enlightening facts. As a short training exercise, start with two job titles: clinical psychologists, and personal and home care aides. In minutes, a student or advisor can assemble impressively detailed profiles for these occupations based on O*NET features called "Descriptors" (or "Other Information"). To show how, I provide instructions for generating selected O*NET output, and next explain what that output means. When you are connected to the Internet, complete these 10 steps:

1. log on to http://www.onetcenter.org
2. click the Visit O*NET OnLine Today! link
3. click the Find Occupations link
4. type a job title in the Quick Search keyword box (e.g., clinical psychologists)
5. click GO
6. click the Clinical Psychologists link (the first line in the list)
7. click the Custom box
8. click the Skills, Tasks, and Job Zone boxes in the O*NET Descriptor list
9. click the Education and Wages and Employment boxes in the Other Information list
10. click GO

Understanding the Information You Get

Assuming everything worked properly, completion of the preceding steps will have resulted in considerable information about the work of clinical psychologists. Here are summaries of what the current O*NET output categories mean. (Information in this section was located at the http://online.onetcenter.org/help/ link in O*NET. Data from searches conducted on different dates may vary due to DOL updates.)

Skills output: This is a set of competencies (e.g., active listening, reading comprehension, social perceptiveness) rank-ordered in terms of the judged importance of each for the job in question. DOL analysts employed rating scales to obtain respondents' estimates. Technically, the numbers and bars to the left of particular skill lines represent conventionally standardized scale scores, having a possible numerical range of 0 to 100. Verbally, the range is not important (0) to extremely important (100).

Tasks output: As in the preceding matter of skills, the importance of various tasks (e.g., diagnose disorders, discuss the treatment of problems) involved in the occupation are rank-ordered in terms of rating scale standardized scores ranging from 0 to 100.

Job Zone output: This output has to do with ways most people get into the work or how much overall experience or education they need to do the job. DOL defines Job Zone 1 as "occupations that need little or no preparation." For Job Zones 2-5, replace "little or no" with the words "some," "medium," "considerable," and "extensive," respectively.

Further, under the rubric of Job Zone, a line appears for SVP Range. SVP stands for Specific Vocational Preparation, and amounts to a 9-item scale of mutually exclusive and non-overlapping levels of required time in vocational training. According to DOL terminology:

1 = short demonstration only

2 = anything beyond demonstration up to and including 1 month

3 = over 1 month up to and including 3 months

4 = over 3 months up to and including 6 months

5 = over 6 months up to and including 1 year

6 = over 1 year up to and including 2 years

7 = over 2 years up to and including 4 years

8 = over 4 years up to and including 10 years

9 = over 10 years

Education output: In various reports, DOL identifies three levels (categories) of formal educational attainment: (1) high school or less, (2) some college, and (3) bachelor's degree or higher. For the job in question, the numbers and bars in this panel express the known percentages of workers from each attainment category.

Wages and Employment Trends output: At the national level, two lines are of immediate interest: median annual wages and projected change in numbers of workers in the decade from 2004 to 2014.

Sample O*NET Output Profile #1: Clinical Psychologists

Based on the site information in mid-2007, for clinical psychologists the three most important skills are active listening (100, the maximum standard score), reading comprehension (91), and social perceptiveness (90). Three important tasks are to identify psychological, emotional, or behavioral issues, and diagnose disorders (92), develop and implement individual treatment plans (91), and interact with clients to assist them in gaining insight (88). Clinical psychologists stem from the highest job zone (5), and their impressive SVP range (8 or above) reflects the need for postgraduate training and licensure. Naturally, almost all (99%) have a bachelor's degree or higher. These professional credentials warranted median annual wages in 2005 of about $57,000, and for the foreseeable future there will be demands for additional practitioners.

Sample O*NET Output Profile #2: Personal and Home Care Aides

Repeat the 10 O*NET search steps described previously for a profile of personal and home care aides. Because care aides help the elderly and disabled, one might expect some similarities between them and clinical psychologists. Even so, some sharp differences seem certain to emerge. Similarities exist in that three important skills for care aides are active listening (82), social perceptiveness (82), and service orientation (76). Further, three important tasks are to perform health care, such as monitoring vital signs and medication (86), administer bedside and personal care, such as ambulation and hygiene assistance (86), and prepare and maintain records of client progress and services performed (80). However, in contrast to their professional counterparts, care aides stem from a much lower job zone (2), and their SVP range is rather modest (4 to < 6). In terms of formal education, fully 60% of care aides reach only the level of high school or less, and as few as 10% have a bachelor's degree or higher. These features correlated with relatively low median annual wages in 2005 of about $17,000. On the bright side, there will be a strong demand for more care aides in the future, possibly because of the aging boomer generation.

A Job List of One's Own

The current training exercise involved two job profiles: clinical psychologists, and personal and home care aides. As a matter of fact, O*NET provides access to equivalent information concerning over 800 different occupational titles. Also, the current exercise involved five O*NET Descriptors or Information features: Education, Job Zone, Skills, Tasks, and Wages and

Employment Trends. Actually, O*NET offers additional types of informative Descriptors, including Interests, Knowledge, Related Occupations, Work Activities, Work Context, and Work Styles. Users can choose any or all options in the program's menu.

An implication of this enormous resource is that students and advisors can use O*NET to investigate job names they encounter anywhere. Look to articles, books, or Web sites for ideas, or even make up your own titles. You may not find an exact match, but something relevant could turn up. In other words, anyone can produce a richly detailed job list of her or his own.

Suggested Job Titles in Three Categories

For a starter list of a range of occupations, I suggest 18 titles likely found in previously published lists of psychology-related jobs. These examples are loosely categorized in terms of expected academic degrees and employee status.

Postgraduate degree holders (PhD, PsyD, masters) work in universities, institutions, and practice as, for example, counseling psychologists, Industrial/Organizational psychologists, marriage and family therapists, psychology teachers (postsecondary), school psychologists, and substance abuse and behavioral disorder counselors.

Some baccalaureates work in managerial and technical positions as, for example, human resources managers, market research analysts, public relations managers, sales managers, social/community service managers, and survey researchers.

Other baccalaureates, along with associates and high school graduates, work, for example, as child care workers, computer operators, loan interviewers or clerks, psychiatric aides, statistical assistants, and teacher assistants.

Further Reading

As described here, O*NET is a great place to start learning about the job market. But useful U.S. government services do not end with O*NET. Other DOL occupational publications are available online that cover roughly the same jobs found in O*NET, but with a somewhat different perspective, emphasis, or level of detail. Consider the following two resources.

Occupational Outlook Handbook (OOH). According to its Web homepage, the OOH "is a nationally recognized source of career information, designed to provide valuable assistance to individuals making decisions about their future work lives." It can be found at http://www.bls.gov/oco/home.htm

Occupational and Training Data (OPTD). According to its Web homepage, the OPTD is the statistical and research supplement to the OOH. It presents information of value to planners, counselors, and job seekers, and can be found at http://www.bls.gov/emp/optd/home.htm

References

Borden, V. M. H., and Rajecki, D. W. (2000). First year employment outcomes of psychology baccalaureates: Relatedness, preparedness, and prospects. *Teaching of Psychology*, 27, 164-168.

Gallucci, N. T. (1997). An evaluation of the characteristics of undergraduate psychology majors. *Psychological Reports*, 81, 879-889.

Rajecki, D. W. (2007). Job lists for entry-level psychology baccalaureates: Occupational recommendations that mismatch qualifications. Manuscript submitted for publication.

Rajecki, D. W., Appleby, D., Williams, C. C., Johnson, K., and Jeschke, M. P. (2005). Statistics can wait: Career plans activity and course preferences of American psychology undergraduates. *Psychology Learning and Teaching*, 4, 83-89.

Informational Interviewing Tutorial

QuintCareers.com

Identify an Occupation(s) for Informational Interviews

Identify one or more occupations you would like to investigate. Assess your own interests, abilities, values, and skills, and evaluate labor conditions and trends to identify the best fields to research. Read all you can about the field before the interview.

Decide what information you would like to obtain about the occupation/industry.

Prepare a list of questions that you would like to have answered. Find out as much information as you can about each place before setting up an interview.

Identify People to Interview for Informational Interviews

Start with lists of people you already know: friends, fellow students, present or former co-workers, supervisors, neighbors, etc. Professional organizations, the yellow pages from the phone book, organizational directories, and public speakers are also good resources. You may also call an organization and ask for the name of the person by job title. There's no one in the world who you can't try contacting. People like to help students out with job information. One student whose dream job was to run a Fortune 500 company called the president of Levi Strauss and Co., asked for an informational interview, and got it.

To find a working professional, go to your college career center or alumni office [at Stetson, you will have more success at Career Services, even though the alumni database is not up-to-date.] and ask for a list of people who are working in the field that interests you. Locate alumni, people you've read about, or people your parents know.

You should be prepared. Research the organization, person you'll be speaking with, product produced by the organization, etc. If your contact is an alumnus/alumna, look him/her up in the Alumni Office's biographical material (Be aware, however, that Stetson's alumni office gives out limited, if any information). Try easily accessible periodicals, such as local and large metropolitan newspapers.

The more you know, the better you'll be able to formulate questions pertaining to the organization and job. The more knowledge you have, the more confident you will feel about your ability to communicate effectively. Write to organizations for brochures and pamphlets for additional information. Ask yourself what it is you want to know and then figure out who has an investment in knowing that sort of information. Use the university library.

Never Ask for a Job

Don't mix informational interviewing with job seeking. Employers will grant informational interviews when they firmly trust that you will not hit them up for a job. The minute you begin trying to get a job, the employer will feel misled. If you discover a job that you do want to apply for during the interview, wait until the informational interview is over. The next day, call the employer and tell your contact that the informational interview not only confirmed your interest in the field, but also made you aware of a position that you would like to formally apply for.

Sometimes the interviewee may offer you an internship or job. It's happened on numerous occasions. Many people have conducted informational interviews and have done nothing but ask questions and yet have been offered employment. What do you do if they offer you an internship or job? If it sounds good, take it! Suddenly your life changes in an instant!

The typical job searcher is going around asking for a job instead of asking questions to find out more about the job and the employer. A job searcher needs to know the basics about the employer and what the company is about. The fact that you are seeking only information will help set you apart from the hundreds of others who are walking in asking for jobs and being told no. Approach the employer with the attitude that you are seeking career advice. It is, therefore, usually a good idea to set up an informational interview with a resource person before there is an actual job opening in your area of interest. Most managers and supervisors feel uneasy or uncomfortable talking with a potential candidate when the organization is actively recruiting to fill the position. However, you may find it helpful for future reference to find out the name of the manager or the person who does the hiring. (Be sure the information you get is accurate!)

Prepare Ahead of Time for Your Interview

Ask only those questions that are appropriate and important to you. You will convey your motivation and interest to the employer by acknowledging that the information the interviewee is giving you is important.

A list of suggested questions can be found a little later in this tutorial.

Scheduling the Informational Interview

Contact the resource person preferably by telephone or letter. You can also try to have someone who knows the interviewer make the appointment for you.

Guidelines for contacting the resource person by:

- Letter
- Phone or in Person

Scheduling the Informational Interview by Letter

An introductory letter, written much like a cover letter without the job pitch, is a great way to get your name out there. Although an introductory letter should be typed, neat printing is acceptable. Your letter should include:

- A brief introduction about yourself;
- Why you are writing to this individual;
- A brief statement of your interests or experiences in the person's field, organization or location;
- Why you would like to converse. Be straightforward; tell him/her you are asking for information and advice.
- The last paragraph of the letter should always include a sentence about how and when you will contact this person again.

Make sure to follow up the letter as you said! Usually this follow-up involves a phone call to set up a phone appointment or an informational interview. Never expect the person to phone you. If you have difficulties contacting the person, ask the receptionist for a convenient time to phone again.

Finally, *proofread all correspondence and save copies!*

Requesting an Informational Interview in Person or by Phone

People who grant informational interviews are generally willing to share 20–30 minutes of their time to-explain their expertise in their field. Please remember to be flexiblein your scheduling, as these volunteer interviewees may have prior commitments.If your prospective interviewee seems too busy to talk to you, ask a convenienttime when you could call back to discuss scheduling an appointment. Althoughthere are many techniques to requesting the informational interview, the following are good approaches:

1. "Hello, my name is _______. I'm conducting career research in your field. I would like to meet and talk with you for about 30 minutes so that I can find out more about your field of expertise."

2. "Hi, my name is _______ and I'm a student at _______ University. I got your name from __________. You're in a line of work that I'm interested in, and I was hoping that you could help me gain insights into the profession. I'm sure that my questions could be answered in a 20–30-minute informational interview."

3. If you prefer to arrange an appointment in person and cannot get past the front desk, treat receptionists as resources. They hold the key to getting inside the unit or section ofthat organization if you do not already have an inside contact or referral. Ask them some of your questions. You will usually get good information. Receptionists and other support staff know much more about their company than we often realize. They know how it works, the names of key people, job requirements, etc. It is important that they understand what you want. If you ask them something that they feel could be more fully answered by someone else, they will usually give you a referral.

4. You can use your own creativity, but the most important thing is to emphasize that you are simply trying to get first-hand information, and whatever they share with you will be appreciated.

Most of the time, your prospective interviewee will be more than willing to take 20–30 minutes to answer your questions. Sometimes the person will want to talk over the phone, but often he or she will invite you to his or her workplace. When you can, choose that the interview be at their workplace because you'll learn more and make a stronger connection with the person.

You may want to schedule some of your interviews with managers and supervisors who have the authority to hire. Identify yourself and explain that you are researching careers in the contact's field, and that you obtained the person's name from ________ (if you were referred).

Scheduling the Informational Interview by Letter

An introductory letter, written much like a cover letter without the job pitch, is a great way to get your name out there. Although an introductory letter should be typed, neat printing is acceptable. Your letter should include:

- A brief introduction about yourself;
- Why you are writing to this individual;
- A brief statement of your interests or experiences in the person's field, organization or location;

- Why you would like to converse. Be straightforward; tell him/her you are asking for information and advice.
- The last paragraph of the letter should always include a sentence about how and when you will contact this person again.

Make sure to follow up the letter as you said! Usually this follow-up involves a phone call to set up a phone appointment or an informational interview. Never expect the person to phone you. If you have difficulties contacting the person, ask the receptionist for a convenient time to phone again.

Finally, *proofread all correspondence and save copies!*

Preparing for an Informational Interview

The day before the interview, call to confirm your appointment with the contact person. If you have questions regarding the location of the contact's office, this is the time to ask. Plan to arrive 10 minutes early for your interview.

Carry a small notebook and pen. Be polite and professional. Refer to your list of prepared questions; stay on track, but allow for spontaneous discussion.

Dressing Appropriately for an Informational Interview

Because 90 percent of all jobs are never advertised, you will uncover job openings that never make it to the newspaper or employment office. Thus, be prepared to make a good impression and to be remembered by the employer.

Dress as you would for a regular job interview.

Be Prepared to Take Notes at an Informational Interview

Pretend you are a reporter. You don't need to write down everything, but there may be names, phone numbers or other information that you may want to remember.

Be enthusiastic and show interest. Employ an informal dialogue during the interview. Be direct and concise with your questions and answers and do not ramble. Have good eye contact and posture. Be positive in your remarks, and reflect a good sense of humor.

Questions to Ask at the Informational Interview

You have arrived and are greeted by the individual at the front desk. When the interviewee comes out to meet you, introduce yourself. Thank your contact for his or her willingness to meet with you, and re-emphasize that you are there to learn and gather information about his or her career field. Use an informal dialogue duringthe interview.

Below are some typical informational interview questions. Remember that you won't have time to ask anywhere nearly all of these questions, so target the ones you feel will be most useful to you personally. Pick a dozen or so that get at what you most want to know.

Feel free to skip some—even most—of these questions or to substitute questions of your own—as long as you don't come off sounding like you're there for a job interview.

You may want to get permission from your interviewees to tape-record the conversations, but be aware that transcribing taped conversations can be very time-consuming.

- What is your job like?
- A typical day?
- What do you do? What are the duties/functions/responsibilities of your job?
- What kinds of problems do you deal with?
- What kinds of decisions do you make?
- What percentage of your time is spent doing what?
- How does the time use vary? Are there busy and slow times or is the work activity fairly constant?
- How did this type of work interest you and how did you get started?
- How did you get your job? What jobs and experiences have led you to your present position?
- Can you suggest some ways a student could obtain this necessary experience?
- What are the most important personal satisfactions and dissatisfactions connected with your occupation? What part of this job do you personally find most satisfying? Most challenging? What do you like and not like about working in this industry?
- What things did you do before you entered this occupation?
- Which have been most helpful? What other jobs can you get with the same background?
- What are the various jobs in this field or organization?
- Why did you decide to work for this company?
- What do you like most about this company?
- Do you find your job exciting or boring? Why?
- How does your company differ from its competitors?
- Why do customers choose this company?
- Are you optimistic about the company's future and your future with the company?
- What does the company do to contribute to its employees' professional development?
- How does the company make use of technology for internal communication and outside marketing? (Use of e-mail, Internet, intranets, World Wide Web page, video conferencing, etc.)
- What sorts of changes are occurring in your occupation?
- How does a person progress in your field? What is a typical career path in this field or organization?
- What is the best way to enter this occupation? What are the advancement opportunities? What are the major qualifications for success in this occupation?
- What were the keys to your career advancement? How did you get where you are and what are your long-range goals?
- What are the skills that are most important for a position in this field?
- What particular skills or talents are most essential to be effective in your job? How did you learn these skills? Did you enter this position through a formal training program? How can I evaluate whether or not I have the necessary skills for a position such as yours?
- How would you describe the working atmosphere and the people with whom you work?
- Is there a basic philosophy of the company or organization and, if so, what is it? (Is it a people, service or product oriented business?)
- What can you tell me about the corporate culture?
- What is the average length of time for an employee to stay in the job you hold? Are there incentives or disincentives for staying in the same job?
- Is there flexibility related to dress, work hours, vacation schedule, place of residence, etc.?
- What work-related values are strongest in this type of work (security, high income, variety, independence)?
- If your job progresses as you like, what would be the next step in your career?
- If your work were suddenly eliminated, what kinds of work do you feel prepared to do?

- With the information you have about my education, skills, and experience, what other fields or jobs would you suggest I research further before I make a final decision?
- How is the economy affecting this industry?
- What can you tell me about the employment outlook in your occupational field? How much demand is there for people in this occupation? How rapidly is the field growing? Can you estimate future job openings?
- What obligations does your employer place have on you outside of the ordinary work week? What social obligations go along with a job in your occupation?
- Are there organizations you are expected to join? Are there other things you are expected to do outside work hours?
- How has your job affected your lifestyle?
- What are the salary ranges for various levels in this field? Is there a salary ceiling?
- What are the major rewards aside from extrinsic rewards such as money, fringe benefits, travel, etc.?
- From your perspective, what are the problems you see working in this field?
- What are the major frustrations of this job?
- What interests you least about the job or creates the most stress?
- If you could do things all over again, would you choose the same path for yourself? Why? What would you change?
- What are the educational, requirements for this job? What other types of credentials or licenses are required? What types of training do companies offer persons entering this field? Is graduate school recommended? An MBA? Does the company encourage and pay for employees to pursue graduate degrees?
- Does your work relate to any experiences or studies you had in college?
- How well did your college experience prepare you for this job?
- What courses have proved to be the most valuable to you in your work? What would you recommend for me?
- How important are grades/GPA for obtaining a job in this field?
- How do you think my university's reputation is viewed when it comes to hiring?
- How do you think graduation from a private (or public) university is viewed when it comes to hiring?
- How did you prepare for this work? If you were entering this career today, would you change your preparation in any way to facilitate entry?
- What abilities or personal qualities do you believe contribute most to success in this field/job?
- What are the typical entry-level job titles and functions? What entry level jobs are best for learning as much as possible?
- Who is the department head or supervisor for this job? Where do you and your supervisor fit into the organizational structure?
- Who else do you know who is doing similar kinds of work or uses similar skills? What other kinds of organizations hire people to perform the functions you do here? Do you know of other people whom I might talk to who have similar jobs?
- Do you have any advice for someone interested in this field/job? Are there any written materials you suggest I read? Which professional journals and organizations would help me learn more about this field?
- What kinds of experience, paid or unpaid, would you encourage for anybody pursuing a career in this field?
- What special advice do you have for a student seeking to qualify for this position?

- Do you have any special words of warning or encouragement as a result of your experience?
- These are my strongest assets (skills, areas of knowledge, personality traits and values): ___________. Where would they fit in this field? Where would they be helpful in this organization? Where might they fit in other fields? Where might they be helpful in other organizations?
- How would you assess the experience I've had so far in terms of entering this field?
- [If you feel comfortable and it seems appropriate:] Would you mind taking a look at my resume?

The whole interview could be spent finding answers to the dozen or so questions you decide to ask. But as you practice and move further toward your target, questions will probably pop into your head spontaneously based on what you need to know.

Pay careful attention to what's said by the person you interview. Ask questions when something isn't clear. People are often happy to discuss their positions and willing to provide you with a wealth of information.

Try to keep the conversation friendly, brief, and focused on the contact person's job and career field.

If Only I Knew Then What I Know Now

Perspectives of a Woman of Color

By Melba J.T. Vasquez and Carla J. Reyes

Learning from a psychologist who is willing to share personal experiences with others can be extremely beneficial. They have lived and learned and are willing to pass on the knowledge so that you can learn from their struggles and make it different for yourself. Dr. Vasquez shared her thoughts and wisdom, which come from her culmination of life experiences from the past 25-30 years with the audience at RMPA. She discussed the challenges to success, happiness, and well-being as an undergraduate student, emphasizing that this can be one of the most stressful periods of one's life. Diverse students face additional stresses, "The slights and oppressive behaviors toward us serve as powerful barriers—externally, and which we have to struggle against internalizing—to be able to develop and keep our ability to be confident and maintain high levels of self-esteem." Dr. Vasquez spoke from the heart as she shared the following.

I grew up as the first born of two first-borns, and was essentially treated like a princess by parents, grandparents, 16 aunts, and uncles! It wasn't perfect, because we were poor, but I did not know that until I was 6 or 7. However, when I entered elementary school, I experienced discrimination and bad treatment for the first time in my life. I grew up in a socially segregated period of time and did not really have a white friend until after I graduated from college. For example, I had a white boyfriend in the second grade; it may have only lasted a few days, I don't remember for certain, but one day this boyfriend came up to me and told me that his mother (the school nurse) said that he could not be my boyfriend anymore because I was "Mexican." I remember going home and asking my mother what was wrong with being Mexican. She got very angry, and I learned to not share those kind of painful experiences with her much more.

I did learn how to interact in the white world. Being a good student was my ticket for approval. I was an officer in high school, and was in national honor society, student council, homecoming royalty, a cheerleader (one of the first Latinas in my small central Texas town of San Marcos). But I did not trust my white peers or most of my teachers, based on good reason. I was often left out of events. I would find out that my fellow high school cheerleaders had slumber parties, but did not include me.

One day, for example, my high school teacher pulled me out of class and told me how sorry and ridiculous she thought it was that the guys in the homecoming royalty, including her son, did not want to have to be my escort (I was the only person of color among the five men and five women selected). She told her son that if no one else was willing to do so, he should. She meant well, and did not realize that I had had no notion of what was going on. One cannot go through those mixed experiences, painful, sad, lonely, without being affected!

These oppressive experiences can be very demoralizing, rejecting, painful, and lead to silencing of ourselves and questioning of our voices. Of course, we can't stay in our sadness; we have to then allow our anger and frustration to be experienced so that it can help transform us into constructive action.

One of the myths, of course, is that status, credentials, and salaries will pave the way to a life free of problems. How many have discovered that that is a myth? Don't get me wrong. Status, credentials, and money are indeed forms of power and make us more visible. However, the glass ceiling is alive and especially working for most of us; we are each reminded on a regular basis that those credentials and status don't protect us from hurts and offenses.

In case you think that my experiences are "old" and that doesn't happen anymore, I see evidence of it daily in my psychotherapy office. Last week, I had a young Latina in her 20s, very successfully employed in the corporate world, with graduate degrees, who wept in recollection of her immigrant parents being called "dirty Mexicans" when her father accidentally bumped into someone at a store. She is still working through the feelings of inferiority, despite her clear achievements.

So when we experience the pain of failure and oppression, it is often shameful—we can erroneously feel that we have erred in ways that extend and affect our families and communities, which is an incredible burden. Each of us has countless stories of a range of failure and oppressive experiences. They include almost imperceptible slights and subtle dismissal by bosses, waiters, clients, classmates, colleagues, or strangers we might meet or interact with across a conference table, at a restaurant, at a party. They assume that we have nothing to say, or do not want to speak. We might be mistaken for one of the wives or girlfriends or even workers or servants; we are seen as a marginalized member or guest who may not even be able to speak English. At best, we spice up the crowd with exotic ethnicity.

Examples: a professor who refuses to understand simple questions once he detects a slight accent. A teller who makes us wait while she takes a short break, assuming that a woman of color won't complain as others might. A boss or coworker's over-willingness to criticize our work when that criticism would not be given as freely to other workers. Employees who refuse to take directives that they would not question if we were White men. The African American or Latina or Asian American member of the 20-person corporate team whose new board member assumes she is a secretary and nonchalantly asks her to make a copy of something. These are all painful dilemmas about which, we have a choice to act or let go of. In either case, we can't let those define us ... yet, they take a toll.

Challenges to Success: External

Studies show that discrimination is more likely to occur when competition for jobs or promotions occur with those who hold similar qualifications (highly qualified blacks with highly qualified Whites; highly qualified women with highly qualified men) (Jones, 1996).

- Studies also show that that racism among Whites is subtle, often unintentional and unconscious, but that its effects are systematically damaging to race relations by fostering miscommunication and distrust (Dovidio Gaertner, Kawakami, and Hodson, 2002), and we are affected and discouraged by that discrimination when we experience it in our APA volunteer activities.
- Lack of mentoring and other support can make for a very lonely ordeal. I have learned to take brief mentoring moments when I can

with people. I don't have the expectation that someone will be in long-term contact with me; I may not even know them well, but I expect that they may be available for input or advice at times. (I seek those mentoring experiences from psychologists of color, White women, White men, peers, etc.)

- Also, the backlash that exists in society to the few gains that women and minorities have made is pervasive, including in our profession of psychology. I have some anxieties about the impact of those conservative members in APA whose philosophies do not allow them to support or perhaps even understand the basis for promotion of diversity. Some letters to the editor in the APA *Monitor* are often chilling in the anger expressed about APA's activities in support of diversity. So the more I see people of color involved in all levels of the pipeline-from undergraduates to serving as leaders in academia and in the professional organizations-the more at ease I feel. My hope is that our continued involvement will inoculate the profession from most of the backlash phenomenon occurring in society.
- Another challenge involves the perception that women and ethnic minorities' contributions aren't as valued. Evidence exists that devaluation of women's work occurs on a regular basis (Lott, 1985); documented evidence demonstrates the undermining of an ethnic minorities' performance by an employer when they unconsciously communicate a negative expectation about the person based solely on that person's race or gender (Jones, 1996).

Challenges to Success: Internal

- The way women and ethnic minorities are socialized often leaves us with a lack of confidence and with a fear of risk taking in new uncharted territories.
- Internalized oppression may even cause us to question the viability of our or others' ability to perform well in a variety of activities related to success. Doubts about our own abilities may be the result of those internal barriers. But various strategies can help counteract that socialization that most of us have experienced.

So, one of our tasks is to understand the negative experiences and messages that we have received from society. We also have to be aware of the messages and axioms that are transmitted through our histories and our cultural and familial expectations, and to determine which and when to accept and live those because they are positive and constructive messages in our lives, and when to transform them, because living by those can be destructive at times. It is up to us as individuals, as groups, and in our organizations, to take steps to become more empowered and visible. Let me share some strategies for success, confidence, and well-being.

Strategies for Success, Confidence, and Well-Being

Nobody can make you feel inferior without your permission.

— Eleanor Roosevelt

- **Take risks.** Allow curiosity and energy to give direction to areas in which you wish to explore your power and salience. Eng, in her book, *Warrior Lessons,* states that "... sometimes we've got to force ourselves into battle-for beliefs, for our boundaries, and to defend big pictures. Becoming a wise fighter, after all, is less about shouting and more about strategy" (p. 197). She also suggests that learning to fight the good fight means understanding that our successes do not imply the failure of others. We must believe that there is plenty to go around. Risk takers often find that true fearlessness is not the elimination of fear, but the transcendence of fear, the movement through it and not against it. Fearlessness means the willingness to "lean into the anxiety and fear."

I work with a lot of graduate students and young professionals who avoid and procrastinate for all the various reasons one does so: perfectionism, fear of failing to do a difficult job well, fear of the hard work and drudgery involved, etc. My basic mantra is to go directly to the task, lean into the anxiety, move into it. Before you know it, it is done, and the worst part was the avoidance. It is only through risk taking that you can lay foundation after foundation of confidence. It is also how you learn where you "fit" in regard to your strengths and weaknesses.

- **Allow for imperfections and mistakes.** Mistakes are part of life. Acknowledge them to yourself (to others, if necessary), learn from them, fix them as much as possible, move on. Do not let them define you. They are a part of every human's experience.

  Men tend to attribute success to themselves, failures to others. Women tend to attribute success to luck and the support of others, and failure to (guess who?) themselves. We have to let go of shame and learn the philosophy of "bummer, oh well!" We must transcend the fear of failure, cast it aside, and listen to our kinder selves. There isn't a person alive, nor in leadership, who hasn't made mistakes. Do not crawl away with the conclusion that you are incapable after one mistake (unless it is in an area that you know you dislike); that would be allowing one negative experience to define you or the whole experience.
- **Understand that emotional pain is a part of life.** Related to the notion that mistakes are a part of life is the notion that emotional pain is also a part of life. Many people avoid taking risks or other activities because they fear emotional pain. The pain of failure, loneliness, embarrassment, criticism, loss, etc., are certainly annoying at best, uncomfortable, and at times devastating. However, all pain passes, and we can learn to cope in healthy ways by getting support and by utilizing other healthy options.
- **Focus in areas about which you have passion.** If you are working in areas that are near and dear to you, your energy and motivation to contribute will be high. Furthermore, the energy that comes from engaging with others in exciting and meaningful tasks is very rewarding. We tend to "fit best" and our natural talents tend to come to the forefront when we work in areas that we love or about which we have interest or energy.
- **Persistence** is a very important quality. Persisting to try for an elected position or to get your agenda on the table will pay off. Persistence is one of the major qualities that employers, admissions committees, and others assess in selection processes.
- **Networking** is a skill that comes easily for some and is more challenging for others, but connections with people can help. A recent study indicated that more successful employees are those who were liked by their supervisors and colleagues—they reached out to everyone they came in contact with and had a diverse network of people across the board, in a variety of departments, from top to bottom of the hierarchy (Kleiman, 2001).
- **Develop skills and confidence.** Confidence building is a life-long process, in my opinion, which is partly helped by ongoing skill development. Technical skills as well as publications, presentations, or other demonstrations of your work are helpful. Assertive expressions of your perspective, whether you feel confidant or not, is important. I am a big believer in acting confidently-the feelings will follow. We must constantly practice how to hold

ourselves out with confidence, how to articulate our ideas, how to face creative conflict in order to reach resolutions. These are simply skills that can be developed through practice. Acquire skills, take classes, gain credentials if necessary as part of the process of developing confidence.

- **Find activities and projects that will enhance your sense of self.** Take care of your responsibilities and find ways to contribute to that about which you feel passionate. Volunteerism is one of the best antidepressants there is. Find ways to helping others. Don't be afraid to take action or try a project because you don't think you have the right position.
- **Stand up for yourself.** Develop assertiveness skills and learn to work through and live through conflict. If you are "too kind," timid, or fearful to the point of being a doormat, change that. It is impossible to avoid conflict in life and in relationships, and when we don't engage in assertiveness, we often violate our dignity and integrity. Don't be afraid of acting out of your strengths; we can become the best of what women and men have to offer. Gloria Steinem said, "Some of us are becoming the men we wanted to marry."
- **Articulate the value of diversity and inclusion in decision making and power, etc.** We need individuals who are able and willing to articulate commitment to diversity issues. Eng (1999) talks about modern-day warrior women of color. She believes that "Power-from-within" (confidence) is based on the inherent value in each of us, separate from that which represents us to others. Power-from-within recognizes that groups and alliances are strong and balanced only when each of the members is strong and balanced. If we have "power-from-within" we are relatively freed from the weight of outside expectations, downward pressure, and confining stereotypes. We can be released to act genuinely and freely.

"Our lives begin to end the day we are silent about things that matter."
— Martin Luther King, Jr.

- **Observe role models and mentors.** Mentors are scarce. Use them situationally and at a distance. I have received much mentoring and guidance from my peers, and sometimes have learned lots from watching younger students and professionals. I have also been fortunate to learn from various senior people, of color, White, some male, others women. ... Observe skills and strengths of others and decide whether you wish to cultivate those as well.
- **Engage in self care.** You are the only one who can ensure that you exercise; eat healthily; have a good balance of work, rest, play, relationships; set appropriate boundaries; and so on.We have to be able to treat ourselves as preciously as we do anyone else. Women in particular must learn how to apply the same standard of care that they provide to others.
- **Use your frustration and anger to empower your lives**. Our upbringing and social codes can make it difficult to allow us to experience anger, or we may express it destructively. Many of us haven't learned how to translate that to create change in the situations around us. We may assume that if we are good and respectful to others, those behaviors will be reciprocated. This expectation can interfere with our right to anger that can be transformed into healthy, assertive expressions that say, "We count." "I am to be respected." "You may not mistreat me." "I am deserving." Anger is a healthy signal that tells us and those around us where our boundaries are, what we instinctively feel is tolerable or intolerable, and can signal when those limits

have been trespassed. Conflict is necessary because difference is inherent in every endeavor.

- **Understand why you have chosen to rein yourself in, if you have.** Often, we experience many of what Clarissa Pinkola-Estes, author of *Women Who Run With the Wolves,* identified as "small deaths and big deaths," "las muertes chiquitas, and las muertes grandotas," which include experiences of loss, all the times when roads were not taken or paths were cut off. The "little deaths" can be subtle, wounding slights, belittling comments, painful rejections. Years of those can take a toll. "Big deaths" include more major betrayals, harassment, sexual assaults, etc. Pinkola-Estes suggests a ritual "descansos" where you draw a life line, identify those and allow yourself to acknowledge the pain, anger, forgiveness and move on. Stop reining yourself in!

  By the way, this happens to everyone, including White men, in varying degrees. My clinical work has informed me of this. How we interpret, internalize those varies according to our position in society, histories, coping strategies, etc.
- **Identify to what extent the values of modesty, reserve, and humility serve as barriers or strengths for you.** Do you experience a cultural tradition against loudness, aggression, domination of others? And does it feel that we're engaging in those activities when we say yes to jobs with intimidating titles and important-sounding duties? Do our values keep us from disagreeing because it might seem rude, from expressing dissatisfaction because it might offend someone?
- **Engage in activism**. We can depend on ourselves as individuals and groups to make a difference. We must also develop alliances with power structures and set up policies and structures to make a difference. Affirmative action types of strategies are absolutely necessary for continued change in my very strong opinion.
- **Support each other and connect with each other.** Empowering others can be the same as empowering ourselves. The precious and powerful standing up for each other is the one of the most exquisite gifts to give and to receive. Make sure you surround yourself with supportive people in your life. Family, friends, and acquaintances with whom you come away feeling good and zestful about life and yourself are the kind to spend time with.

  Jean Baker Miller of the Stone Center says that a healthy interaction is one in which we come away feeling energized, zestful, happy, with the motivation to connect again, not only with that individual or group, but in general! The hurt, pain and betrayal from the words of an enemy are nothing compared to the silence of a friend (rephrased, Martin Luther King).
- **Cultivate qualities of care, compassion, and kindness.** Be a supportive person. How often do we think good things about people, but fail to articulate them? Kindness and generosity evoke kindness and generosity. Apply those same standards to yourself.

  If you are a critical person, you're probably also harsh with yourself. Caring, compassion and kindness can help shape behavior. I know that we all learn in different ways, but I believe that we can set high expectations, boundaries, rules, and even consequences and communicate those with care, compassion, and kindness. The resilience literature shows us that individuals exposed to harsh conditions can evolve into embittered, angry, hostile, sarcastic, and cynical individuals. And that others exposed to the same conditions cope by becoming caring, compassionate, and kind people.

  The attachment literature informs us of the importance of bonding, and the resiliency literature tells us of the importance of caring, confiding relationships as important in the enhancement of health and vitality among children and adolescents, even into late adolescence (Spencer, Jordan, Sazama, 2002). I am an "n" of one, but kindness and caring from key people throughout my life during adverse periods has had tremendous impact on my capacity to thrive as well as to motivate me to respond in kind, caring ways to others.

The modeling of coping strategies, including the way people think about and respond to harsh conditions and experiences, is powerful, in my opinion. This process—of providing a connecting, caring relationship and shaping people's cognitions, skills, and behaviors in response to their difficulties and pain, is what we try to do in psychotherapy as well as in supervision! If people have a context of support, caring, compassion during difficult periods, that may be one factor that facilitates enhancement of psychological health, including the capacity to be caring, compassionate, and kind to others.

Not everyone responds to care, compassion, and kindness in the same way; some people cannot perceive it or accept it; others may take advantage. We may all need a variety of experiences to learn what we need to learn. However, these qualities and virtues should be in the repertoire of every ethical professional. If we don't see it modeled, or if we don't often experience the effects of caring, compassion and kindness, then those are less likely to be in our options of responding.

I love the following quote:

> *"It's a bit embarrassing to have been concerned with the human problem all one's life and find at the end that one has no more to offer by way of advice than 'Try to be a little kinder.'"*
>
> — Aldous Huxley, English novelist and critic

In summary, I would like to encourage you all to engage in these strategies to acquire success, confidence, happiness, and a strong sense of well-being. Life is an exciting process, and the field of psychology, whether you are directly in it, or it serves as a foundation for your work and life, is fascinating. I hope my words have been inspiring, helpful, and supportive to you. I'd like to end with two quotes which I think are relevant. The first is one I like to remember when I feel discouraged or disempowered.

In the words of Adrienne Rich:

> *My heart is moved by all I cannot save, so much has been lost ... so much has been destroyed. I have to cast my lot with those who, age after age, perversely, with no extraordinary power ... reconstitute the world."*

The next quote is one I want you to remember when you do gain power. When you do, use it well.

In the Words of Martin Luther King, Jr.: *"Now, we've got to get this thing right. What is needed is a realization that power without love is reckless and abusive, and love without power is sentimental and anemic. Power at its best is love implementing the demands of justice, and justice at its best is power correcting everything that stands against love. It is precisely the collision of immoral power with powerless morality which constitutes the major crisis of our times."* (Last Southern Christian Leadership Council presidential address, 1967).

As I sat listening to Dr. Vasquez' invited talk at RMPA, so many thoughts raced through my mind. For every example she gave of either a personal experience or one of her clients, I had a similar example that would continue to illustrate or accentuate her point that came from my life experience. For each piece of knowledge she passed on to inspire or rejuvenate, I nodded my head in agreement. By her sharing of herself and her process of making her way in this profession, she helped solidify my belief that mentorship plays a vital role in one's success. As a student, support from family and friends can be essential to alleviating stress in one's life. A mentor can be in this support system. However, a mentor should also be able to provide you with a different aspect of support, knowledge, and guidance that helps you find those successes allowing you to meet your goals and dreams.

Mentoring should not stop when one stops being a student. As a young professional, I soaked up everything Dr. Vasquez had to offer. I felt that every minute was sacred and that she may not know she was mentoring me or the audience, but she was. Each piece of wisdom shared was a moment of evaluation on my part to see how I was doing in this rat race of making a career in psychology.

Can I and have I put into play in my life these important life lessons learned and shared from this wise elder? Yes and yes. Now the question for me to answer was "Am I passing along these valuable lessons to the students I mentor?" My students and mentees know the answer to this. So, I take with me the knowledge that mentoring moments can happen in many forms, durations, and contexts. No matter what stage of the game you are engaged in, if we could always see ourselves as a mentor or a potential mentor, students may get further down the path of being successful, having happiness, and a positive well-being. Wouldn't this make us all "a little kinder"?

References

Delgado, J. L. (1997). *Salud! A Latino's guide to total health—Body, mind, and spirit.* New York: HarperCollins.

Dovidio J. F., Gaertner, S. L, Kawakami, K. and Hodson, G. (2002). Why can't we just get along? Interpersonal biases and interracial distrust. *Cultural Diversity and Ethnic Minorily Psychology. 8,* 88–102.

Duenwald, M. (2002, September 17). Students find another staple of campus life: Stress. *New York Times.* Retrieved from www.newyorktimes.com

Eng. P. (1999). *Warrior Lessons: An Asian American woman's journey into power.* New York: Pocket Books.

Jones, J. M. (1996). *Prejudice and racism* (2nd ed.). New York: McGraw-Hill.

Kieiman, C, (2001, August 12). Schmoozing may improve your ratings. *Austin American Statesman,* p. E1.

Lott, B. (1985). The devaluation of women's competence. *Journal of Social Issues. 41,* 43–60.

Vasquez, M. J. T. (1994). Latinas. In L. Comas-Diaz and B. Greene (eds.). *Women of Color: Integrating Ethnic and Gender Identities in Psychotherapy.* New York: Guilford Press. 114–138.

How Do I Become Culturally Competent?

By Rebecca A. Clay

Both research and practice-oriented psychology students can benefit from a healthy dose of self-reflection, experts say.

As a former Asian-American studies minor with an interest in diversity and a minority-group member himself, Ali M. Mattu thought that he was ready to tackle just about any cultural issue when he began doctoral studies in clinical psychology at the Catholic University of America five years ago. As it turned out, the future diversity chair for APAGS was flummoxed by one of his first clients.

"He was going on and on about confession, using a lot of Catholic lingo that I'm not familiar with," says Mattu, now chair-elect of APAGS. "Then he looked at me and asked point blank, 'Have you been to confession here?'" Instead of owning up to not being Catholic, Mattu sidestepped the question and missed an opportunity to explore a topic that meant so much to his client.

Since then, Mattu has taken an intensive course on cultural issues in clinical psychology, which included lectures, self-reflection and community service. But while APA accreditation requires programs to cover cultural competence, and many states require such training for licensure, not all psychology programs offer the thorough grounding Mattu received.

"Traditional models of training don't focus very much on learning how to adapt one's skills to different populations," says Janet E. Helms, PhD, director of the Institute for the Study and Promotion of Race and Culture at Boston College. "People still have a tendency to make cultural competence the topic they cover at the end of the semester, so they really don't cover it very well."

That won't do, says Helms, who wants cultural competence integrated into every aspect of graduate training. "We're becoming an increasingly culturally complex country," she says, adding that training in cultural competence should include race and ethnicity, sexual orientation, age, gender, disability status, and other demographic characteristics.

Fortunately, say Helms and other experts, there are plenty of ways to get that training and experience on your own:

- **Learn about yourself.** Get started by exploring your own historical roots, beliefs and values, says Robert C. Weigl, PhD, a psychologist at the Franklin Center in Alexandria, Va., who described a protocol for such self-reflection in a 2009 paper in the *International Journal of Intercultural Relations* (Vol. 33, No. 4). The eight-step process includes such exercises as describing your ancestors and their experiences, thinking about how your family functions as a group, and characterizing your most representative style of thought as emotional or rational, "me-centered" or "we-centered," and the like.

Self-assessment makes participants realize the pervasive role culture plays in their lives, says Weigl. It also makes people aware of their own biases while sparking open-minded curiosity about other cultures. Plus, it's fun, he says, adding that students are "sometimes swept away by healthy narcissism" as they explore their own backgrounds.

- **Learn about different cultures.** If you know you're going to be researching or providing therapy to people with unfamiliar backgrounds, seek cultural insight through journal articles and academic books, says Mattu. But don't stop there. "There's a richness to memoirs, for example, that scientific journal articles just cannot capture," he says. He also recommends novels such as "The God of Small Things"—an examination of India's caste system—and such documentaries as "Divided We Fall," about post-9-11 hate crimes against South Asians.

  However, one of the best ways to immerse yourself in another culture's worldview is to learn a second language, says private practitioner Pamela A. Hays, PhD, of Soldotna, Alaska, and author of "Addressing Cultural Complexities in Practice: Assessment, Diagnosis, and Therapy" (APA, 2008). "One of the most mind-expanding experiences is to learn a word or concept that doesn't exist in your own language," she says. "Plus, learning a language means you're more able to reach out and connect with people who speak that language."

- **Interact with diverse groups.** Arranging a research project, practicum experience or internship where you work with people from a culture that's unfamiliar to you is a great way to enhance your cultural competence. Depending on the kinds of cultural experiences you're seeking, you may want to volunteer at community centers, religious institutions or soup kitchens, says Mattu. Take a friend or two with you, he recommends, and spend some time afterward discussing how the experience may have changed your views.

  It's also important to supplement work and volunteer experience with nonclinical social interactions, recommends Hays. Instead of solely interacting with members of diverse groups who are seeking help, get a fuller picture by interacting with them as peers at parties, religious services and cultural events. "Put yourself in social situations where you're the only one of your cultural group," she recommends.

- **Attend diversity-focused conferences.** Get formal training on diversity-related research and practice issues, learn about the latest research, and meet potential collaborators at APA's Annual Convention, as well as conferences that are focused specifically on diversity issues. Check APA's online events calendar for news about upcoming meetings. One such conference, the biennial National Multicultural Conference and Summit, will take place Jan. 27–28 in Seattle. "We'll be exploring how science can be more sensitive to diversity, as well as how science can have an impact on diverse communities that have been marginalized in the past," says Francisco J. Sánchez, PhD, the summit's lead coordinator and a psychology research fellow at the University of California, Los Angeles, School of Medicine.

  Interested students who are short on cash can often volunteer at conferences in exchange for reduced fees, or apply for a travel grant. Check out APA's searchable database of scholarships, grants and awards.

- **Lobby your department.** If your program isn't giving you the training you need, push the faculty to do better, says Helms. Whether you plan to send the departmental chair a formal letter with concrete suggestions and complaints or handle the matter more informally, be sure to gather allies—students from within and outside your department—to help you make your case. That way, says Helms, "the program gets the message that this is something important to students."

And remember: These steps are just the beginning, says Hays.

"Cultural competence is a lifelong project," she says, adding that competence with one group doesn't mean you're competent with another. "You have to keep finding ways to expand your learning."

Section Four

Personal Reflections

1. Based on the readings in this section, list four types of jobs of interest thus far. List them in rank order, beginning with the job of most interest to you.
2. Go to the website **www.online.onetcenter.org**.
   - Click on FIND OCCUPATIONS.
   - Type a job title of your choice in the box labeled KEYWORD OR O*NET-SOC CODE (don't change anything in the other boxes).
   - Click GO.
   - Click on one of the links of interest to you.
   - Read the information, then click on the CUSTOM tab at the top.
   - Click on the following four boxes: TASKS, SKILLS, JOB ZONE, WAGES & EMPLOYMENT.
   - Click GO.
3. What occupation title did you search? Was what you found in your search consistent with your expectations of what the job duties, work environment, required skills, and wages would be like? Explain.
4. Since you will be conducting two informational interviews by the end of the semester, begin to consider the type of worker you want to interview. Begin to consider the questions you will ask each person, based on the readings in this section.

Section Five

Deconstructing Graduate Degree Options

If you are starting as a psychology major you might be feeling pretty darn confident about what you want to be "when you grow up" (e.g., child psychologist) but you might not have a clue how to get there. Should I apply to a master's degree program? A doctorate degree program? What kind? How long will it take? How do I prepare? Alternatively you might be overwhelmed by the possibilities and not know how to narrow them down. The good news about pursuing an advanced degree in psychology is that there are many graduate school options open to psychology students—the bad news is that there are SO many options to choose from. This section aims to provide you with data from the U.S. Bureau of Labor Statistics on education levels associated with various career options, and information about the educational and licensing requirements for professional counselors, therapists, and psychologists, all with the goal of helping you decide which graduate degree might be best for your occupational path. Use this section initially to help you think about the possibilities, but also return to this section to revisit what you have learned. As you proceed through your education you may find your preferences and ideas change, and will want to take a second (or third) look at this information.

Stats on Counseling Professions

Bureau of Labor Statistics

Counselors

Significant Points

- People interested in counseling should have a strong desire to help others and should be able to inspire respect, trust, and confidence.
- Education and training requirements vary by State and specialty, but a master's degree is required to become a licensed counselor.
- Projected job growth varies by specialty, but job opportunities should be favorable as job openings are expected to exceed the number of graduates from counseling programs.

Nature of the Work

Counselors work in diverse community settings designed to provide a variety of counseling, rehabilitation, and support services. Their duties vary greatly, depending on their specialty, which is determined by the setting in which they work and the population they serve. Although the specific setting may have an implied scope of practice, counselors frequently are challenged with children, adolescents, adults, or families that have multiple issues, such as mental health disorders and addiction, disability and employment needs, school problems or career counseling needs, and trauma. Counselors must recognize these issues in order to provide their clients with appropriate counseling and support.

Educational, vocational, and school counselors provide individuals and groups with career, personal, social and educational counseling. School counselors assist students of all levels, from elementary school to postsecondary education. They advocate for students and work with other individuals and organizations to promote the academic, career, personal, and social development of children and youth. School counselors help students evaluate their abilities, interests, talents, and personalities to develop realistic academic and career goals. Counselors use interviews, counseling sessions, interest and aptitude assessment tests, and other methods to evaluate and advise students. They also operate career information centers and career education programs. Often, counselors work with students who have academic and social development problems or other special needs.

Elementary school counselors provide individual, small-group, and classroom guidance services to students. Counselors observe children during classroom and play activities and confer with their teachers and parents to evaluate the children's strengths, problems, or special needs. In conjunction with teachers and administrators, they make sure that the curriculum addresses both the academic and the developmental needs of students. Elementary school counselors do less vocational and academic counseling than high school counselors do.

High school counselors advise students regarding college majors, admission requirements, entrance exams, financial aid, trade or technical schools, and apprenticeship programs. They help students develop job search skills, such as resume writing and interviewing techniques. College career planning and placement counselors assist alumni or students with career development and job-hunting techniques.

School counselors at all levels help students to understand and deal with social, behavioral, and personal problems. These counselors emphasize preventive and developmental counseling to enhance students' personal, social, and academic growth and to provide students with the life skills needed to deal with problems before they worsen. Counselors provide special services, including alcohol and drug prevention programs and conflict resolution classes. They also try to identify cases of domestic abuse and other family problems that can affect a student's development.

Counselors interact with students individually, in small groups, or as an entire class. They consult and collaborate with parents, teachers, school administrators, school psychologists, medical professionals, and social workers to develop and implement strategies to help students succeed.

Vocational counselors, also called *employment counselors* or *career counselors,* usually provide career counseling outside the school setting. Their chief focus is helping individuals with career decisions. Vocational counselors explore and evaluate the client's education, training, work history, interests, skills, and personality traits. They may arrange for aptitude and achievement tests to help the client make career decisions. They also work with individuals to develop their job-search skills and assist clients in locating and applying for jobs. In addition, career counselors provide support to people experiencing job loss, job stress, or other career transition issues.

Rehabilitation counselors help people deal with the personal, social, and vocational effects of disabilities. They counsel people with both physical and emotional disabilities resulting from birth defects, illness or disease, accidents, or other causes. They evaluate the strengths and limitations of individuals, provide personal and vocational counseling, offer case management support, and arrange for medical care, vocational training, and job placement. Rehabilitation counselors interview both individuals with disabilities and their families, evaluate school and medical reports, and confer with physicians, psychologists, employers, and physical, occupational, and speech therapists to determine the capabilities and skills of the individual. They develop individual rehabilitation programs by conferring with the client. These programs often include training to help individuals develop job skills, become employed, and provide opportunities for community integration. Rehabilitation counselors are trained to recognize and to help lessen environmental and attitudinal barriers. Such help may include providing education, and advocacy services to individuals, families, employers, and others in the community. Rehabilitation counselors work toward increasing the person's capacity to live independently by facilitating and coordinating with other service providers.

Mental health counselors work with individuals, families, and groups to address and treat mental and emotional disorders and to promote mental health. They are trained in a variety of therapeutic techniques used to address issues such as depression, anxiety, addiction and substance abuse, suicidal impulses, stress, trauma, low self-esteem, and grief. They also help with job and career concerns, educational decisions, mental and emotional health issues, and relationship problems. In addition, they may be involved in community outreach, advocacy, and mediation activities. Some specialize in delivering mental health services for the elderly. Mental health counselors often work closely with other mental health specialists, such as psychiatrists, psychologists, clinical social workers, psychiatric nurses, and school counselors. (Information on psychologists, registered nurses, social workers, and physicians and surgeons, which includes psychiatrists, appears elsewhere in the *Handbook*.)

Substance abuse and behavioral disorder counselors help people who have problems with alcohol, drugs, gambling, and eating disorders. They counsel individuals to help them to identify behaviors and problems related to their addiction. Counseling can be done on an individual basis, but is frequently done in a group setting and can include crisis counseling, daily or weekly counseling, or drop-in counseling supports. Counselors are trained to assist in developing personalized recovery programs that help to establish healthy behaviors and provide coping strategies. Often, these counselors also will work with family members who are affected by the addictions of their loved ones. Some counselors conduct programs and community outreach aimed at preventing addiction and educating the public. Counselors must be able to recognize how addiction affects the entire person and those around him or her.

Marriage and family therapists apply family systems theory, principles, and techniques to address and treat mental and emotional disorders. In doing so, they modify people's perceptions and behaviors, enhance communication and understanding among family members, and help to prevent family and individual crises. They may work with individuals, families, couples, and groups. Marriage and family therapy differs from traditional therapy because less emphasis is placed on an identified client or internal psychological conflict. The focus is on viewing and understanding their clients' symptoms and interactions within their existing environment. Marriage and family therapists also may make appropriate referrals to psychiatric resources, perform research, and teach courses in human development and interpersonal relationships.

Work environment. The work environment can vary greatly, depending on the occupational specialty. School counselors work predominantly in schools, where they usually have an office but also may work in classrooms. Other counselors may work in a private practice, community health organizations, day treatment programs, or hospitals. Many counselors work in an office where they see clients throughout the day, although counselors may frequently be required to provide services out in the community.

Counselors work in diverse community settings designed to provide a variety of counseling, rehabilitation, and support services.

Training, Other Qualifications, and Advancement

Education and training requirements for counselors are often very detailed and vary by State and specialty, but a master's degree usually is required to become a licensed counselor. Prospective counselors should check with State and local governments, prospective employers, and national voluntary certification organizations to determine which requirements apply.

Education and training. Education requirements vary with the occupational specialty and State licensure and certification requirements. A master's degree usually is required to be licensed or certified as a counselor. Counselor education programs in colleges and universities often are found in departments of education, psychology, or human services. Fields of study may include college student affairs, elementary or secondary school counseling, education, gerontological counseling, marriage and family therapy, substance abuse or addictions counseling, rehabilitation counseling, agency or community counseling, clinical mental health counseling, career counseling, and related fields. Courses frequently are grouped into core areas, including human growth and development, social and cultural diversity, relationships, group work, career development, counseling techniques, assessment, research and program evaluation, and professional ethics and identity. In an accredited master's degree program, 48 to 60 semester hours of graduate study, including a period of supervised clinical experience in counseling, typically are required.

Some employers provide training for newly hired counselors. Others may offer time off or tuition assistance to complete a graduate degree. Often, counselors must participate in graduate studies, workshops, and personal studies to maintain their certificates and licenses.

Licensure. Licensure requirements differ greatly by State, occupational specialty, and work setting. Some States require school counselors to hold a State school counseling certification and to have completed at least some graduate coursework; most require the completion of a master's degree. Some States require school counselors to be licensed, which generally entails completing continuing education credits. Some States require public school counselors to have both counseling and teaching certificates and to have had some teaching experience.

For counselors based outside of schools, 49 States and the District of Columbia have some form of counselor licensure that governs the practice of counseling. In addition, all 50 States and the District of Columbia have some licensure requirement for marriage and family therapists. Requirements for both counselors and marriage and family therapists typically include the completion of a master's degree in counseling or marriage and family therapy, the accumulation of 2 years or 3,000 hours of supervised clinical experience beyond the master's degree level, the passage of a State-recognized exam, adherence to ethical codes and standards, and the completion of annual continuing education credits. However, counselors working in certain settings or in a particular specialty may face different licensure requirements. For example, a career counselor working in private practice may need a license, but a counselor working for a college career center may not. In addition, substance abuse and behavior disorder counselors generally are governed by a different State agency or board than are other counselors. The criteria for their licensure can vary greatly, and in some cases these counselors may need only a high school diploma and certification. Those interested in entering the field must research State and specialty requirements to determine what qualifications are necessary.

Other qualifications. People interested in counseling should have a strong desire to help others and should be able to inspire respect, trust, and confidence. They should be able to work independently or as part of a team. Counselors must follow the code of ethics associated with their respective certifications and licenses.

Counselors must possess high physical and emotional energy to handle the array of problems that they address. Dealing daily with these problems can cause stress.

Certification and advancement. Some counselors elect to be certified by the National Board for Certified Counselors, which grants a general practice credential of National Certified Counselor. This national certification is voluntary and is distinct from State licensing. However, in some States, those who pass the national exam are exempt from taking a State certification exam. The board also offers specialty certifications in school, clinical mental health, and addiction counseling.

The Commission on Rehabilitation Counselor Certification offers voluntary national certification for rehabilitation counselors. Many State and local governments and other employers require rehabilitation counselors to have this certification. To become certified, rehabilitation counselors usually must graduate from an accredited educational program, complete an internship, and pass a written examination. Certification requirements vary, however, according to an applicant's educational history. Employment experience, for example, is required for those with a counseling degree in a specialty other than rehabilitation. To maintain their certification, counselors must successfully retake the certification exam or complete 100 credit hours of acceptable continuing education every 5 years.

Other counseling organizations also offer certification in particular counseling specialties. Usually, becoming certified is voluntary, but having certification may enhance one's job prospects.

Prospects for advancement vary by counseling field. School counselors can become directors or supervisors of counseling, guidance, or pupil personnel services; or, usually with further graduate education, they may become counselor educators, counseling psychologists, or school administrators. (Psychologists and education administrators are covered elsewhere in the *Handbook*.) Some counselors choose to work for a State's department of education.

Some marriage and family therapists, especially those with doctorates in family therapy, become supervisors, teachers, researchers, or advanced clinicians in the discipline. Counselors also may become supervisors or administrators in their agencies. Some counselors move into research, consulting, or college teaching or go into private or group practice. Some may choose to pursue a doctoral degree to improve their chances for advancement.

Employment

Counselors held about 665,500 jobs in 2008. Employment was distributed among the counseling specialties as follows:

Educational, vocational, and school counselors	275,800
Rehabilitation counselors	129,500
Mental health counselors	113,300
Substance abuse and behavioral disorder counselors	86,100
Marriage and family therapists	27,300
Counselors, all other	33,400

A growing number of counselors are self-employed and work in group practices or private practice, due in part to laws allowing counselors to be paid for their services by insurance companies and to the growing recognition that counselors are well-trained, effective professionals.

Job Outlook

Employment is expected to grow faster than the average for all occupations. Projected job growth varies by specialty, but job opportunities should be favorable because job openings are expected to exceed the number of graduates from counseling programs, especially in rural areas.

Employment change. Overall employment of counselors is expected to increase by 18 percent between 2008 and 2018, which is faster than the average for all occupations. However, growth is expected to vary by specialty.

Employment of substance abuse and behavioral disorder counselors is expected to grow by 21 percent, which is much faster than the average for all occupations. As society becomes more knowledgeable about addiction, more people are seeking treatment. Furthermore, drug offenders are increasingly being sent to treatment programs rather than to jail.

Employment for educational, vocational, and school counselors is expected to grow by 14 percent, which is faster than the average for all occupations. Demand for vocational or career counselors should grow as multiple job and career changes become common and as workers become increasingly aware of counseling services. States require elementary schools to employ counselors. Expansion of the responsibilities of school counselors also is likely to lead to increases in their employment. For example, counselors are becoming more involved in crisis and preventive counseling, helping students deal with issues ranging from drug and alcohol abuse to death and suicide. Although schools and governments

Projections data from the National Employment Matrix

Occupational Title	SOC Code	Employment, 2008	Projected Employment, 2018	Change, 2008-18	
				Number	Percent
Counselors	21-1010	665,500	782,200	116,800	18
Substance abuse and behavioral disorder counselors	21-1011	86,100	104,200	18,100	21
Educational, vocational, and school counselors	21-1012	275,800	314,400	38,600	14
Marriage and family therapists	21-1013	27,300	31,300	3,900	14
Mental health counselors	21-1014	113,300	140,400	27,200	24
Rehabilitation counselors	21-1015	129,500	154,100	24,500	19
Counselors, all other	21-1019	33,400	37,800	4,400	13

Note: Data in this table are rounded. See the discussion of the employment projections table in the *Handbook* introductory chapter on *Occupational Information Included in the Handbook.*

realize the value of counselors in helping their students to achieve academic success, budget constraints at every school level will dampen the job growth of school counselors. Federal grants and subsidies may help to offset tight budgets and allow the reduction in student-to-counselor ratios to continue.

Employment of mental health counselors is expected to grow by 24 percent, which is much faster than the average for all occupations. Under managed care systems, insurance companies increasingly are providing for reimbursement of counselors as a less costly alternative to psychiatrists and psychologists. In addition, there has been increased demand for mental health services as individuals become more willing to seek help.

Jobs for rehabilitation counselors are expected to grow by 19 percent, which is faster than the average for all occupations. The number of people who will need rehabilitation counseling will increase as the size of the elderly population, whose members become injured or disabled at a higher rate than other age groups, increases and as treatment for mental health related disabilities increases.

Marriage and family therapists will experience growth of 14 percent, which is faster than the average for all occupations, in part because of an increased recognition of the field. It is becoming more common for people to seek help for their marital and family problems than it was in the past.

Job prospects. Job opportunities should be favorable because job openings are expected to exceed the number of graduates from counseling programs, particularly in rural areas. Substance abuse counselors should enjoy particularly good job prospects.

Earnings

Median annual wages of educational, vocational, and school counselors in May 2008 were $51,050. The middle 50 percent earned between $38,740 and $65,360. The lowest 10 percent earned less than $29,360, and the highest 10 percent earned more than $82,330. School counselors can earn additional income by working summers in the school system or in other jobs. Median annual wages in the industries employing the largest numbers of educational, vocational, and school counselors were as follows:

Elementary and secondary schools	$57,800
Junior colleges	50,440
Colleges, universities, and professional schools	43,980
Vocational rehabilitation services	35,220
Individual and family services	33,780

Median annual wages of substance abuse and behavioral disorder counselors in May 2008 were $37,030. The middle 50 percent earned between $29,410 and $47,290. The lowest 10 percent earned less than $24,240, and the highest 10 percent earned more than $59,460. Median annual wages in the industries employing the largest numbers of substance abuse and behavioral disorder counselors were as follows:

General medical and surgical hospitals	$44,130
Local government	41,660
Outpatient care centers	36,650
Individual and family services	35,210
Residential mental retardation, mental health and substance facilities	31,300

Median annual wages of mental health counselors in May 2008 were $36,810. The middle 50 percent earned between $28,930 and $48,580. The lowest 10 percent earned less than $23,580, and the highest 10 percent earned more than $63,100. Median annual wages in the industries employing the largest numbers of mental health counselors were as follows:

Local government	$45,510
Offices of other health practitioners	40,880
Outpatient care centers	37,590
Individual and family services	36,130
Residential mental retardation, mental health and substance abuse facilities	29,950

Median annual wages of rehabilitation counselors in May 2008 were $30,930. The middle 50 percent earned between $24,110 and $41,240. The lowest 10 percent earned less than $20,150, and the highest 10 percent earned more than $56,550. Median annual wages in the industries employing the largest numbers of rehabilitation counselors were as follows:

State government	$45,350
Local government	38,800
Vocational rehabilitation services	29,060
Individual and family services	28,290
Residential mental retardation, mental health and substance facilities	25,950

Median annual wages of marriage and family therapists in May 2008 were $44,590. The middle 50 percent earned between $34,840 and $56,320. The lowest 10 percent earned less than $27,810, and the highest 10 percent earned more than $70,830. Median annual wages in the industries employing the largest numbers of marriage and family therapists were as follows:

State government	$50,770
Local government	48,220
Outpatient care centers	46,830
Offices of other health practitioners	41,220
Individual and family services	39,690

Self-employed counselors who have well-established practices, as well as counselors employed in group practices, usually have the highest earnings.

Licensed Professional Counselor

Education Requirements and Duties

Education-Portal.com

Licensed professional counselors help people with emotional, mental and behavioral issues. They typically work with individuals, groups or families. Licensed professional counselors hold a graduate degree in counseling and are licensed in their state of employment.

Education Requirements

To become a licensed professional counselor (LPC), you must hold a master's or doctoral degree in counseling or psychology from an accredited college or university. Coursework in graduate level programs includes counseling techniques and theories, testing and measuring models, research and counseling ethics. Students are required to complete a counseling practicum and supervised fieldwork. Completing a counseling program prepares graduates to sit for national exams.

Certification Information

Graduates wanting to become licensed should sit for the National Counselor Examination (NCE), which is administered by the National Board for Certified Counselors (NBCC). This exam is meant to assess skills, knowledge and abilities of individuals wanting to practice as professional counselors.

The NCE tests general areas of counseling like human growth and development, group work, social and cultural foundations, counseling fundamentals, professional practice issues and counseling ethics. Passing the NCE leads to National Certified Counselor (NCC) credentials. Many states request these test scores for the licensing process.

Licensing Requirements

All states require counselors to be licensed. Individual state requirements vary, though individuals must have a graduate degree from an accredited program and a minimum number of hours of clinical practicum. License renewal usually requires continuing education coursework.

Job Duties

Licensed professional counselors are educated and trained to provide mental health therapy to those in need. These professionals work with individuals, groups, couples and families to provide assistance in dealing with life issues. They might counsel on emotional or behavioral problems, career or health concerns, addiction or related issues. Typically, a LPC uses what is known as client-centered therapy, which is intended to encourage individual growth and well being for a client.

Skills

Aspiring licensed professional counselors should have patience and willingness to help people. Additionally, a LPC must demonstrate reliability to clients while building trust and comfort. This work can be stressful, so having the ability to handle stress and maintain both physical and emotional stamina are essential.

Courses and Classes Overview

Those interested in becoming licensed professional counselors should pursue a graduate degree or post-master's certificate in counseling or a related field. Courses in these programs typically prepare students for the National Board for Certified Counselors (NBCC) certification exam. Most states require the National Certified Counselor (NCC) credential as one of their qualifications for licensure.

List of Licensed Professional Counselor Courses

Human Growth and Development Course

This course offers an overview of human development at all stages of life. Students consider physical, emotional and social development. Additional topics might include intellectual growth, aging and prenatal development.

Counseling Theories Course

Students survey several counseling theories, discussing their effectiveness and comparing times and ways to apply them. Course assignments typically assist students in developing a theoretical framework to guide their counseling practices. Discussions address person-centered, cognitive and psychoanalytic therapy. Other topics generally include behavioral, existential and Adlerian therapies.

Abnormal Psychology Course

This class examines the symptoms, causes and treatments of mental disorders. Students rely on the American Psychiatric Association's current version of the Diagnostic and Statistical Manual for definitions of mental disorders. Course assignments place particular importance on understanding psychoactive substance use disorders. Topics typically include psychopathology testing, treatment planning and diagnostic interviewing techniques.

Individual and Group Counseling Course

Instructors and students review the techniques and principles used in effective counseling. Assignments explore the differences between counseling a group and an individual. Specific topics often include group dynamics and effective communications skills.

Ethical Principles in Counseling, Assessment and Research Course

This course discusses the legal and ethical duties of counselors, therapists and researchers. Course assignments examine code of ethics formulation, professional responsibilities and legal aspects of counselor and client interactions. Materials highlight the counselor's role in changing a client's high-risk behaviors, intervention effectiveness and privacy guidelines. Additional topics might include identifying issues in practice, applying ethical guidelines and following laws pertaining to addiction therapy.

Research Methods Course

Participants examine behavioral science research methods commonly used in current American practice. They discuss the weaknesses and advantages of experimental methods and quasi-experimental approaches to behavioral science research. Course discussions generally address issues of validity, sensitivity and reliability when critically reviewing research reports.

Alternative Master's Degree Programs for Psychology Majors

By Linda L. Walsh

The number of students pursuing master's degrees has been on the rise and those degrees need not be in psychology or counseling. Graduate programs in social work, occupational or physical therapy, marriage and family, or student affairs are other options psychology majors should consider. Many students choose to major in psychology anticipating careers that involve helping others, but few realize just how many ways there are to do so. Although I have told advisees that those with bachelor's degrees in psychology are welcomed in a wide variety of graduate and professional programs, I myself did not realize until recently just how many alumni from my department pursued master's programs other than those in psychology or counseling. In the remainder of this article, I describe the alternative master's degree programs they most often selected.

Master's in Social Work (MSW) Programs

Would you like to help individuals or families struggling with the social problems so often encountered in today's world, such as family strife, poverty, unemployment, disability, violence, substance abuse, or illness? Social workers are often the professionals in the front lines of those fighting to improve the lives of others. An undergraduate degree in social work is not an admission requirement for MSW programs. A psychology major provides good preparation, especially if complemented by additional courses in areas like social work, sociology, political science, and urban studies. Relevant paid or volunteer experiences in social services, residential or care facilities, shelters, or other human service settings are important, if not essential, when applying to these graduate programs. Generally MSW programs require two years of course work plus many hours (~900 hours) of supervised fieldwork. All MSW programs offer foundation courses on the social work profession. Some then provide several different tracks allowing students to specialize or develop an area of concentration preparing them for work in a particular setting (e.g., healthcare, schools, substance abuse treatment, social service administration) or with a particular client population (e.g., children, disabled, elderly, disadvantaged) or on a particular social problem (e.g., homelessness, child abuse, poverty). A MSW degree from an accredited program is a highly marketable degree; the U.S. Department of Labor (2006) predicts that employment of social workers will increase faster than the average for all occupations into the next decade. For additional information see the print or online resources listed below.

Linda L. Walsh, "Alternative Master's Degree Programs for Psychology Majors," *Eye on Psi Chi*, vol. 11, no. 1, pp. 21–23.

Council of Social Work Education. (n.d.). *Member program directory.* Retrieved May 9, 2006, from http://www.cswe.org/

Ginsburg, L. H. (2001). *Careers in social work* (2nd ed.). Boston, MA: Allyn and Bacon.

National Association of Social Workers. (n.d.). *Choices: Careers in social work.* Retrieved May 9, 2006, from http://www.socialworkers.org/pubs/choices/choices.htm

U.S. Department of Labor Bureau of Labor Statistics. (2006). *Occupational outlook handbook - Social workers.* Retrieved May 9, 2009, from http://www.bls.gov/oco/ocos060.htm

Wittenberg, R. (2003). *Opportunities in social work careers.* Lincolnwood, IL: VGM Career Books (McGraw-Hill Publishing).

Master's Degrees in Allied Health Professions

Do you enjoy natural science classes and the biological aspect as well as the helping aspect of psychology? Then you might want to consider one of the following types of masters programs in allied health areas. Allied health professionals work in clinical healthcare settings providing specialized services that complement and extend the efforts of physicians and nurses. The particular allied health areas that draw the most psychology students are occupational therapy (OT) and physical therapy (PT).

Master's in Occupational Therapy (MOT) Programs

Occupational therapists are certified professionals who help their clients regain or master the activities of daily living and other perceptual-motor tasks to develop as much independence and self-sufficiency at home, school, and/or work as possible. Clients might include individuals with physical or behavioral limitations due to injury or health problems as well as those with developmental disabilities, and they may range in age from infants to elderly. Some clients may be adapting to prosthetic or orthotic devices or may be working to maintain functioning in the face of a progressive disorder. Occupational therapists may work in hospitals and other medical, rehabilitation, or special care settings, schools, residential facilities, social service agencies, or in private practice. For additional information see the print or online resources listed below.

Abbott, M., Franciscus, M., and Weeks, Z. (2001). *Opportunities in occupational therapy careers.* Lincolnwood, IL: VGM Career Books (NTC/Contemporary Publishing Group).

The American Occupational Therapy Association. (2005). *Consumer information.* Retrieved May 9, 2006, from http://www.aota.org/featured/area6/index.asp

The American Occupational Therapy Association (2005). *O-T programs – Accredited.* Retrieved May 9, 2006, from http://www.aota.org/nonmembers/area13/links/LINK28.asp

U.S. Department of Labor Bureau of Labor Statistics. (2005). *Occupational outlook handbook: Occupational therapists.* Retrieved May 9, 2006, from http://www.bls.gov/oco/ocos078.htm

Master's in Physical Therapy (MPT) Programs

Physical therapists work primarily in healthcare settings to maximize muscle strength and comfortable movement in those whose motor function is less than optimal. They make use of therapeutic exercise and a variety of physical treatment approaches (such as ultrasound, hydro therapies, cold and heat therapies, electrical stimulation) to improve flexibility, fitness, and healthy motion patterns and to decrease muscle and joint pain. Physical therapy clients may be those suffering from disability or health problems or individuals who have recently had surgery or been injured in an accident. For additional information see the print or online resources listed below.

American Physical Therapy Association. (2006). http://www.apta.org

Hawkins, T. (2001). *Careers in physical therapy.* New York, NY: Rosen Publishing Group, Inc.

U.S. Department of Labor Bureau of Labor Statistics. (2005). *Occupational outlook handbook: Physical therapists.* Retrieved May 9, 2006, from http://www.bls.gov/oco/ocos080.htm

Both occupational therapists and physical therapists are in high demand and admission to graduate programs in OT or PT is highly competitive. Psychology majors interested in either area should take a year or more of biology courses, including anatomy and physiology, and course work on the nervous system and neurological disorders, if available. Campus advising offices may have a list of other recommended courses for those preparing to enter OT or PT. These are, again, areas of graduate study where admission is not based solely on academic record and GRE scores; it is particularly important that applicants have a record of relevant volunteer or work experiences, with diverse populations if possible. Work with individuals with disabilities is especially valued.

Master's Programs in Marriage and Family

Although you could do graduate work preparing you to work with couples and families in departments of counseling, psychology, or social work, a large number of the graduate programs in this area are offered by departments of family studies, family science, or human development. The particular advanced degrees offered vary from campus to campus—some award the Master's in Family Therapy (MFT), others award Master of Arts or Master of Science degrees in family studies/family science, and some have several degree options. Professionals with master's degrees in this area find work in most of the same settings that employ those with degrees in psychology, counseling, or social work. These professionals might be providing family-related education (e.g., parent education, prenatal support, writing for family publications, family support in a healthcare setting), serving as an advocate (e.g., for children, women, or families), providing social services (e.g., abuse protection, victim support, hospice or gerontological services), or lobbying for or seeking funding for family related programs. Those who earn the master's degree in Family Therapy (and, in most states, pass a licensing exam) will most often be providing family-centered interventions, helping couples or families deal with a variety of issues (e.g., psychological disorders, substance abuse, criminal offenses, violence and abuse, family discord, or broken families). They might work in a treatment setting, a social service agency, a school system, or the criminal justice system. For more information on family studies/family science, see the list of resources below.

American Association for Marriage and Family Therapy. (n.d.). *A career as a marriage and family therapist.* Retrieved May 9, 2006, from http://www.aamft.org/resources/Career_PracticeInformation/career.htm

American Association for Marriage and Family Therapy. (2002). *Directory of MFT training programs.* Retrieved May 9, 2006, from http://www.aamft.org/cgi-shl/TWServer.exe/Run:COALIST

Educational Directories Unlimited. (n.d.) *Family and consumer sciences - family studies.* Retrieved May 9, 2006, from http://www.gradschools.com/programs/family_home_science.html

Educational Directories Unlimited. (n.d.). *Human development – child development.* Retrieved May 9, 2006, from http://www.gradschools.com/listings/menus/human_develop_menu.html

Family science. (2002). Retrieved May 9, 2006, from http://issues.families.com/family science 629 635 iemf

Hans, J. D. (2005). *Graduate and undergraduate study in marriage and family: A guide to bachelor's, master's, and doctoral programs in the United States and Canada, 2005-2007.* Columbia, MO: Family Scholar Publications.

Touliatos, J. (1999). *Graduate study in marriage and the family: A guide to master's and doctoral programs in the United States and Canada.* Fort Worth, TX: Human Sciences Publications.

Master's Programs in Student Affairs

Have you enjoyed your time in an academic environment? Would you like to work at a university helping students have a full and successful college experience? Have you perhaps enjoyed working as a resident assistant, peer advisor, or leader in a student organization? A master's program preparing you for a career in student affairs (also known as the area of college student development or college student personnel) may be a good choice for you. Student affairs professionals are found all across campus—admissions, financial aid, student residences, academic advising, career and placement centers, student unions and student activity offices, and many other offices offering support services to different student populations (e.g., international, disabled, minority, Greek system, academically challenged, or gifted). For additional information see the print or online resources listed below.

Coomes, M. D., and Gerda, J. J. (Eds.). (2005). *Directory of graduate programs preparing student affairs professionals.* Retrieved May 9, 2006, from http://www.myacpa.org/c12/directory.htm

National Association of Student Personnel Administrators. (2006-2007). *Grad prep.* Retrieved May 9, 2006, from http://www.naspa.org/gradprep/search.cfm

StudentAffairs.com. (n.d.). Retrieved June 20, 2006, from http://www.studentaffairs.com

Summary

One must earn a doctoral degree to become a psychologist and the employment opportunities for those with master's degrees in psychology are therefore more limited. In contrast, in each of the areas briefly described in this article, the master's degree is the most common advanced degree. Doctoral degrees may be available, primarily for those most interested in careers in research or higher education, but it is the master's degree that is required for access to most of the positions in social work, family science, occupational therapy, physical therapy, or student affairs. Each of these areas makes use of psychological principles and research findings. Master's programs in these areas offer important graduate school options for psychology students interested in becoming helping professionals.

Clinical versus Counseling Psychology

What's the Diff?

By John C. Norcross

The majority of psychology students applying to graduate school are interested in clinical work, and approximately half of all graduate degrees in psychology are awarded in the subfields of clinical and counseling psychology (Mayne, Norcross, and Sayette, 2000). But deciding on a health care specialization in psychology gets complicated. The urgent question facing each student—and the question frequently posed to academic advisors—is "What are the differences between clinical psychology and counseling psychology?" Or, as I am asked in graduate school workshops, "What's the diff?"

This article seeks to summarize the considerable similarities and salient differences between these two psychology subfields on the basis of several recent research studies. The results can facilitate your informed choice in the application process, enhance matching between the specialization and your interests, and sharpen the respective identities of psychology training programs.

Considerable Similarities

The distinctions between clinical psychology and counseling psychology have steadily faded in recent years, leading many to recommend a merger of the two. Graduates of doctoral-level clinical and counseling psychology programs are generally eligible for the same professional benefits, such as psychology licensure, independent practice, and insurance reimbursement. The American Psychological Association (APA) ceased distinguishing many years ago between clinical and counseling psychology internships: there is one list of accredited internships for both clinical and counseling psychology students. Both types of programs prepare doctoral-level psychologists who provide health care services and, judging from various studies of their respective professional activities, there are only a few meaningful differences between them (e.g., Gaddy, Charlot-Swilley, Nelson, and Reich, 1995; Norcross, Karg, and Prochaska, 1997; Watkins, Lopez, Campbell, and Himmell, 1986).

Put differently, students interested in a career in psychological health care should certainly consider both clinical psychology and counseling psychology in their initial deliberations. Of course, we are addressing here *counseling psychology*, a doctoral-level field in psychology, not the master's-level profession of *counseling*.

John C. Norcross, "Clinical Versus Counseling Psychology: What's the Diff?" *Eye on Psi Chi*, vol. 5, no. 1, pp. 20–22.

Salient Differences

At the same time, a few differences between clinical psychology and counseling psychology are still visible and may impact your application decisions. Here are thumbnail sketches of these differences.

Size

Clinical psychology doctoral programs are more numerous than counseling psychology doctoral programs: In 1999, there were 194 APA-accredited doctoral programs in clinical psychology and 64 APA-accredited doctoral programs in counseling psychology. Clinical psychology programs produce approximately 2,000 doctoral degrees per year (1,300 PhD and 600 to 700 PsyD), while counseling psychology programs graduate approximately 500 new psychologists per year.

Location

Clinical psychology graduate programs are almost exclusively housed in departments or schools of psychology, whereas counseling psychology graduate programs are located in a variety of departments and divisions. A 1995 survey of APA-accredited counseling psychology programs found that 18% of them were housed in colleges of art and science, 75% were housed in schools of education, and 6% in interdepartmental or interinstitutional settings (Woerheide, 1996).

Professional Activities

The daily activities of clinical and counseling psychologists are highly similar. They devote the bulk of their day to psychotherapy, teaching, research, and supervision (Mayne et al., 2000). But there are a few robust differences: Clinical psychologists tend to work with more seriously disturbed populations and are more likely trained in projective assessment, whereas counseling psychology graduates work with healthier, less pathological populations and conduct more career and vocational assessment (Brems and Johnson, 1997; Fitzgerald and Osipow, 1986; Watkins, Lopez, Campbell, and Himmell, 1986).

Theoretical Orientations

In one of our recent studies (Bechtoldt et al., 2000), we compared the theoretical orientations and employment settings of APA's Division 12 (Clinical) and 17 (Counseling) psychologists (N = 1,389). … Again, the convergence was more impressive than the divergence: 29% of both divisions embraced the eclectic/integrative orientation and 26% endorsed the cognitive orientation. However, clinical psychologists more frequently favored the behavioral and psychoanalytic (but not psychodynamic) persuasions, and counseling psychologists the client-centered and humanistic traditions.

The same pattern holds true for the theoretical orientations of faculty members. In one of our studies (Norcross et al., 1998) examining the theoretical orientations of faculty in doctoral clinical and counseling psychology programs, we found a higher percentage of psychodynamic faculty in clinical PsyD programs, a higher percentage of humanistic faculty in counseling PhD programs, and a higher percentage of cognitive-behavioral faculty in clinical PhD programs.

Employment Settings

Previous research has consistently found that clinical and counseling psychologists are employed in similar settings, with private practice and universities leading the way. But here, too, we find salient differences. Counseling psychologists are more frequently employed in university counseling centers, whereas clinicians are more frequently employed in hospital settings (Gaddy, Charlot-Swilley, Nelson, and Reich, 1995; Watkins, Lopez, Campbell, and Himmell, 1986).

... Division 12 clinical psychologists were more often employed in private practice, hospitals, and medical schools. By contrast, Division 17 counseling psychologists were more likely to be located in universities (particularly university counseling centers) and other human service settings.

Graduate Admissions

In a large study, colleagues and I set out to obtain critical information on the admission statistics and student characteristics of APA-accredited programs in counseling and clinical psychology (see Norcross et al., 1998, for details). We secured the following information: Graduate Record Examination (GRE) scores and grade point averages (GPAs), number of applicants and acceptances, percentages of incoming students entering with a baccalaureate only and those with a master's degree, and the percentages of incoming students who were women and minorities. The results from 178 clinical psychology programs and 61 counseling psychology (response rates of 99% and 95%, respectively) provide the empirical basis for these conclusions:

- The mean GRE scores of accepted applicants in clinical and counseling psychology doctoral programs were similar overall with a few differences favoring the clinical programs. For all programs, verbal scores averaged 621 (*SD* = 45), quantitative scores averaged 627 (*SD* = 45), and analytical scores averaged 648 (*SD* = 53). The average score on the Psychology Subject Test was 641 (*SD* = 47). The only significant differences emerged between PhD clinical programs and PhD counseling programs on the verbal and quantitative scores. In both cases, the incoming students of the clinical PhD programs had higher mean scores (638 verbal and 664 quantitative).
- Similarly, the grade point averages of incoming students were quite similar across clinical and counseling doctoral programs: The overall GPA averaged 3.5 (*SD* = .2) and the psychology GPA averaged 3.7 (*SD* = .1).
- The programs accepted, on average, 6 to 8% of the 239 (*SD* = 123) applicants. The acceptance rate refers to the percentage of applicants who were accepted to the programs, not to the number of students who eventually enrolled in the program. The clinical programs received a significantly higher number of applications than did counseling programs (270 vs. 130), but the acceptance rates were virtually identical between clinical PhD and counseling PhD programs.
- For both types of programs, two thirds of the entering doctoral students were women and one fifth were ethnic minorities. Counseling psychology programs, however, accepted a significantly higher percentage of ethnic minorities (25%) than their clinical counterparts (18%).
- For both clinical and counseling programs, approximately two thirds of incoming doctoral students were baccalaureate level and one third master's level. However, this generic conclusion was tempered by the fact that counseling psychology programs accepted a far higher proportion of master's-degree students than PsyD programs, which in turn accepted a far higher proportion than the PhD clinical programs (67% vs. 40% vs. 21%).

Research Areas

In the same study, we took a close look at the frequency of research areas for clinical and counseling psychology doctoral programs. For all programs, the most frequently listed areas of faculty research, in descending order, were: behavioral medicine/health psychology, minority/cross-cultural psychology, psychotherapy process and outcome, family therapy and research, child clinical/pediatric psychology, neuropsychology, mood disorders, anxiety disorders, eating disorders, and assessment. In order to discern patterns of probable differences in research areas between clinical and counseling programs, we examined the frequency of listings for departures from the expected ratio.

By far, the largest differences occurred in minority/cross-cultural psychology and vocational assessment: 69% and 62% of counseling psychology programs listed these, respectively, compared to only 32% and 1% of the clinical programs. Counseling psychology programs more frequently provided research training and mentorship in human diversity (e.g., gender differences, homosexuality, minority/cross-culture, women's studies), and professional issues (e.g., ethics, professional training). Conversely, clinical psychology program offered, as a group, more research opportunities in psychopathological populations (e.g., attention deficit hyperactivity disorder, autism, affective disorders, chronic mental illness, personality disorders, posttraumatic stress disorder, schizophrenia) and in activities traditionally associated with medical and hospital settings (e.g., pediatric, neuropsychology, pain management, psychophysiology).

Concluding Comments

Choosing between counseling psychology and clinical psychology has been difficult for graduate school applicants given the paucity of published studies and their considerable overlap. As a resource to applicants and advisors, this article has attempted to review the similarities and highlight their differences.

The specific credentials, characteristics, and interests of students should guide applications, of course. Counseling psychology programs seem best suited for those with established interests in the vocational and career processes, human diversity, and professional training. Similarly, students possessing master's degrees and those seeking more intensive exposure to humanistic theory and practice would find these the "norm" in counseling psychology.

Conversely, students with an abiding interest in psychopathological populations and in behavioral health will more likely find these in clinical psychology programs. While all APA-accredited programs expect their incoming students to manifest relatively high GREs and GPAs (Norcross, Hanych, and Terranova, 1996), the PhD clinical psychology programs expect them a bit higher. Students with a cognitive-behavioral orientation should also find PhD clinical programs most amenable to their interests.

Distinctive emphases between PhD counseling psychology and PhD clinical psychology programs ought not to be rigidly interpreted as absolute or unique characteristics. With the robust overlap in these programs, qualified students should consider all options and then tailor their applications to those specializations that match their academic credentials, research interests, career trajectories, and theoretical orientations. We hope that the systematic comparisons provided in this article will assist students and advisors in doing just that.

References

American Psychological Association Research Office. (1997). *Demographic characteristics of Division 12 members by membership status: 1997.* Washington, DC: Author.

American Psychological Association Research Office. (1997). *Demographic characteristics of Division 17 members by membership status: 1997.* Washington, DC: Author.

Bechtoldt, H., Wyckoff, L. A., Pokrywa, M. L., Campbell, L. F., and Norcross, J. C. (2000, March). *Theoretical orientations and employment settings of clinical and counseling psychologists: A comparative study.* Poster presented at the 71st annual convention of the Eastern Psychological Association, Baltimore, MD.

Brems, C., and Johnson, M. E. (1997). Comparison of recent graduates of clinical versus counseling psychology programs. *Journal of Psychology, 131,* 91-99.

Fitzgerald, L. F., and Osipow, S. H. (1986). An occupational analysis of counseling psychology: How special is the specialty? *American Psychologist, 41,* 535-544.

Gaddy, C. D., Charlot-Swilley, D., Nelson, P. D., and Reich, J. N. (1995). Selected outcomes of accredited programs. *Professional Psychology: Research and Practice, 26,* 507-513.

Mayne, T. J., Norcross, J. C., and Sayette, M. A. (2000). *Insider's guide to graduate programs in clinical and counseling psychology* (2000-2001 ed). New York: Guilford.

Norcross, J. C., Hanych, J. M., and Terranova, R. D. (1996). Graduate study in psychology: 1992-1993. *American Psychologist, 51,* 631-643.

Norcross, J. C., Karg, R., and Prochaska, J. O. (1997). Clinical psychologists in the 1990's. II. *The Clinical Psychologist, 50,* 4-11.

Norcross, J. C., Sayette, M. A., Mayne, T. J., Karg, R. S., and Turkson, M. A. (1998). Selecting a doctoral program in professional psychology: Some comparisons among PhD counseling, PhD clinical, and PsyD clinical psychology programs. *Professional Psychology: Research and Practice, 29,* 609-614.

Watkins, C. E., Lopez, F. G., Campbell, V. L., and Himmell, C. D. (1986). Counseling psychology and clinical psychology: Some preliminary comparative data. *American Psychologist, 41,* 581-582.

Woerheide, K. (1996). *1995 summary of characteristics and outcomes of university-based, clinical doctoral programs.* Washington, DC: American Psychological Association Office of Program Consultation and Accreditation.

Appreciating the PsyD: The Facts

By John C. Norcross and Patricia H. Castle

Students contemplating doctoral studies in clinical psychology are confronted with a confusing diversity of training opportunities. Boulder model or Vail model, PhD or PsyD? Without a firm understanding of the differences in these training models, many applicants will waste valuable time and needlessly experience disappointment. In this article, we distinguish between the two prevalent training models in clinical psychology—the Boulder model and the Vail model—and then outline the research-based differences between PhD and PsyD programs. Our objective is to help you appreciate the PsyD degree, whether or not you ultimately find it to your taste, by acquainting you with the facts.

The Boulder Model (PhD)

The first national training conference on clinical psychology was held during 1949 in Boulder, Colorado (hence, the Boulder model). At this conference, equal weight was accorded to the development of both research competencies and clinical skills. This dual emphasis resulted in the notion of the clinical psychologist as a scientist-practitioner.

The Boulder conference was a milestone for several reasons. First, it established the PhD as the required degree, as in other academic fields. To this day, all Boulder-model programs in clinical psychology award the PhD degree. Second, the conference reinforced the idea that the appropriate location for training was within a university department, not a separate school or institute as in medicine and dentistry. And third, clinical psychologists were trained to be scientist -practitioners—prepared for work in both the academic world and the practice world.

The important implication for students and advisors alike is to know that Boulder-model programs provide rigorous education as a researcher along with training as a clinician. Consider this dual thrust carefully before applying to Boulder-model programs. Some first-year graduate students undergo undue misery because they dislike research-oriented courses and the research projects that are part of the degree requirements. These, in turn, are preludes to the formal dissertation required by Boulder-model, PhD programs.

The Vail Model (PsyD)

Dissension with the recommendations of the Boulder conference culminated in a 1973 national

John C. Norcross and Patricia H. Castle, "Appreciating the PsyD: The Facts," *Eye on Psi Chi*, vol. 7, no. 1, pp. 22–26.

training conference held in Vail, Colorado (hence, the Vail model). The Vail conferees endorsed different principles, leading to an alternative training model (Peterson, 1976, 1982). Psychological knowledge, it was argued, had matured enough to warrant creation of explicitly professional programs along the lines of professional programs in medicine, dentistry, and law. These professional programs were to be added to, not replace, Boulder-model programs. Further, it was proposed that different degrees should be used to designate the scientist role (PhD) from the practitioner role (PsyD—Doctor of Psychology). Graduates of Vail-model professional programs are scholar - professionals: the focus is primarily on clinical practice and less on research.

This revolutionary conference led to the emergence of two distinct training models typically housed in different settings. Boulder-model programs are almost universally located in graduate departments of universities. However, Vail-model programs can be housed in three organizational settings: within a psychology department, within a university-affiliated psychology school, and within an independent, freestanding psychology school. The latter programs are not affiliated with universities; rather, they are independently developed and staffed.

Table 1 lists the 56 APA-accredited PsyD programs as a function of their institutional setting. As seen there, 17 PsyD programs are housed in university departments, 23 in university professional schools, and 16 in freestanding institutions. Clinical psychology programs represent the largest segment, with 82% of the PsyD programs. For this reason, we focus in this article on the PsyD programs in clinical and counseling psychology, recognizing, of course, that there are a handful of PsyD programs in school psychology.

Two Training Models

Clinical psychology now has two established and complementary training models. Although Boulder-model, PhD programs still outnumber PsyD programs, PsyD programs enroll, as a rule, three times the number of incoming doctoral candidates per school (Mayne, Norcross, and Sayette, 1994). This creates almost a numerical parity in terms of psychologist graduates.

The differences between clinical PhD and clinical PsyD programs are quantitative, not qualitative. The primary disparity is in the relative emphasis on research: Boulder programs aspire to train producers of research; Vail programs train consumers of research. PsyD programs require some research and statistics courses; you simply cannot avoid research sophistication in any APA-accredited program. The clinical opportunities are very similar for students in both types of programs. Indeed, research has substantiated that PsyD programs provide slightly more clinical experience and clinical courses but less research experience than Boulder-model, PhD programs (Tibbits-Kleber and Howell, 1987).

Several studies demonstrated that initial worries about stigmatization, employment difficulties, and licensure uncertainty for PsyDs never materialized (Hershey, Kopplin, and Cornell, 1991; Peterson, Eaton, Levine, and Snepp, 1982). Nor are there discernible differences of late in employment except, of course, that the research-oriented, PhD graduates are far more likely to be employed in academic positions and medical schools (Gaddy, Charlot-Swilley, Nelson, and Reich, 1995). Although PsyD graduates may still be seen in some quarters as second-class citizens by Boulder-model traditionalists, this is not the case among health care organizations or individual consumers.

Vive la Différence!

Two training models present attractive diversity and alluring choices for students. But with choice comes the responsibility of being informed about actual differences between PhD programs and PsyD programs, as opposed to antiquated stereotypes or personal biases. Our colleagues and I have been systematically collecting data on PsyD programs over the past decade in order to present such objective, contemporary information (e.g., Mayne et al., 1994; Norcross, Hanych, and Terranova, 1996; Norcross, Sayette, Mayne, Karg, and Turkson, 1998).

Here we present many of "the facts" about PsyD programs in clinical and counseling psychology, particularly in comparison to PhD clinical psychology programs. All of the comparisons are based solely on APA-accredited programs; generalizations to non-APA-accredited programs cannot be made.

Acceptance Rates

Table 2 summarizes the application and acceptance rates for APA-accredited PsyD programs. In general, PsyD programs average 141 applications and 53 acceptances, but there are significant differences as a result of institutional location.

Freestanding programs, on average, receive twice the number of applications as university department programs (with university professional schools in between).

Similarly, the freestanding programs accept significantly more of the applicants than both types of university-based programs.

The average acceptance rate for PsyD programs is 40-41%. That is, 4 out of 10 applicants to a PsyD program are accepted.

By contrast, the average acceptance rate for clinical PhD programs is 11-15%. That is, 1 or 1.5 out of 10 applicants to a PhD program is accepted.

Enrollments

Table 2 also shows that freestanding PsyD programs typically enroll far more students per year (46) than university PsyD professional schools (31) and university PsyD departmental programs (16). PsyD programs have relatively large incoming classes each year.

By contrast, the number of incoming students in a clinical PhD program is much smaller (about 9 per year).

Financial Assistance

Although PsyD programs afford easier (but not easy) admission, they provide less financial assistance than PhD programs. Table 3 summarizes the financial assistance awarded to incoming students in APA-accredited PsyD programs, listing the percentage of students receiving a tuition waiver only, an assistantship only, or both tuition and assistantship. Across all PsyD programs, 18% of students receive both. University-based departmental PsyD programs tend to offer more aid: 31% of their students receive both tuition waiver and assistantship compared to 14% and 12% of incoming students in university professional schools and freestanding programs, respectively.

By contrast, clinical PhD programs provide 70-80% of their students with full financial assistance (tuition waiver plus assistantship stipend). In other words, more rigorous admission standards and acceptance odds translate into increased probability of substantial financial aid (Kohout, Wicherski, and Plon, 1991; Mayne et al., 1994).

The proliferating number of APA-accredited programs and the increasing number of acceptances in psychology doctoral programs during a period of economic downsizing raises difficult questions about internal funding of students. Our findings on financial aid portend a "pay as you go" expectation for three fourths of PsyD students. This is particularly true, as we have seen, for students in freestanding PsyD programs. The explicit expectation, as is true in such other practice disciplines as medicine and law, is that graduates will repay their debt after they are engaged in full-time practice.

Student Debt

Doctoral students' debt can be substantial. Research demonstrates that 74% of recent graduates in clinical psychology have debt related to graduate studies. Graduates of PsyD programs reported a median debt of $53,000 to $60,000. Recipients of Boulder-model clinical PhDs, by contrast, reported a median debt of $22,000 (Kohout and Wicherski, 1999). In large part, this difference in debt between PsyD and PhD graduates is attributable to the huge differences in financial aid between them. The APA researchers (Kohout and Wicherski, 1999) who compiled these data conclude, "It is important to disseminate this information to students who may be considering a career in psychology—so that their decisions can be fully informed" (p. 10). We wholeheartedly agree.

Student Characteristics

The educational and demographic characteristics of PsyD and PhD students are quite similar with one exception. Seventy percent of all clinical psychology doctoral students are now women, and about 20% are members of ethnic or racial minorities. The difference is that students in PsyD programs are far more likely to have master's degrees already (and concurrently tend to be a little older) than PhD students. About 35% of incoming PsyD students possess a master's degree, compared to about 20% in PhD programs.

Faculty Theoretical Orientations

PsyD faculty are impressively diverse in their theoretical orientations. About 30% of PsyD faculty subscribe to the psychodynamic/psychoanalytic orientation, another 30% to the cognitive-behavioral orientation, and about 20% to systems/family systems. The remainder of the faculty favor humanistic and behavioral theories.

By contrast, cognitive-behavioral faculty dominate PhD programs in clinical psychology. In fact, about 65% of the faculty are cognitive-behavioral. PhD programs afford less theoretical variety, certainly fewer psychoanalytic and humanistic faculty on staff.

Length of Training

Another crucial difference between PhD and PsyD programs concerns the length of training. Students in PhD programs take significantly longer, approximately 1 to 1.5 years longer, to complete their degrees than do PsyD students. This finding has now been replicated in our research and that of others (Gaddy et al., 1995). Various interpretations are given to this reliable difference, from PsyD training is more focused and efficient on one hand, to PhD training is more comprehensive and rigorous on the other.

Licensure Exam

One disconcerting trend is that PsyD graduates do not perform as well as PhD graduates on the national licensing examination for psychologists (Kupfersmid and Fiala, 1991; McGaha and Minder, 1993; Yu et al., 1997). That is, doctoral students who graduate with PsyDs score lower, on average, than doctoral students who graduate with PhDs on the Examination for Professional Practice in Psychology (EPPP), the national licensing test. Higher EPPP scores have been reliably associated with smaller-sized clinical programs and larger faculty-to-student ratios, in addition to traditional PhD curricula.

This replicated difference probably applies more to the larger, freestanding PsyD programs than to the smaller, university-based PsyD programs. But the lesson is clear: smaller sized programs with proportionally more faculty are important factors to consider in selecting a doctoral program.

Informed Diversity

Whenever we present on graduate school admissions, we are asked, "Which degree do you personally favor?" and "Which training model do clinical psychologists prefer?" We answer by sharing the results of one of our studies (Norcross, Gallagher, and Prochaska, 1989) on this question. We found that 50% of clinical psychologists favored the Boulder model, 14% the Vail model, and the remaining 36% both models equally. But these general preferences varied as a function of the psychologists' own doctoral program: 93% of the psychologists trained in a strong Boulder tradition preferred the Boulder model or both equally, and 90% of the psychologists trained in a strong Vail tradition preferred the Vail model or both equally.

Thus, our answer during our workshops and in concluding this article is that we prefer both PhD and PsyD programs—for the right person. The key task for you as a potential applicant is to recognize the diversity in training and the inevitable tradeoffs between PsyD and PhD programs. This article has outlined many of the pivotal differences, as well as noting several important commonalities.

As a potential applicant, make it your business to investigate the attributes, strengths, and weaknesses of any graduate program. Carefully read the program's website and application materials with an eye to those features that impact you. Refer to the APA's (2002) *Graduate Study in Psychology* for general data on graduate departments and to our *Insider's Guide to Graduate Programs in Clinical and Counseling Psychology* (Norcross, Sayette, and Mayne, 2002) for information on GRE requirements and acceptance rates of individual doctoral programs, as well as financial assistance provided by these programs.

The bottom line for applicants to clinical and counseling psychology programs is one of choice and matching. PsyD programs are numerous, well established, and popular. You have the choice of two training models (and all the programs in between; Conway, 1988). The choice should be matched to your strengths and interests. The choices are yours, but please make informed decisions based on "the facts."

References

American Psychological Association. (2002). *Graduate study in psychology* (2003 ed.). Washington, DC: Author.

Conway, J. B. (1988). Differences among clinical psychologists: Scientists, practitioners, and scientist - practitioners. *Professional Psychology: Research and Practice, 19,* 642-655.

Gaddy, C. D., Charlot-Swilley, D., Nelson, P. D., and Reich, J. N. (1995). Selected outcomes of accredited programs. *Professional Psychology: Research and Practice, 26,* 507-513.

Hershey, J. M., Kopplin, D. A., and Cornell, J. E. (1991). Doctors of Psychology: Their career experiences and attitudes toward degree and training. *Professional Psychology: Research and Practice, 22,* 351-356.

Kohout, J., and Wicherski, M. (1999). *1997 doctorate employment survey.* Washington, DC: American Psychological Association Research Office.

Kohout, J., Wicherski, M., and Plon, G. (1991). *Characteristics of graduate departments of psychology: 1988-89.* Washington, DC: American Psychological Association Research Office.

Kupfersmid, J., and Fiala, M. (1991). Comparison of EPPP scores among graduates of varying psychology programs. *American Psychologist, 46,* 534-535.

Mayne, T. J., Norcross, J. C., and Sayette, M. A. (1994). Admission requirements, acceptance rates, and financial assistance in clinical psychology programs: Diversity across the practice-research continuum. *American Psychologist, 49,* 806-811.

McGaha, S., and Minder, C. (1993). Factors influencing performance on the Examination for Professional Practice in Psychology (EPPP). *Professional Psychology: Research and Practice, 24,* 107-109.

Norcross, J. C., Gallagher, K. M., and Prochaska, J. O. (1989). The Boulder and/or the Vail model: Training preferences of clinical psychologists. *Journal of Clinical Psychology, 45,* 822-828.

Norcross, J. C., Hanych, J. M., and Terranova, R. D. (1996). Graduate study in psychology: 1992-1993. *American Psychologist, 51,* 631-643.

Norcross, J. C., Sayette, M. A., and Mayne, T. J. (2002). *Insider's guide to graduate programs in clinical and counseling psychology* (2002-2003 ed.). New York: Guilford Press.

Norcross, J. C., Sayette, M. A., Mayne, T. J., Karg, R. S., and Turkson, M. A. (1998). Selecting a doctoral program in professional psychology: Some comparisons among PhD counseling, PhD clinical, and PsyD clinical psychology programs. *Professional Psychology: Research and Practice, 29,* 609-614.

Peterson, D. R. (1976). Need for the Doctor of Psychology degree in professional psychology. *American Psychologist, 31,* 792-798.

Peterson, D. R. (1982). Origins and development of the Doctor of Psychology concept. In G. R. Caddy, D. C. Rimm, N. Watson, and J. H. Johnson (Eds.), *Educating professional psychologists* (pp. 19-38). New Brunswick, NJ: Transaction Books.

Peterson, D. R., Eaton, M. M., Levine, A. R., and Snepp, F. P. (1982). Career experiences of doctors of psychology. *Professional Psychology: Research and Practice, 13,* 268-277.

Tibbits-Kleber, A. L., and Howell, R. J. (1987). Doctoral training in clinical psychology: A students' perspective. *Professional Psychology: Research and Practice, 18,* 634-639.

Yu, L. M., Rinaldi, S. A., Templer, D. I., Colbert, L. A., Siscoe, K., and Van Patten, K. (1997). Score on the Examination for Professional Practice in Psychology as a function of attributes of clinical psychology graduate programs. *Psychological Science, 8,* 347-350.

Stats on Ph.D.-Level Psychologists

Bureau of Labor Statistics

Significant Points

- About 34 percent of psychologists are self-employed, mainly as private practitioners and independent consultants.
- Employment growth will vary by specialty; for example, clinical, counseling, and school psychologists will have 11 percent growth; industrial-organizational psychologists, 26 percent growth; and 14 percent growth is expected for all other psychologists.
- Acceptance to graduate psychology programs is highly competitive.
- Job opportunities should be the best for those with a doctoral degree in a subfield, such as health; those with a master's degree will have good prospects in industrial-organization; bachelor's degree holders will have limited prospects.

Nature of the Work

Psychologists study mental processes and human behavior by observing, interpreting, and recording how people and other animals relate to one another and the environment. To do this, psychologists often look for patterns that will help them understand and predict behavior using scientific methods, principles, or procedures to test their ideas. Through such research studies, psychologists have learned much that can help increase understanding between individuals, groups, organizations, institutions, nations, and cultures.

Like other social scientists, psychologists formulate theories, or hypotheses, which are possible explanations for what they observe. But unlike other social science disciplines, psychologists often concentrate on individual behavior and, specifically, in the beliefs and feelings that influence a person's actions.

Research methods vary with the topic which they study, but by and large, the chief techniques used are observation, assessment, and experimentation. Psychologists sometimes gather information and evaluate behavior through controlled laboratory experiments, hypnosis, biofeedback, psychoanalysis, or psychotherapy, or by administering personality, performance, aptitude, or intelligence tests. Other methods include interviews, questionnaires, clinical studies, surveys, and observation— looking for cause-and-effect relationships between events and for broad patterns of behavior.

Research in psychology seeks to understand and explain thought, emotion, feelings, or behavior.

The research findings of psychologists have greatly increased our understanding of why people and animals behave as they do. For example, psychologists have discovered how personality develops and how to promote healthy development. They have gained knowledge of how to diagnose and treat alcoholism and substance abuse, how to help people change bad habits and conduct, and how to help students learn. They understand the conditions that can make workers more productive. Insights provided by psychologists can help people function better as individuals, friends, family members, and workers.

Psychologists may perform a variety of duties in a vast number of industries. For example, those working in health service fields may provide mental health care in hospitals, clinics, schools, or private settings. Psychologists employed in applied settings, such as business, industry, government, or nonprofit organizations, may provide training, conduct research, design organizational systems, and act as advocates for psychology.

Psychologists apply their knowledge to a wide range of endeavors, including health and human services, management, education, law, and sports. They usually specialize in one of many different areas.

Clinical psychologists—who constitute the largest specialty—are concerned with the assessment, diagnosis, treatment, and prevention of mental disorders. While some clinical psychologists specialize in treating severe psychological disorders, such as schizophrenia and depression, many others may help people deal with personal issues, such as divorce or the death of a loved one. Often times, clinical psychologists provide an opportunity to talk and think about things that are confusing or worrying, offering different ways of interpreting and understanding problems and situations. They are trained to use a variety of approaches aimed at helping individuals, and the strategies used are generally determined by the specialty they work in.

Clinical psychologists often interview patients and give diagnostic tests in their own private offices. They may provide individual, family, or group psychotherapy and may design and implement behavior modification programs. Some clinical psychologists work in hospitals where they collaborate with physicians and other specialists to develop and implement treatment and intervention programs that patients can understand and comply with. Other clinical psychologists work in universities and medical schools, where they train graduate students in the delivery of mental health and behavioral medicine services. A few work in physical rehabilitation settings, treating patients with spinal cord injuries, chronic pain or illness, stroke, arthritis, or neurological conditions. Others may work in community mental health centers, crisis counseling services, or drug rehabilitation centers, offering evaluation, therapy, remediation, and consultation.

Areas of specialization within clinical psychology include health psychology, neuropsychology, geropsychology, and child psychology. *Health psychologists* study how biological, psychological, and social factors affect health and illness. They promote healthy living and disease prevention through counseling, and they focus on how patients adjust to illnesses and treatments and view their quality of life. *Neuropsychologists* study the relation between the brain and behavior. They often work in stroke and head injury programs. *Geropsychologists* deal with the special problems faced by the elderly. Work may include helping older persons cope with stresses that are common in late life, such as loss of loved ones, relocation, medical conditions, and increased care-giving demands. Clinical psychologists may further specialize in these fields by focusing their work in a number of niche areas including mental health, learning disabilities, emotional disturbances, or substance abuse. The emergence and growth of these, and other, specialties reflects the increasing participation of psychologists in direct services to special patient populations.

Often, clinical psychologists consult with other medical personnel regarding the best treatment for patients, especially treatment that includes medication.

Projections data from the National Employment Matrix

Occupational Title	SOC Code	Employment 2008,	Projected Employment, 2018	Change 2008–2018	
				Number	Percent
Psychologists	19-3030	170,200	190,000	19,700	12
Clinical, counseling, and school psychologists	19-3031	152,000	168,800	16,800	11
Industrial-organizational psychologists	19-3032	2,300	2,900	600	26
Psychologists, all other	19-3039	15,900	18,300	2,300	14

(NOTE) Data in this table are rounded. See the discussion of the employment projections table in the *Handbook* introductory chapter on *Occupational Information Included in the Handbook.*

Clinical psychologists generally are not permitted to prescribe medication to treat patients; only psychiatrists and other medical doctors may prescribe most medications. (See the statement on physicians and surgeons elsewhere in the *Handbook.)* However, two States—Louisiana and New Mexico—currently allow appropriately trained clinical psychologists to prescribe medication with some limitations.

Counseling psychologists advise people on how to deal with problems of everyday living, including problems in the home, place of work, or community, to help improve their quality of life. They foster well-being by promoting good mental health and preventing mental, physical, and social disorders. They work in settings such as university or crisis counseling centers, hospitals, rehabilitation centers, and individual or group practices. (See also the statements on counselors and social workers elsewhere in the *Handbook.)*

School psychologists work with students in early childhood and elementary and secondary schools. They collaborate with teachers, parents, and school personnel to create safe, healthy, and supportive learning environments for all students. School psychologists address students' learning and behavioral problems, suggest improvements to classroom management strategies or parenting techniques, and evaluate students with disabilities and gifted and talented students to help determine the best way to educate them.

They improve teaching, learning, and socialization strategies based on their understanding of the psychology of learning environments. They also may evaluate the effectiveness of academic programs, prevention programs, behavior management procedures, and other services provided in the school setting.

Industrial-organizational psychologists apply psychological principles and research methods to the workplace in the interest of improving the quality of worklife. They also are involved in research on management and marketing problems. They screen, train, and counsel applicants for jobs, as well as perform organizational development and analysis. An industrial psychologist might work with management to reorganize the work setting in order to enhance productivity. Industrial psychologists frequently act as consultants, brought in by management to solve a particular problem.

Developmental psychologists study the physiological, cognitive, and social development that takes place throughout life. Some specialize in behavior during infancy, childhood, and adolescence, or changes that occur during maturity or old age. Developmental psychologists also may study developmental disabilities and their effects. Increasingly, research is developing ways to help elderly people remain independent as long as possible.

Social psychologists examine people's interactions with others and with the social environment. They work in organizational consultation, marketing research, systems design, or other applied psychology fields. Many social psychologists specialize in a niche area, such as group behavior, leadership, attitudes, and perception.

Experimental or *research psychologists* work in university and private research centers and in business, nonprofit, and governmental organizations. They study the behavior of both human beings and animals, such as rats, monkeys, and pigeons. Prominent areas of study in experimental research include motivation, thought, attention, learning and memory, sensory and perceptual processes, effects of substance abuse, and genetic and neurological factors affecting behavior.

Forensic psychologists use psychological principles in the legal and criminal justice system to help judges, attorneys, and other legal professionals understand the psychological findings of a particular case. They are usually designated as an expert witness and typically specialize in one of three areas: family court, civil court, and criminal court. Forensic psychologists who work in family court may offer psychotherapy services, perform child custody evaluations, or investigate reports of child abuse. Those working in civil courts may assess competency, provide second opinions, and provide psychotherapy to crime victims. Criminal court forensic psychologists often conduct evaluations of mental competency, work with child witnesses, and provide assessment of juvenile or adult offenders.

Work environment. Psychologists' work environments vary by subfield and place of employment. For example, clinical, school, and counseling psychologists in private practice frequently have their own offices and set their own hours. However, they usually offer evening and weekend hours to accommodate their clients. Those employed in hospitals, nursing homes, and other health care facilities may work shifts that include evenings and weekends, and those who work in schools and clinics generally work regular daytime hours. Most psychologists in government and industry have structured schedules.

Psychologists employed as faculty by colleges and universities divide their time between teaching and research and also may have administrative responsibilities; many have part-time consulting practices.

Increasingly, a good number of psychologists work as part of a team, consulting with other psychologists and medical professionals. Many experience pressures because of deadlines, tight schedules, and overtime.

Training, Other Qualifications, and Advancement

A master's or doctoral degree, and a license, are required for most psychologists.

Education and training. A doctoral degree usually is required for independent practice as a psychologist. Psychologists with a Ph.D. or Doctor of Psychology (Psy.D.) qualify for a wide range of teaching, research, clinical, and counseling positions in universities, health care services, elementary and secondary schools, private industry, and government. Psychologists with a doctoral degree often work in clinical positions or in private practices, but they also sometimes teach, conduct research, or carry out administrative responsibilities.

A doctoral degree generally requires about 5 years of full-time graduate study, culminating in a dissertation based on original research. Courses in quantitative experimental methods and research design, which include the use of computer-based analysis, are an integral part of graduate study and are necessary to complete the dissertation. The Psy.D. degree may be based on practical work and examinations rather than a dissertation. In clinical, counseling, and school psychology, the requirements for the doctoral degree usually include an additional year of post-doctoral supervised experience.

A specialist degree or its equivalent is required in most States for an individual to work as a school psychologist, although some States credential school psychologists with master's degrees. A specialist (Ed.S.) degree in school psychology requires a minimum of 2 years of full-time graduate study (at least 60 graduate semester hours) and a 1-year full-time internship during the third year. Because their professional practice addresses educational and mental health components of students' development, school psychologists' training includes coursework in both education and psychology.

People with a master's degree in psychology may work as industrial-organizational psychologists. They also may work as psychological assistants conducting research under the direct supervision of doctoral-level psychologists. A master's degree in psychology requires at least 2 years of full-time graduate study. Requirements usually include practical experience in an applied setting and a master's thesis based on an original research project.

Competition for admission to graduate psychology programs is keen. Some universities require applicants to have an undergraduate major in psychology. Others prefer only coursework in basic psychology with additional courses in the biological, physical, and social sciences, and in statistics and mathematics.

A bachelor's degree in psychology qualifies a person to assist psychologists and other professionals in community mental health centers, vocational rehabilitation offices, and correctional programs. Bachelor's degree holders may also work as administrative assistants for psychologists. Many, however, find employment in other areas, such as sales, service, or business management.

In the Federal Government, candidates must have a bachelor's degree with a minimum of 24 semester hours in psychology, or a combination of education and experience to qualify for entry-level positions. However, competition for these jobs is keen because this is one of the few ways in which one can work as a psychologist without an advanced degree.

The American Psychological Association (APA) presently accredits doctoral training programs in clinical, counseling, and school psychology, as well as institutions that provide internships for doctoral students in school, clinical, and counseling psychology. The National Association of School Psychologists, with the assistance of the National Council for Accreditation of Teacher Education, helps to approve advanced degree programs in school psychology.

Clinical psychologists in Louisiana and New Mexico who prescribe medication are required to complete a post-doctoral master's degree in clinical psychopharmacology and pass a National exam approved by the State Board of Examiners of psychologists.

Licensure. Psychologists in a solo or group practice or those who offer any type of patient care—including clinical, counseling, and school psychologists—must meet certification or licensing requirements in all States and the District of Columbia. Licensing laws vary by State and by type of position and require licensed or certified psychologists to limit their practice to areas in which they have developed professional competence through training and experience. Clinical and counseling psychologists usually need a doctorate in psychology, an approved internship, and 1 to 2 years of professional experience. In addition, all States require that applicants pass an examination. Most State licensing boards administer a standardized test, and many supplement that with additional oral or essay questions. Some States require continuing education for renewal of the license.

The National Association of School Psychologists (NASP) awards the Nationally Certified School Psychologist (NCSP) designation, which recognizes professional competency in school psychology at a national, rather than State, level. Currently, 31 States recognize the NCSP and allow those with the certification to transfer credentials from one State to another without taking a new certification exam. In

States that recognize the NCSP, the requirements for certification or licensure and those for the NCSP often are the same or similar. Requirements for the NCSP include the completion of 60 graduate semester hours in school psychology; a 1,200-hour internship, 600 hours of which must be completed in a school setting; and a passing score on the National School Psychology Examination.

Other qualifications. Aspiring psychologists who are interested in direct patient care must be emotionally stable, mature, and able to deal effectively with people. Sensitivity, compassion, good communication skills, and the ability to lead and inspire others are particularly important qualities for people wishing to do clinical work and counseling. Research psychologists should be capable of detailed work both independently and as part of a team. Patience and perseverance are vital qualities, because achieving results in the psychological treatment of patients or in research may take a long time.

Certification and advancement. The American Board of Professional Psychology (ABPP) recognizes professional achievement by awarding specialty certification in 13 different areas, such as psychoanalysis, rehabilitation, forensic, group, school, clinical health, and couple and family. To obtain board certification in a specialty, candidates must meet general criteria which consist of having a doctorate in psychology, as well as State licensure. Each candidate must then meet additional criteria of the specialty field, which is usually a combination of postdoctoral training in their specialty, several years of experience, and professional endorsements, as determined by the ABPP. Applicants are then required to pass the specialty board examination.

Psychologists can improve their advancement opportunities by earning an advanced degree and by participation in continuing education. Many psychologists opt to start their own private practice after gaining experience working in the field.

Employment

Psychologists held about 170,200 jobs in 2008. Educational institutions employed about 29 percent of psychologists in positions other than teaching, such as counseling, testing, research, and administration. About 21 percent were employed in health care, primarily in offices of mental health practitioners, hospitals, physicians' offices, and outpatient mental health and substance abuse centers. Government agencies at the State and local levels employed psychologists in correctional facilities, law enforcement, and other settings.

After several years of experience, some psychologists—usually those with doctoral degrees—enter private practice or set up private research or consulting firms. About 34 percent of psychologists were self-employed in 2008—mainly as private practitioners.

In addition to the previously mentioned jobs, many psychologists held faculty positions at colleges and universities and as high school psychology teachers. (See the statements on teachers—postsecondary and teachers—kindergarten, elementary, middle, and secondary elsewhere in the *Handbook.)*

Job Outlook

Employment of psychologists is expected to grow as fast as average. Job prospects should be the best for people who have a doctoral degree from a leading university in an applied specialty, such as counseling or health, and those with a specialist or doctoral degree in school psychology. Master's degree holders in fields other than industrial-organizational psychology will face keen competition. Opportunities will be limited for bachelor's degree holders.

Employment change. Employment of psychologists is expected to grow 12 percent from 2008 to 2018, about as fast as the average for all occupations. Employment will grow because of increased demand for psychological services in schools, hospitals, social service agencies, mental health centers, substance abuse treatment clinics, consulting firms, and private companies.

Demand for school psychologists will be driven by a growing awareness of how students' mental health and behavioral problems, such as bullying, affect learning. School psychologists will also be needed for general student counseling on a variety of other issues, including working with students with disabilities or with special needs, tackling drug abuse, and consulting and managing personal crisis.

Spurring demand for clinical psychologists will continue to be the rising healthcare costs associated with unhealthy lifestyles, such as smoking, alcoholism, and obesity, which have made prevention and treatment more critical. An increase in the number of employee assistance programs, which help workers deal with personal problems, also should lead to employment growth for clinical and counseling specialties. More clinical and counseling psychologists will be needed to help people deal with depression and other mental disorders, marriage and family problems, job stress, and addiction. The growing number of elderly will increase the demand for psychologists trained in geropsychology to help people deal with the mental and physical changes that occur as individuals grow older. There also will be increased need for psychologists to work with returning veterans.

Industrial-organizational psychologists also will be in demand to help to boost worker productivity and retention rates in a wide range of businesses. Industrial-organizational psychologists will help companies deal with issues such as workplace diversity and antidiscrimination policies. Companies also will use psychologists' expertise in survey design, analysis, and research to develop tools for marketing evaluation and statistical analysis.

Job prospects. Job prospects should be best for people who have a doctoral degree from a leading university in an applied specialty, such as counseling or health, and those with a specialist or doctoral degree in school psychology. Psychologists with extensive training in quantitative research methods and computer science may have a competitive edge over applicants without such background.

Master's degree holders in fields other than industrial-organizational psychology will face keen competition for jobs because of the limited number of positions that require only a master's degree. Master's degree holders may find jobs as psychological assistants or counselors, providing mental health services under the direct supervision of a licensed psychologist. Still, others may find jobs involving research and data collection and analysis in universities, government, or private companies.

Opportunities directly related to psychology will be limited for bachelor's degree holders. Some may find jobs as assistants in rehabilitation centers or in other jobs involving data collection and analysis. Those who meet State certification requirements may become high school psychology teachers.

Earnings

Median annual wages of wage and salary clinical, counseling, and school psychologists were $64,140 in May 2008. The middle 50 percent earned between $48,700 and $82,800. The lowest 10 percent earned less than $37,900, and the highest 10 percent earned more than $106,840. Median annual wages in the industries employing the largest numbers of clinical, counseling, and school psychologists were:

Offices of other health practitioners............................ $68,400
Elementary and secondary schools......................................65,710
State government.......................63,710
Outpatient care centers.............59,130
Individual and family services....57,440

Median annual wages of wage and salary industrial-organizational psychologists were $77,010 in May 2008. The middle 50 percent earned between $54,100 and $115,720. The lowest 10 percent earned less than $38,690, and the highest 10 percent earned more than $149,120.

In 2008, about 31 percent of all psychologists were members of a u+nion.

Section Five

Personal Reflections

1. In your own words, describe the differences among a licensed professional counselor, a licensed marriage family therapist, and a licensed clinical social worker.
2. In your own words, describe the differences between a doctor of philosophy in psychology (PhD) and a doctor of psychology (PsyD).
3. Choose <u>one</u> of these websites to explore and describe two aspects of it that may be helpful to you during your college career.
    - **www.aamft.org**
    - **www.socialworkers.org**

Section Six

Applying to Graduate School

Do you know that about a third of psychology majors probably will pursue a graduate education? Although you have options as a college-educated individual in the workforce (see Section Four), many of you may need to plan on a graduate education to perform the type of work you desire or to pursue a specific career. If you want to practice psychotherapy, for example, you will need to be licensed, and you will need a graduate education. If you want to be a professor of psychology, you also will need to hold an advanced degree. For many psychology majors, graduate studies are the next logical step. For others, the prospect may seem daunting. So should you pursue graduate school? And if you decide the answer is yes, regardless of the type of graduate education you decide to pursue, do you know how to get there? Do you know what is involved? Do you know what to include in an application, what not to include? Do you know what to expect once you have submitted your application? If you don't, then do not fear. The goal of the next section is to demystify the graduate school application process. To this end, we have collected resources that may help you decide whether graduate school is right for you, and then guide you to prepare a successful application free from common mistakes. We know these tips will be fruitful, so we have also included readings that describe the experiences of others to give you a sense of the challenges and rewards you can expect from the graduate school experience.

Graduate School

By Amira Rezec Wegenek and William Buskist

If you have decided on a career path that requires education beyond the associate's or bachelor's degree, you will need to apply to graduate school programs. This chapter addresses questions and issues relevant to the graduate school program application and selection process and offers advice for anyone considering application to experimental psychology or clinical psychology master's and/or doctoral programs. [...] Experimental psychology programs differ from other programs in that they provide primarily research training, whereas clinical psychology doctoral programs provide training in both research and therapy to prepare students as researchers and clinicians. This chapter offers critical information you can use that may give you an edge when it comes to choosing, applying to, and getting accepted into the right experimental psychology graduate program that suits you and your professional goals. The doctor of psychology (PsyD), master of social work (MSW), and marriage and family therapy (MFT) degree programs [...] do not emphasize research training but do value both research and practicum training in applicants [...].

Graduate Schools and Graduate Programs

A graduate school is an administrative body, usually directed by a dean, and creates policies regarding all graduate programs within a college or university. A graduate program is a group of faculty members organized around a particular subfield or subdiscipline, such as a graduate program in cognitive psychology or clinical psychology. These programs create their own admissions processes and criteria. At colleges and universities that have a centralized graduate school the application for a particular program is submitted to the graduate school. At schools that do not have centralized graduate schools, the application is submitted to the department in which the program resides (e.g., psychology or cognitive science) and then is forwarded to a selection committee within the graduate program. If you are applying for a doctor of philosophy (PhD) in psychology, you should decide on which program area(s) you want to specialize in before applying for admission.

Students often think that if they apply to a graduate school program that is ranked higher in national graduate school rankings than another graduate school overall it is necessarily a better program. For example, the National Research Council and U.S.

News and World Report both provide annual national rankings for graduate programs in psychology based on overall statistics, such as amount of grant money obtained and number of publications written by faculty. However, it is not true that a graduate school's national rankings necessarily reflect the esteem of each of its individual programs. For example, a very prestigious Ivy League school may have an excellent social psychology program with several faculty members who are famous in that field, but it may not have a very well-developed biological psychology or cognitive psychology program. Different graduate schools offer different strengths and weaknesses within each of their program's areas that are not always evident in overall graduate school rankings. However, individual program reputations can be discovered through a little research, as we describe later in this chapter.

The Graduate School Program Admissions Process

The typical graduate school program admissions process requires several components and involves multiple stages. Undergraduate applicants should e-mail departments requesting admissions materials no later than September of their senior year. Waiting longer may make it impossible for you to meet some of the earlier deadline requirements (e.g., January 1). The application is usually not considered complete until the graduate school receives the following items:

- application form,
- letter of intent,
- transcripts,
- letters of recommendation,
- GRE scores,
- Other materials required by the program, and
- an application fee.

Graduate schools forward completed applications to the appropriate admissions committee, which is usually made up of departmental administrators, faculty, and, sometimes, graduate student representatives. Admissions committees or the graduate program coordinator usually prescreen applications and then select some applicants to be interviewed by faculty. Some programs conduct interviews over the phone, whereas others conduct them in person. Students usually incur some travel costs to attend on-campus interviews, though some programs may subsidize these costs.

How Difficult Is It to Get into Graduate School?

Acceptance to graduate programs is extremely competitive, especially for highly regarded PhD programs. Clinical programs often have the most competitive entrance requirements. These very competitive programs typically admit students with a grade-point average (GPA) of 3.8 to 4.0, and the typical GRE score may be in the 1300 plus range. Other programs are less competitive, although the typical GPA of their students is still fairly high—generally in the 3.3 to 3.5 range.

If your GPA is in the lower range, you may wish to consider applying to master's programs if you do not get admitted into a PhD program. Performing at the "A" level in these programs can put you in a better position to be accepted into a PhD program in the future. Some undergraduate programs offer a master's program called a "5th-year program." The 5th-year program allows you to earn both your bachelor's and master's degree by adding 1 more year to the time it would normally take you to complete the bachelor's degree. During this year, you would take graduate-level courses and possibly complete a research project. Some 5th-year programs are accelerated graduate programs in which you earn your master's degree in 1 year. Whether you choose a 5th-year or traditional 2-year master's degree program, be aware that most PhD programs will require you to have completed a thesis in your master's program. The thesis is a written report of independent research. If you complete a master's program that does require a thesis and later apply to a graduate PhD program, the program may require you to complete a thesis after admission. There is another caution to consider if you plan to apply to a PhD or PsyD program after completing a master's program: Some doctorate programs do not accept transfer credits or master's thesis work completed in other programs and may require students to start over, increasing the time spent in school and cost.

If your GPA is low and you still wish to consider applying to PhD programs, there are some factors that might compensate for your low GPA. If you have a modest GPA (e.g., 3.2) but high GRE scores (1200 plus), a strong letter of intent, strong clinical or research experience, and great letters of recommendation, you may still be a viable applicant to competitive programs. However, high GRE scores do not necessarily make up for weak letters of recommendation or a weak letter of intent.

What Admissions Committees Look for in Applicants

Admissions committees are looking for applicants who are well prepared to begin graduate-level studies, are a good match to work with at least one faculty member in their program, have a good likelihood of success in the program, and know what they are getting themselves into. You can work to attain all of these attributes in almost any undergraduate program, big or small. You should try to perform your best academically to become well prepared for graduate-level studies and earn a high GPA. You should research programs carefully to gauge whether a program and its faculty members might be a good fit for you. Doing well academically, scoring high on standardized tests such as the GRE, and obtaining great letters of recommendation will serve as indicators of your potential for success in a graduate program.

One important step that you can take to become a stronger candidate (and that will help you to get a better idea of what is likely in store for you as a future graduate student) is to become involved in research during your undergraduate years. In fact, a survey in the 1990s asked clinical psychology admissions committees what the most important factors besides GPA and GRE scores were in developing the appropriate credentials for becoming a graduate student. Admissions committees listed research experience and letters of recommendation as the most heavily weighted factors (Stroup and Benjamin, 1982). These results likely reflect the feelings of many or most faculty that serve on admissions committees, not just clinical faculty.

Getting Involved in Research

Whether your own personal goal is to become a research psychologist, clinical psychologist, or educator or to go into industry, one of the most important things that you can do as an undergraduate psychology major is become involved with a research project. Do not be shy about contacting your professors or their graduate students in person or via e-mail to inquire about becoming involved in their research. You should ask them whether they have any volunteer, paid, or course-credit-earning positions open in their laboratory. If so, you should meet with them to discuss what type of project you can get involved with and what your duties would include to decide whether a particular laboratory position seems right for you. It may be more difficult to get research experience at some institutions than others. For this reason, do not feel as if the project that you work on has to be one that you are particularly interested in or the ideal project because your objective is to gain research experience in general. Any research experience is better than no research experience, and it will allow you to discover elements of the research process that you do and do not enjoy as well as to understand better what type of research you would or would not like to pursue in the future.

Research involvement allows you to get a firsthand look at what the research process is like, learn analytical

EXHIBIT 5.1

One Student's Perspective

Michelle Robison, BA, MA (Experimental Psychology), California State University Fullerton, "How Volunteering in Research Helped Me"

Getting involved as an undergraduate research assistant in different psychology laboratories was advantageous for me in a number of ways. First, I got to dabble in all aspects of the research process. I got the experience of doing a literature review, contributing ideas for methodology, collecting data, analyzing data, and writing parts of a paper. These research skills are essential to have, especially for somebody like me, who was considering entering graduate school. Second, I had an opportunity to establish relationships with professors I worked with and other students in the laboratory. These relationships have created opportunities and networking tools helpful for gaining graduate school admission and jobs. Third, being a research assistant allowed me to explore different areas of psychology to figure out where my interests fit best, which increased my knowledge of the field of psychology and helped me realize that I wanted to continue doing research in the field in which I had initially started. Finally, being a research assistant created a sense of responsibility and empowerment in me. It gave me the ability to contribute collaboratively and independently to important research projects and to prove my commitment to the field of psychology to myself and others.

and computer skills, and work with others. All these are practical skills that are applicable in the "real world" and academia. Becoming involved in research also allows you to get to know faculty members on a personal level. Most laboratories have regular meetings or regular journal discussion group meetings. Laboratory meetings usually involve all laboratory members, including the principle investigator (PI; usually the faculty who heads the laboratory), gathering to discuss ongoing projects. Journal club meetings usually involve a group meeting to discuss selected journal articles that are related to the group's research interests. In either type of meeting, it is common for a member to present research or lead a discussion on a research-related topic and for the faculty to interact with attendees. If you join a laboratory, you may end up working closely with a faculty member's graduate student or postdoctoral researcher. Although you will receive experience in research working mostly with this person, the laboratory and journal club meetings are great opportunities to interact with the PI directly. You may also wish to schedule personal appointments with the PI or attend appointments with your mentor (graduate student or postdoctoral supervisor) and the PI that are related to the project to which are assigned. Knowing the PI will give you more personal exposure to what it is like to be a faculty member at your college and will likely result in the PI writing you a more powerful and personal letter of recommendation (see the "Who to Ask for Letters of Recommendation" section). You can read about how volunteering in a laboratory was beneficial to one student in Exhibit 5.1.

What if You Attend a Small Undergraduate Institution?

If you come from a small undergraduate college that is not a major research institution and hope to be admitted to an experimental psychology or clinical psychology PhD program, do not fret. It is not usually the reputation or size of the school from which you obtain your undergraduate degree that is the most important factor in determining how an admissions committee views your application. Rather, it is what you do during your time as an undergraduate that is often considered more important. Did you excel among the top students in your department or college? Did you get involved in research at your school? If these opportunities were not available to you in your undergraduate program, did you seek out opportunities to be involved in research at other institutions besides your own undergraduate college? These considerations are important if you wish to apply to a graduate program but do not attend an undergraduate program with a strong reputation for research. Remember, admissions committees are looking for applicants who know what they are getting themselves into, are well prepared to embark on graduate studies, are a good match to work with faculty in the program, and have a strong likelihood of succeeding in the program. You can strive to acquire all of these attributes at most undergraduate programs if you are proactive in doing so.

Why You Should Join Clubs and Honor Societies

Colleges often have student organizations such as psychology clubs and psychology honor societies that you can join. These organizations may have GPA and other requirements for joining. Membership in these societies is considered to be an honor and is sometimes even noted on official transcript records as such. Examples of these clubs are Psi Chi (at the 4-year university level) and Psi Beta (at the community college level). Having such a distinction is a positive addition to your list of extracurricular experiences and to your resume. A more important reason to join than recognition is for the many other types of rewards that these organizations can offer. Both Psi Chi and Psi Beta provide academic recognition and professional growth to their members. Membership also includes benefits such as eligibility for research awards at regional conferences, student grants and awards, subscriptions to newsletters filled with helpful information regarding graduate school and other issues important to undergraduate psychology majors (e.g., *Eye on Psi Chi* quarterly newsletter), and more. Honor societies and clubs promote professional development by bringing in speakers to talk about their own careers in psychology or topics such as academic success, GRE preparation, and other topics relevant to undergraduates in psychology. Honor societies and clubs also foster community service opportunities.

Whether you join an honors or a nonhonors psychology club, you will undoubtedly be exposed to new learning experiences related to psychology, leadership opportunities, and friends who share a common interest—all of which might not have been available to you otherwise. You can not only potentially be exposed to valuable information by joining these organizations, but also attain important leadership skills. If you want to set yourself apart from other graduate school applicants, you should get involved in a leadership role within your honor society or club. Mere membership alone will not necessarily set you apart from other applicants against whom you are competing for a few open slots in a given graduate program. Leadership positions will help you to develop important skills, such as organizational, writing, and speaking skills. These abilities are useful in almost every type of career and can benefit you socially as well.

Speaking of your social life, being a part of an honor society or psychology club allows you to meet other psychology majors with interests similar to yours. Members often network with one another and alumni, use the club to form study groups, compare notes about instructors and classes, and sometimes even investigate potential careers together.

If your school does not have a psychology club or psychology honor society, you may be able to find a club in a related field that can meet these needs (e.g., look for a human development, communications, sociology, or biology student club). Find one that is right for you, and reap the benefits! Go to http://www.psichi.org and http://psibeta.org/site for more information about Psi Chi and Psi Beta, respectively.

How to Research Graduate School Programs

The best place to start when trying to find out which graduate school programs best meet your educational and career goals is the American Psychological Association's (2009) book *Graduate Study In Psychology 2010*. This book can be purchased or may be found in the reference section of your college or university library. This book contains information about over 600 graduate programs, including the number of applications received by a program, number of individuals accepted in each program, dates for applications and admission, types of information required for an application (e.g., GRE scores, letters of recommendations, documentation concerning volunteer or clinical experience), in-state and out-of-state tuition costs, availability of internships and scholarships, employment information of graduates, orientation and emphasis of departments and programs, and more. The American Psychological Association also provides information regarding graduate study as well as many resources for current graduate students at the American Psychological Association for Graduate Students (APAGS) web site (http://www.apa.org/apags/). APAGS offers many resources for current graduate students and even publishes an online magazine geared specifically toward graduate students (gradPSYCH: see http://gradpsych.apags.org/). Graduate students who join, have many other resources available to them, including discounted journal subscriptions, the ability to purchase access to PsycINFO, scholarships, internship and career services, listserv subscriptions, and access to liability insurance for graduate students. It may be worthwhile to visit the APAGS web site to learn more about topics and issues that are pertinent to graduate students, even if you are not a current graduate student but considering the prospect of entering graduate school.

You should also ask faculty whom you know for suggestions regarding which graduate school programs might best suit your needs as well as research different programs on your own via the Internet. Carefully read program descriptions and the various faculty members' biographies and consider how many faculty members a program has who specialize in different subdisciplines. This research will give you a good idea of how well represented your chosen subdiscipline is at the prospective school. This datum also is important because it may give you a clue as to whether there would be many resources in terms of potential mentors and funding devoted to that subdiscipline. In addition, it is important to make sure that there are at least one or two faculty members in the program with whom you share common interests and with whom you would like to study.

Of course, in a perfect world, you could be 100% logical in your decision-making process and not factor in variables such as your preference for geographic location when deciding where to apply to graduate school. You will be in graduate school for a limited time, which may provide you a great opportunity to live in a new city. If you are willing to move for a few years rather than staying close to home, then you will have many more options for attending graduate school. However, it would be a waste of time to apply and interview at schools that you would never truly consider attending because of location. See Exhibit 5.2 to learn about how one student found the right graduate school fit.

Can You Contact Faculty at Prospective Graduate Programs?

You should consider contacting faculty members in prospective graduate programs to ask them about their research and whether they plan to take on graduate

EXHIBIT 5.2

One Student's Perspective

Rebecca Hetey, BA, doctoral student, Stanford University "Finding the Right Graduate School Fit"

Early in my undergraduate career, I did not really know what graduate school was. After a few years of being a psychology major and working in a number of labs alongside graduate students and professors, I gained more insight into what graduate school entailed. In my junior year, as my passion for psychology blossomed and my interests became more refined, I knew that the next step in my career was to apply to doctor of philosophy (PhD) programs in social psychology.

Just as I had not originally known what graduate school was, I was not sure how to go about finding programs to which I could apply. There were so many programs scattered about the country with vastly different philosophies of graduate education and a seemingly infinite number of potential advisors with whom I could work. I needed to start somewhere, so I thought about the authors whose work had inspired me most in terms of the direction my own independent research had taken. I scanned the bibliographies of some of the most personally meaningful papers I had written in college and found that a few professors popped up again and again. Research, I realized, was an ongoing dialogue, an ongoing debate. I wanted my own voice as a scholar to be shaped by those whose voices I found most compelling and most enlightening.

I made a list of these potential advisors and started looking up details of the programs at their home institutions. The Internet has greatly aided in this process, as virtually all psychology graduate programs have very detailed web sites that spell out the admissions requirements and the requirements of the program itself. By examining the information on these web sites, I started to piece together what it would be like to be a student at a particular school. [*Continued on next page.*]

students in their laboratory in the near future. As long as your interaction with faculty is professional and not seen as an attempt to win them over or unduly influence them, contact is appropriate. You can ask faculty whether they recommend any readings for you that will help you to learn more about their work as well. Consider the following situation as an example of why it is wise to contact a graduate program's faculty members before applying to a graduate program. Suppose you apply to a program and list Professor Jones and Professor Smith as your preferred potential major professors (i.e., faculty advisors). Little do you know that Professor Jones is nearing retirement and not taking on new students, and Professor Smith is going on sabbatical the next year and not planning on taking on any new students until the following year. This information would be very useful to have before applying to a program in a particular year. Alternatively, you may apply to this particular program because Professor Jones's biography on the department's web site stares that she has published on a specific research topic that greatly interests you. Then you do not learn until meeting her at an official interview that although she is well known for her research on that particular research topic, her laboratory has since shifted its focus to a completely different topic and she no longer conducts research on the topic that initially interested you in her work. There is no way that you could have known any of this information without personally contacting prospective faculty advisors. Contacting faculty members before you apply

EXHIBIT 5.2 (cont'd)

The process by which you select a graduate school is very different from the process by which you selected an undergraduate institution to attend. Deciding where to apply to college is often largely driven by the overall reputation of the university. The quality of any particular graduate program in a specific field of psychology, however, is not reliably gleaned from the reputation of an entire institution. The best programs might be at universities you might never have heard of, and the most reputable university might not have a strong program. Beyond this consideration, you would likely be unhappy at the best program in the world if it had no professors who shared your research interests and with whom you could work.

I did not know this all-important information when I first started my graduate school search. I quickly realized that to find the proverbial "needle in the haystack" that is the perfect graduate program in psychology, I would need to tap into all of the resources I had at my disposal, including professors with whom I had worked and graduate student mentors whom I met within their laboratories.

They explained to me how graduate students at schools I would be applying to would be important resources for me and instructed me to ask these potential peers about the overall atmosphere of the program, funding issues, living in the area, and how the faculty and students interacted in the program. I was told to specifically seek out and speak with students who worked with the professors I was interested in having as my potential major advisors, as the student-major advisor relationship can have such a great impact on one's graduate school experience.

The time I invested in my careful and thorough search for the best programs to apply to made all the difference when it came time for me to decide which school I would ultimately attend. I had a number of good options from which to choose, and after recently completing my first year of graduate school at Stanford University, I can honestly say that I could not be happier with my choice.

to graduate programs can save you valuable time and help to inform your decision as to which programs to apply.

Who to Ask for Letters of Recommendation

Most graduate programs require at least three letters of recommendation. It is wise to select letter writers who can speak to your preparedness for graduate studies in their letters of recommendation. Before you ask professors to write a letter of recommendation on your behalf when you apply to a graduate program, consider whether they really know you or whether you are just one of the students in the crowd who earned an "A" in their course. Can they speak to your intelligence, communication skills, organizational abilities, creativity, maturity, knowledge in the field, ability to work well with others, or anything else? It is to your advantage to request letters from professors who know you personally through working with you in a laboratory or internship setting. Your letter of recommendation will be more personal and more informative. (On a side note, it is common practice for professors to collaborate with their graduate students or postdoctoral researchers in writing letters of recommendation on behalf of an undergraduate student if that student actually worked more closely with one of those laboratory members.)

Next, you can ask other professors who know your academic ability, maturity level, and so on to write letters for you. You might want to ask current or past supervisors from related positions that you have held to write a letter. Your letter writers should be able to speak to why you are well prepared to continue your education in psychology at the graduate level. It does not make sense to have a swimming coach write you a letter that says how devoted and hardworking of a person you are in general because this information does not directly address your preparedness or potential to succeed in a psychology graduate program. It is a good idea to set up a short appointment to meet with each of your letter writers and to talk about your goals and education plans. Another helpful step to take is to provide your letter writers with an unofficial copy of your transcripts, a resume or list of college activities, and/or a short narrative about yourself and your career goals. This information will give them a more well-rounded picture of you as an individual that they can incorporate into their letter along with the usual facts regarding how they know you, how well you performed as a student or worker, and what skills you demonstrated in that capacity.

Be sure to ask for your letters of recommendation well in advance of your application due dates. Four to 6 weeks is a reasonable amount of advance notice to provide a letter writer. If you provide your letter writers a list, of graduate schools to which you are applying, be sure to include on that list a bolded, all caps, underlined "**<u>APPLICATION DUE DATE</u>**" next to each graduate school's name. For those schools that do not yet accept electronic applications and request that you submit letters via surface mail, always include stamped, addressed envelopes and any supplemental paperwork or special directions necessary to include with the letter. Do not worry too much about having to ask you letter writers for another letter later on should you decide to apply to another program unexpectedly. They will usually be happy to do so and can simply modify or mail out the original letter that they wrote on your behalf. Be sure to thank them for their help personally with a letter or phone call. It is also considered courteous to keep your letter writers posted on your progress.

What to Include in Your Letter of Intent

The letter of intent is a brief letter of introduction that is included with your application that should include information about your educational and career goals, your academic background, and why you plan to pursue graduate studies. It should be no longer than two typed (single-spaced) pages and should be written clearly and concisely. Be sure to proofread your letter of intent for typos and grammatical, errors, as these mistakes will reflect poorly on you as an applicant. There is no strict format for the letter of intent, but there are critical pieces of information that should be included. It should contain a clear statement of your educational and career goals, a brief description of how your interest in your chosen area of psychology developed, a description of your academic history and special skills you may have acquired during your undergraduate years (e.g., statistical skills, computer programming skills, research or clinical skills), how your undergraduate educational or work experiences have led you to pursue graduate studies in the field, and why you have chosen to apply to that particular program.

Although some applications may call the letter of intent an autobiographical or personal statement, it is best to avoid including personal stories that have to do with friends or family members and to keep your letter professional. Avoid stating that you are interested in psychology because you "want to help others," as this statement is cliche and does not speak to your potential or desire to be a research scientist. Faculty members who read your statement of intent are scientists who have devoted their lives to science and academic endeavors and are more likely to want to read about why you are interested in psychology for reasons of scientific curiosity rather than your personal reasons for wishing to pursue a graduate degree. It is appropriate to list the names of faculty members in the potential graduate school program whose research interests match your interests. Be sure that you express your interests so that they are specific enough to show you have seriously considered the program and research area in which you want to work but not so narrow as to make you appear closed minded. The following are some good reference sources to use to help you write your letter of intent.

Books:

- *Getting In: A Step-by-Step Plan for Gaining Admission to Graduate School in Psychology* (American Psychological Association, 2007).
- *Graduate Study in Psychology 2010* (American Psychological Association, 2009).
- *Preparing for Graduate Study in Psychology*: 101 Questions and Answers (Buskist and Burke, 2007).
- *Applying to Graduate School in Psychology: Advice From Successful Students and Psychologists* (Kracen and Wallace, 2008).
- *Insider's Guide to Graduate Programs in Clinical and Counseling Psychology* (Norcross, Sayette, and Mayne, 2008).

Web sites:

- American Psychological Association "A Guide to Getting Into Graduate School" (http://www.apa.org/ed/getin.html).
- The Association for Psychological Science *Observer* online articles (http://www.psychologicalscience.org/observer).

GREs and the Psychology Subject Test

The GRE is a standardized test that is required by almost all graduate programs. This computerized test focuses on measuring abstract thinking skills in the areas of math, vocabulary, and analytical writing. Some graduate programs will also require you to take a specific subject area test in psychology as well. There is no need to get overly nervous about these tests (as many students do) because there are many ways to prepare for them. On each subsection of the exam, there are a finite number of types of questions that you can practice answering. Once you learn strategies for approaching each type of question, you will be ready to handle all of the questions that could possibly be asked on the exam. Free practice GRE exams and access to practice question banks are available at the GRE web site (http://www.ets.org). There are also GRE preparation books and software programs that you can purchase. Check these resources out at your local bookstore. Private companies and some university extension offices also offer GRE preparation classes or workshops. Popular courses are offered by Kaplan Educational Center Ltd. (http://www.kaptest.com), Princeton Review (http://www.princetonreview.come/home.asp), and Number 2 (online only; http://number2.com). Choosing the option to take a prep course is more costly than preparing via books and software, but you should choose the route that is best for you.

You can also find books and software programs to help you prepare for the Psychology Subject Test at bookstores and online. You may also wish to prepare by looking over your old course materials and reviewing a good introductory psychology textbook. According to the GRE web site, the Psychology Subject Test consists of 140 multiple-choice questions, some of which are based on sets of questions related to a description of an experiment or graphs of psychological functions. According to the site, about 40% of questions are experimental or natural science oriented, covering topics including learning, language, memory, thinking, sensation and perception, physiological psychology, ethology, and comparative psychology. About 43% of test questions are social or social science oriented, covering topics including clinical and abnormal, developmental, personality, and social psychology. About 17% of questions are general psychology questions covering topics including the history of psychology, applied psychology, measurement, research designs, and statistics. Practice tests and preparation tips are available at the GRE web site (http://www.ets.org).

What if You Do Not Ace the GRE?

If you do not perform as well as you had hoped on the GRE, you may retake it. You should definitely focus on improving your GRE scores to make your application more competitive, but do not think that all schools treat these scores in the same way. It is true that some schools may use these scores as screening devices to weed out applicants. However, if you do not perform well on the GRE, there are other factors that may outweigh this particular element in your application. First, strong letters of recommendation and research experience can compensate for low GRE scores. In addition, having a faculty member in the program to which you have applied recommend that you be given an interview may overshadow low GRE scores in some cases. A strong statement of intent that reflects your experience and potential to succeed in the program is also important.

If you want to retake the GRE for any reason, you may only do so on certain dates and times of the year (see http://www.ets.org). Be sure to find out whether the graduate school programs to which you are applying will average the scores from multiple attempts of the GRE or will take the highest scores from different attempts. Determining this information should play a role in your decision about whether to retake the GRE and what strategy to use in preparing to retake it. For example, you may perform poorly on the verbal subsection of the GRE and be content with your score on the math subsection. If all the programs to which you are applying take the highest score on each subsection from each attempt, then you can plan to spend most of your preparation time focusing on how to improve your verbal score. However, if the programs to which you are applying take the average of scores on each subsection from multiple attempts, then you should attempt to increase your scores on all subsections of the test. This way, you can avoid potentially lowering your score on one or more subsections as the result of retaking the exam. The graduate program coordinator at prospective graduate school programs should be able to provide the answers to these questions.

What to Do at Your Interviews

If you are invited to a school for an interview, keep in mind that the interview serves a specific purpose for both you and the admissions committee at the prospective program. The program admissions committee wants you to be able to meet with prospective advisors and for both of you to discern whether you would work well together if you were to be offered admission to the program. Second, the committee wants you to get an accurate view of the university, program, its faculty, and its students so that you can make an informed decision should they decide to admit you. As such, the goals of the admissions committee also serve you well. You will have a chance to ask questions and learn as much as you can about the prospective program and your potential faculty mentors in the program while you are there, which should surely help you to make your decision about whether to accept an offer of admission. The best thing you can do is to be yourself, behave professionally throughout the entire visit, be prepared to talk intelligently about what research-related experiences you have had in the past or hope to have in the future, and be ready to show your interest and learn about the program by being prepared to ask questions. In the following sections, we offer several tips on questions that you may wish to consider asking different people while on your visit. These questions are organized into two main categories, those about financial support and those about mentorship available in the program.

Questions to Ask About Financial Support

Most PhD programs offer financial support to their students. In some programs, financial support is guaranteed to all students in the program for a certain number of years. In other programs, the amount and guarantee of financial support are tied to the students' major professor (i.e., official advisor of record). In these latter programs, student funding may come from the major professor's grants and not from departmental funds. Master's programs typically do not provide financial support guarantees but may offer opportunities for students to earn money through teaching assistantships and/or research assistantships. The following questions address important funding issues that you should ask program representatives about during your interview:

- How are students supported financially?
- Does the program provide general funding to all students from the same source, or is a student's funding tied to the specific major professor with whom he or she works?
- If funding is provided by the program, are students required to serve as teaching assistants or research assistants as a condition for funding? If so, what is the typical time commitment required for such positions?
- For how many years is funding guaranteed? Does funding typically discontinue after a certain number of years in the program?
- Do students typically receive support in the summer?
- Are paid teaching assistantships or research assistantships available during the summer?
- Where do students obtain funds to attend professional conferences? Do students have to be presenting work at the conference to receive funding?
- Is there subsidized student housing available? If so, is there a waiting list for this housing?

Questions to Ask About Faculty Advisors

The relationship that you have with your faculty advisor (also called major professor) is important, as it can greatly influence your entire graduate school experience. This person is going to be your mentor, your colleague, and your "boss." He or she is going to determine whether you continue in the program by reviewing your performance every year via written report and/or grades and, at least to some extent, determine the course of your career. You will want to ask graduate students or postdoctoral researchers who work with your potential faculty advisor(s) questions to get a sense of what it might be like to work closely with this person. Of course, you should take into account that their answers will reflect their personal experiences and will not necessarily be completely representative of the professor because we all have unique personalities that differentially affect our working relationships with others. However, you can glean a lot of information and see potential red flags easily when asking these questions. The following is a list of potential questions that you might consider tactfully asking graduate students and postdoctoral researchers during your interview:

- What is it like to work for this faculty member?
- Is the faculty member a hands-off supervisor or a micromanager?
- Does the professor provide guidance when needed, or is he or she too busy to mentor students?
- Is the professor pleasant and reasonable to work alongside?
- Does the professor allow students the freedom to develop their own ideas?
- Is credit and authorship assigned to students fairly when it comes to publishing joint research?
- Is the professor eager to publish or slow to publish with students?
- Does the professor give students the freedom to work on their dissertation or thesis projects to complete the degree program in a timely manner?
- Does the professor require students to work on laboratory grant projects that are not related to the students' own publications or graduate work or interests?

Should You Go to Graduate School Now or Wait?

By Tara Kuther

You've planned on attending graduate school, but with graduation just around the corner, are you ready for another three to eight years of graduate education? Should you take time off before graduate study? This is a personal decision and there's no definitive right or wrong answer. However, if you have any doubts about your educational and career aspirations take your time and rethink your goals. What are your reasons for taking time off before attending graduate school?

You're Exhausted

Are you tired? Exhaustion is understandable. After all, you've just spent 16 or more years in school. If this is your primary reason for taking time off, consider whether your fatigue will ease over the summer. You've got two or three months off before grad school starts; can you rejuvenate? Depending on the program and degree, graduate school takes anywhere from three to eight or more years to complete. If you're certain that graduate school is in your future, perhaps you shouldn't wait.

You Need to Prepare

There are also many good reasons for taking time off. If you feel unprepared for grad school, a year off may enhance your application. For example, you might take a prep-course for GRE or other standardized tests required for admission. Improving your scores on standardized tests is essential for at least two reasons. First, it will enhance your chances of being accepted to the program of your choice. Perhaps more importantly, financial aid in the form of scholarships and awards are distributed based on standardized test scores.

You Need Research Experience

Research experience will also enhance your application. Maintain contacts with the faculty at your undergraduate institution and seek research experiences with them. Such opportunities are beneficial because faculty members can write more personal letters of recommendation. Plus you gain insight into what it's like to work in your field.

You Need Work Experience

Other reasons for taking a year or two off between undergraduate and graduate school include gaining work experience. Some fields, such as nursing and business, recommend and expect some work experience. In addition, the lure of money and the chance to save is hard to resist. Saving money often is a good idea because grad school is expensive and it's unlikely that you'll be able to work many hours, if any, while you're in school.

Many students worry whether they'll return to school after a year or two away from the grind. That's a realistic concern, but take the time that you need to be sure that grad school is right for you. Graduate school requires a great deal of motivation and the ability to work independently. Generally, students who are more interested and committed to their studies are more likely to be successful. Time off may increase your desire and commitment to your goals.

Finally, recognize that attending grad school several years after completing the BA is not unusual. More than one-half of grad students in the US are over age 30. If you wait before going to grad school, be prepared to explain your decision, what you learned, and how it improves your candidacy. Time off can be beneficial if it enhances your credentials and prepares you for the stresses and strains of grad school.

Organizing Your Personal Statement

An Outline to Get You Started

By Merry J. Sleigh

One of the biggest challenges when applying to graduate school is writing the personal statement, particularly given that the personal statement is one of the most important criteria for graduate admission (Norcross, Kohout, and Wicherski, 2006). Applicants have a restricted amount of space to describe their past accomplishments, future plans, and interest in a particular graduate program. Despite impressive credentials and experiences, students often don't know how to get started. As suggested below, getting started can begin with organizing the information that needs to go into your personal statement.

Opening Paragraph: 4–6 Sentences

The selection committee will read many personal statements each year, and the majority of these statements start in a similar fashion. Students tend to describe themselves in terms of their academic work, high level of motivation, or desire to help others. Because these characteristics are common among applicants, they will not distinguish you as an individual. I must admit that when I had the opportunity to review graduate applicants, it was challenging to remember which details of the many applications went with which individual.

Think of the opening paragraph as an opportunity for you to paint a "mental picture" of yourself for your readers. Identify something about you or your experiences that make you unique and well-suited for graduate training—a fact that illustrates the type of person you are. Incorporate this element into the opening paragraph. Your goal is for the committee to be interested enough in the information to retain it and use it as a central point around which to organize the other details in your packet and to help them remember you. For example, you might have traveled extensively, been raised in a foster home, led a service project in your community, paid for your own college education, overcome a physical challenge, survived a great loss, or double-majored. Be thoughtful about the mental picture that you choose; you do not want to invoke pity, raise a red flag, or create a complicated self-portrait. Keep the paragraph short and focused, four to six sentences in length. The point is to help the selection committee see you as a person, not just another folder.

Tips

- Keep this section short and organized. Your goal is to briefly introduce yourself.

Merry J. Sleigh, "Organizing Your Personal Statement: An Outline to Get You Started," *Eye on Psi Chi*, vol. 13, no. 4.

- You have a limited amount of space, so avoid stating ideas that your readers already know (e.g., "I love learning about psychology" or "I want to get a graduate degree in psychology so that I can continue to learn about why people do the things they do"). Your application to a psychology graduate program is evidence that you enjoy the field of psychology and would like to obtain a graduate degree.
- Don't begin your statement with a quotation unless it is impossible to express the idea better.
- First impressions matter, so take the time to create a strong opening. Good writing is a process, requiring feedback and multiple drafts.
- You might choose to write this section last. Put together the rest of the paper, and then think about the overall image you would like to present to introduce yourself and the upcoming credentials.
- Read Osborne (1996), and Appleby and Appleby (2007) for advice about how to appropriately incorporate personal information into your statement.

Academic Accomplishments: 5–7 Sentences

You might choose to have a second paragraph that emphasizes aspects of your academic work. Many students make the mistake of repeating information that can be found elsewhere in the application. Remember, the selection committee will have your transcript, GPA, and GRE score. You do not need to repeat this information unless repeating it serves a purpose. For example, if you want to address why your GRE score does not represent your ability or how your grades dramatically improved after your first year, this paragraph might be the ideal place to do so. Otherwise, use this paragraph to expand on, or supplement, the information you have already provided.

As you write about the work you have done in college, link the activities to skills and qualities that you possess. Avoid simply listing activities you have done or classes you have taken. Such lists do not tell the reader much beyond the fact that you stayed busy. Similarly, don't list a series of adjectives that you feel describe you. Instead, offer evidence that leads the reader to conclude that those adjectives fit you. For example, you could explain that you intentionally selected challenging coursework because you are willing to work hard and are motivated to learn. You might reveal that you worked full-time while maintaining a high GPA to show that you have good time management skills and the ability to multi-task. This presentation is more effective than simply writing something like, "I am willing to work hard, am motivated to learn, and have good time management skills."

Tips

- Share your accomplishments honestly, but maintain a humble tone. You may be competing against other applicants who have a higher GPA or stronger GRE scores than you.
- Quantify your accomplishments when possible. For example, provide your class rank (e.g., 15 out of 475; top 10%) rather than making vague statements such as "high GPA" or "top student."
- Feel free to share activities not directly related to your field, especially if they reveal positive aspects of who you are. • Be specific. "I helped our Psi Chi officers organize a book drive for a local children's shelter" is more informative than "I was an active member of Psi Chi."
- See Appleby (2003) for an examination of transcript features that may need to be addressed in a personal statement.
- Start concentrating on writing smooth transition sentences to start each paragraph. Show the reader how this paragraph logically follows the preceding one. Your reader should understand

your overall organization as well as the main idea of each paragraph.

Research Experience: 5–8 Sentences

Most graduate programs include a research component and research experience as an important factor in admission decisions (Collins, 2001; Norcross, et al., 2006). Thus, documenting your research experiences can be a critical aspect of your application. The term "research experience" can include a range of participation from entering data to publishing independent work. You need to be specific about the research skills you have acquired. "I worked in a child development lab during my senior year" needs additional details such as, "I was responsible for greeting parents, explaining informed consent, and videotaping parent-baby conversations." Graduate programs appreciate students who understand and are prepared for research training—from the mundane to the more challenging aspects. Thus, even limited exposure to research may be useful to include in this paragraph.

You also can use this paragraph to share your other relevant characteristics. For example, let the reader know if you took the initiative to create a research opportunity or were given additional laboratory responsibilities as a result of your efforts. Make sure to quantify the length and/or level of participation. Working in a laboratory for three semesters reveals a higher level of commitment and perseverance than one semester of effort. As you focus on your research experience, make sure to share credit where it is due. Your selection committee includes faculty who will serve as research mentors for incoming students and will appreciate a student who respects the lab team and faculty advisor.

Tips

- Keep in mind that you will be conveying your attitude toward research alongside your research experiences. Be thoughtful about the attitude you want to express (e.g., Do you work well independently? Are you a strong team player?).
- Your research experience does not have to directly relate to your field of interest in graduate school, as many research skills are transferable.
- Don't forget to include research-related activities, such as applying for grants, receiving travel funding for a conference, or being nominated for an award.

Employment/Volunteer Work/Clinical Experience: 5–8 Sentences

Graduate programs invest a great deal of time and money in their students; therefore, selection committees want to choose students who are knowledgeable about and prepared for training. Each program might place its training emphasis in a slightly different area. You need to think about each program to which you are applying and identify the qualities that are desired by that program. For example, if you are applying to an industrial/organizational program, the school is likely to be interested in any statistical skills, legal training, or management experience you have. If you are applying to a clinical program, the school will want applicants who understand issues such as confidentiality, professional boundaries, and mirroring. Being able to identify these qualities demonstrates to the program that you are knowledgeable about the training they provide.

After you have identified the qualities desired by your program, carefully consider how your work, either paid or volunteer, has helped you develop these skills and an awareness of the issues related to your field of interest (see Appleby, Keenan, and Mauer, 1999, for a list of characteristics valued by graduate programs). You may not have direct experience in your field of interest, so think broadly about how the work you have done translates to graduate training. Perhaps you held a position which required you to do public speaking; those speeches may have helped you develop an awareness of your audience, an ability to communicate complex ideas in an accessible fashion, develop rapport with a diverse group of people, project a professional demeanor, or showcase technological savvy. Write about the aspects that are most relevant to the degree you are seeking. When possible, clarify to the selection committee how your capabilities will benefit you and your program during graduate training.

Graduate committees recognize that the skills you can acquire as an undergraduate are limited, so don't exaggerate what you have done. The committee is looking for students who have a good foundation on which to build during graduate school. They are not seeking applicants who believe they have already mastered the necessary skills. Instead of phrasing an idea as "Because of my exceptional people skills, I was asked to do intake interviews for new clients," you might want to use, "Handling the intake interviews for new clients challenged me to build rapport with a variety of personalities and strengthened my time management skills." Show humility and a willingness to learn.

Tips

- Avoid using local abbreviations or jargon that will be unfamiliar to your committee. Use the full name of places where you have worked or positions you have held (e.g., Mount Holly Juvenile Detention and Attention Center vs. Attention Center; Resident Counselor vs. R.C.).
- Look for overall strengths as well as specific skills. If you are involved in a wide range of activities, emphasize the breadth of your experiences. If you have devoted yourself to a particular cause, emphasize depth and commitment.
- Read Landrum (2002) for a variety of activities that prepare students for graduate training and Khemlani (2008) for suggestions about how to consider your personal statement from the perspective of your readers.

Future Plans/Goodness-of-Fit: 6–9 Sentences

Typically, graduate programs will ask you to state your future plans. This paragraph allows you to describe your goals and explain how you are a good fit for a particular graduate program. In order to explain fit, you need to investigate each program to which you are applying. If you have done your homework, then you will have picked each program because it has characteristics that appeal to you. Show the selection committee that you are familiar with these characteristics, and that these characteristics are a good match with your career goals. Selection committees will not be impressed with over-the-top flattery that praises features that apply to most graduate programs (e.g., "I would love to learn from your very accomplished faculty"). Instead, consider unique elements that attracted you to that specific program. Perhaps the location of the program will afford you a professional experience that you would not get otherwise. Perhaps the program's heavy focus on practical experience matches your future goals. Perhaps your interests match the program's specialization. Reveal your familiarity with the program and closely tie those facts to your career goals. You want to explain how the program meets your training needs and how you are a good fit for the structure of that specific program.

Some schools will ask you to mention specific faculty members whose expertise matches your current interests. If asked, a good rule of thumb is to mention two or three faculty members with similar research programs. Demonstrate that you are familiar with their expertise while avoiding excessive name-dropping or flattery. "My current interests match most closely with Dr. Susan Doe's work with fetal alcohol exposure in rats" is preferable to "I am impressed with Dr. Susan Doe's many publications in prestigious journals dealing with rats and alcohol." Mentioning more than one faculty member is useful, as individual faculty members may retire, move, go on sabbatical, or have full labs. Although you may have very defined interests, be careful about seeming narrow or close-minded. Just as you may have changed majors in college, it is possible that your research/training focus may shift slightly in graduate school.

Tips

- Avoid writing a generic paragraph and using it for every program to which you apply. The selection committee easily will identify this strategy. If you can't figure out what is special about the program, then why apply?
- Have plans for your future with defined interests. Recent research suggests that successful versus unsuccessful statements are more likely to emphasize the applicant's identity as a young scientist, rather than primarily focusing on the applicant's past accomplishments (Brown, 2004).
- Have realistic plans for your future. For example, it is unlikely that you will open a private practice in clinical psychology immediately following graduation. You do not want the selection committee to perceive you as naïve and/or unprepared.
- Read Birchmeier, Shore, and McCormick (2008) and Dirlam (1998) for information about identifying the characteristics of graduate programs and assessing your fit.

Concluding Paragraph: 4 or 5 sentences

If you have done your job, the selection committee should have a clear idea of who you are and what you would bring to their program by this point in the paper. Thus, your goal for the last paragraph is to close the paper on a strong note. One option is to return to the original picture that you painted in the opening paragraph. Reference the idea again as a bookend, connecting the imagery at the end of the paper to the imagery that opened the paper. This reminder helps package all of the information in the body of the paper around a central idea of who you are.

This paragraph also affords you the opportunity to express your willingness to meet with the selection committee and/or provide them with additional information. Show enthusiasm about the possibility of being accepted to the program, but don't write as though your acceptance is guaranteed. "I would welcome the opportunity to express my interest in your program in person" is better than "I look forward to being a graduate student in your program" or "I will work very hard in your graduate program." This paragraph is your last chance to make a lasting impression.

Tips

- Stay short and focused. The last paragraph is not the place to insert important, new information.
- Seek feedback from professors once your paper is written. Your paper ultimately needs to reflect you; however, you should consider the input from multiple reviewers.
- Revise, revise, and revise. Good writing is a process that takes time. Many students submit the first or second draft of their personal statement; revising beyond that might just give you a competitive edge.

References

Appleby, D. (2003, Winter). What does your transcript say about you, and what can you do if it says things you don't like? *Eye on Psi Chi, 7*(2), 21-23.

Appleby, D. C., and Appleby, K. M. (2007, Spring). How do avoid the kisses of death in the graduate school application process. *Eye on Psi Chi, 11*(3), 20-21.

Appleby, D., Keenan, J., and Mauer, B. (1999, Spring). Applicant characteristics valued by graduate programs in psychology. *Eye on Psi Chi, 3*(3), 39.

Birchmeier, Z., Shore, C., and McCormick, S. (2008, Summer). Getting in: Finding your fit in a graduate program. *Eye on Psi Chi, 12*(4), 24-27.

Brown, R. M. (2004). Self composed: Rhetoric in psychology personal statements. *Written Communication, 21*(3), 242-260.

Collins, L. H. (2001, Winter). Does research experience make a significant difference in graduate admissions? *Eye on Psi Chi, 5*(2), 26-28.

Dirlam, D. K. (1998, Fall). Applications that make the schools you want, want you. *Eye on Psi Chi, 3*(1), 29-30.

Khemlani, S. (2008). Bolstering an application. In A. Kracen and J. L. Wallace (Eds.) *Applying to graduate school in psychology: Advice from successful students and prominent psychologists* (pp. 129-149). Washington, DC: American Psychological Association.

Landrum, R. E. (2002, Winter). Maximizing undergraduate opportunities: The value of research and other experiences. *Eye on Psi Chi, 6*(2), 15-18.

Norcross, J. C., Kohout, J. L., and Wicherski, M. (2006, Winter). Graduate admissions in psychology: I. The application process. *Eye on Psi Chi, 10*(2), 28-29, 42-43.

Osborne, R. E. (1996, Fall). The "personal" side of graduate school personal statements. *Eye on Psi Chi, 1*(1), 14-15.

Kisses of Death in the Graduate School Application Process

By Drew C. Appleby and Karen M. Appleby

A survey of psychology graduate admissions committee chairs revealed 5 categories of mistakes applicants make that diminish their probability of acceptance. We discuss 3 strategies that psychology departments can use to decrease the likelihood that students will commit these mistakes in their graduate school applications and provide suggestions that will help students avoid these mistakes.

The ideal student, seen through the eyes of graduate faculty, is gifted and creative, very bright and extremely motivated to learn, perfectly suited to the program, eager to actively pursue the lines of inquiry valued by the faculty, pleasant, responsible, and devoid of serious personal problems.

—Keith-Spiegel and Wiederman (2000, p. 32)

This statement indicates that applicants must convey these impressions to graduate school admissions committees throughout the application process to gain acceptance into graduate programs. Numerous authors have offered advice to undergraduate psychology majors about gaining admission to graduate programs during the past decade (Appleby, 2003a; Buskist and Sherburne, 1996; Keith-Spiegel and Wiederman, 2000; Kinder and Walfish, 2001; Kuther, 2003, 2004; Landrum and Davis, 2003; Lloyd, 2001; Morgan and Korschgen, 2005; Peterson's, 2001; Sayette, Mayne, and Norcross, 2004; Taylor-Cooke and Appleby, 2002). Despite this wealth of valuable information, few authors advise students about what they should *not* do when applying to graduate school. When authors do offer this advice, few support it with data.

We surveyed chairs of graduate school admissions committees in psychology about the characteristics of graduate school candidates that decrease their chances for acceptance (i.e., kisses of death [KODs]). Our data provide faculty who mentor, advise, and teach psychology majors with strategies to enable their students to avoid KODs when they apply to graduate school.

Drew Appleby and Karen Appleby, "Kisses of Death in the Graduate School Application Process," *Teaching of Psychology,* vol. 33, no. 1, pp. 19–24.

Method

We mailed a letter addressed to the Chair of the Graduate Admissions Committee to each of the 457 psychology graduate programs listed in the American Psychological Association's (2001) *Graduate Study in Psychology 2001*. The letter explained the purpose of the study and asked participants to provide "one or two examples of kisses of death you have encountered during your career." We defined KODs in the letter as "aberrant types of information that cause graduate admissions committees to reject otherwise strong applicants."

Data Analysis

Eighty-eight of the 457 chairs (19%) returned their surveys, and these responses yielded 156 examples of KODs. This relatively low response rate is common in qualitative research that uses open-ended questions because, although this type of question gives respondents freedom to "expand on ideas," it often "requires more time to answer than closed questions" (Thomas and Nelson, 2001, p. 263). We qualitatively analyzed the 156 examples of KODs according to the following procedures (Miles and Huberman, 1994; Patton, 1990). First, we independently inductively analyzed each example (McCracken, 1988). This approach required us to consider each response individually and to identify its central theme (poorly written application, harmful letter of recommendation, or lack of interest in research). Second, we independently grouped these inductive findings into categories, or "words, phrases, sentences, or whole paragraphs, connected ... to a specific setting" (Miles and Huberman, 1994, p. 56), that described broad situations in which several similar KODs occurred (e.g., we placed an example identified as an inappropriate letter of recommendation author under the major heading for harmful letters of recommendation). Third, we conducted "analyst triangulation" (Patton, 1990, p. 468) by comparing our findings from Step 1 and our categories from Step 2. This procedure yielded a set of themes that were both internally consistent (i.e., all categories contained numerous similar responses) and externally representative of broad examples of KODs (Patton, 1990).

Results

We identified the following five major KOD categories: (a) damaging personal statements, (b) harmful letters of recommendation, (c) lack of program information, (d) poor writing skills, and (e) misfired attempts to impress. We subsequently describe these categories in descending order of frequency accompanied by illuminating examples.

Damaging Personal Statements

The personal statement section of a graduate school application is an opportunity to inform an admissions committee about personal and professional development, academic background and objectives, research and field experiences, and career goals and plans (Keith-Spiegel and Wiederman, 2000). We found 53 responses related to damaging personal statements, which we sorted into four subcategories: personal mental health, excessive altruism, excessive self-disclosure, and professional inappropriateness.

Personal mental health. The discussion of a personal mental health problem is likely to decrease an applicant's chances of acceptance into a program. Examples of this particular KOD in a personal statement included comments such as "showing evidence of untreated mental illness," "emotional instability," and seeking graduate training "to better understand one's own problems or problems in one's family." More specifically, one respondent stated that a KOD may occur "when students highlight how they were drawn to graduate study because of significant personal problems or trauma. Graduate school is an academic/

career path, not a personal treatment or intervention for problems."

Excessive altruism. Several respondents described personal statements that expressed excessively altruistic professional goals as KODs. Admissions committees are not impressed by statements such as "I want to help all people," "I'm destined to save the world," or "I think I am a strong candidate for your program because people have always come to me with their problems; I am viewed as a warm, empathetic, and caring person." One respondent offered the following advice: "Everybody wants to help people. That's assumed. Don't say the reason you want to go into clinical psychology is to help people." Thus, a personal statement should focus on the student's professional activities such as research interests and pursuits, academic strengths, and professional experiences rather than on purely personal characteristics and motives. It is better to allow letter of recommendation authors to describe strong personal qualities than to include them as self-perceptions in a personal statement.

Excessive self-disclosure. Promiscuous self-disclosure characterized another KOD in personal statements. An example of such disclosure was "a long saga about how the student had finished [school] over incredible odds. Much better to have a reference allude to this." However, one committee chair noted that graduate admissions committees do not always view this type of information negatively if an applicant has written it in a professional manner that is appropriate for the context of a formal application.

> The applicant mentions in the personal statement that he/she decided to pursue a career in clinical psychology due to personal family experience with psychopathology. This isn't always a kiss of death, but a sensitive area such as this should be communicated carefully. If the applicant is "spilling" overly personal information in a written statement, I often view this as a "worry sign" or an indication of poor interpersonal boundaries.

Professionally inappropriate. A final example of a KOD that can occur in a personal statement is any professionally inappropriate information that does not match the context of the application. One applicant admitted to feeling "a thrill of excitement every time he/she steps into a morgue." Another wrote "a 10-page narrative of herself as Dorothy on the yellow-brick road to graduate school." A third indicated that he or she "had performed (acted?) in pornographic movies, which was not well received by the admissions department in consideration for acceptance into graduate school." Other types of professionally unsuitable content include using excessive or inappropriate humor, "cutesy/clever stuff," and excessively religious references (e.g., "I am a gifted therapist naturally. God has given me natural talents that make me a very good clinician. This was recently demonstrated when I helped my devil-worshipping brother go on the right path, God's path."). As one respondent noted, "Being religious is OK, but it has little relevance to research or psychology graduate school."

Harmful Letters of Recommendation

A total of 45 KOD examples centered on letters of recommendation. The two most harmful aspects of these documents centered on undesirable applicant characteristics and letters from inappropriate sources.

Undesirable applicant characteristics. To excel in graduate school, a student must possess fundamentally positive personal characteristics such as intelligence, motivation, responsibility, and agreeableness (Keith-Spiegel and Wiederman, 2000). Therefore, any letter of recommendation suggesting that a student does not possess these qualities can be a KOD. Statements such as "arrogant, not a team player, and self-centered"; "unreliable, manipulative, and immature"; "strong will and imposing character"; "does not like research"; and "scattered and needs some direction" are detrimental to a student's acceptance chances. One respondent noted that a KOD can occur if the letter included "a lack of superlatives. The student has to rise above competency." Finally, a personality characteristic deemed vital for a graduate student was the ability to work independently. For example, a KOD may occur if

> The letter of recommendation somehow suggested that the applicant has trouble working independently and is not clearly intrinsically motivated. Then that person would be at a serious disadvantage. Admissions committees believe that graduate school is a challenging and demanding experience. Successful applicants must have the motivation to succeed and the perseverance to carry through even when obstacles are encountered.

Inappropriate sources. Applicants should choose their letter of recommendation authors carefully. "Letters of recommendation should be from professors or other individuals who have been involved in the student's education and research activities . they should NOT be from relatives or employees." Participants suggested that "letters of recommendation from odd sources such as ministers or family friends and letters of recommendation from faculty members who did not know the applicant well" are KODs. Other inappropriate— and therefore damaging—authors included "therapists," "travel agents," "parents," "boyfriend[s] or girlfriend[s]," "family friends," and "the applicant." Letters of recommendation should come from people who can truthfully describe the applicant's work habits and potential as a graduate student (Buskist and Sherburne, 1996).

Lack of Information About the Program

A total of 22 KOD examples identified applicants' lack of knowledge about the program to which they were applying. These examples included not researching the general focus of the program and not exploring how the applicant's research interests fit the focus of the program.

Program focus. Advisors cannot overemphasize the importance of researching the focus of the programs to which their students apply. For example, KODs occur when applicants "demonstrate no clue regarding what the foci of the program are" or "haven't bothered to see what kind of work is done in our program." Studying the current research interests of graduate faculty at schools to which they apply is also crucial. One respondent advised, "applicants should do some background reading on the faculty, read their publications, and be able to say how their research interests and career goals fit with Dr. X." Another respondent supported this point with the following statement:

> Students who express an interest in research activity that does not correspond to the research interests of our faculty are not likely to be admitted. This is especially true if the student appears set on doing research in his or her area of interest.

This idea was further supported by another respondent, who stated that a KOD occurs when "students note that they wish to work with a specific faculty member who has retired, died, or relocated."

Fit into the program. A crucial aspect of researching a graduate program involves applicants' comparison of their research interests with the research activities of a program's faculty. The importance of applicant-program fit is crucial for both the professor and the student to receive maximum professional gains from the relationship (Buskist and Sherburne, 1996). One participant noted

> I'm very attentive to whether a student's interest matches our training. I expect a statement of personal interest that displays a convincing, compelling desire for what we have to offer from its start to finish. It's

> a kiss of death when I read a personal essay that describes an applicant's life-long goal of serving humankind and has a paragraph tacked on to the end that "personalizes" the essay for the particular school to which it was sent.

Another participant noted that students must "do homework on each program. Statements from applicants that state the program is just perfect for them, without evidence they know much about the program other than its specialty name" are KODs.

Poor Writing Skills

Completing an application for graduate school is much like writing a manuscript. The application must include appropriate content, but it must also be cohesive, organized, concise, written skillfully, and proofread thoroughly (Buskist and Sherburne, 1996). A total of 21 KOD examples pertained to poorly written applications, which we divided into two major subcategories: spelling and grammatical errors and poorly written applications.

Spelling and grammatical errors. According to several respondents, spelling and grammatical errors found anywhere in the application are an immediate KOD. Comments such as "writing that abuses the rules of grammar," "misspellings," and "letters that display grammar and punctuation errors" all point to the importance of proofreading materials included in an application packet. Another respondent elaborated on this point by saying, "It is not so much the student's lack of writing ability, but rather the carelessness of sending such sloppy work to an admissions committee that bodes ill."

Poorly written application materials. Poorly written material or material weak in content is another KOD. Students should write their personal statements concisely, but in enough detail to reflect their research, educational, and professional goals clearly. One respondent stated that a KOD occurs when he or she reads "overly long and detailed statements of purpose that are poorly edited." Overall structure is also important because a statement of purpose is a chance to demonstrate strong writing skills, a crucial characteristic of successful graduate students. One respondent succinctly stated that a KOD exists in applications that "lack structure. People who want to get their doctorate should already know how to write."

Misfired Attempts to Impress

The final KOD category included six examples of students' misfired attempts to impress admissions committees. Applicants should assiduously avoid the following failed efforts to make a positive impression on admissions committees.

Admissions committees do not respond favorably to applicants who attempt to impress them by being critical of their undergraduate programs or offering unsupported praise for the graduate program to which they are applying. For example, one applicant said "My undergraduate program was really bad because of x, y, and z. I didn't really learn anything, so I'm applying to your program so that I will actually learn something." One participant mentioned, "the candidate will give a very bad impression if he/she blames others for his/her poor academic record. Example: Faculty here at X university were unwilling to help me succeed in this course." Another respondent cited a similar KOD when he or she suggested that, "statements in the personal statement that are openly and overly critical of one's undergraduate institution or quality of preparation are [a kiss of death]."

Attempting to impress admissions committees by name dropping influential practitioners of psychology or other well-known public officials may be an unsuccessful strategy to gain admission to graduate school. For example, statements of purpose that "elaborate on [the applicant's] family's work history in the area of psychology or mental health and/or namedrop some recognized practitioner without any substantive evidence of having a real connection" are often a KOD. Another example included obtaining letters of recommendation from political sources who may be influential within government agencies, but who are inappropriate candidates to recommend the applicant for graduate study in psychology. For example, one KOD occurred when

> an applicant included a letter of recommendation from a state senator who was a friend of the family and only knew the applicant as a child and adolescent. The letter said little about the applicant and described the senator's powerful role in overseeing the funding of higher education in the state.

Discussion and Recommendations

Although the KODs identified in this study reflect unwise choices on the part of applicants, we believe many of these KODs resulted more from a lack of appropriate advising and mentoring than from a lack of applicants' intelligence. Unless undergraduate psychology programs provide appropriate advising and mentoring opportunities, their majors are likely to commit many of these KODs because of a lack of exposure to information that would otherwise enable them to understand the graduate school culture, the requirements of the graduate school application process, and the exact nature of some of its components. For example, an unmentored psychology major may interpret a personal statement at face value by perceiving it as an opportunity to share personal (i.e., private) information with the members of a graduate admissions committee. Unless applicants know that a personal statement should address issues such as research interests and perceived fit with a program, they may misinterpret its purpose and write personal statements that inadvertently doom their applications. Similarly, an unmentored student may interpret a letter of recommendation as a request for information from a person who knows her or him well and can vouch for her or his admirable traits and strong values (e.g., a family member or a member of the clergy).

We believe undergraduate psychology programs can prepare their students to construct successful graduate school applications that do not contain KODs in the following three ways: (a) mentoring, (b) academic advising, and (c) teaching classes designed to prepare students for their lives after undergraduate school. Keith-Spiegel and Wiederman (2000) defined a mentor as "an established professional in the student's general study area who facilitates the student's undergraduate accomplishments and the path to graduate school" (p. 67). Although some departments may have official mentoring programs, most mentor-protege relationships are likely to develop when students participate in research conducted by faculty. Departments can help their students understand the importance of research participation in the graduate school selection process by sponsoring informal social gatherings for undergraduates to talk with graduate students (Appleby, 2000b). Likewise, departments can promote mentoring by engaging in community-building strategies that encourage closer relationships among students and faculty (Appleby, 2000a). Effective mentoring of undergraduate students can help them attain the research and classroom experiences that facilitate strong letters of recommendation, compelling personal statements, and proficient writing skills. These experiences can help students avoid KODs in their graduate applications.

Academic advising is a second strategy that departments can use to help their undergraduates avoid KODs. Ware et al. (1993) described the role of advisers in preparing their advisees for their postbaccalaureate educational aspirations:

> Advisers may encourage students to seek a match between personal characteristics (e.g., values, interests, skills, etc.) and characteristics of the graduate program.

Table 1. How to Avoid the Kisses of Death in the Graduate School Application Process

Personal statements

• Avoid references to your mental health. Such statements could create the impression you may be unable to function as a successful graduate student.

• Avoid making excessively altruistic statements. Graduate faculty could interpret these statements to mean you believe a strong need to help others is more important to your success in graduate school than a desire to perform research and engage in other academic and professional activities.

• Avoid providing excessively self-revealing information. Faculty may interpret such information as a sign you are unaware of the value of interpersonal or professional boundaries in sensitive areas.

• Avoid inappropriate humor, attempts to appear cute or clever, and references to God or religious issues when these issues are unrelated to the program to which you are applying. Admissions committee members may interpret this type of information to mean you lack awareness of the formal nature of the application process or the culture of graduate school.

Letters of recommendation

• Avoid letters of recommendation from people who do not know you well, whose portrayals of your characteristics may not objective (e.g., a relative), or who are unable to base their descriptions in an academic context (e.g., your minister). Letters from these authors can give the impression you are unable or unwilling to solicit letters from individuals whose depictions are accurate, objective, or professionally relevant.

• Avoid letter of recommendation authors who will provide unflattering descriptions of your personal or academic characteristics. These descriptions provide a clear warning that you are not suited for graduate study. Choose your letter of recommendation authors carefully. Do not simply ask potential authors if they are willing to write you a letter of recommendation; ask them if they are able to write you a strong letter of recommendation. This question will allow them to decline your request diplomatically if they believe their letter may be more harmful than helpful.

Lack of information about the program

• Avoid statements that reflect a generic approach to the application process or an unfamiliarity with the program to which you are applying. These statements signal you have not made an honest effort to learn about the program from which you are saying you want to earn your graduate degree.

• Avoid statements that indicate you and the target program are a perfect fit if these statements are not corroborated with specific evidence that supports your assertion (e.g., your research interests are similar to those of the program's faculty). Graduate faculty can interpret a lack of this evidence as a sign that you and the program to which you are applying are not a good match.

Poor writing skills

• Avoid any type of spelling or grammatical errors in your application. These errors are an unmistakable warning of substandard writing skills, a refusal to proofread your work, or willingness to submit careless written work.

• Avoid writing in an unclear, disorganized, or unconvincing manner that does not provide your readers with a coherent picture of your research, educational, and professional goals. A crucial part of your graduate training will be writing; do not communicate your inability to write to those you hope will be evaluating your writing in the future.

Misfired attempts to impress

• Avoid attempts to impress the members of a graduate admissions committee with information they may interpret as insincere flattery (e.g., referring to the target program in an excessively complimentary manner) or inappropriate (e.g., name dropping or blaming others for poor academic performance). Graduate admissions committees are composed of intelligent people; do not use your application as an opportunity to insult their intelligence.

> Additional advising tasks include establishing a realistic time line, preparing applications (including a goals statement), taking the Graduate Record Examination (or other standardized test), and selecting faculty to write letters of recommendation. (p. 58)

This process, known as developmental advising (Crookston, 1972), reflects the conscious effort of advisors to help advisees understand how their undergraduate program can help them develop into the people they wish to become (Appleby, 2002). Unfortunately, this type of time-consuming, one-on-one advising may not be available to all psychology majors because many departments lack the human resources to provide it.

The third strategy to help students avoid KODs is to provide them with a class that familiarizes them with the nature of graduate education and the graduate application process. Oles and Cooper (1988) described a class titled Professional Seminar that allowed "one faculty member, together with volunteer help, to provide 150 students with 13-14 hours of academic advising each semester for a total of 1400 contact hours" (p. 63). Although the primary focus of this class was to familiarize students with their program's faculty, curriculum, and research opportunities, it also included information about graduate school and required its enrollees to write a paper that included "their plans for graduate school" (p. 62). Classes of this nature have increased in the 17 years since Oles and Cooper described their pioneering seminar. Now 34.2% of psychology departments that answered a survey about this type of class reported offering one (Landrum, Shoemaker, and Davis, 2003).

The purpose of these classes is to provide students with academic and career advising information that may otherwise be unavailable, overlooked, or ignored. When taught well and taken seriously, these classes provide students with the guidance and encouragement they need to identify their career goals and understand how they can use their undergraduate curricular and extracurricular opportunities to accomplish these goals (Appleby, 2003b). When Landrum et al. (2003) asked departments that offered such a class how important it was for enrollees to gain knowledge about 33 issues typically taught in these classes, the ratings (on a 0 to 3 scale, with 3 being *extremely important)* were 2.50 for "know the information needed to apply to graduate programs," 2.30 for "know how to apply to graduate school," and 2.11 for "know the value of letters of recommendation" (p. 49). Students who possess this type of knowledge are much less likely to commit KODs than their peers who are unaware of this information.

Not all psychology departments possess the resources to offer their students a full range of mentoring, advising, and academic opportunities designed to prevent them from committing KODs in the graduate school application process. However, we believe that most departments can provide at least a subset of these types of support. To facilitate these ends, we provide a condensed, student-friendly version of the results of our study in Table 1. We encourage faculty to use this as a handout they can distribute to their students who display an interest in graduate school.

References

American Psychological Association. (2001). *Graduate study in psychology 2001.* Washington, DC: Author.

Appleby, D. C. (2000a, November). Academic community building. *Monitor on Psychology, 31,* 37-41.

Appleby, D. C. (2000b, May/June). Facilitating undergraduate—graduate student communication: "Family" meals. *American Psychological Society Observer,* pp. 27, 29.

Appleby, D. C. (2002). The teaching—advising connection. In S. F. Davis and W. Buskist (Eds.), *The teaching of psychology: Essays in honor of Wilbert J.*

McKeachie and Charles L. Brewer (pp. 121-139). Mahwah, NJ: Lawrence Erlbaum Associates, Inc.

Appleby, D. C. (2003a). *The savvy psychology major.* Dubuque, IA: Kendall/Hunt.

Appleby, D. C. (2003b, August). Transforming psychology majors into book authors at IUPUI. In B. T. Loher (Chair), *Overview of orientation and career planning courses in psychology.* Symposium conducted at the annual meeting of the American Psychological Association, Toronto, Ontario, Canada.

Buskist, W., and Sherburne, T. R. (1996). *Preparing for graduate study in psychology: 101 questions and answers.* Boston: Allyn and Bacon.

Crookston, B. B. (1972). A developmental view of academic advising as teaching. *Journal of College Student Personnel, 13,* 12-17.

Keith-Spiegel, P., and Wiederman, M. W. (2000). *The complete guide to graduate school admission: Psychology, counseling, and related professions.* Mahwah, NJ: Lawrence Erlbaum Associates, Inc.

Kinder, B. N., and Walfish, S. (2001). Perspectives on applying to graduate school. In S. Walfish and A. K. Hess (Eds.), *Succeeding in graduate school* (pp. 61-73). Mahwah, NJ: Lawrence Erlbaum Associates, Inc.

Kuther, T. L. (2003). *The psychology major's handbook.* Belmont, CA: Wadsworth.

Kuther, T. L. (2004). *Graduate study in psychology: Your guide to success.* Springfield, IL: Thomas.

Landrum, R. E., and Davis, S. F. (2003). *The psychology major: Career options and strategies for success* (2nd ed.). Upper Saddle River, NJ: Prentice Hall.

Landrum, R. E., Shoemaker, C. S., and Davis, S. F. (2003). Important topics in an introduction to the psychology major course. *Teaching of Psychology, 30,* 48-51.

Lloyd, M. (2001). *Graduate school: The application process.* Retrieved November 26, 2004, from http://www.psywww.com/careers/applicat.htm

McCracken, G. (1988). *The long interview.* Newbury Park, CA: Sage.

Miles, M. B., and Huberman, A. M. (1994)- *Qualitative data analysis: An expanded sourcebook* (2nd ed.). Thousand Oaks, CA: Sage.

Morgan, B. L., and Korschgen, A.J. (2005). *Majoring in psych?: Options for psychology undergraduates* (3rd ed.) Boston: Allyn and Bacon.

Oles, H. J., and Cooper, R. G., Jr. (1988). The professional seminar: A new method for student advisement. In P. J. Woods (Ed.), *Is psychology the major for them?* (pp. 61-63). Washington, DC: American Psychological Association.

Patton, M. Q. (1990). *Qualitative evaluation and research methods* (2nd ed.). Newbury Park, CA: Sage.

Peterson's. (2001). *Graduate programs in psychology 2002.* Lawrenceville, NJ: Author.

Sayette, M. A., Mayne, T. J., andNorcross, J. C. (2004). *Insider's guide to graduate programs in clinical and counseling psychology: 2004/2005 edition.* New York: Guilford.

Taylor-Cooke, P., and Appleby, D. C. (2002). *The graduate school application process.* Retrieved January 9, 2005, from http://www.psynt.iupm.edu/Users/dappleby/undergrad/images/process.ppt

Thomas, J. R., andNelson, J. K. (2001). *Research methods in physical activity* (4th ed.). Champaign, IL: Human Kinetics.

Ware, M. E., Busch-Rossnagel, N. A., Crider, A. B., Gray-Shellberg, L., Hale, K., Lloyd, M. A., Rivera-Medina, E., andSgro,J. A. (1993). Developing and improving advising: Challenges to prepare students for life. In T. V. McGovern (Ed.), *Handbook for enhancing undergraduate education in psychology* (pp. 47-70). Washington, DC: American Psychological Association.

Notes

1. We thank Becky May for her help during the data collection process and three anonymous reviewers for their helpful suggestions.

2. Send correspondence to Drew C. Appleby, Department of Psychology, Indiana University-Purdue University Indianapolis, 402 North Blackford Street, Indianapolis, IN 46202-3275; email: dappleby@iupui.edu.

Graduate Study in Psychology: 1971–2004

By John C. Norcross, Jessica L. Kohout, and Marlene Wicherski

Table 4: *Minimum Required and Actual Scores of First-Year Graduate Students by Year and Level of Department*

	Minimum required							Actual						
	1979–1980[a]		1992–1993[a]		2003–2004			1979–1980[a]		1992–1993[a]		2003–2004		
Measure	*M*	*Mdn*	*M*	*Mdn*	*M*	*Mdn*	n	*M*	*Mdn*	*M*	*Mdn*	*M*	*Mdn*	*n*
						Doctoral departments								
GRE														
Verbal	560	550	546	550	529	528	76	608	609	593	593	571	571	233
Quantitative	556	550	548	550	538	550	76	592	588	613	610	626	630	233
Analytical			543	550	547	550	28			638	640	636	640	124
Verbal + Quantitative	1,122	1,100	1,090	1,100	1,066	1,050	103	1,202	1,205	1,206	1,204	1,183	1,200	172
Psychology Subject Test	562	550	565	580	552	550	30	614	620	624	629	633	638	93
GPA														
Overall	3.09	3.00	3.09	3.00	3.11	3.00	200	3.46	3.46	3.50	3.50	3.54	3.56	232
Psychology	3.22	3.20	3.26	3.25	3.17	3.00	69	3.60	3.63	3.66	3.67	3.66	3.70	65
Last 2 years	3.18	3.00	3.18	3.00	3.16	3.00	78	3.53	3.53	3.59	3.60	3.67	3.70	89
						Master's departments								
GRE														
Verbal	511	500	489	500	449	450	53	537	540	517	520	504	500	72
Quantitative	509	500	490	500	453	450	50	532	530	533	540	549	540	70
Analytical			485	500	456	450	17			555	550	552	550	27
Verbal + Quantitative	1,017	1,000	984	1,000	952	1,000	57	1,065	1,068	1,033	1,040	1,055	1,050	57
Psychology Subject Test	519	522	505	500	495	500	12	556	558	549	550	577	570	24
GPA														
Overall	2.86	3.00	2.86	3.00	2.92	3.00	129	3.20	3.26	3.27	3.25	3.37	3.40	99
Psychology	3.07	3.00	3.05	3.00	3.05	3.00	58	3.48	3.46	3.42	3.45	3.48	3.50	54
Last 2 years	3.01	3.00	3.00	3.00	3.03	3.00	50	3.43	3.43	3.38	3.41	3.44	3.50	37

Note. The academic years correspond to the 1981–1982, 1994, and 2005 editions of *Graduate Study in Psychology*, respectively. GRE = Graduate Record Examination; GPA = grade point average. [a] Data from Stoup and Benjamin (1982) and Norcross, Hanych, and Terranova (1996).

Table 7: *2003–2004 Acceptance and Enrollment Percentages for Doctoral Programs by Subfield*

		Acceptance rate				Enrollment rate				Total students enrolled
Subfield	*N* of programs	*M*	*Mdn*	Q1	Q3	*M*	*Mdn*	Q1	Q3	Sum
Clinical	211	21.2	11.1	6.2	32.4	14.3	7.4	4.1	20.9	3,324
Clinical neuropsychology	20	25.8	22.4	13.3	40.5	17.2	14.6	8.6	23.1	213
Community	12	31.0	26.4	18.7	47.6	21.2	14.3	8.6	30.2	43
Counseling	64	21 5	17.0	9.3	25.2	15.4	10.2	7.1	19.3	447
Health	12	30.9	21.5	6.1	48.8	21.4	15.0	5.5	39.3	87
School	52	37.4	31.2	18.3	47.8	27.8	18.5	13.4	33.3	392
Other health service provider subfields	49	25.7	21.9	7.7	38.8	19.4	14.3	6.6	27.6	477
Cognitive	88	32.4	26.1	14.4	43.4	22.0	14.3	7.8	29.4	351
Developmental	99	27.2	20.7	12.5	34.8	19.0	14.0	8.5	21.7	374
Educational	31	50.0	50.0	33.3	70.0	34.0	30.0	16.7	48.3	170
Environmental	2	39.1	39.1	11.5	66.7	29.1	24.8			10
Experimental	31	37.6	30.0	16.7	50.0	26.7	18.2	11.8	30.0	163
Industrial/organizational	53	25.7	17.4	12.1	31.6	16.3	11.0	5.9	16.7	281
Neuroscience	49	26.9	25.0	13.9	32.5	19.7	16.0	8.3	25.0	148
Personality	15	19.2	12.5	7.1	19.5	9.0	8.7	3.8	11.4	45
Physiological	4	39.4	33.9	11.9	72.5	27.0	20.0	8.5	52.5	12
Psychobiology	13	25.0	25.0	11.2	35.2	13.7	8.3	7.0	17.6	34
Quantitative	14	42.6	36.0	21.1	64.6	27.0	20.0	6.7	51.9	32
Social	80	19.4	15.0	9.4	27.1	11.3	8.0	5.3	15.0	270
Other research subfields	76	33.2	27.3	16.7	50.0	24.2	20.0	11.3	33.1	339
Other fields	8	22.9	22.5	9.6	36.6	14.7	13.6	4.7	20.0	36
Total	981	27.4	20.8	10.6	38.9	18.8	13.0	6.7	25.0	7,247

Note. Acceptance rates are computed by dividing the number of students accepted to a program by the number of applications. Enrollment rates are the number of students who enrolled in a program divided by the number of applications. Q = quartile.

Table 8: *2003–2004 Acceptance and Enrollment Percentages for Master's Programs by Subfield*

		Acceptance rate				Enrollment rate				Total students enrolled
Subfield	*N* of programs	*M*	*Mdn*	Q1	Q3	*M*	*Mdn*	Q1	Q3	Sum
Clinical	98	52.7	49.5	33.9	72.3	35.5	32.0	22.3	47.7	1,671
Community	22	53.8	55.8	22.6	81.4	41.8	41.4	20.0	60.6	416
Counseling	108	65.5	67.3	50.0	84.6	51.8	50.0	33.0	66.4	2,764
Health	3	70 3	72.7	38.2		56.2	36.4	32.4		23
School	49	48.9	47.8	28.3	72.5	39.7	34.3	19.3	56.1	682
Other health service provider subfields	64	64.5	69.5	43.1	83.2	49.2	40.0	30.8	66.3	1,395
Cognitive	10	52.8	45.8	31.8	77.7	27.3	31.7	11.3	40.0	25
Developmental	19	47.9	50.0	31.2	66.7	33.0	33.3	17.9	48.1	166
Educational	15	57.3	56.5	46.2	70.6	41.6	38.1	30.0	54.2	149
Experimental	38	55.4	50.8	40.0	71.9	38.0	34.5	19.8	50.0	261
Industrial/organizational	76	56.6	60.0	32.5	75.5	38.6	35.0	19.4	50.0	849
General	59	58.0	53.8	40.0	75.0	41.3	33.8	23.4	59.4	972
Neuroscience	6	32.3	35.9	8.8	52.6	25.8	25.3	9.1	38.6	50
Quantitative	5	72.7	83.3	47.2	92.9	63.5	61.9	47.6	81.0	18
Social	8	47.6	47.5	26.2	65.0	27.5	28.6	22.2	30.0	29
Other research subfields	41	60.7	60.9	42.9	78.8	43.1	39.4	32.3	58.2	443
Other fields	2	33.3	33.3			33.3	33.3			12
Total	624	57.4	57.9	38.8	76.5	41.9	37.5	25.0	55.0	9,925

Note. Acceptance rates are computed by dividing the number of students accepted to a program by the number of applications. Enrollment rates are the number of students who enrolled in a program divided by the number of applications. Q = quartile.

Minority Students of Color and the Psychology Graduate Pipeline

Disquieting and Encouraging Trends, 1989–2003

By Kenneth I. Maton, Jessica L. Kohout, Marlene Wicherski, George E. Leary and Andrey Vinokurov

The underrepresentation of persons of color in psychology has received increasing attention during the past 40 years (cf. American Psychological Association [APA], 1963; Commission on Ethnic Minority Recruitment, Retention, and Training in Psychology [CEMRRAT], 1997; Dulles Conference Task Force, 1978; Highlen, 1994; Howard et al., 1986; Pickren, 2004; Stricker et al., 1990). Many reasons have been offered for the critical importance of increasing levels of minority representation in psychology. These include enhanced quality and sensitivity of services and education provided to ethnic minority clients and students, respectively; new perspectives generated for theory development and application related to contemporary social issues; and greater congruence with the field's commitment to social justice (e.g., CEMRRATT, 1997; Lott, 2005; Sue, Bingham, Porche-Burke, and Vasquez, 1999). In this article we examine trends in the minority graduate pipeline during the last decade of the 20th century and the early years of the 21st century. This has been a period of dramatic change in the ethnic makeup of the U.S. population, as well as in attitudes and policies concerning affirmative action in higher education (cf. Bowen and Bok, 1998; Bowen, Kurzweil, and Tobin, 2005; Malcom, Van Horne, Gaddy, and George, 1998; Vasquez and Jones, 2006). It has also been a time of increasing attention to professional degrees and practice in psychology and of generally declining enrollments in doctoral programs (Syverson, 2001). Each of these developments underscores the importance of a systematic examination of recent trends in the minority pipeline.

The change in the ethnic makeup of the U.S. population is well documented. The percentage of Whites in the United States decreased between 1990 and 2000 from 75.7% to 69.4%. Conversely, the percentage of persons of Hispanic origin increased sharply from 9.0% to 12.6%, surpassing that of African Americans (12.2%). The percentage of Asian Americans (i.e., Asians and Pacific Islanders) also increased, from 2.8% to 3.8%. Non-Hispanic individuals identifying with two or more races and Native Americans (i.e., American Indians and Alaskan Natives) represented 1.2% and 0.8% of the U.S. population, respectively (U.S. Census Bureau, 2002, 2005). In certain states

Kenneth I. Matson, Jessica L. Kohout, Marlene Wicherski, George E. Leary and Andrey Vinokurov, "Minority Students of Color and the Psychology Graduate Pipeline: Disquieting and Encouraging Trends, 1989–2003," *American Psychologist,* vol. 61, no. 2, pp. 117–119, 123–131.

the demographic changes were especially dramatic (e.g., California). It is safe to say that every aspect of U.S. society, ranging from schools and urban life to media and business, has been influenced by the rapidly increasing ethnic diversity in the country.

Attitudes and policies concerning affirmative action in higher education emerged as a highly contentious public issue in the mid-1990s, an issue that remains so to this day. The early anti-affirmative action decisions severely limiting (e.g., *Hopwood v. State of Texas,* 1996) or outlawing (e.g., Proposition 209 in California in 1996) the use of race for admissions or financial support in higher education have been followed by additional, related actions in other states (e.g., Washington, Georgia, Florida). The Supreme Court decisions addressing the anti-affirmative action lawsuits in Michigan again galvanized national attention on the issue (Lemann, 2003). Although the Court provided a positive ruling in favor of affirmative action strategies during the next several decades, the rates of African American student admissions at the undergraduate level at the University of Michigan and at a number of other major state universities around the country have surprisingly fallen sharply (Dobbs, 2005). The extent to which shifting attitudes and practices will ultimately affect the graduate minority pipeline in psychology is, to date, unclear.

The 1990s also brought important developments to undergraduate and graduate education in psychology. Rapid growth in the number of individuals receiving bachelor's and master's degrees during the 1990s was especially evident. Bachelor's degree receipt in psychology increased by about 50% from 1989 to 2000, with almost 25,000 additional students receiving degrees each year by the end of the decade (49,854-74,654). Proportionally, master's degree receipt increased to an even greater extent, by 80% during this period, adding almost 7,000 additional degree recipients to the annual count by 2000 (8,652-15,540). In contrast, receipt of PhD degrees in psychology expanded slowly, up only 13% from 1989 to 2000, with 410 additional students receiving degrees (3,208-3,618). Similarly, full-time faculty in psychology departments increased only 12% during this period (National Science Foundation [NSF], 2000 [see NSF Tables 4, 7, and 10], 2004a [see NSF Tables 4 and 7], 2004b, 2004c).

During the 1990s, the focus on training for professional practice was a continuing development within the field. The number and visibility of PsyD programs dramatically increased; available data indicate that the number of PsyD recipients more than doubled from less than 650 in 1988-1989 to over 1,500 in 2003-2004. Overall, more than 3,300 doctorates are currently awarded yearly by U.S. graduate schools in health service provider subfields (APA, 2005; Hoffer et al., 2005). In terms of graduate training and education, a watershed event was the passage of the multicultural training guidelines by APA's (2003) Council of Representatives. Moreover, the need for ethnically diverse (and competent) practitioners, educators, and researchers within psychology to serve an increasingly diverse clientele and student body and to meet pressing research and public interest needs was often emphasized (e.g., Bernal and Castro, 1994; Comas-Diaz, 1990; Highlen, 1994; National Advisory Mental Health Council Workgroup, 2001; Rabasca, 2000; Sue et al., 1999), encompassing myriad areas of the field, ranging from behavior therapy (Olatunji, 2003) to neuropsychology (Hills-Briggs, Evans, and Norman, 2004).

We must regularly examine emerging trends in the minority pipeline as part of our goal as psychologists to enhance diversity. On the basis of an understanding of these trends, extant strategies and tactics to enhance the pipeline can be refined and, as necessary, new ones developed. Conceptually, the graduate pipeline is best viewed from an ecological or systemic perspective, in that its parts are interrelated, and each part is affected by developments in the larger society. Simply put, increasing the percentage of minorities who receive bachelor's degrees increases the potential pool of candidates for graduate study. As more minorities attend psychology graduate programs, the presence of a critical mass of students can facilitate recruitment of new minority graduate students. At the master's program level, an increased number of minorities who receive degrees, including those not fully competitive for doctoral study at the time of bachelor's degree receipt, enlarges the pool of eligible minority students for doctoral programs. The greater the pool of minorities who receive the doctoral degree, the larger the potential pool of qualified minority faculty applicants.

The presence of minority faculty in a department, in turn, can enhance the recruitment, retention, and achievement of both undergraduate and graduate minority students and fellow minority faculty. For prospective graduate students, the presence of a critical mass of minority faculty likely increases perceptions that the department will provide cultural congruity, a trusted and valued faculty mentor, and opportunities for research in ethnic-congruent areas (Jones, 1990; Munoz-Dunbar and Stanton, 1999; Rogers, Hoffman and Wade, 1998; Speight, Thomas, Kennel, and Anderson, 1995). The increased presence of minority faculty in a department also enhances the pool of available mentors for undergraduate majors preparing for graduate school, completing the cycle. Finally, all aspects of the pipeline are influenced by external factors such as changing societal demographics, public attitudes toward ethnic minorities and affirmative action in education, competing career possibilities attractive to minorities, and availability of financial support.

To date, there has been little research examining factors that contribute to minority underrepresentation in the psychology pipeline (cf. Lott, 2005). More research exists in the natural science fields, especially research focused on factors that contribute to high levels of undergraduate success (e.g., College Board, 1999). Four sets of factors that research indicates are especially important for underrepresented minority student success in the sciences are academic and social integration, knowledge and skills development, support and motivation, and monitoring and advising (Maton and Hrabowski, 2004). Such individual and environmental resources can help counteract the barriers researchers have identified that contribute to occupational segregation and marginalization, including occupational stereotyping, limited perceptions of structural opportunity, discrimination, and limited access to influential networks and mentoring (cf. Cockley, Dreher, and Stockdale, 2004; Xu and Leffler, 1996).

Earlier reviews of minority pipeline trends in psychology have consistently demonstrated underrepresentation of minorities at all levels, with underrepresentation increasing as one moves up the pipeline from college entrance to receipt of the doctorate degree. In the mid-1990s the APA's CEMRRAT provided an in-depth look at changes from 1976 to 1993 in the psychology pipeline (CEMRRAT, 1997). They reported, for example, that in 1993 ethnic minorities accounted for 16.2% of all bachelor's degree recipients, an increase from 11.5% in 1976. At the other end of the pipeline, ethnic minorities accounted for 9.4% of all doctoral degree recipients, a dramatic increase from 4.2% in 1976 but still substantially below that of bachelor's degree recipients and still further below their 26.4% representation in the U.S. population.

Of note, reviews of minority representation trends in psychology, including the CEMRRAT report, have tended to focus on, in addition to change in the percentage of minorities receiving degrees, the change in the percentage of minorities enrolled in graduate programs. The latter data provide a snapshot of current graduate representation based on data regularly reported over the years by federal agencies. Unfortunately, year-to-year changes in graduate program enrollment levels do not provide a sensitive, "front-end" view of emerging trends because the number of new students entering and the number of students graduating are confounded. Emerging trends are better examined through changes over time in first-year enrollments, an indicator not regularly included in previous federal surveys. The present article includes, along with 1989-2003 trends in degree receipt, the findings of a recent analysis of 1989-2003 first-year enrollments, based on entering student enrollment data collected routinely from graduate departments by APA for their student guides to graduate programs. Taken together, new enrollment and degree receipt trends provide an encompassing, up-to-date view of emerging pipeline developments. This article also goes beyond previous reviews by examining not only whether minorities are under-represented in the pipeline but also the extent of their underrepresentation (i.e., by use of a numerical indicator of representation level).

Given the dramatic changes in societal demographics and attitudes during the past decade and the evolving changes in graduate education in psychology, a review of emerging trends in minority representation in the graduate pipeline is timely. The current review examines trends in minority representation since 1989, with special focus on recent trends. Trend data related to bachelor's degrees awarded, entry into master's-degree-granting departments, master's degrees awarded, entry into PsyD-granting departments, entry into PhD-degree-granting departments, PhD degrees awarded, and full-time minority faculty, in turn, are examined. The extent to which current levels of minority representation are commensurate with minority representation in the U.S. population is also examined for each level of the pipeline. We hope that the resulting overview of minority representation status in psychology will provide a basis for serious conversation and reflection and will contribute further to efforts to increase minority representation—thus helping to increase the contributions of psychology to ethnically diverse students, clients, communities, and society.

Bachelor's Degree Receipt

There was a substantial increase in the percentage of bachelor's degrees awarded to minority students from 1989 (13.6%) to 2002 (24.3%; see Table 1). In 2002, degree receipt representation for minorities was slightly more than three quarters (0.77) of their U.S. population representation, up from less than three fifths (0.57) representation in 1989. Of some concern, however, was the finding that growth in minority students' receipt of bachelor's degrees halted from 2000 to 2002. If this remains the case in the upcoming years, further progress toward minority degree receipt commensurate with U.S. population representation will likely not occur.

The overall increase in degree receipt from 1989 to 2002 was distributed relatively evenly across ethnic groups. The percentage of African American recipients of bachelor's degrees increased from 5.6% to 10.1%; Hispanics/Latinos(as), from 4.4% to 7.9%; Asian Americans, from 3.2% to 5.5%; and Native Americans, from 0.4% to 0.7%. However, in recent years, growth for all four ethnic groups has halted. If this trend continues, African American (0.83), Hispanic/Latino(a) (0.59), and Native American (0.88) students will likely make little further progress toward degree representation commensurate with their representation in the U.S. population. Asian American recipients of bachelor's degrees have already surpassed representation (1.34) relative to their U.S. population representation.

Students Entering Master's-Granting Departments and Receiving Master's Degrees

For the minority population overall, from 1989 to 2003 there was a substantial increase in the number of students entering departments granting master's degrees (11.0%— 23.0%), and from 1989 to 2002, in the number of students receiving master's degrees (10.6%—21.5%; see Table 2). Pipeline representation relative to the U.S. population currently stands at 0.71 for entry and 0.68 for receipt (up from 0.46 and 0.44, respectively, in 1989). It is interesting to note that the lull in growth in student entry from 1999 to 2000 appears to be reflected in the lull in growth in degree receipt from 2001 to 2002 (on average, master's students receive their degrees in two years; APA, 2005). However, if the sharp increase in student entry between 2000 and 2003 (18.7%—23.0%) is sustained, degree receipt can be expected to resume its growth.

There was substantial variation in trends across the different ethnic groups at the master's level. African Americans did not show growth in entry into master's-granting departments between 1997 (7.3%) and 2003 (7.0%). In 2003 their pipeline representation for entry was less than three fifths (0.57) of their U.S. population representation. Surprisingly, however, the number of African American recipients of master's degrees nonetheless grew steadily over this time period, reaching 11.4% in 2003—nearly commensurate (0.93) with their population representation. This success apparently reflects a high level of retention of and degree completion by African Americans relative to other students entering master's departments. As long as this continues, degree receipt for African American students may remain close to being commensurate with their representation in the population.

For Hispanic/Latino(a) students, the 1997 (5.0%) to 1999 (5.8%) rise in student entry appeared to have contributed to the 1999 (5.3%) to 2001 (6.6%) rise in master's degree receipt. However, from 1999 (5.8%) to 2000 (6.0%), there was little change in student entry, which appears, in turn, to be linked to the cessation of growth (and actual decline) in master's degree receipt from 2001 (6.6%) to 2002 (5.7%). As of 2002, Hispanics/Latinos(as) had achieved degree receipt less than half (0.43) of their population representation. The sharp rise in entering Hispanic/ Latino(a) students (5.7% to 9.0%) from 2002 to 2003, though, may contribute to an increase in degree receipt in the years ahead, especially if it is not a random, isolated surge but part of an ongoing trend. The rise in Hispanic/ Latino(a) student entry brought their representation up to two thirds (0.66) of population representation and was a primary contributor to the 2002 to 2003 rise noted previously for minorities overall.

The rates of both student entry and degree receipt for Asian American students have been relatively constant since 1999. Currently, Asian Americans' levels of representation in both entry (1.02) and degree receipt (0.90) are either at or somewhat below their level of population representation, respectively. Native American students have shown somewhat more fluctuation over time, especially in terms of student entry, perhaps because of their small base number. Currently, Native American students' levels of representation in both entry (0.88) and degree receipt (0.88) are not yet commensurate with their population representation levels. The rise in entry from 2002 to 2003 (0.9%-2.0%) for multiethnic students contributed to the overall rise in minority students' entry into master's departments. In 2003, multiethnic students (1.54) achieved one-and-a-half times their representation in the U.S. population. Unfortunately, data on master's degree receipt were not available for multiethnic students.

Overall, consistent with trends at the bachelor's level, minority progress over the years at the master's level of the pipeline has been encouraging.

Students Entering PsyD-Granting Departments and Schools

A strong period of growth from 1993 to 1999 (12.6%–20.1%) for minority students entering PsyD departments and schools came to a halt in recent years, with no growth achieved from 1999 to 2003 (20.1%–20.0%; see Table 3). In 2003, pipeline representation for minority students was below two thirds (0.62) of their population representation, about the same as it was in 1989 (0.65).

African American students achieved little change in PsyD entry from 1997 (6.3%) to 2003 (6.5%). If this lack of growth continues, they will have difficulty moving beyond the current level of one half (0.53) of population representation. Hispanic/Latino(a) students similarly showed little change in student entry from 1997 to 2002, but as was the case at the master's level, an increase in entry occurred from 2002 (5.4%) to 2003 (6.1%). Again, if this is not a random fluctuation but part of a new growth trend, their current pipeline representation level of less than one half (0.45) of their population representation can be expected to move upward.

Both Asian American and Native American students showed a fair amount of fluctuation between 1997 and 2003 in terms of entry rates. For Asian American students the percentage of entry in both 2002 (5.3%) and 2003 (5.4%) was lower than it had been in the three previous years. Nonetheless, in 2003 they still achieved a pipeline representation level more than one-and-a-quarter times higher (1.29) than their representation in the population. Native American students between 1997 (1.0%) and 2003 (0.5%) were higher some years and lower other years in entry than their representation in the U.S. population. As at the master's level, multiethnic students showed an increase in entry from 2002 to 2003; in 2003 they were commensurate (1.08) with their population representation.

Students Entering PhD-Granting Departments and Receiving PhD Degrees

There was a steady increase in the percentage of minority students entering PhD departments from 1989 (13.1%) to 1995 (17.6%), no growth in student entrance from 1995 to 2000, and then a renewed period of growth from 2000 (17.5%) to 2003 (22.1%; see Table 4). In 2003, the pipeline representation of minority students was somewhat more than two thirds (0.69) of their population representation (up from 0.55 in 1989).

PhD receipt among minority students increased from 1989 (8.0%) to 2000 (15.7%) but has not increased since then. The 14.8% minority PhD receipt level in 2003 was less than half (0.46) of population representation (up from 0.33 in 1989).

It is noteworthy that the 2.8% increase in PhD-level student entry from 1989 to 1993 appears to be reflected in the 2.6% increase in PhD receipt from 1995 to 1999. If this linkage between student entry and degree receipt continues, the lack of growth in minority student entry from 1995 to 1999 can be expected to result in little increase in degree receipt from 2001 to 2005, but the increase in minority student entry from 1999 to 2003 should be reflected in increased degree receipt from 2005 to 2009.

The recent growth in minority students' entry into doctoral degree programs from 1999 to 2003, however, is due almost entirely to an increase in two groups: entering Asian American (6.5%-8.7%) and multiethnic (n/a-1.5%) students. During this period, African American, Hispanic/ Latino(a), and Native American student entry achieved modest or no growth. Furthermore, African American and Hispanic/Latino(a) students have not shown any evidence of sustained growth over the six-year period that individual ethnic group data have been available (beginning in 1997). As of 2003, African American students had not yet surpassed one half of their population representation in entry (0.49) or receipt (0.42), and Hispanic/Latino(a) students had only just surpassed one third of their population representation in either area (0.37 and 0.38, respectively). These are disconcerting findings, indeed, as there appears little evidence suggesting that either group will progress in terms of levels of entrance into PhD-granting departments or degree receipt in the years immediately ahead.

In contrast, in 2003 Asian American students had achieved levels of representation in PhD departmental entry that were twice their population representation (2.07), and Native American (1.00) and multiethnic (1.15) students' levels of entry were commensurate with their population representation. Asian American (0.90) and Native American (0.88) students, however, had not yet achieved their population representation in terms of degree receipt.

Trends concerning entry into top-ranked doctoral-research departments from 1989 to 2003 (see Table 5) in most cases paralleled those for doctoral programs in general. African American students' levels of entry, however, instead of showing no change, actually declined from 1997 (4.9%) to 2003 (3.8%). Hispanic/Latino(a) students' levels of entry again did not show any growth from 1997 (5.9%) to 2003 (5.5%). Asian American students' levels of entry again showed strong growth from 1997 (6.5%) to 2003 (11.6%). Their sharp one-year increase from 2002 (7.8%) to 2003 (11.6%) single-handedly accounted for most of the growth in 2003 for minorities overall. In 2003, Asian American students achieved a level of representation more than two-and-three-quarters above (2.76) their representation in the U.S. population. In contrast, African American (0.31), Hispanic/Latino(a) (0.40), and multiethnic (0.23) students only achieved between one fifth and two fifths of their representation in the U.S. population. Native American students achieved three quarters of their population representation in 2003. Overall, the findings for PhD department entry and PhD receipts raise substantial concern for the field.

Full-Time Faculty

There has been a small but steady increase in the percentage of minority faculty from 1989 (6.9%) to 2003 (12.0%; see Table 6). In 2003, however, faculty pipeline representation was still less than two fifths (0.37) of population representation.

African American and Hispanic/Latino(a) faculty showed small but steady increases from 1989 to 2001, but as of 2001, African American faculty representation was only two fifths (0.40) of their population representation, and Hispanic/Latino(a) faculty was about one quarter (0.27) of theirs. Asian American and Native American faculty showed relatively little gain from 1989 to 2003 in representation. As of 2001, Asian American (0.56) and Native American (0.50) faculty representation was only about one half of their respective U.S. population representations.

Summary and Implications

The trends reported present a mix of disquieting and encouraging information concerning the minority graduate pipeline. Encouraging trends outweighed disquieting ones at the lower levels of the pipeline, with the reverse the case at higher levels. Encouraging developments include the steady increase in the percentage of minority students receiving bachelor's degrees from 1989 to 2000, with minorities representing nearly one quarter of degree recipients in 2000, 2001, and 2002. In addition, there has been a steady increase over time in the number of ethnic minority students entering master's-granting departments and receiving master's degrees; ethnic minorities represented more than one fifth of master's degree recipients in 2001 and 2002. In 2002, Asian American, African American, and Native American students each received master's degrees at levels approaching their respective U.S. population representations.

At the upper end of the pipeline, however, there has been no growth in the percentage of minority students receiving doctoral degrees since 1999, and the percentage of African American and Hispanic/Latino(a) students entering PhD-granting departments has shown little or no growth since 1997. As of 2003, both Hispanic/Latino(a) and African American students had achieved only one half or less of their population representation in terms of PsyD program entry, PhD program entry, and PhD degree receipt. Furthermore, although the percentage of minority faculty grew at a steady rate from 1989 to 2003, the rate of growth has been modest, such that in 2003, minority faculty had still not attained two fifths of their U.S. population representation.

At the lower levels of the pipeline, the overall positive trends in bachelor's receipt and master's department entry and degree receipt are substantive indicators of the progress made in the field toward diversification. Undergraduate minority students apparently find psychology an engaging and important area of study. Furthermore, the steadily increasing percentage of students who have entered master's departments and received master's degrees reflects the interest minority students have in developing a career in psychology. Various factors may contribute to these positive trends, including the increased percentage of minorities attending college over the years and a parallel, increased commitment on the part of departmental and graduate program faculty to recruit and support minority students.

Although master's degree receipt for African American, Asian American, and Native American students has grown to levels close to commensurate with their U.S. population representation, the same is not true for His-panic/Latino(a) students. In part, this may reflect their lower entrance rates into master's-granting departments—as of 2003, Hispanic/Latino(a) representation in master's entry was less than half of their U.S. population representation, whereas Asian American and Native American students have consistently been at or near their population representation. The reason for the lower rates for Hispanic/Latino(a) students is not clear, and a unique combination of factors including family responsibilities, financial needs, language, and perceived discrimination may play a part (Gandara, 1995). However, these factors may be changing, as reflected in the sharp increase in rates of Hispanic/Latino(a) students entering departments granting master's degrees in 2003 (9.0%, up from 5.7% in 2002). If this represents a substantive, enduring change, enhanced master's degree receipt among Hispanic/Latino(a) students can be expected to ensue in the years ahead.

There was a sharp increase from 1993 to 1999 in the percentage of minority students entering PsyD-granting departments. One factor that may have contributed to this large gain was the concerted minority recruitment efforts made by professional schools in the early and mid-1990s (cf. Hammond and Yung, 1993; Stricker et al., 1990). A second factor may be the location of many newly developed PsyD programs in states and in cities with large and/or growing numbers of minority residents; geographic location has been emphasized as an important consideration for minority students (Jones, 1990; Munoz-Dunbar and Stanton, 1999; Rogers et al., 1998). An additional factor may be the strong appeal of practice-oriented careers and training for many minority students. Some support for this latter factor is present in the leveling-off of growth in minority students' entry into PhD-granting departments in the latter half of the 1990s, concurrent with their increased entrance into PsyD-granting schools and departments.

From 2000 to 2003, trends related to students' entry into PsyD- and PhD-granting departments were the mirror image of those from 1993 to 1999. Entry into PhD-granting departments increased for minority students during 2000–2003 but leveled off for PsyD-granting departments. In part, this shift reflects changing entry patterns among Asian American students. During this time they increased from 6.2% to 8.7% of entering students in PhD departments while decreasing from 7.5% to 5.5% of entering students in PsyD-granting departments. The reason for this shift is not clear; it may reflect, in part, increased interest in and/or preparation for research-oriented training, given the sharp increase in Asian American students entering top-ranked PhD departments during this period.

Extremely disquieting trends at the PhD level concern the lack of growth in entrance to PhD-granting departments from 1997 onward for African American and Hispanic/ Latino(a) students, and their similar lack of growth in PhD receipt from 2000 onward. Unfortunately, levels of both degree receipt and entry into PhD-granting departments appear "stuck" at 50% or less of each group's representation in the U.S. population. Furthermore, there was an actual decline among African American students from 1997 to 2003 in entry to highly ranked PhD departments. Various factors may contribute to these disconcerting trends in the PhD domain, including greater interest in other fields or PsyD programs among qualified African American and Hispanic/Latino(a) students; reduced flexibility in admissions criteria due to changing attitudes, concerns, and practices related to affirmative action; decreased availability of financial support geared to African American and Hispanic/Latino(a) students; and/or insufficient faculty and departmental educational and personal support provided to admitted students (cf. Lott, 2005; Malcom et al., 1998; Smedley, Butler, and Bristow, 2004; Woodrow Wilson National Fellowship Foundation, 2005).

Of note, the recent disconcerting trends in doctoral degree receipt are not limited to psychology but are generally present across disciplines (NSF, 2000 [see NSF Table 10], 2004b). Across all PhD-granting fields, the percentage of minority students receiving doctorates (of all recipients, including international students) declined from 14.1% in 1999 to 13.4% in 2003, due primarily to the 6.1%-5.1% decline among Asian American/Pacific Islander students. The latter decline was centered primarily in the physical science, biological science, and engineering fields (8.8%-7.0%); there was little change in these fields for the other three ethnic groups. The social science fields as a whole (excluding psychology) evidenced an increase from 1999 to 2003 in the percentage of Hispanic/Latino(a) students receiving doctorates but showed slight declines among the other three ethnic groups. The humanities also experienced an increase in representation during this period for Hispanic/Latino(a) students only. Finally, in terms of professional degree fields, the percentage of African American and Hispanic/Latino(a) students receiving medical degrees has declined since the late 1990s (American

Table 1 *Percentage of Minority Students Receiving Bachelor's Degrees in Psychology: 1989–2002*

Group	1989	1991	1993	1995	1997[a]	1999	2000	2001	2002	% 2002 U.S. pop.	2002 representation relative to U.S. pop.
Minority total	13.6	14.5	16.5	19.3	22.1	23.8	24.7	24.9	24.3	31.7	0.77
African American/ Black	5.6	6.3	6.9	7.9	8.9	10.0	10.1	10.2	10.1	12.2[b]	0.83
Hispanic/Latino(a)	4.4	4.7	5.3	6.3	7.1	7.3	8.2	8.3	7.9	13.4	0.59
Asian/Pacific Islander	3.2	3.2	3.8	4.6	5.4	5.7	5.6	5.6	5.5	4.1[b]	1.34
American Indian/ Alaskan Native	0.4	0.4	0.5	0.6	0.7	0.7	0.7	0.8	0.7	0.8[b]	0.88

Note. Data sources for 1989–1991 degree receipt: National Science Foundation ([NSF] 2000, Table 4). 1993–1997 and 2000–2001 degree receipt: NSF (2004a, Table 4). 1999 degree receipt: National Center for Education Statistics ([NCES] 2001a). 2002 degree receipt: NCES (2003a). 2002 population: U.S. Census Bureau (2005).

[a]Number with unknown ethnicity was missing from NCES data and was estimated. [b] Persons who indicated one or more additional races were excluded and counted as multiethnic instead (not shown, 1.3%).

Association of Medical Colleges, 2005a, 2005b), as has the percentage of African American students receiving law degrees (American Bar Association, 2005).

Research is needed to determine the factors that are unique to given fields and those that are common across fields in order to explain minority representation trends. Of note, one factor that appears to be playing a more salient role in the physical, biological, and social science fields and in engineering than in psychology is the increase in the percentage of international students receiving doctorates (e.g., from 31.5% in 1999 to 36.9% in 2003 in the physical sciences; from 24.7% to 29.4% in the social sciences). In psychology, in contrast, the increase in international student representation (4.2% in 1999 to 6.0% in 2003) is much smaller, as is the level of representation.

The extremely slow rate of growth in full-time minority faculty is an additional disquieting trend. In 2003, the percentage of minority faculty was still only two fifths of their representation in the U.S. population. Again, a combination of factors may have contributed to the low level of growth achieved. These include limited growth in the number of qualified degree recipients interested in academic instead of applied careers, limited growth in the number of academic job openings in geographic locales and departments attractive to minorities, increased numbers competing for a limited number of academic openings, and insufficient commitment on the part of departments and universities to the hiring and success of minority faculty of color (cf. Cole and Barber, 2003).

The current research, unfortunately, cannot provide insight into which of the these possible explanations, or set of explanations, are at play for the various trends observed. Future research is needed to examine the factors that influence the decisions made by minority psychology majors about graduate school and alternative career options. Research is similarly needed to examine the size and nature of the minority and nonminority applicant pools for graduate school doctoral programs, including the quality of the academic preparation of the growing numbers of students of color who receive bachelor's and master's degrees and their resulting competitiveness for entry into doctoral-level programs. Research on the changing availability of targeted funds for minority students and the decision-making processes and criteria of graduate admissions committees and faculty hiring committees are also critical. Equally crucial to research on factors related to admissions and hiring is research focused on factors that contribute to the retention and high level of achievement of minority students and minority faculty, including support and mentoring, departmental climate, peer relationships, stereotype threat, academic and social integration, knowledge and skills development, and decisions made by promotion and tenure committees. Research in each of these areas will need to carefully delineate sources and mechanisms of influences that are common across ethnic groups and those that are specific to ethnic groups (cf. Lott, 2005; Rogers and Molina, 2006). A recently conducted study, including a Web-based survey and follow-up interviews of a large national sample of ethnic minority and White students at various levels of the psychology pipeline, promises to provide initial insight into some of these areas (Maton et al., 2006).

Underlying many of the institutional factors that influence the minority pipeline appears to be the level of commitment of the department and the larger university to enhancing minority representation—when commitment levels are extremely strong, the action steps necessary to enhance representation will likely be forthcoming. Systematic evidence of the potential of sustained, concerted efforts on the part of committed faculty, staff, and university administrators to make a substantive difference in the minority pipeline has begun to appear in recent years, especially in the biological and physical science fields (cf. BEST [Building Engineering and Science Talent], 2004).

One national model of a long-term, successful programmatic effort to strengthen the minority pipeline is the Meyerhoff Scholars Program at the University of

Table 2 *Percentage of Minority Students Entering Psychology Master's-Granting Departments and Receiving Master's Degrees: 1989–2003*

Group	1989	1991	1993	1995	1997	1999[a]	2000	2001	2002[a]	2003	%U.S. pop.	Representation relative to U.S. pop.
Master's department entry												
											2003	
Minority total	11.0	12.8	13.2	14.6	16.4	18.3	18.7		19.6	23.0	32.2	0.71
African American/Black					7.3	7.4	7.3		7.7	7.0	12.2[b]	0.57
Hispanic/Latino(a)					5.0	5.8	6.0		5.8	9.0	13.7	0.66
Asian/Pacific Islander					3.5	4.5	4.4		4.7	4.3	4.2[b]	1.02
American Indian/Alaskan Native					0.6	1.2	1.0		0.6	0.7	0.8[b]	0.88
Multiethnic									0.9	2.0	1.3	1.54
Master's degree receipt												
											2002	
Minority total	10.6	10.9	11.4	13.6	16.4	17.9	19.6	21.5	21.5		31.7	0.68
African American/Black	4.6	4.6	4.9	6.2	7.8	8.6	9.6	10.9	11.4		12.2[b]	0.93
Hispanic/Latino(a)	4.2	4.0	4.2	4.7	5.3	5.3	6.2	6.6	5.7		13.4	0.43
Asian/Pacific Islander	1.5	1.7	1.7	2.1	2.6	3.5	3.3	3.3	3.7		4.1[b]	0.90
American Indian/Alaskan Native	0.4	0.5	0.5	0.6	0.7	0.6	0.5	0.7	0.7		0.8[b]	0.88

Note. Data sources for 1989–1999 department entry: data extracted from American Psychological Association ([APA] 1990, 1992, 1994, 1996, 1998, 2000). 2000, 2002, 2003 department entry: APA (2005) graduate study departmental survey databases. 1989–1991 degree receipt: National Science Foundation ([NSF] 2000, Table 7). 1993–1997 and 2000–2001 degree receipt: NSF (2004a, Table 7). 1999 degree receipt: National Center for Education Statistics ([NCES] 2001b). 2002 degree receipt: NCES (2003b). 2002 and 2003 population: U.S. Census Bureau (2005).

[a]Number with unknown ethnicity was missing from NCES data and was estimated. [b]Persons who indicated one or more additional races were excluded and counted in the multiethnic category instead (not shown for 2002, 1.3%).

Maryland Baltimore County (UMBC; BEST, 2004). The goal of the program is to substantially increase the number of undergraduate minority students who enter and complete science PhD programs (Maton and Hrabowski, 2004). This comprehensive program includes scholarship support, a summer bridge program, study groups, summer research internships, an extensive program community, highly involved full-time program staff, and high-level university support. To date, this comprehensive initiative has produced over 100 African American students who have entered science PhD programs, and if current PhD receipt rates continue, UMBC will likely become the leading predominantly White baccalaureate-origin university for Black recipients of PhDs in the sciences. The other articles in this special section address in more detail the factors and programmatic efforts that appear critical to enhancing minority representation (cf. Rogers and Molina, 2006; Vasquez and Jones, 2006; Vasquez et al., 2006).

Several limitations of the data sources used in the current article warrant repeating. The APA (2005) graduate study survey data were not developed for research purposes but rather to provide prospective graduate students with information about graduate programs. Concerns with this data set include the unknown accuracy of the information on entering students that was provided by departmental respondents; several changes in key survey items and data collection methods during the period assessed; lack of information on how multiethnic students, international students, and students of unknown ethnicity were counted; the differing subset and number of departments responding to the survey any given year; and, especially in the case of master's and PsyD departments, the relatively low percentage of extant

Table 3 *Percentage of Minority Students Entering PsyD-Granting Departments: 1989–2003*

Group	1989	1991	1993	1995	1997	1999	2000	2002	2003	% 2003 U.S. pop.	2003 representation relative to U.S. pop.
Minority total	15.6	15.3	12.6	16.8	18.9	20.1	20.2	18.8	20.0	32.2	0.62
African American/ Black					6.3	8.2	6.5	6.1	6.5	12.2[a]	0.53
Hispanic/ Latino(a)					5.4	5.0	5.3	5.4	6.1	13.7	0.45
Asian/Pacific Islander					6.2	6.5	7.5	5.5	5.4	4.2[a]	1.29
American Indian/ Alaskan Native					1.0	0.5	0.8	1.1	0.5	0.8[a]	0.63
Multiethnic								0.7	1.4	1.3	1.08

Note. Data sources for 1989–1999 department entry: data extracted from American Psychological Association ([APA] 1990, 1992, 1994, 1996, 1998, 2000). 2000, 2002, 2003 department entry: APA (2005) graduate study departmental survey databases. 2003 population: U.S. Census Bureau (2005).

[a]Persons who indicated one or more additional races were excluded and placed in the multiethnic category instead.

departments responding to the survey most survey years. Several of these concerns apply as well to the NCES and NSF data. These concerns notwithstanding, the general consistency in trends depicted in the primary analyses with those from the secondary analyses provides support for the minority representation trends reported.

The extant Census Bureau data do not provide an optimal means for categorizing multiethnic persons. The exclusion of multiethnic individuals for Native Americans in particular—given Native Americans' small U.S. population size—resulted in substantive consequences for determination of pipeline representation relative to population representation (i.e., almost twice the pipeline representation level than if double-counting had been employed). This fact should be kept in mind when considering the findings reported for Native Americans.

Future research on national trends in minority representation will benefit from enhanced data collection tools and methods. Departmental surveys should include state-of-the-art indicators of ethnicity, including separate categories for international students and students of unknown ethnicity. Such information ideally should be obtained annually for each graduate program in a department, with information obtained from entering students, students leaving the program, and students receiving their degrees. Finally, special efforts need to be made to ensure high response rates across departments.

Conclusions

We believe that the data examined advance an understanding of longer term and newly emerging trends in the minority graduate pipeline. Generally encouraging trends exist at lower levels of the pipeline, but a number of disquieting trends are present at higher levels. Ethnic groups with low levels of representation are of special concern. It is important to continue to monitor trends in the future to see if the trends reported, including recent, emerging trends, continue over time. Our hope is that this study will provide further impetus for psychology's development of a comprehensive, systematic approach to enhancing minority representation in the field, one that can help to counter the troubling trends and help to sustain and enhance the promising ones.

One facet of such a comprehensive approach is to increase the number of high-achieving minority youth in general and those with interests in psychology in particular, both in high school and in college (cf. Dittmann, 2005; Hammond and Yung, 1993; Kohout and Pion, 1990). A second is to develop academic support programs at the undergraduate level that contribute to achievement and preparation for graduate school, especially doctoral study. As noted earlier, potential models in this context include the highly successful, comprehensive programs for minority students of color that have been developed in natural science areas (cf. BEST, 2004). A third focus is to enhance recruitment, retention, and achievement of minority students at the graduate school level, which is the focus of a number of other articles in this special section (Rogers and Molina, 2006; Vasquez and Jones, 2006; Vasquez et al., 2006). An emphasis on enhanced recruitment and retention of minority faculty is also essential, given the critically important role of minority faculty in every facet of the graduate minority pipeline and in the future of psychology more generally. Finally, student and faculty activism in this area may be necessary to ensure that substantive progress continues to be made, harkening back to early efforts to combat underrepresentation (cf. Pickren, 2004). To make a difference, we need a core of committed psychologists working together, united by the vision of a psychology in which all minority groups are fully represented.

Table 4 *Percentage of Minority Students Entering Psychology PhD Departments and Receiving PhD Degrees: 1989–2003*

Group	1989	1991	1993	1995	1997	1999	2000	2001	2002	2003	% 2003 U.S. pop.	2003 representation relative to U.S. pop.
PhD department entry												
Minority total	13.1	14.2	15.9	17.6	16.7	17.5	17.5		20.0	22.1	32.2	0.69
African American/Black					5.8	6.0	6.1		6.4	6.0	12.2[a]	0.49
Hispanic/Latino(a)					4.8	4.3	4.7		5.9	5.1	13.7	0.37
Asian/Pacific Islander					5.6	6.5	6.2		6.5	8.7	4.2[a]	2.07
AmericanIndian/Alaskan Native					0.5	0.6	0.5		0.5	0.8	0.8[a]	1.00
Multiethnic									0.7	1.5	1.3	1.15
PhD receipt												
Minority total	8.0	10.0	9.9	12.5	13.1	15.1	15.7	14.2	15.6	14.8	32.2	0.46
African American/Black	3.0	4.0	3.5	4.4	4.3	4.7	5.2	5.1	5.3	5.1	12.2[a]	0.42
Hispanic/Latino(a)	2.9	3.8	3.8	4.3	4.8	5.9	5.8	5.1	5.8	5.2	13.7	0.38
Asian/Pacific Islander	1.7	1.8	2.1	3.5	3.5	3.6	4.0	3.5	4.0	3.8	4.2[a]	0.90
American Indian/ Alaskan Native	0.3	0.4	0.4	0.4	0.5	1.0	0.6	0.5	0.5	0.7	0.8[a]	0.88

Note. Data sources for 1989–1999 department entry: data extracted from American Psychological Association ([APA] 1990, 1992, 1994, 1996, 1998, 2000). 2000, 2002, 2003 department entry: APA (2005) graduate study departmental survey databases. 1989–1993 degree receipt: National Science Foundation ([NSF] 2000, Table 10). 1995–2003 degree receipt: NSF (2004b, Tables 3 and 5). 2003 population: U.S. Census Bureau (2005).

[a]Persons who indicated one or more additional races were excluded and placed in the multiethnic category instead.

References

American Association of Medical Colleges. (2005a). *Total graduates by gender and race/ethnicity (1992–2002).* Retrieved July 15, 2005, from www.aamc.org/data/facts/archive/famg92002.htm

American Association of Medical Colleges. (2005b). *Total graduates by sex and race/ethnicity (2004).* Retrieved July 15, 2005, from www. aamc.org/data/facts/2004/factsgrads1.htm

American Bar Association. (2005). *Minority degrees awarded (by ethnic group) 1980-2004.* Retrieved July 10, 2005, from www.abanet.org/_legaled/statistics/mindegrees.html

American Psychological Association. (1963). Proceedings of the American Psychological Association. *American Psychologist, 18,* 757-776.

American Psychological Association. (1990, 1992, 1994, 1996, 1998, 2000). *Graduate study in psychology.* Washington, DC: Author.

American Psychological Association. (2003). Guidelines on multicultural education, training, research, practice, and organizational change for psychologists. *American Psychologist, 58,* 377-402.

American Psychological Association, Research Office. (2005). Surveys of graduate departments of psychology, 1989-1990 through 2003-2004 [Unpublished data]. Washington, DC: Author. (Available from the APA Research Office)

Bernal, M. E., and Castro, F. G. (1994). Are clinical psychologists prepared for service and research with ethnic minorities? Report of a decade of progress. *American Psychologist, 49,* 797-805.

BEST. (2004, February). *A bridge for all: Higher education design principles to broaden participation*

Table 5 Percentage of Minority Students Entering Highly Ranked Doctoral-Research Departments: 1989–2003

Group	1989	1991	1993	1995	1997	1999	2000	2002	2003	% 2003 U.S. pop.	2003 representation relative to U.S. pop.
Minority total	13.6	14.0	17.9	17.1	17.9	17.4	19.0	17.0	21.7	32.2	0.68
African American/ Black					4.9	3.8	5.7	4.0	3.8	12.2[a]	0.31
Hispanic/Latino(a)					5.9	3.5	3.9	4.4	5.5	13.7	0.40
Asian/Pacific Islander					6.5	9.5	9.0	7.8	11.6	4.2[a]	2.76
American Indian/ Alaskan Native					0.7	0.6	0.4	0.2	0.6	0.8[a]	0.75
Multiethnic								0.5	0.3	1.3	0.23

Note. Data sources for 1989-1999 department entry: data extracted from American Psychological Association ([APA] 1990, 1992, 1994, 1996, 1998, 2000). 2000, 2002, 2003 department entry: APA (2005) graduate study departmental survey databases. 2003 population: U.S. Census Bureau (2005).

[a]Persons who indicated one or more additional races were excluded and placed in the multiethnic category instead.

in science, technology, engineering, and mathematics. Retrieved March 8, 2004, from www.bestworkforce.org/PDFdocs/BEST_High_Ed_Rep_48pg_02_25.pdf

Bowen, W. G., and Bok, D. (1998). *The shape of the river: Long-term consequences of considering race in college and university admissions.* Princeton, NJ: Princeton University Press.

Bowen, W. G., Kurzweil, M. A., and Tobin, E. M. (2005). *Equity and excellence in American higher education.* Charlottesville: University of Virginia Press.

Cockley, K., Dreher, G. F., and Stockdale, M. S. (2004). Toward the inclusiveness and career success of African Americans in the workplace. In M. S. Stockdale and F. J. Crosby (Eds.), *Psychology and management of workplace diversity* (pp. 168 -190). Malden, MA: Blackwell.

Cole, S., and Barber, E. (2003). *Increasing faculty diversity: The occupational choices of high-achieving minority students.* Cambridge, MA: Harvard University Press.

College Board. (1999). *Reaching the top.* New York: College Board Publications.

Comas-Díaz, L. (1990). Ethnic minority health: Contributions and future directions of the American Psychological Association. In F. C. Serafica, A. E. Schwebel, R. K. Russell, P. D. Isaac, and L. B. Myers (Eds.), *Mental health of ethnic minorities* (pp. 275-301). New York: Praeger.

Table 6 *Percentage of Minority Psychology Faculty: 1989–2003*

Group	1989	1991	1993	1995	1997	1999	2000	2001	2003	% U.S. pop.	Representation relative to U.S. pop.
										2003	
Minority total	6.9	7.3	7.7	8.0	9.6	10.5	11.1	11.1	12.0	32.2	0.37
										2001	
African American/ Black	3.0	3.4	3.1	3.0	3.4	4.6		4.9		12.2[a]	0.40
Hispanic/Latino(a)	1.5	1.5	2.1	2.5	3.4	3.2		3.5		13.0	0.27
Asian/Pacific Islander	2.0	1.9	2.1	2.0	2.4	2.3		2.2		3.9[a]	0.56
American Indian/ Alaskan Native	0.5	0.5	0.5	0.5	0.5	0.5		0.4		0.8[a]	0.50

Note. Data sources for 1989–1999 and 2001 faculty: National Science Foundation (2004c). 2000 and 2003 faculty: American Psychological Association (2005] graduate study departmental survey databases. 2001 and 2003 population: U.S. Census Bureau (2005).

[a]Persons who indicated one or more additional races were excluded and counted as multiethnic instead (not shown, 1.2%).

Commission on Ethnic Minority Recruitment, Retention, and Training in Psychology. (1997). *Visions and transformations ... The final report.* Washington, DC: American Psychological Association.

Dittmann, M. (2005). Attracting minority students early: Psychology faculty and undergraduates reach out to minority high school students. *APA Monitor on Psychology, 36,* 30-31.

Dobbs, M. (2005, November 22). Universities record drop in black admissions. *The Washington Post,* p. A1.

Dulles Conference Task Force. (1978). *Expanding the roles of culturally diverse peoples in the profession of psychology* (Report submitted to the Board of Directors of the American Psychological Association). Washington, DC: Author.

Gandara, P. (1995). *Over the ivy walls: The educational mobility of low-income Chicanos.* Albany, NY: SUNY Press.

Hammond, W. R., and Yung, N. (1993). Minority student recruitment and retention practices among schools of professional psychology: A national survey and analysis. *Professional Psychology: Research and Practice, 24,* 3-12.

Highlen, P. (1994). Racial/ethnic diversity in doctoral programs of psychology: Challenges for the 21st century. *Applied and Preventive Psychology, 13,* 91-108.

Hills-Briggs, F., Evans, J. D., and Norman, M. A. (2004). Racial and ethnic diversity among trainees and professionals in psychology and neuro-psychology: Needs, trends, and challenges. *Applied Neuropsychology, 11,* 13-22.

Hoffer, T., B., Welch, V., Jr., Williams, K., Hess. M., Weber, K., Lisek, B., et al. (2005). *Doctorate recipients from United States universities: Summary report 2004* (Appendix A, Table A-1). Retrieved January 4, 2006, from norc.uchicago.edu/issues/sed-2004.pdf

Hopwood v. State of Texas, 78F.3d 932 (5th Cir. 1996).

Howard, A., Pion, G. M., Gottfredson, G. D., Oskamp, S., Pfafflin, S. M., Bray, D. W., and Burstein, A. G. (1986). The changing face of American psychology. *American Psychologist, 41,* 1311-1327.

Jones, J. M. (1990). Who is training our ethnic minority psychologists, and are they doing it right? (Invitational address). In G. Stricker, E. E. Davis-Russell, E. Bourg, E. Duran, W. R. Hammond, J. McHolland, et al. (Eds.), *Toward ethnic diversification in psychology education and training* (pp. 17-34). Washington, DC: American Psychological Association.

Kohout, J., and Pion, G. (1990). Participation of ethnic minorities in psychology: Where do we stand today? In G. Stricker, E. E. Davis- Russell, E. Bourg, E. Duran, W. R. Hammond, J. McHolland, et al. (Eds.), *Toward ethnic diversification in psychology education and training* (pp. 153-165). Washington, DC: American Psychological Association.

Lemann, N. (2003, June 29). A decision that universities can relate to. *The New York Times,* p. 4 -14.

Lott, B. (2005). *Strategies for enhancing the pipeline for students of color in psychology graduate programs.* Unpublished manuscript.

Malcom, S., Van Horne, V. V., Gaddy, C. D., and George, Y. S. (1998). *Losing ground: Science and engineering graduate education of Black and Hispanic Americans.* Washington, DC: American Association for the Advancement of Science.

Maton, K. I., Grant, S., Lott, B., Rogers, M. R., Vasquez, M. J. T., Vazquez, L., and Witting, M. (2006). *The minority pipeline study.* Manuscript in preparation.

Maton, K. I., and Hrabowski, F. A., III. (2004). Increasing the number of African American PhDs in the sciences and engineering: A strengths-based approach. *American Psychologist, 59,* 629 - 654.

Munoz-Dunbar, R., and Stanton, A. L. (1999). Ethnic diversity in clinical psychology: Recruitment and admission practices among doctoral programs. *Teaching of Psychology, 26,* 259 -264.

National Advisory Mental Health Council Workgroup on Racial/Ethnic Diversity in Research Training and

Health Disparities Research. (2001). *An investment in America's future: Racial/ethnic diversity in mental health research careers.* Retrieved February 8, 2005, from www.nimh.nih.gov/council/diversity/pdf

National Center for Education Statistics. (2001a). *Digest of education statistics tables and figures, 2001* (Table 270). Retrieved January 15, 2005, from http://nces.ed.gov/programs/digest/d01/dt270.asp

National Center for Education Statistics. (2001b). *Digest of education statistics tables and figures, 2001* (Table 273). Retrieved January 15, 2005, from http://nces.ed.gov/programs/digest/d01/dt273.asp

National Center for Education Statistics. (2003a). *Digest of education statistics tables and figures, 2003* (Table 265). Retrieved January 15, 2005, from http://nces.ed.gov/programs/digest/d03/tables/dt265.asp

National Center for Education Statistics. (2003b). *Digest of education statistics tables and figures, 2003* (Table 268). Retrieved January 15, 2005, from http://nces.ed.gov/programs/digest/d03/tables/dt268.asp

National Research Council. (1995). *Research-doctorate programs in the United States: Continuity and change.* Washington, DC: National Academies Press.

National Science Foundation. (2000). *Science and engineering degrees by race/ethnicity of recipients: 1989-97* (Tables 4, 7, and 10). Retrieved January 10, 2005, from www.nsf.gov/statistics/nsf00311/pdf/sectb.pdf

National Science Foundation. (2004a). *Science and engineering degrees by race/ethnicity of recipients: 1992-2001* (Tables 4 and 7). Retrieved January 10, 2005, from www.nsf.gov/statistics/nsf04318/pdf/sectb.pdf

National Science Foundation. (2004b). *Science and engineering doctorate awards: 2003* (Table 5). Retrieved January 12, 2005, from www.nsf .gov/statistics/nsf05300/pdf/tables.pdf

National Science Foundation. (2004c). *Science and engineering indicators 2004* (Appendix Table 5-24). Retrieved January 19, 2005, from www.nsf.gov/statistics/seind04/append/c5/at05-24.pdf

Olatunji, B. O. (2003). Increasing diversity in psychology: A call for the involvement of ethnic minority graduate students. *Behavior Therapist, 26* 288 -289.

Pickren, W. (2004). Between the cup of principle and the lip of practice: Ethnic minorities and American psychology, 1966 -1980. *History of Psychology, 7,* 45-64.

Rabasca, L. (2000, March). Attracting more minority students to psychology programs. *APA Monitor on Psychology,* 56 -57.

Rogers, M. R., Hoffman, M. A., and Wade, J. (1998). Notable multicultural training in APA-approved counseling psychology and school psychology programs. *Cultural Diversity and Mental Health, 4,* 212-226.

Rogers, M. R., and Molina, L. E. (2006). Exemplary efforts in psychology to recruit and retain graduate students of color. *American Psychologist, 61,* 143-156.

Smedley, B. D., Butler, A. S., and Bristow, L. R. (Eds.). (2004). *In the nation's compelling interest: Ensuring diversity in the health-care workforce* (Committee on institutional and policy-level strategies for increasing the diversity of the U.S. health care workforce, Board on health sciences policy). Washington, DC: National Academies Press.

Speight, S. L., Thomas, A. J., Kennel, R. G., and Anderson, M. E. (1995). Operationalizing multicultural training in doctoral programs and internships. *Professional Psychology: Research and Practice, 26,* 401-406.

Stricker, G., Davis-Russell, E. E., Bourg, E., Duran, E., Hammond, W. R., McHolland, J., et al. (Eds.). (1990). *Toward ethnic diversification in psychology education and training.* Washington, DC: American Psychological Association.

Sue, D. W., Bingham, R. P., Porche-Burke, L., and Vasquez, M. (1999). The diversification of psychology: A multicultural revolution. *American Psychologist, 54,* 1061-1069.

Syverson, P. (2001). What can application trends tell us about the future demand for graduate education? In D. E. Chubin and W. Pearson Jr. (Eds.), *Scientists and engineers for the new millennium: Renewing the human resource* (pp. 55-59). New York: Alfred P. Sloan Foundation.

U.S. Census Bureau. (2002). *Statistical abstract of the United States: 2002* (Table 15. Resident population by Hispanic origin status, p. 17). Retrieved February 9, 2005, from www.census.gov/prod/2002pubs/01statab/pop/pdf

U.S. Census Bureau. (2005). *Statistical abstract of the United States: 2004–2005* (Table 13. Resident population by sex, race, and Hispanic origin status, p. 14). Retrieved February 9, 2005, from www.census.gov/prod/2004pubs/04statab/pop/pdf

Vasquez, M. J. T., and Jones, J. M. (2006). Increasing the number of psychologists of color: Public policy issues for affirmative diversity. *American Psychologist, 61,* 132-142.

Vasquez, M. J. T., Lott, B., Garcia-Vazquez, E., Grant, S. K., Iwamasa, G. Y., Molina, L. E., et al. (2006). Personal reflections: Barriers and strategies in increasing diversity in psychology. *American Psychologist, 61,* 157-172.

Woodrow Wilson National Fellowship Foundation. (2005). *Diversity and the PhD: A review of efforts to broaden race and ethnicity in U.S. doctoral education.* Princeton, NJ: Author.

Xu, W., and Leffler, A. (1996). Gender and race effects on occupational prestige, segregation, and earnings. In E. N. Chow and D. Y. Wilkinson (Eds.), *Race, class, and gender: Common bonds, different voices* (pp. 107-124). Thousand Oaks, CA: Sage.

Personal Reflections

Barriers and Strategies in Increasing Diversity in Psychology

By Melba J.T. Vasquez, Bernice Lott, Enedina Garcia-Vazquez, Sheila K. Grant, Gayle Y. Iwamasa, Ludwin E. Molina, Brian L. Ragsdale, Elise Vestal-Dowdy

Our objective in this article is to give voice to the personal experiences and problems encountered by students and faculty of color in departments of psychology—in their training and in their current workplaces. Six such faculty and students talk about the barriers they encountered as related to the intersections of ethnicity and race, gender, sexual orientation, social class, and physical disabilities. They also discuss strategies that were useful and positive in their doctoral programs and in their current work environments.

The contributors were invited to participate in a panel held in January 2003 at the third National Multicultural Conference and Summit, which was sponsored by several divisions of the American Psychological Association (APA). The group is diverse with respect to ethnicity and race, gender, sexual orientation, social class background, physical disability, area of specialization, training institution, and type of current employment. Three of the contributors are experienced psychology faculty members, and three are recent PhD recipients or current doctoral program students.

The general focus of the panel (as well as of all the articles in this special section) was on how to go about changing psychology's dominant European American perspective in the United States by increasing the numbers of students of color in psychology graduate programs. The more specific focus was to relate personal experiences to strategies and prescriptions for change relevant to recruitment, retention, and achievement. The ultimate goal of identifying barriers and strategies is to increase diversity among psychologists

Melba J.T. Vasquez, Bernice Lott, Enedina Garcia-Vazquez, Sheila K. Grant, Gayle Y. Iwamasa, Ludwin E. Molina, Brian L. Ragsdale and Elise Vestal-Dowdy, "Personal Reflections: Barriers and Strategies in Increasing Diversity in Psychology," *American Psychologist*, vol. 61, no. 2, pp. 157–163, 165–172.

in the educational pipeline and in the profession. The panelists describe their relationships with dominant-group and minority peers and colleagues in graduate school and in their current employment and how they dealt with issues of stereotyped beliefs and inhospitable environments. The impact of affirmative action policies on the experiences of some is also noted. This article is presented as a personal complement to others in this special section of the *American Psychologist* in order to illustrate, through the bravely voiced experiences of colleagues, what it means to be a minority of color in psychology.

Personal Reflections

Enedina Garcia-Vazquez: A Chocolate Drop in a Sea of Vanilla

Graduate school experiences are influenced by the color of one's skin, and phenotypic features can moderate many life experiences (Codina and Montalvo, 1994). Hall (1994) described skin color as the "master status" that impacts employment, income, and self-concept. As a result, graduate students of color who choose a life in academia may have experiences different from those of their White counterparts.

In graduate school, although my experiences were generally positive, I experienced racism, subtle and overt, often simply because of the color of my skin. I was the only non-White student in my school psychology program and was the first Latina to graduate from the program in 1990. I had heard that another student of color had graduated from the program, but no one could provide me with details. My dark skin seemed to confuse my peers, and I was frequently asked, "What country are you from?" My response of "Texas!" did not seem to be an acceptable answer. Some believed I was African American; after all, my caramel skin must have come from somewhere. Some children in a rural town referred to me as the "Japanese lady." While the color of my skin appeared to confuse individuals, the lack of diversity added to my less than positive experiences. Because there was a lack of ethnic diversity in psychology, I often felt like a stranger in my classes, like I didn't belong. As Lewis (2004) pointed out in his study with African Americans, students of color may feel like uninvited guests. I, too, felt like an uninvited guest, and when I searched for others like myself, I didn't find anyone. In addition, I did not have anonymity in my classes. After all, how can you miss the only chocolate drop in a sea of vanilla? At the same time, I worried how others might perceive me, because light skin has historically been considered better than dark skin (DuBois, 1969). As a woman with Mestizo features and darker skin, I did not fit the ideal of White beauty.

Not all students of color are recruited as affirmative action admits. No one recruited me directly, although some of my peers believed that I had been admitted because of my ethnicity. My admission was seen as a result of affirmative action instead of my ability. This is not unusual. Research has shown that status and achievement by White Americans are perceived to be a result of their own efforts, whereas status and achievement by people of color are attributed to affirmative action (Carter, 1995; McIntosh, 1992). My program was flexible with admissions criteria, but I never felt that I was extended special privileges because of the color of my skin or ethnicity. I believed that my application was competitive, and I was awarded graduate assistantships and a scholarship that provided me with tuition and a small stipend.

I had good interactions with my primary program professors and other faculty. I believed that my previous experiences, a master's degree and two years of teaching, aided my admission and subsequent success. These helped me create my own networks and support systems, which included other students, none of whom were of color, and a friend who eventually became my spouse. I also relied on the teachings of my ancestors and my parents.

Support is important. There were no faculty members of color in my graduate program. As a result, I saw the commitment to diversity as superficial. The graduate school did provide financial support in the form of funding for students of color who wanted to visit the university and for admitted students. Financial support is an important variable in increasing retention and timely graduation. This was an excellent recruitment and retention tool (Maher, Ford, and Thompson, 2004), yet other ways to support students of color were also needed. More emphasis was placed on recruiting and retaining international students because of the interests of some faculty members. In general, the administration neither encouraged nor discouraged particular recruitment efforts, and assistantships were tough to come by.

Support for diversity can also be shown by offering a curriculum that presents a multicultural perspective. In my case, the curriculum was not inclusive, and discussion of minority issues seemed to center on stereotypes (Vazquez, 1997). Mexicans have mustaches, take naps, don't make eye contact, are all family oriented (so plan on having things for the kids to do when they meet for parent conferences), and so forth. Once when I was advocating for bilingual education and bilingualism, a professor noted, "You could have gone further if you had not been in bilingual education." The irony is that I was never in a bilingual education program and the professor made an incorrect assumption, so his comments were based on stereotypes.

Education does not automatically make a person White. While I worried about how I would be perceived and treated by White Americans, I also had to address the fears of my Latino peers and family. My family worried that I would lose my ethnicity and become White. They worried that I would be too different from them and become fully assimilated (Keefe and Padilla, 1987). Of course I became different from my family—I am the only one with a PhD—but I did not lose my language or my ethnicity. In fact, I became more steadfast in keeping those aspects of my life alive. Even more interesting were my interactions with a peer in another doctoral program who felt I had "sold out"—until he discovered that I cooked complicated traditional Latino meals, knew the songs of my ancestors, and spoke Spanish flawlessly. He seemed to believe that in order to obtain academic success, the culture of origin would be lost. Simply put, education would lead to assimilation.

It's every faculty member's job to recruit and train graduate students of color. When I became a faculty member in the department where I received my PhD, recruiting students of color became my responsibility. It became my job to facilitate the road for students of color. Other faculty of color were angry that a faculty member of color was the one responsible for recruiting and retaining students of color. Yet I felt that it needed to be done. The other program faculty members were supportive, helpful, and committed, but I was the first and only person of color to be hired in my program.

As the department worked on increasing the number of students of color, admissions criteria became very flexible, and students with very low GRE scores were admitted. Progress through the program for the students with low GREs was very difficult. It was important that faculty members were committed to helping these students develop their skills. Initially, graduation rates for people of color were low, but this changed. The program won the American Psychological Association's Suinn Minority Achievement Award, given to doctoral programs judged to be committed to diversity through funding, recruitment, retention, mentoring, curriculum, faculty-student collaborations, and graduation rates.

Faculty of color and allies make a difference. In my current position, we have three faculty of color in a department of nine, all Latino and bilingual. Yet 66% of the department consists of White Americans.

Two faculty members represent sexual orientation diversity. Multicultural issues are discussed and infused in the majority of courses, although the curriculum is not completely inclusive. We are pretty open and pride ourselves on being a safe place for diversity, including diversity in terms of disability, sexual orientation, and social class. Our departmental efforts in recruiting, retaining, and graduating students of color have been effective. More students of color now apply to our program, and they indicate that their primary reason is the program's commitment to diversity. Often the students specifically request to work with our faculty of color. Support and guidance for discussion of diversity issues are provided.

Final comments. My life as a student and an academic has been challenging. Many things I heard from administrators created an uncomfortable environment for me. One questioned whether I would be doing "real research" or research without a multicultural emphasis. One dean questioned why a college should make special efforts to recruit faculty of color. His statement "We are not a social system" implied that special consideration should not be given to faculty of color. A few years ago, a White administrator did not have any qualms about insulting me in front of other faculty. In response to my question about the process for applying for awards, he said that I needed to do something credible to be considered for an award. Since then I have won several awards.

Although some of my experiences have been negative as a result of the color of my skin, I believe that the educational environment is the best place to develop diversity of ideas. In addition, the goal of affirming diversity seems to have become more prevalent and more positive than simple tolerance of differences.

The most profound lesson I have learned is that although I may choose not to be the spokesperson or to address racist or discriminatory comments every time I hear them, the more often I stay silent, the more often I show tolerance for such statements. Yes, I may get tired of always having to be the one to remind others of multicultural issues, but if I do not do so, I contribute to my own oppression. And I refuse to be oppressed. In my work with students, I urge them to express their own voices. And aren't we all in the business of empowering the powerless?

Helpful strategies. There are a number of strategies that can be incorporated in order to enhance success among students and faculty of color. First of all, students of color should not become spokespeople for all persons of color. Students of color can feel isolated and unwelcome in college (Lewis, 2004), but having them be spokespersons for all students of color is not the best approach. As the only graduate student of color, I often was seen as the expert on all Latino issues. At some point I became the expert on all people of color, a hefty role I often chose not to take. Mentoring is a better approach to increasing students' sense of belongingness and success (Valverde and Rodriguez, 2002). Mentoring helps faculty learn about students, assess their needs, and learn how to provide moral and other support.

A second strategy is to provide financial support. Financial support is a must. Students with stable financial aid have been found to be more likely to graduate on time (Maher et al., 2004). Johnson (1996) added that a 1994 report by the American Society for Engineering Education emphasized that fellowships are beneficial to students because, as opposed to assistantships, they allow students to concentrate on their studies. When time to study is increased, completion rates increase and time needed to earn a degree decreases. Lewis (2004) noted that the research experience students gain from research assistantships increases their chances of completing their dissertations.

Another strategy is to make the curriculum more multicultural. The APA has approved guidelines for multicultural competencies (APA, 2003), and programs are urged to infuse multicultural issues into their curriculum and practices. To advance the field of psychology toward diversity, it is important to apply critical pedagogy in the teaching of multiculturalism (Vazquez and Garcia-Vazquez, 2003).

For faculty members, it is important to remember that faculty of color cannot be on every committee. Given that critical masses of faculty of color have not been reached, departments, colleges, and universities tend to call on their few faculty of color to serve on every committee. A department needs to protect the time of faculty members so that they can write manuscripts and achieve tenure and promotion successfully. I am often pulled in many different directions. Even in a Hispanic-serving institution, faculty of color are not in the majority, and I am still asked to serve on too many committees because I fit many categories: female, Latina, faculty senator. Until this year, I was the only Latina faculty senator in a group of over 100 senators. And as of my last count, there are only three other senators of color.

Faculty members will not become sensitive to multicultural issues simply because they are called racists. Calling someone a racist is not a gentle push. Multicultural development is a process.

Sheila K. Grant: A Difficult Dialogue

My grandmother often said to me, "Sheila, you have to work twice as hard to be thought half as good." My grandmother was speaking from her experience as a colored woman born in the late 1800s, descended from parents who were slaves, but her statement seems to still hold true today! As a woman faculty member of color who has just completed 11 years at my university, I can speak about the sociocultural barriers I continue to face, as well as about some of the recruitment, retention, and achievement strategies used on my behalf.

Recruitment. I was a beneficiary of creative recruitment strategies as both a graduate student and a faculty member. I received a four-year fellowship as well as a "forgivable doctoral loan" to supplement my education, and I was recruited and hired at my university as part of its faculty development affirmative action program.

My university still complies with federal affirmative action requirements, but California's Proposition 209 has necessitated different approaches to and strategies for achieving diversity among our faculty and staff. We now need to "recast diversity" in the hiring process by focusing on diversity in knowledge, skills, and experience. Every search committee is supposed to have an equity and diversity advocate, who is usually the chair of the search committee. In my experience, however, faculty search committees often have titular equity advocates who may lack a true commitment to diversity and be uninformed about how to "recast diversity" in the recruitment process.

Oh, Grandma, I'm getting so tired of working twice as hard to be thought half as good because now they don't even see me! My experiences are illustrated by two recent national reports (Menges and Associates, 1999; Rice, Sorcinelli, and Austin, 2000) that highlight the role of departmental social climate in the success and satisfaction of new faculty. The findings of those reports suggest that inexperienced faculty rarely succeed in teaching and scholarship without the support of more experienced faculty as friends, role models, and mentors. Without guidance, faculty newcomers are unable to decipher the expectations of the institution with respect to retention, tenure, and promotion. Devoid of community, new faculty often find themselves anxious and stressed, may feel a sense of loneliness and competition, and report being intellectually understimulated (Boice, 1999; Sorcinelli, 2000). This lack of support and guidance is a greater problem for minority faculty than for their majority counterparts, especially at predominantly White institutions.

I will share my perception of the climate I encountered in my early experiences in academia. As an African American woman with disabilities since the age of 12, I have come to view my recruitment as the easy part. The retention and achievement aspects of being a university professor have been much more difficult.

Retention and achievement. One significant barrier has been my innocence and lack of acculturation to the world of academia. As a student, I believed my family's watchwords "Knowledge is power!" and that if I learned my discipline well and became a proficient teacher and mentor, I would be successful as a faculty member. But cracking academia's code of conduct has been more difficult than that. Like a stranger in a foreign land, I experienced difficulty in comprehending the rules for promotion and tenure. I struggled to reconcile the dilemma between being a faculty member at a teaching institution with an increasing course load and increasing classroom size and responding to a growing emphasis on research, publications, and extramural grant procurement. I enjoyed and excelled in teaching, developed creative techniques to reach and motivate a diverse student population, and successfully mentored numerous students of color into competitive psychology PhD programs (more than a full-time job in my opinion). Yet, I felt compelled to spread myself extremely thin by engaging in numerous research projects in search of publications and grants.

My satisfaction as a faculty member has been compromised by experiences of isolation and alienation. As a student, I had been idealistic about the ivory tower and put my professors on pedestals. After being hired at my alma mater, I was quickly disabused of these notions and instead began to feel that I was working on an academic plantation, where my voice and my existence were marginalized by the good old boys' and girls' network (Paul, 2001). For example, when I would speak during faculty meeting discussions during the first seven years, I would notice that everyone would politely stop talking, seemingly to give me their attention, but when I finished they would pick right up where they left off, as if I had never spoken. Because of this surreal experience of invisibility, I felt a desperate need to protect my self-esteem. I vacillated between self-blame and using the self-protective strategy of attributional ambiguity (Crocker, Voelkl, Testa, and Major, 1991), and I questioned whether it was prejudice and discrimination or my lack of anything worthwhile to contribute to faculty meetings that was at work.

Another example of painful invisibility occurred immediately after my first year, when my deteriorating physical condition required that I have sequential bilateral hip replacements during the school break. Since my department was notified about my pending surgeries before I left for the summer, I was dumbfounded to receive no contact (not to mention concern) from any of my colleagues during my convalescence. In the absence of concern about my welfare from my colleagues, I had to fall back on my grandmother's advice that I "work twice as hard to be thought half as good." I discharged myself from the hospital against doctors' orders on a Friday and reported to work and a full teaching schedule (four classes) on Monday (still in a wheelchair, unable to bear my own weight, and in considerable pain). I realize now how martyrlike this behavior was, but at the time, I saw no other way to maintain my tenure-track position; I was too proud to ask for help since none was offered. I was learning about the department culture, which appeared cold, to say the least.

Several years ago, I hurt my back while already dealing with multiple disabling conditions, and I was having difficulty physically keeping up with my faculty duties. When I asked my department chair what type of accommodations might be available to help me, I was told in an e-mail message that I "should go out on disability leave because there was nothing the department nor the college ... could do" for me.

Grandma, now they don't even want to give me a chance to work at all!!! Other incidents have contributed to my perception of a cold and unwelcoming departmental climate. During a committee meeting in my first semester, in discussing the type of new faculty hires to consider as aging faculty retire, I heard a White male colleague say, "Well, we certainly don't want a diversity hire." When I asked for clarification, I was told, "You know, someone substandard and not up to caliber." I felt anger and threat from the stereotype he was promoting (Steele, 1997) and felt compelled to try to "educate" him. Why should minority faculty have to defend their credentials at every turn (a truly exhausting task) while majority faculty can rest on their laurels by virtue of their privileged ethnic status?

I have overheard majority faculty make racist comments about minority colleagues and students. One faculty member (who is well-liked and respected by colleagues and adored by students) regularly uses racial epithets in lectures, speeches, and conversations. His defense is that he is "desensitizing" all of us to these words so that they will no longer hurt! Students came to me in anger and/or tears about this teacher, but I was a vulnerable junior faculty member at the time. More senior faculty members, aware of this behavior, had done nothing about it for 30 years (either turning a blind eye or supporting the behavior, I know not which). Again, the culture of the department was one that appeared to accept prejudice in the air.

Another colleague once complimented me on my hair with the comment that I "must be mixed with something else (White or Indian) because I couldn't be all Black!"—as if that would be a "bad" thing. When discussing diversity from my perspective as an African American or as a person with disabilities, I have had numerous well-educated majority faculty members (European American and nondisabled) repeat this mantra to me: "But I don't think of you as an African American [Black]" or "But I don't think of you as disabled." I perceive both types of comments, which are offered as compliments, as painful denials of my real, authentic existence and of my multiple identities. Such incidents of unintentional racism (Ridley, 1995) have had profoundly negative consequences on my psychological and physical well-being. I have often felt alone, anxious, angry, and depressed.

The positive experiences. I have also had many positive interactions with majority faculty. I have benefited from the mentoring of two women faculty allies who have gone to bat for me, encouraged me professionally and personally, exposed me to the grant writing process (a missing piece in my education), and hired me as a consultant on funded research projects. These have led to publications that helped me to achieve early tenure and promotion. I could not have been this successful without their belief in me and in my potential as an academic.

In addition, my department has undergone a metamorphosis as it lost significant numbers of the "old guard" through retirement and replaced them, for the most part, with young, recent doctoral recipients with more commitment to equity and diversity. I believe that I have made a difference as the first and only African American tenure-track faculty member hired in the department's more than 40-year history. I have contributed to the work of university-wide committees and boards dedicated to improving equity for ethnic minorities and persons with disabilities. A few good lifelong faculty friends have let me know that I am not alone in this fight to make a better, more equitable department for faculty, students, and staff.

Grandma, maybe things really are changing? These examples from my experiences as a faculty member of color with disabilities are anecdotal, and I have no evidence that they are systemic. My decade-long experiences do suggest to me, however, that a lessening of inequality and discrimination may very well be generalizable to other California universities and perhaps to others across the country.

In summary, I encourage ethnic and nonethnic minorities to enter into the discipline of psychology, to persist up the educational pipeline to the doctorate, and to contribute their much-needed cultural insight to enrich the entire field, from theory development, to empirical research, and on to application and social change. This enrichment will benefit the field as a whole and both majority and minority members by encouraging a cross-pollination of ideas and by promoting multicultural understanding, appreciation, and competence.

To survive emotionally in a stigmatizing world, ethnic and nonethnic minority individuals may adopt self-protective strategies, but we must either resist developing or consider dismantling the proverbial "chips" on our shoulders that often arise after years of hurt and rejection resulting from prejudice and discrimination. This is no easy feat, but I believe it is necessary for us to take a higher road so that this assault does not irreparably change our character and hearts and move us from a positive place of hope and possibility to a negative place of defensive hate, despair, and surrender. Even though I believe ethnic and nonethnic minorities will still feel pressured to work twice as hard to be thought half as good, I urge them to resist martyrdom. We must take better care of ourselves by actively developing support networks, by realizing that we cannot be all things to every minority student or colleague, and by understanding that we cannot serve on every committee that requests a diversity person.

It is important for ethnic and nonethnic minority faculty to pick their battles, because it is unwise to take upon oneself the education and consciousness raising of the White faculty body without experiencing burnout. And we cannot make progress alone without the support from majority allies. I entreat existing and potential majority allies to "work twice as hard" at confronting their biases and reaching out to minority faculty and students with genuine care and support in an effort to prevent their marginalization, while taking care not to patronize them.

And finally, I believe that we should continue to listen to our ethnic and cultural elders like my Grandma (alive and in memory or history), either biological or extended, as they encourage us (if we listen) through the revelation of their wisdom, their strength of character, and their steadfast perseverance against much more difficult sociocultural barriers than we face today. In turn, we can become positive role models for those who follow us by demonstrating broadened possibilities and providing encouragement. As we walk in the footsteps of our forebears, we can light the path to lead many more ethnic and nonethnic minority scholars up the educational pipeline to the doctorate and beyond—to successful careers in psychology.

Ludwin E. Molina: A Perspective from a Student of Color

As I write this, I am beginning my second year in a social psychology doctorate program at a research university. I am glad to have this opportunity to reflect on my impressions of the recruitment process and on my first year in a graduate program, because these two important periods have set the tone and expectations for the remainder of my graduate student experience. I will highlight some relevant topics (e.g., initial contact, funding, diversity within the program) and discuss the barriers I encountered and some effective strategies for increasing diversity.

Initial contact. Initial contact by my department took place during the recruitment phase when ethnic minority professors and students contacted me to inform me about the program and answer my questions (see Hammond and Yung, 1993, for a review of minority student recruitment practices). I thought this was a good idea on the part of the department because it gave me the opportunity to ask the students about their experiences as some of the few persons of color in a program that is predominantly White. This was a concern of mine because I had reservations about entering an environment that might be uncomfortable for the next five to six years. Moreover, I knew I would have a unique status as one of just a handful of Latino graduate students within my program, and this caused me some anxiety (see work by Sekaquaptewa and Thompson,

2002, on solo status). The general response I received was that the atmosphere within the department was comfortable for ethnic minorities.

Funding. Funding was a significant issue for me because I come from a low socioeconomic background (Lott, 2005; Rogers and Molina, 2006, this issue). My decision to apply to graduate school was not easy given the likelihood that I might have to finance a good portion of it myself; this was a daunting prospect. However, I was fortunate that the program I was deciding to attend secured a two-year fellowship for me well before the decision deadline. The intramural fellowship I was awarded is given to entering graduate students conducting research on ethnic minority issues. Knowing that I would receive fellowship support my first two years put my focus squarely on whether the program was a good fit for me in terms of my research interests, departmental resources, faculty, students, and department atmosphere.

Diversity within the program. One of my impressions of the department after completing my first year was that it could improve its commitment to diversity. It was interesting to hear people in the department talk about its dedication to diversity while it was my experience that there was a lack of numerical representation or a "critical mass" of Latino/Latina, African American, and Native American students and faculty (see Rogers, Hoffman, and Wade, 1998; Rogers and Molina, 2006). The gender composition of the faculty in the department seems to be pretty good, although it could still be improved in particular areas.

Mentoring. In general, the mentoring I have received in my doctoral program has been good. The program ensures that first-year graduate students are paired with a "student buddy" (i.e., a continuing graduate student within the same area) to act as a peer mentor and help with the transition during the first year. I thought it was a good decision by the department to pair me with a student buddy who was a person of color because it allowed me to discuss openly some worries I had about being one of the few Latinos in the program. I have also been able to work with a primary advisor who both has research interests similar to mine and comes from a similar social class background. She has been a person to whom I turn for research and career advice. In addition, I have been able to discuss with her particular concerns I have about the program and about planning a career in academia. I am also impressed by the opportunities graduate students have to present their research (e.g., in labs, in class) and to receive critical and constructive feedback. I believe the mentoring I have received within the department has been quite exceptional.

Student integration into the program. My program attempts to integrate graduate students into the social psychology "family" through weekly colloquia at which invited speakers present their research, a weekly happy hour following the colloquium that is an informal time where faculty and students can talk, and quarterly celebrations. Some faculty members also have social gatherings at their homes during the year or the quarter for the graduate students they advise. These occasions encourage social networking and friendship among students and faculty within the program. For students of color who want to network with other minorities, there is no formal organization at the department level, but such organizations and clubs can be found at the university level.

Diversity within the curriculum. There are few classes in my program that have an emphasis on ethnic minority issues. Moreover, there is not much emphasis or discussion of ethnic minority issues within required classes except where directly relevant (e.g., intergroup relations). If class discussions sometimes do turn to ethnic minority issues, this is more the exception than the rule. An alternative for interested students is to enroll in classes outside of the department on ethnic minority issues that have psychological relevance.

Relationships with people in the program

My relationships and interactions with people in the department are generally positive, and I don't typically feel that my ethnicity is an issue. Times when my ethnicity has been salient to me have been when there is an area gathering, for example, and I realize that I am one of the few Latino students in my program (see Thompson and Sekaquaptewa, 2002). One instance of discomfort I can recall was when I was in a class one day and I became the default expert on ethnic minority issues because I was the only person of color in the class.

I don't interact much with other Latino or African American students because there are not many of us in the program. Furthermore, the ethnic minority students who are in the program are not necessarily part of my area or cohort. Outside of my student buddy, I can count on one hand the number of conversations I have had with other ethnic minority students in my program about being a student of color. It appears to be a norm in the department not to discuss such issues. This norm results in what I refer to as a "deafening silence." As much as I would like to discuss my concerns openly with other ethnic minority students I do not because I assume others in the program do not want to talk about these issues. It is likely that there are situational constraints (e.g., departmental norms, the perceived silence of ethnic minority students regarding such issues) that influence their behavior (see Jones and Harris, 1967, and Ross, 1977, on fundamental attribution error). It would not surprise me if the other students of color would like to discuss some of these issues but don't because, like me, they overlook the situational pressures and assume that other people's silence indicates they are doing just fine or that the issue is irrelevant. For this reason, I believe it is important that psychology programs foster norms that encourage open discussion.

An unforeseen issue. Social class became salient to me when I realized that my particular upbringing and socioeconomic background were not typical of most other graduate students in my program. It became clear that many of the students in my graduate program came from families in which college degrees, professional careers, and a moderately good standard of living were the norm. My background was quite different: I am one of the first in my family to get a college education, the end of most months means a time of financial struggle for my family, and in the neighborhood where I grew up, gangs, drugs, and violence were part of the scenery. This social class difference is alienating at times because there are moments at school or conferences when I view my upbringing as a stigma rather than as providing a unique perspective in my discipline.

How is social class made salient in my academic life? It can occur in a variety of ways, including being asked questions as commonplace as what countries I have traveled to and questions with a little more depth such as what my parents do. Although my responses to such questions are formed easily enough, it is their implications for my academic identity that I am still coming to terms with. It has been my experience that social class differences are another issue not discussed much among students and faculty. I sometimes wonder whether the silence surrounding this issue is because of its irrelevance to most graduate students and faculty or whether it is due to the discomfort associated with talking about such sensitive issues. I suspect the lack of discussion regarding social class is similar to the "deafening silence" surrounding ethnic minority concerns. That is, the silence surrounding such issues may be a poor gauge of the resonance or importance these issues have among people within the program and instead may reflect the norms of the department.

Closing remarks. My experience within the psychology graduate program has been invaluable in many ways. I have met many interesting and brilliant people who I have come to admire and respect. The training I have received, while at times difficult, has influenced my way of thinking at a level that I didn't anticipate. In general, I also believe my program has done many things that are effective strategies for increasing diversity. Putting me in touch with faculty and students of color was a good idea. The amount of funding they provided me with at the outset and well ahead of the decision deadline was very important given my financial circumstances, and the type of mentoring and student integration into the program have been exceptional.

There is room for improvement, however. More of an effort needs to be made to recruit a "critical mass" of students of African American, Latino/Latina, and Native American backgrounds. There can also be a greater emphasis on ethnic minority issues within the curriculum. Finally, I believe people in the program should be more sensitive to the norms of the departmental culture that may stifle open discussion of sensitive issues. This knowledge can serve as leverage to revise such norms or at least lead to a recognition that some things have been left out of the conversation altogether.

Brian L. Ragsdale: Sometimes My Soul Just Aches!

In 1994, when I began my doctoral studies, I was the only Black man and Black gay man in the psychology department, although there were other openly gay and lesbian Whites and one transgendered student. I distinguish between being a Black man and a Black gay man because the former is how I experience myself. I have experienced much more racism than homophobia in my life, and I have grown up in a home where developing a Black consciousness was highly valued.

Having come out later in life at the age of 29, I have been struck by the ways in which some Whites and some people of color have related to the domains and to the "intersectionality" of my dual identity as a Black and gay man. For example, my White peers and some White professors tended to relate to my gay side, asking me questions about my partner, sharing with me that they had a gay or lesbian in their family, or asking me if I was going to the gay pride parade, and so forth. There would often be an awkward silence when I changed the topic to talk about my experiences as a Black man. In contrast, some people of color would talk to me about being an ethnic minority, with only casual mentioning or little engaged discussion about my experience as a gay man. Some professors and graduate students had pink triangles on their office doors (and if my memory serves me correctly, those stickers had a saying on them that went something like "This is a gay friendly and supportive environment"). These stickers helped me to feel more comfortable. I also remember those professors who didn't have these stickers on their doors. This White versus people of color way of relating to my dual identity continued as I entered into other professional arenas.

I do not want to give the impression that my experiences were without moments of fear, trepidation, and mistrust. They were, and it is still difficult to decipher when a person may be both homophobic and racist toward me. There is a real sense of professional and personal vulnerability that I experience by being openly gay and what some might perceive as outspokenly Black. I never really believed that the department would ever graduate me, given my sexual orientation and ethnicity, so as I studied, I kept fearing secretly that I would be kicked out of the program. In order to calm these feelings, I looked for like-minded people, people who were divergent in their own thinking, who listened, and who were supportive.

It was also helpful for me to make friendships with other students of color in psychology departments in other universities. It didn't matter that they were in Massachusetts and I was in Rhode Island. Finding and listening to other students who were having similar experiences relating to differences and hearing how they navigated through their graduate school experiences were extremely important. The best advice I can give any graduate student or early professional who is both a person of color and one who celebrates their sexual orientation is to find someone who cares about your life story, your experience in life, and to not be encumbered by distance. It doesn't matter if they don't get all of it; if they are willing to listen with an open heart, you are halfway there.

Overall, the psychology department tried to be welcoming, but it was seriously struggling with how to institutionalize its commitment to diversity. There was one untenured African American female professor among 20 or more faculty members. The department implicitly expected her to get along with 10 ethnic minority students with very different personalities, solely on the basis of her ethnicity. There is far too much pressure on sole ethnic minority faculty members to be everything to all minority students.

A major problem that I see in psychology as a whole is the predominance and pervasiveness of Whiteness (hooks, 1995; Lipsitz, 1998; Rothenberg, 2002). There are subtle and not so subtle ways that Whiteness often dominates discourse, clinical practice, and ways of knowing without leaving room for other viewpoints (Morawski, 1997; Sue, 2003). Here, I make a distinction between a general and shared cultural way of knowing (conferred by Whiteness) and the subscription to and support of White supremacist ideology (hooks, 1995; Johnson, 2001; Ross and Mauney, 1997). I encountered both Whiteness and White supremacy in my graduate program, during my predoctoral internship, and beyond.

Whiteness is not completely foreign to me, and I suspect that I have been influenced by it (Johnson, 2001). In general, Whiteness manifests itself in the inability of some of my peers and some previous professors to be sensitive to how their overvalued ideas about White superiority might influence their teaching or the development of their course syllabi (Dalton, 2002). In clinical work, this Whiteness often reveals itself when White supervisors, who have been the overwhelming majority of my supervisors, are overconfident about how my cultural background might influence client-therapist transference and counter-transference issues (Williams and Halgin, 1995). Yet they focus little attention on how their Whiteness and their perspective affect our supervisory relationship and the dynamics of the client-therapist relationship (Williams and Halgin, 1995).

Whiteness, a socially dominant force, affected my education through the lack of inclusion of multicultural issues within the curriculum (Dyer, 2002). In statistics classes, for example, there were few illustrations of research with ethnic minority participants. And instructors often failed to discuss how ethnicity or acculturation might be measured or analyzed and failed to mention the impact of poverty (Sabnani and Ponterotto, 1992).

I am very tired of having to deal, interact, and be on a team with White psychologists who do not give me the same level of respect White PhDs are afforded. Just recently, a White male psychologist, when introducing me to an organizational outsider, addressed me by using my first and last name, after having introduced a White male psychologist as "Dr. so and so." This may seem like a petty example, but I share it with the hope that it will illustrate how language supports a belief system of who is superior and afforded status and who is denied status and marginalized (Morrison, 1992). I am also disappointed by the many White researchers and clinicians I have met who work with African American clients and research participants and have never read the *Journal of Black Psychology.*

Now I turn to positive thoughts and some ideas to hasten change. I was fortunate to receive a one-year tuition graduate fellowship and additional summer financial support from my university. The Dean of the Graduate School, who is African American and a tenured biology professor, was a good role model and very supportive.

During my graduate school years, I found wonderful mentors in several professors. Both my master's and doctoral dissertation chairs were well versed in ethnic minority issues and were supportive of my clinical and research interests with African American populations. A gender and ethnicity research group that met at the home of two professors offered a rich and nurturing learning environment. These professors were not people of color but had done their homework on minority issues. Majority professors who have demonstrated a good track record of supporting minority students should be given more attention and support. This support should not replace recruitment and retention of professors of color but complement it. The APA *Monitor on Psychology* and other publication outlets should highlight and document how these majority professors learned to support minority students.

In my own case, prayer and meditation continue to play a powerful role in my development as a psychologist. I suggest that APA, as part of the accreditation and reaccreditation process, require program and department chairs to conduct exit interviews with ethnic and nonethnic minority students. The American Psychological Association of Graduate Students and APA should also provide support for the development of formal mentoring networks. APA should increase support for the Office of Ethnic Minority Affairs in APA and should consider ways that members could designate a portion of their membership dues to go to this office. And APA should develop a formal complaint process, provide mediation guidelines, and/or publish procedures for how graduate students or new PhD recipients could report various levels of discrimination.

In conclusion, being both Black and gay means that the road I am traveling will be different than that of many of my psychology foremothers and forefathers. Being supportive of someone who is different doesn't have to be hard, belabored, or confusing. Some people in the gay community want to minimize my Blackness, and parts of the Black community want to minimize my gayness. Celebrating multiple or dual identities is important not in just one context but in all contexts: the classroom, in research, in teaching, in psychotherapy, and in developing our own self-knowledge.

Themes in the Personal Reflections

Several themes are evident in the narratives presented by the contributors. One theme is that the challenges faced by graduate students and young professionals of color are still pervasive. The experiences of most illustrate the adage that women and people of color have to work twice as hard to be considered half as good. Research supports this experience. Studies of the devaluation of women (cf. Lott, 1985) and negative beliefs about people of color (Dovidio and Gaertner, 2000; Steele, 1997) document the serious consequences of biased and stereotypic evaluations and interactions in the classroom, workplace, and elsewhere.

Voiced by some was the experience of having to deal with the perception of others that their acceptance as a graduate student or their hiring as a faculty or staff member was less a validation of their competence and accomplishment than a result of affirmative action. The sad reality seems to be that many do not understand how affirmative action policies assist in the making of admissions and hiring decisions that are truly based on merit. The frustration of being devalued presents an added burden for graduate students and professional psychologists of color, whose minority status per se presents sufficient challenges.

Another theme in the narratives is the importance of finding allies and mentors, primarily among other students and faculty of color but also among any academics who share in the goals of diversity and behave as agents of social change. Such allies were seen as helping reduce isolation, providing assistance in new environments, buffering the stress of "difference" in a pervasively White culture, serving as role models, and helping to counter stereotypes. Faculty who have a nonambivalent belief in the capacity of persons of color to achieve provide encouragement to students and young professionals and have constructive and empowering effects in graduate school and employment settings.

Some of the narratives speak of how social class issues add to the challenges faced by many persons of color in the educational pipeline. Working-class students lack financial support as well as the experiences and opportunities that money provides, such as travel and exposure to varied situations. Many life experiences of low-income people that are different from those in the majority culture tend to be devalued and disrespected (Lott, 2002). Financial support to graduate students of color is clearly necessary.

Other challenges accompany being a person of color and being gay, or disabled, or presenting multiple diversities. Most programs attempt to provide support for those who feel doubly or multiply alienated, but the pervasiveness of Whiteness and other aspects of the majority culture, in our language and institutions, reinforces White priorities and leaves students of color feeling "tired." That respect is not accorded to them at the same level as it is accorded to those who are White takes its psychological toll, resulting in pain and anxiety.

Each narrative concluded with a positive and optimistic theme in recounting successes and satisfactions. Change, it was agreed, was not only possible but was being reflected in increased multicultural concerns in curriculum development, hiring, professional advancement, and understanding. A number of institutional and departmental strategies for change were credited with having made a difference. Many of these are categorized, discussed, and placed in theoretical and empirical contexts in other articles (see Lott, 2005; Rogers and Molina, 2006). Here we are more focused on the personal strategies that our contributors found useful.

Personal Strategies

Some positive, optimistic themes were described in these narratives. Mentors and allies who believed in the students and young professionals had constructive effects. Most important seemed to be a nonambivalent belief in the capacity of persons of color to achieve. Confidence in a student or colleague can go far to provide encouragement, especially during challenging times. Also noted was the importance of peer mentoring and peer support for empowerment and personal development in graduate school and on the job.

Mentioned by many was the importance of choosing one's battles and deciding when to challenge discrimination and prejudice. Weighing the costs and benefits of challenging inappropriate behavior must take into account one's personal energy, one's level of support from others, the degree to which one's dignity and integrity are affected, and other variables.

Although a student or young professional of color cannot always be the spokesperson for all persons of color, cannot be on every committee, and cannot address every issue, there was agreement that there are times when confronting prejudice and injustice have to be done openly and forthrightly.

A frequently mentioned personal strategy was to make good use of opportunities to be part of social and professional networks in one's program, community, or employment setting and/or in APA and other organizations. Attending conferences and joining with others with whom one shares values and interests were seen as providing both personal gain as well as an opportunity to share one's knowledge and experience with others.

The personal strategy most often alluded to—directly or indirectly—was insistence on respectful treatment in the classroom, at faculty or staff meetings, in committees, and in social settings. When such insistence seems fruitless, too difficult, and painful, supportive allies need to be found and engaged. The narratives illustrate that people of color are multicultural and often have the flexibility and adaptability to adjust to environments that are diverse and complex. Ramirez (1998) has suggested that the complex immigration, international, intercultural, and multicultural experiences of persons of color lead to the development of complex interpersonal skills and abilities.

Final Thoughts

We know that prejudice, racism, and discrimination still exist in our discipline. To counteract the effects of these insidious processes, we must use our knowledge and skills to become truly inclusive in our theories, research, and practice. A vital step in this pursuit is to successfully increase the numbers of students and faculty of color. It is our hope that the stories and rich narratives provided here by a sample of such students and faculty of color will illustrate the importance of pursuing our goals and preventing, as much as possible, the kinds of difficult and discouraging experiences that have been described.

We should be encouraged by the wide range of feasible and effective strategies that can be implemented in the classroom, in the curriculum, in supervision, and in recruitment and retention. In addition to these strategies, and those discussed elsewhere in this special issue, creative new ones can be developed. One contributor, for example, suggested that departments obtain information about graduate student experiences through exit interviews. Perhaps APA can be more effective at holding programs and departments accountable for improving the climate for students and faculty from diverse backgrounds.

Each of our psychology programs is unique and has the capacity to change over time in positive, constructive ways. As psychologists, we value diversity and are committed to efforts to increase and promote multicultural inclusion among our students and faculty and within our profession. Our hope is that faculty can begin to examine their own home institutions for those subtle policies, practices, and norms that promote prejudice and discrimination. Perhaps more of us can engage in self-reflection and analysis of our environments to identify those aspects that are hostile or uninviting and those that are supportive and facilitating.

References

American Psychological Association. (2003). Guidelines on multicultural education, training, research, practice, and organizational change for psychologists. *American Psychologist, 58,* 377-402.

Bernal, M. E. (1994). Integration of ethnic minorities into academic psychology: How it has been and what it could be. In E. J. Trickett, R. J. Watts, and D. Birman (Eds.), *Human diversity: Perspectives of people in context* (pp. 404 -423). San Francisco: Jossey-Bass.

Bernal, M. E., and Castro, F. G. (1994). Are clinical psychologists prepared for service and research with ethnic minorities? Report of a decade of progress. *American Psychologist, 49,* 797-805.

Boice, R. (1999). *Advice for new faculty: Nihil nimus.* Boston: Allyn and Bacon.

Carter, R. T. (1995). *The influence of race and racial identity in psychotherapy: Toward a racially inclusive model.* New York: Wiley.

Codina, G. E., and Montalvo, F. F. (1994). Chicano phenotype and depression. *Hispanic Journal of Behavioral Sciences, 16,* 296-306.

Commission on Ethnic Minority Recruitment, Retention, and Training in Psychology. (1997). *Visions and transformations ... The final report.* Washington, DC: American Psychological Association.

Committee on Women in Psychology and Commission on Ethnic Minority Recruitment, Retention, and Training in Psychology. (1998). *Surviving andthriving in academia: A guide for women andethnic minorities.* Washington, DC: American Psychological Association.

Crocker, J., Voelkl, K., Testa, M., and Major, B. (1991). Social stigma: The affective consequences of attributional ambiguity. *Journal of Personality and Social Psychology, 60,* 218-228.

Dalton, H. (2002). Failing to see. In P. S. Rothenberg (Ed.), *White privilege: Essential readings on the other side of racism* (pp. 15-18). New York: Worth.

Dovidio, J. F., and Gaertner, S. L. (2000). Aversive racism and selection decisions: 1989 and 1999. *Psychological Science, 11,* 315-319.

Dovidio, J. F., Gaertner, S. L., Kawakami, K., and Hodson, G. (2002). Why can't we just get along? Interpersonal biases and interracial distrust. *Cultural Diversity and Ethnic Minority Psychology, 8,* 88 -102.

DuBois, W. E. B. (1969). *The souls of Black folk.* New York: New American Library.

Dyer, R. (2002). The matter of Whiteness. In P. S. Rothenberg (Ed.), *White privilege: Essential readings on the other side of racism* (pp. 9 -14). New York: Worth.

Greene, M. (1993). *Perceived race specific and non-race specific stress and their relationship to social and academic integration in African-American students: A focus on gender differences.* Unpublished master's thesis, University of Maryland Baltimore County.

Hall, P. E. (1994). The "bleaching syndrome": Implications of light skin for Hispanic American assimilation. *Hispanic Journal of Behavioral Sciences, 16,* 307-314.

Hammond, R. W., and Yung, B. (1993). Minority student recruitment and retention practices among schools of professional psychology: A national survey and analysis. *Professional Psychology: Research and Practice, 24,* 3-12.

hooks, b. (1995). *Killing rage: Ending racism.* New York: Henry Holt.

Johnson, A. G. (2001). *Privilege, power, and difference.* Mountain View, CA: Mayfield.

Johnson, I. H. (1996). Access and retention: Support programs for graduate and professional students. *New Directions for Student Services, 74,* 53-67.

Jones, E. E., and Harris, V. A. (1967). The attribution of attitudes. *Journal of Experimental Social Psychology, 3,* 1-24.

Keefe, S. E., and Padilla, A. M. (1987). *Chicano ethnicity.* Albuquerque: University of New Mexico Press.

Lewis, C. W. (2004). The experiences of African American Ph. D. students at a predominately White Carnegie I-research institution. *College Student Journal, June,* 1-5. (Available at http://www.findarticles.com/p/articles/mi_m0FCR/is_2_38/ai_n6146820).

Lipsitz, G. (1998). *The possessive investment in Whiteness: How White people profit from identity politics.* Philadelphia: Temple University Press.

Lott, B. (1985). The devaluation of women's competence. *Journal of Social Issues, 41,* 43-60.

Lott, B. (2002). Cognitive and behavioral distancing from the poor. *American Psychologist, 57,* 100 -110.

Lott, B. (2005). *Strategies for enhancing the pipeline for students of color in psychology graduate programs.* Unpublished manuscript.

Maher, M. A., Ford, M. E., and Thompson, C. M. (2004). Degree progress of women doctoral students: Factors that constrain, facilitate, and differentiate. *The Review of Higher Education, 27*(3), 385-408.

Maton, K. I., Kohout, J. L., Wicherski, M., Leary, G. E., and Vinokurov, A. (2006). Minority students of color and the psychology graduate pipeline: Disquieting and encouraging trends, 1989-2003. *American Psychologist, 61,* 117-131.

McHenry, W. (1997). Mentoring as a tool for increasing minority student participation in science, mathematics, engineering, and technology undergraduate and graduate programs. *Diversity in Higher Education, 1,* 115-140.

McIntosh, P. (1992). White privilege and male privilege: A personal account of coming to see correspondences through work in women's studies. In M. L. Andersen and P. H. Collins (Eds.), *Race, class, and gender: An anthology* (2nd ed., pp. 70-81). Belmont, CA: Wadsworth.

Menges, R. J., and Associates. (1999). *Faculty in new jobs: A guide to settling in, becoming established, and building institutional support.* San Francisco: Jossey-Bass.

Morawski, J. (1997). White experimenters, White blood, and other White conditions: Locating the psychologist's race. In. M. Fine, L. Weis, L. C. Powell, and L. M. Wong (Eds.), *OffWhite: Readings on race, power, and society* (pp. 13-28). New York: Routledge.

Morrison, T. (1992). *Playing in the dark; Whiteness and the literary imagination.* Cambridge, MA: Harvard University Press.

Paul, D. G. (2001). *Life, culture and education on the academic plantation: Womanist thought and perspectives.* New York: Peter Lang.

Ramirez, M., III. (1998). *Multicultural/multiracial psychology: Mestizo perspectives in personality and mental health.* Northvale, NJ: Jason Aronson.

Rice, R. E., Sorcinelli, M. D., and Austin, A. E. (2000). *Heeding new voices: Academic careers for a new generation* (New Pathways Working Paper Series, Inquiry #7). Washington, DC: American Association for Higher Education.

Ridley, C. R. (1995). *Overcoming unintentional racism in counseling and therapy.* Thousand Oaks, CA: Sage.

Rogers, M. R., Hoffman, M. A., and Wade, J. (1998). Notable multicultural training in APA-approved counseling psychology and school psychology programs. *Cultural Diversity and Mental Health, 4*(3), 212-226.

Rogers, M. R., and Molina, L. E. (2006). Exemplary efforts in psychology to recruit and retain graduate students of color. *American Psychologist, 61,* 143-156.

Ross, L. (1977). The intuitive psychologist and his shortcomings. In L. Berkowitz (Ed.), *Advances in experimental social psychology* (Vol. 10, pp. 173-220). New York: Academic Press.

Ross, L. J., and Mauney, M. A. (1997). The changing faces of White supremacy. In R. Delgado and J. Stefanic (Eds.), *Critical White studies: Looking behind the mirror* (pp. 552-557). Philadelphia: Temple University Press.

Rothenberg, P. S. (2002). *White privilege: Essential readings on the other side of racism.* New York: Worth.

Sabnani, H. B., and Ponterotto, J. G. (1992). Racial/ethnic minority-specific instrumentation in counseling research: A review, critique, and recommendations. *Measurement and Evaluation in Counseling and Development, 24,* 161-187.

Sekaquaptewa, D., and Thompson, M. (2002). The differential effects of solo status on members of high- and low-status groups. *Personality and Social Psychology Bulletin, 28,* 694 -707.

Sorcinelli, M. D. (2000). Principles of good practice: Supporting early career faculty: Guidance for deans, department chairs, and other academic leaders. In R. E. Rice, M. D. Sorcinelli, and A. E. Austin (Eds.), *Heeding new voices: Academic careers for a new generation* (New Pathways Working Paper Series, Inquiry #7). Washington, DC: American Association for Higher Education.

Spann, J. (1988). *Achieving faculty diversity: A sourcebook of ideas and success stories.* Madison: University of Wisconsin System, Office of Equal Opportunity Programs and Policy Studies.

Steele, C. M. (1997). A threat in the air: How stereotypes shape intellectual identity and performance. *American Psychologist, 52,* 613-629.

Sue, D. W. (2003). *Overcoming our racism.* San Francisco: Jossey-Bass.

Swoboda, M. J. (1990). *Retaining and promoting women and minority faculty members: Problems and possibilities.* Madison: University of Wisconsin System, Office of Equal Opportunity Programs and Policy Studies.

Thompson, M., and Sekaquaptewa, D. (2002). When being different is detrimental: Solo status and the performance of women and racial minorities. *Analyses of Social Issues and Public Policy,* 2(1), 183-203.

Valverde, M. R., and Rodriguez, R. C. (2002). Increasing Mexican American doctoral degrees: The role of institutions of higher education. *Journal of Hispanic Higher Education,* 1(1), 51-58.

Vasquez, M. J. T., and Jones, J. M. (2006) Increasing the number of psychologists of color: Public policy issues for affirmative diversity. *American Psychologist, 61,* 132-142.

Vazquez, L. A. (1997). A systemic multicultural curriculum model: The pedagogical process. In D. B. Pope-Davis and H. L. K. Coleman (Eds.), *Multicultural counseling competencies: Assessment, education and training, and supervision* (pp. 159-183). Thousand Oaks, CA: Sage.

Vazquez, L. A., and Garcia-Vazquez, E. (2003). Teaching multicultural competence in the counseling curriculum. In D. B. Pope-Davis, H. L. K. Coleman, W. M. Liu, and R. L. Toporek (Eds.), *Handbook of multicultural competencies in counseling and psychology* (pp. 546-561). Thousand Oaks, CA: Sage.

Williams, S., and Halgin, R. P. (1995). Issues in psychotherapy supervision between the White supervisor and the Black supervisee. *Clinical Supervisor, 13,* 39-61.

Yee, A. H., Fairchild, H. H., Weizmann, F., and Wyatt, G. E. (1993). Addressing psychology's problems with race. *American Psychologist, 48,* 1132-1140.

Zuckerman, M. (1990). Some dubious premises in research and theory on racial differences: Scientific, social, and ethical issues. *American Psychologist, 45,* 1297-1303

Section Six

Personal Reflections

1. What potential career paths are you now considering? Do they require a graduate degree?
2. Would you consider pursuing graduate study in psychology? Why or why not?
3. Is your current grade-point average competitive according to the graduate school requirements described in these readings? If not, is there a chance for you to raise it? If so, how do you plan to raise it?
4. Research, discover, and describe how you could take the GRE in your local community.
5. Visit another college or university's psychology department website and view the research interests of the faculty. List at least two faculty members whose research interests you and describe their research projects (do not just cut and paste the information from the website).
6. Based on the "Kisses of death in graduate school application process" article (Appleby and Appleby), list the five biggest mistakes students make when applying to graduate school.
7. Based on the "Kisses of death in graduate school application process" article (Appleby and Appleby), list three strategies for avoiding the mistakes described in question No. 6.
8. Based on the readings in this section, what is your understanding of the underrepresentation of persons of color at the graduate school level in the field of psychology?

Section Seven

Resources

APA Resources for Students

American Psychological Association

The American Psychological Association—an important resource center for psychologists and those studying to be psychologists—has worked for more than 100 years to advance psychology as a science, as a profession, and as a way to promote health and human welfare. APA is the world's largest psychological association, with more than 150,000 members and affiliates.

Student Affiliates

Undergraduate and graduate students taking courses in psychology are eligible for membership in APA as student affiliates. Student affiliates receive subscriptions to the *American Psychologist* and the *Monitor on Psychology*. In addition, members in the American Psychological Association of Graduate Students (APAGS)— all graduate students, and undergraduates who opt to pay the graduate student rate—get *gradPSYCH*, the quarterly magazine written especially for students. Both the *Monitor* and *gradPSYCH* cover information psychologists need to succeed in their careers, as well as extensive job listings. Student affiliates may purchase APA publications at special rates and attend the APA annual convention at a reduced registration fee. For more information, see www.apa.org/about/students.aspx.

APAGS

All graduate student affiliates of APA are automatically members of the American Psychological Association of Graduate Students (APAGS), created in 1988 as a voice for psychology students within the larger association. (Undergraduates can join APAGS by paving a small additional fee.) APAGS was formed by graduate students as a means of establishing communication between students and other members of the psychological community, including universities, training centers, and other members of the APA governance structure, in order to advocate on students' behalf. APAGS represents all graduate study specialties of the discipline and is run by student leaders elected by the APAGS membership. In addition to sponsoring a variety of other initiatives, APAGS sponsors programming at the APA annual convention and distributes a quarterly magazine (*gradPSYCH*) to its members. Please visit ww.apa.org/apags for more information.

Student Membership in APA Divisions

APA student affiliates are encouraged to apply for affiliation in one or more APA divisions. The divisions bring together psychologists of similar or specialized professional interests. You may obtain more information about APA divisions at ww.apa.org/about/division.

APA Office of Ethnic Minority Affairs

The APA Office of Ethnic Minority Affairs (OEMA) is a central resource clearinghouse for students of color interested in pursuing careers in psychology. Information and materials for students who are at any stage in the psychology education pipeline may be accessed via OEMA's Web page www.apa.org/pi/I loema/resources/student.aspx. For example, students of color in community-college might be interested in any one of the *Psychology Education and Careers* guidebooks, a series which includes a guidebook for high school students of color interested in a career in psychology. Undergraduate students of color may find the links to potential funding sources, honor societies in psychology—especially Psi Alpha Omega—and OEMA's internship program useful. Graduate students of color and postdoctorates could benefit from information about the Jeffrey S. Tanaka Memorial Dissertation Award in Psychology; the CEMRRAT Richard M. Suinn Graduate Minority Achievement Award, which honors graduate psychology programs that demonstrate excellence in the recruitment, retention, and graduation of students of color; and other career and professional development opportunities. Links to the four major ethnic minority psychological associations can also be found on the Web page. For more information, visit www.apa.org/pi/oema.

APA Minority Fellowship Program

The APA Minority Fellowship Program (MFP) provides financial support, professional development activities, and guidance to promising doctoral students and postdoctoral trainees, with the goal of moving them toward high achievement in areas related to ethnic minority behavioral health services.

The Mental Health and Substance Abuse Services Fellowship provides fellows with financial support; professional development; mentoring: potential support for tuition, health insurance, and the dissertation; internship application assistance; and lifetime access to the MFP network. Predoctoral fellowships support training for doctoral students in clinical, counseling, school, or related psychology programs that prepare them to provide behavioral health services or develop policy for ethnic minority populations. Postdoctoral fellowships support the training of early career doctoral recipients who have primary interests in the delivery of behavioral health services or policy related to the psychological well-being of ethnic minorities.

The MFP also sponsors the Psychology Summer Institute, a week-long intensive training for advanced doctoral students and early career psychologists that provides mentoring and career development to assist participants in developing projects on ethnic minority issues. More information on psychology fellowships and programs may be found on the MFP Web page: www.apa.org/pi/mfp.

Publications

APA publishes about 60 peer-reviewed journals and more than 800 books in the major interest areas in psychology. APA also produces several electronic databases—PsycHsTO, PsycARTICLES. PsycBOOKS. PsycEXTRA, PsycCRITIQUES, PsycTESTS, and PsycTHERAPY. PsycINFO contains abstracts of the psychological literature from 1887 to present. PsycARTICLES and PsycBOOKS contain the full text of journals and books published by APA and allied organizations from the mid-1800s to the present.

APA produces two magazines: the *Monitor on Psychology*, sent to all members (including student affiliates) 11 times a year, and *gradPSYCH*, APA's graduate student magazine, published 4 times a year. The *Monitor* provides information on the science and practice of psychology and how psychology influences society at large; it also provides extensive job listings. *gradPSYCH* is a membership benefit of APAGS, the student organization within APA. *gradPSYCH* provides timely articles about emerging trends in psychology practice, research, education, and the nation's marketplace and infrastructure as they affect students and their future careers; employment and salary data profiles of innovative psychology careers; cutting-edge information on graduate training and supervision, including internships, postdocs, and dissertations: and classified advertising to help students find internships, fellowships, postdocs, and other career opportunities.

To help individuals negotiate the sequence of activities invoked in becoming a psychology student and a psychologist, APA has developed a line of books for undergraduate and graduate students as well as those who are just now planning to go to college.

Psychology as a Major: Is It Right for Me and *What Can I Do With My Degree?* offers a comprehensive picture of psychology and its subfields and helps prospective and current students better understand themselves and their motivations for pursuing study in the field. *Career Paths in Psychology: Where Your Degree Can Take You* (2nd ed.) offers psychologists' perspectives on 19 different graduate-level careers in psychology. Undergraduates gain a competitive edge by reading *The Insider's Guide to the Psychology Major: Everything You Need to Know About the Degree and Profession*, which, like a good mentor, motivates and empowers them with information and interactive tools to proactively chart their educational careers and increase their chances of success. *What Psychology Students Could (and Should) Be Doing: An Informal Guide to Research Experience and Professional Skills* zeroes in on strategies for actively participating in research and the real world of psychology, so that undergraduates can distinguish themselves in the realms of graduate school and the workforce. *Your Practicum in Psychology: A Guide for Maximizing Knowledge and Competence* prepares undergraduate students for field placement in mental health settings by providing a wide range of both practical and theoretical information.

For psychology students who do not have graduate school in their immediate plans. *Finding Jobs With a Psychology Bachelor's Degree: Expert Advice for Launching Your Career* shows how to leverage their bachelor's degree to find a career with intellectual, emotional, and perhaps even financial rewards.

Students interested in graduate school find that *Getting In: A Step-by-Step Plan for Gaining Admission to Graduate School in Psychology* helps to guide their decision making, structure the application process, and maximize their chances of being accepted and getting financial aid. *Graduate Study in Psychology* complements *Getting In* by summarizing more than 600 programs of study in psychology, requirements for admission for each program, deadlines for applications, and other relevant details about specific programs in the United States and Canada. *Applying to Graduate School in Psychology* inspires readers to home in on their program choices. Through personal accounts from both peer and expert perspectives, it illustrates the ins and outs of applying and preparing for the graduate school experience and the commonalities and differences among student experiences from a variety of academic institutions and programs. . . .

International students considering studying psychology in the United States will find resources tailored to their needs in *Studying Psychology in the United States: Expert Guidance for International Students.* It weighs the pros and cons of studying psychology in the United States and provides direction on finding university resources geared toward international students, financing one's education, handling visa and work permit matters, cultural considerations, mentoring relationships, academic development, internships and training, and whether to pursue employment in the United States or abroad.

The Publication Manual of the American Psychological Association, *Concise Rules of APA Style*, and *Mastering APA Style: Student's Workbook and Training Guide* help both undergraduate and graduate students with their class papers and, for those who go on to graduate school, prepare them to submit articles to psychology journals. The *Publication Manual* is often required reading for students in psychology and many of the other social sciences. Spanish-language versions of each of these essential books are available. Undergraduate students will find detailed, step-by-step help with writing papers in *Undergraduate Writing in Psychology: Learning to Tell the Scientific Story*, including such topics as how to craft a research question or thesis; how to search, analyze, and synthesize the relevant literature; how to draft specific parts of the paper; how to revise; and how instructors gauge the quality of a paper. For undergraduate students in research methods classes, as well as graduate students and early career researchers, *Reporting Research in Psychology* provides practical guidance on journal article reporting standards (JARS) and meta-analysis reporting standards (MARS)—standards which were designed to make the reporting of results comprehensive and uniform. Examples drawn from articles published in APA journals are paired with engaging and helpful commentaries.

Web Sites for Further Exploration in the Field of Psychology

American Association for Marriage and Family Therapy
www.aamftca.org

American Psychological Association
www.apa.org

Association for Psychological Science
www.psychologicalscience.org

California Board of Behavioral Sciences
www.bbs.ca.gov

Careers in Psychology
http://careersinpsychology.org/psychology-careers/

National Association of Social Workers
www.naswdc.org

Psychology Dictionary & Glossary for Students
www.tuition.com.hk/psychology

Psychology Online Resource Central
http://psychcentral.com

Psych Scholar
http://psych.hanover.edu/Krantz/

Psych Web
www.psychwww.com

Web Links by Psychology Subject Area
www.socialpsychology.org/psylinks.htm